GRAPHICS FOR ARCHITECTS AND PLANNERS

James E. Russell

A RESTON BOOK
Prentice-Hall, Inc.
Englewood Cliffs, New Jersey 07632

Library of Congress Cataloging-in-Publication Data

Russell, James E. (James Emmerson)
  Graphics for architects and planners.

  "A Reston book."
  1. Architecture—Graphic methods.   2. Urban renewal—
Graphic methods.   3. City planning—Graphic methods.
I. Title.
NA2590.R8   1986   711'.12   85-19350
ISBN 0-8359-2565-X

Editorial/production supervision and interior design
by Barbara J. Gardetto

A Reston Book
Published by Prentice-Hall
A Division of Simon & Schuster, Inc.
Englewood Cliffs, New Jersey 07632

© 1986 by
Prentice-Hall
Englewood Cliffs, New Jersey 07632

*All rights reserved. No part of this book may be
reproduced in any way, or by any means, without
permission in writing from the publisher.*

10 9 8 7 6 5 4 3 2 1

Printed in the United States of America

For Tina, Lee, Linda Mac,
Hank, Dale, Barbara, and Stephanie—
I couldn't have done it without you.

CONTENTS

	Preface ix
ONE	Graphics in General 1
TWO	Planting Plan 27
THREE	Street Furniture 31
FOUR	Schematic Site Plans 35
FIVE	Subdivisions 49
SIX	Comprehensive Plans 59
SEVEN	Central Business Districts 105
EIGHT	Parks and Recreational Areas 169
NINE	Environmental Analysis 233
TEN	Transportation Planning 239
ELEVEN	Military Plans 259
TWELVE	Miscellaneous Projects 283

PREFACE

Graphic art is an essential tool used to transform highly technical and often abstract ideas into simple visual forms that are accessible to all. Graphics are used on a variety of projects to achieve many goals, including identification of problems; conveying basic ideas; promotion of design concepts, plans, and amenities; definition of objectives and priorities; spotlighting design features; gathering support for planning and design proposals, and other, similar goals inherent to the development or modification of land and property.

Thus, proficiency in the use of graphics is essential to professionals in getting work initially and in conveying information later. Students of architecture and planning usually are required to demonstrate their abilities by way of assigned projects; graphics are essential in communicating what they have learned.

There is much to learn in architecture and planning courses and little time to learn about presentation graphics. *Graphics for Architects and Planners* will save students much time. It shows, by way of example, what the professionals do; what their methods of graphic presentation are for a wide variety of projects.

The projects presented here include commercial projects, redevelopment plans overseas, leisure developments, domestic redevelopments, military master plans, shopping centers, and others. Actual case study examples are used throughout to give the reader an overview while learning specific techniques. In addition, both students and practicing professionals will gain a feel for the vast number of potential clients and projects in their fields and the graphics that are used to present these projects.

James Russell

ACKNOWLEDGMENTS

The author gratefully acknowledges the firm of
Harlan Bartholomew & Associates, Inc.
of Memphis, Tennessee
for supplying the drawings and photographs for
this book. Printed with permission.

GRAPHICS
FOR ARCHITECTS
AND PLANNERS

ONE
GRAPHICS IN GENERAL

INTRODUCTION

To planning and architectural professionals, and to students of these professions, graphic art is an essential tool used to transform highly technical and often abstract concepts into simple visual forms that are accessible to nonprofessionals such as government officials, citizens' groups, bankers, real estate people, investors, potential buyers, clients, and others.

Graphic art is used on a variety of projects to achieve one or more of the following goals:

1. Identify problems
2. Convey basic ideas
3. Promote design concepts, plans, and amenities
4. Define objectives and priorities
5. Spotlight design features
6. Gather support for planning and design proposals
7. Other, similar goals inherent in the development or modification of land and property

The following examples illustrate these basic uses of graphic art.

GRAPHICS IN GENERAL

4 GRAPHICS IN GENERAL

GRAPHICS IN GENERAL 5

6 GRAPHICS IN GENERAL

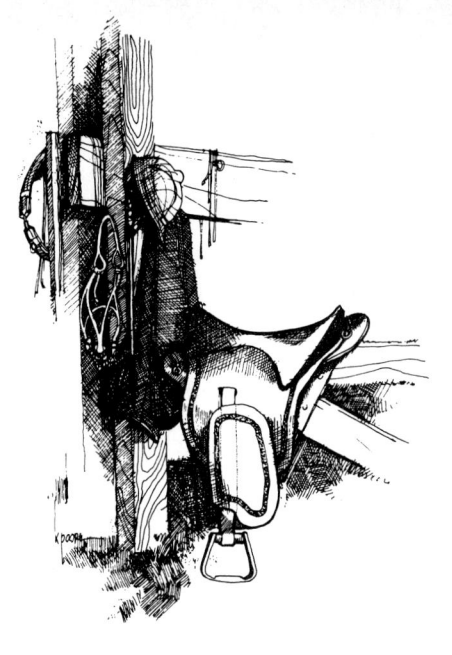

GRAPHICS IN GENERAL

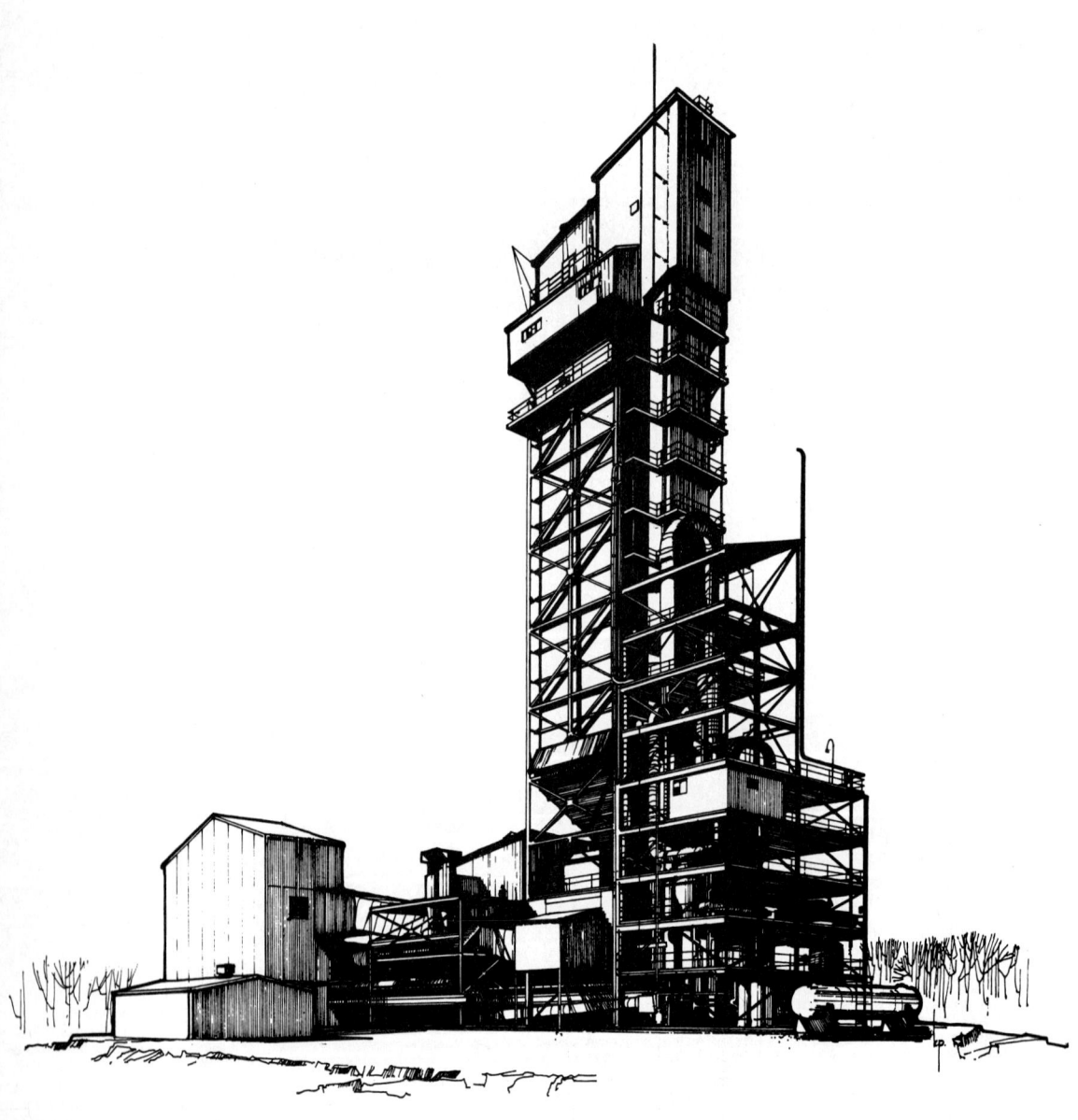

GRAPHICS IN GENERAL 9

10 GRAPHICS IN GENERAL

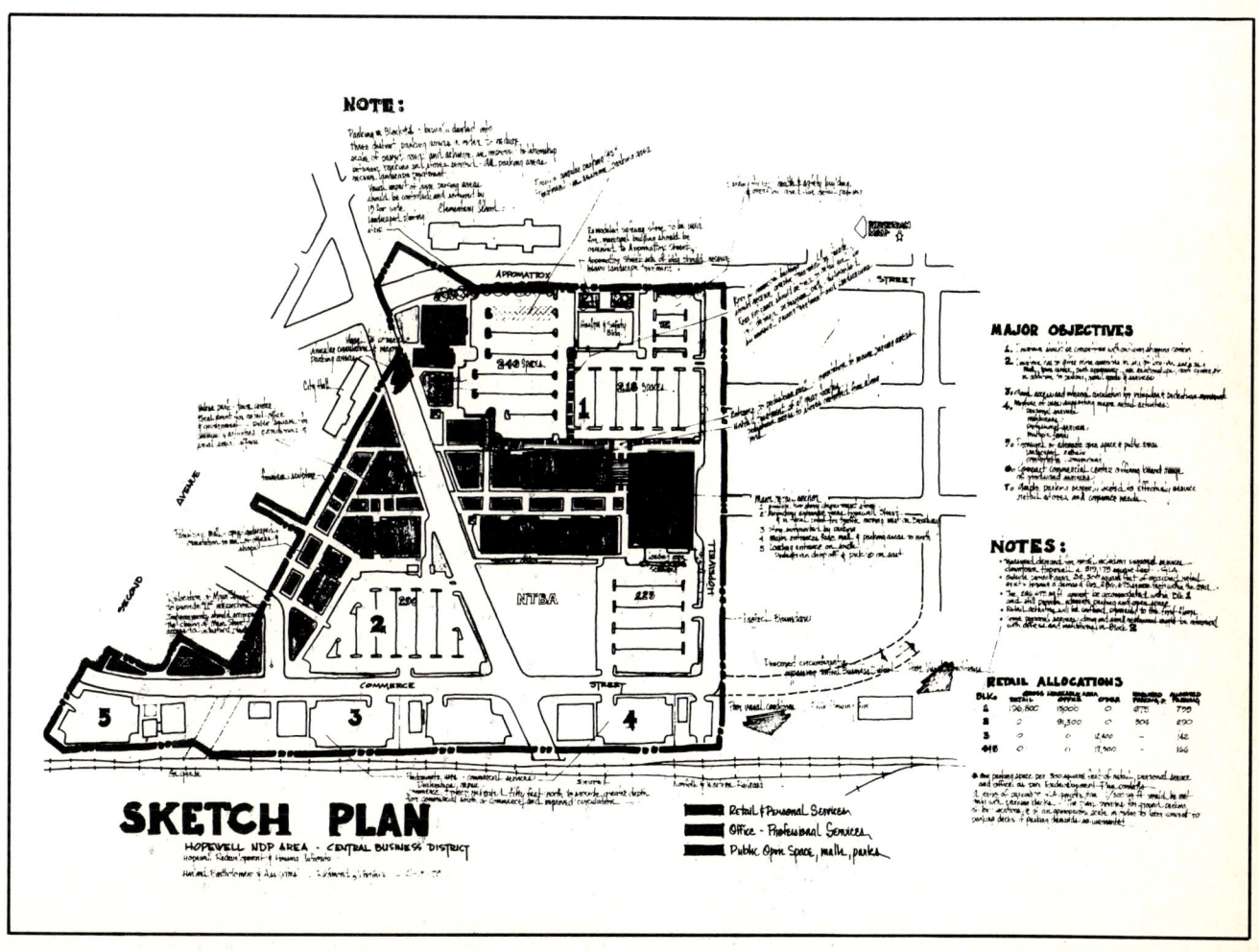

GRAPHICS IN GENERAL 11

Design Concept

POTENTIAL ACTIVITY CENTER IN NEW SUPERBLOCK DEVELOPMENT

Des Plaines, Illinois
Downtown Streetscape and Storefront Rehabilitation Project

Design Concept

TYPICAL APPLICATION TO EXISTING STOREFRONTS
Minor Street west of Pearson Street

Des Plaines, Illinois
Downtown Streetscape and Storefront Rehabilitation Project

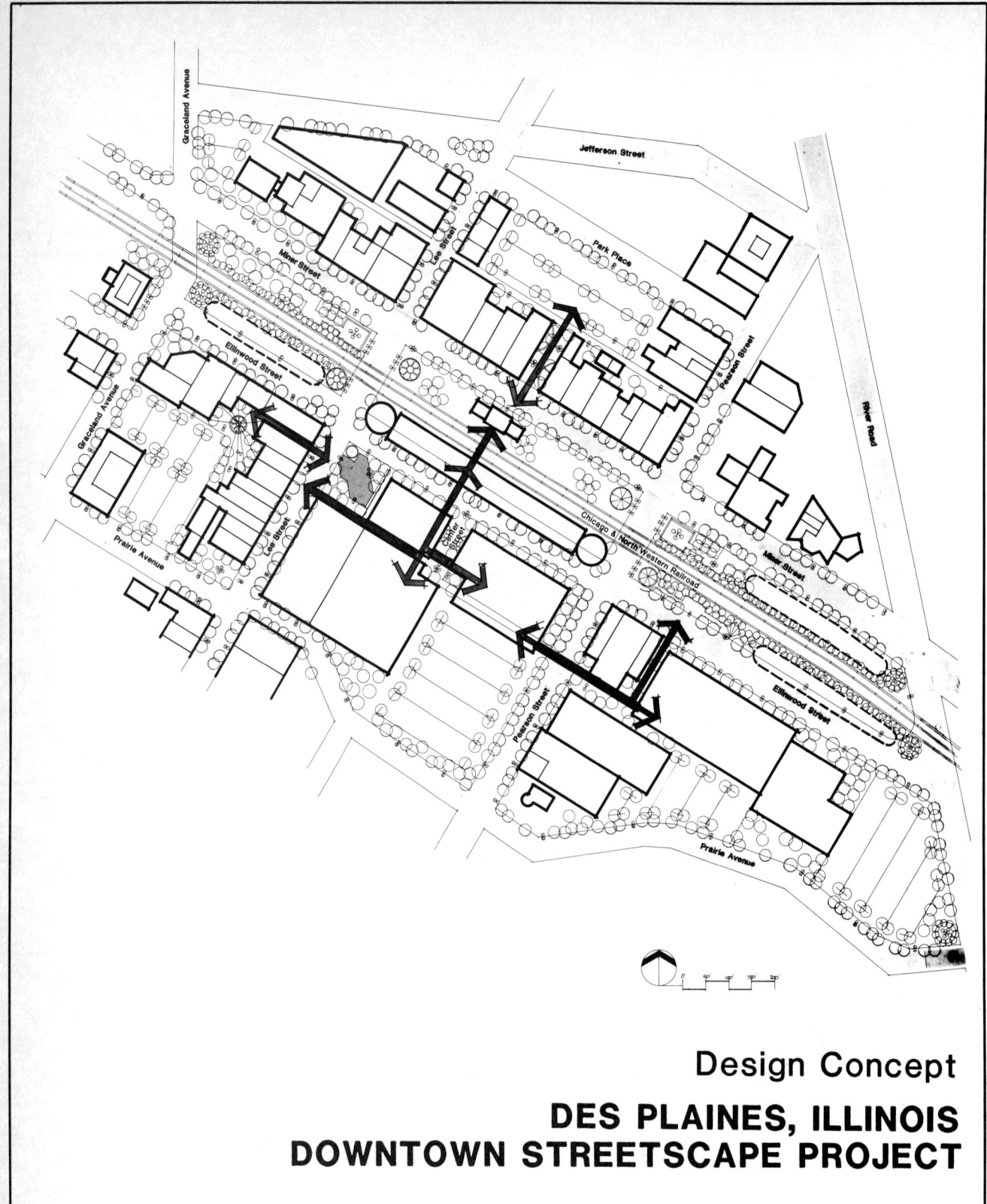

Design Concept
DES PLAINES, ILLINOIS DOWNTOWN STREETSCAPE PROJECT

Prepared by:
Harland Bartholomew & Associates, Inc

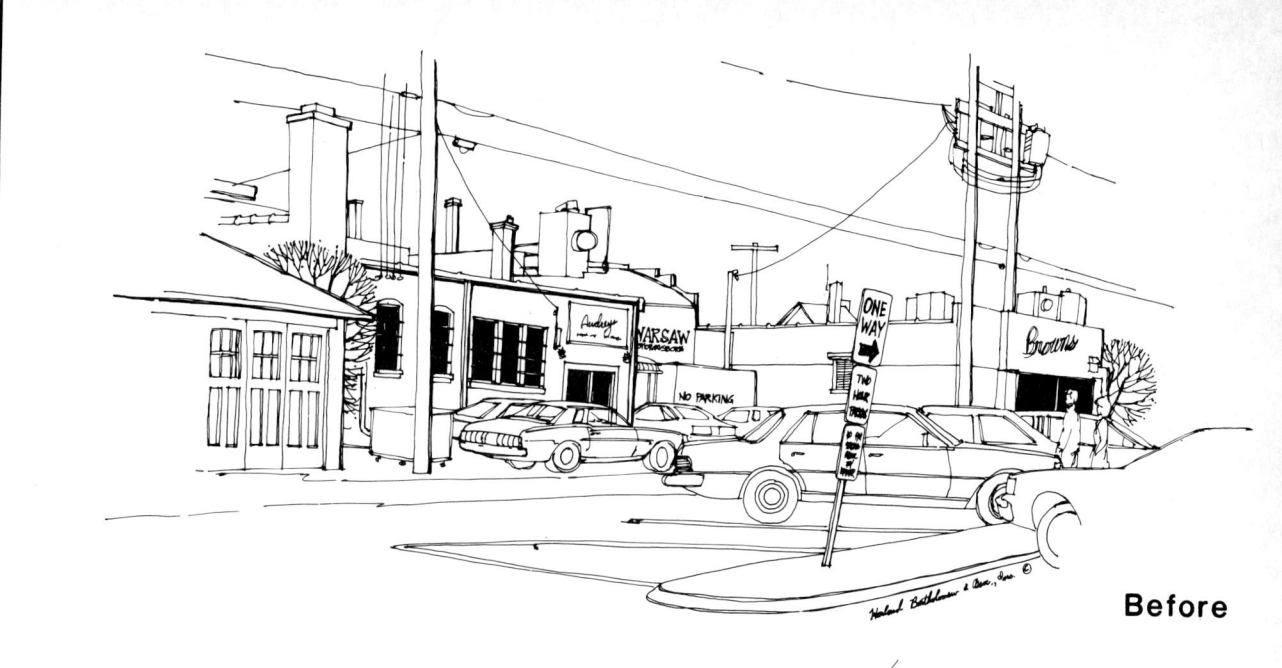

Before

After

Design Concept

TYPICAL APPLICATION TO REAR STOREFRONT AREA
Minor Street west of Pearson Street

Des Plaines, Illinois
Downtown Streetscape and Storefront Rehabilitation Project

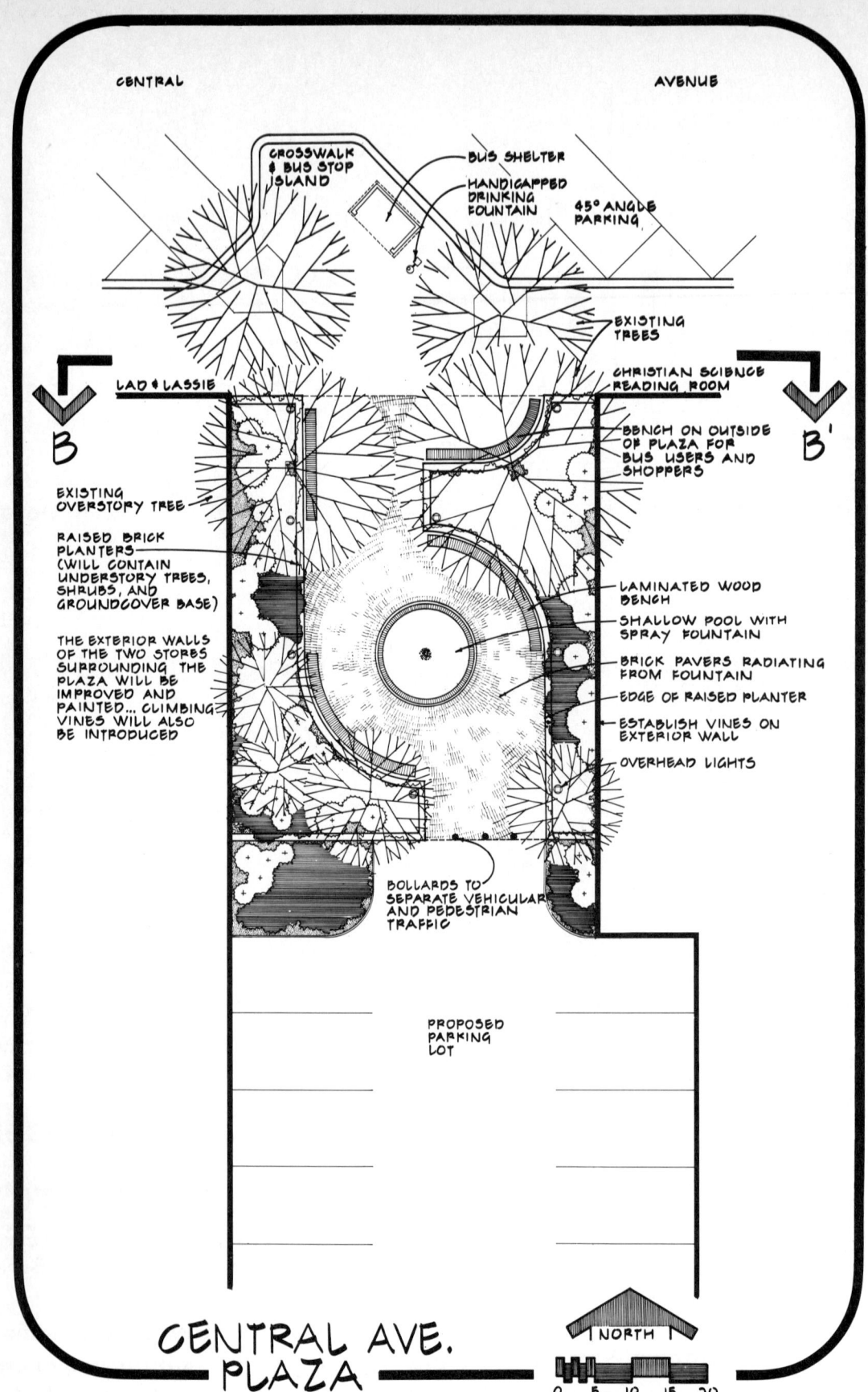

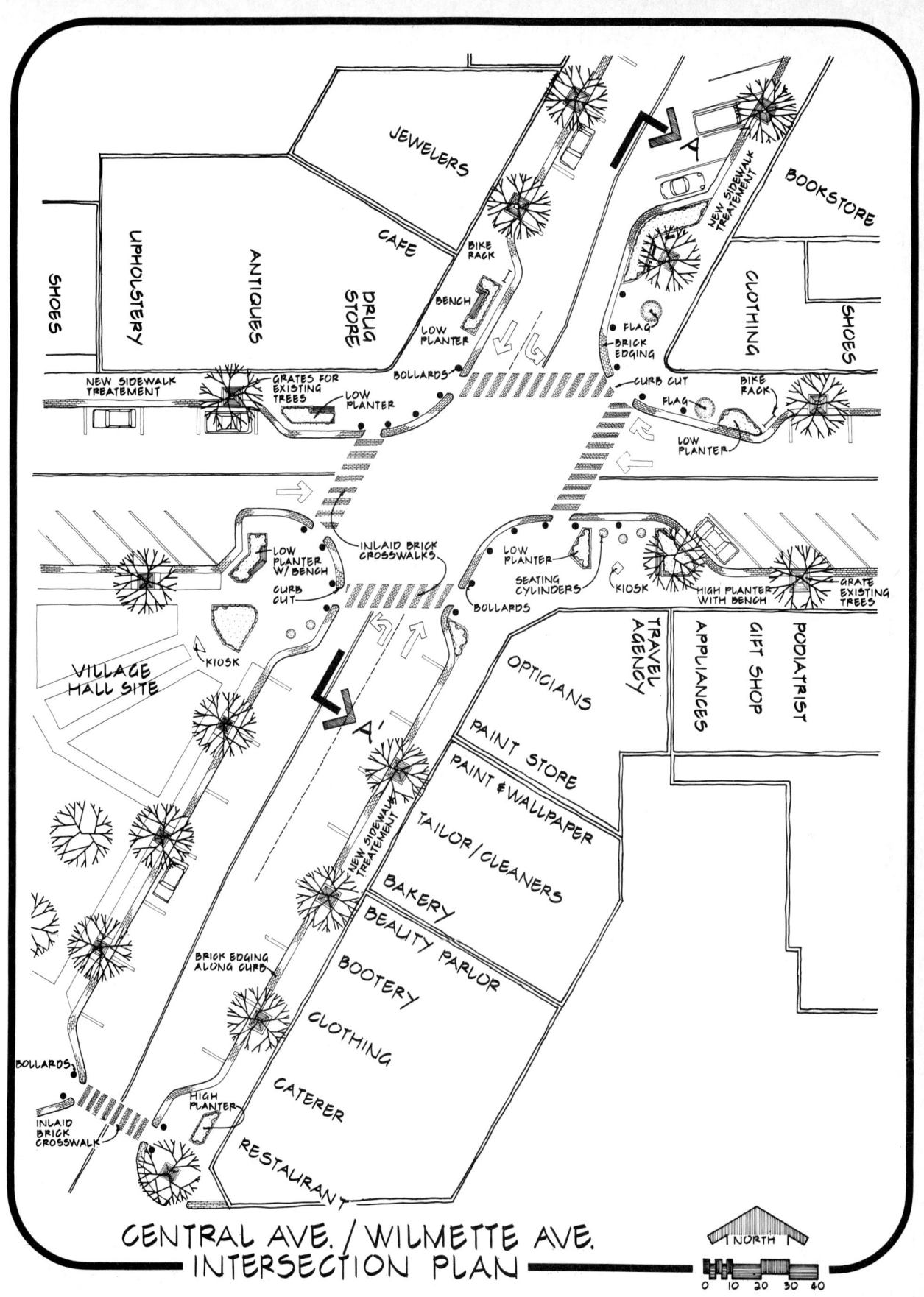

GRAPHICS IN GENERAL 17

18 GRAPHICS IN GENERAL

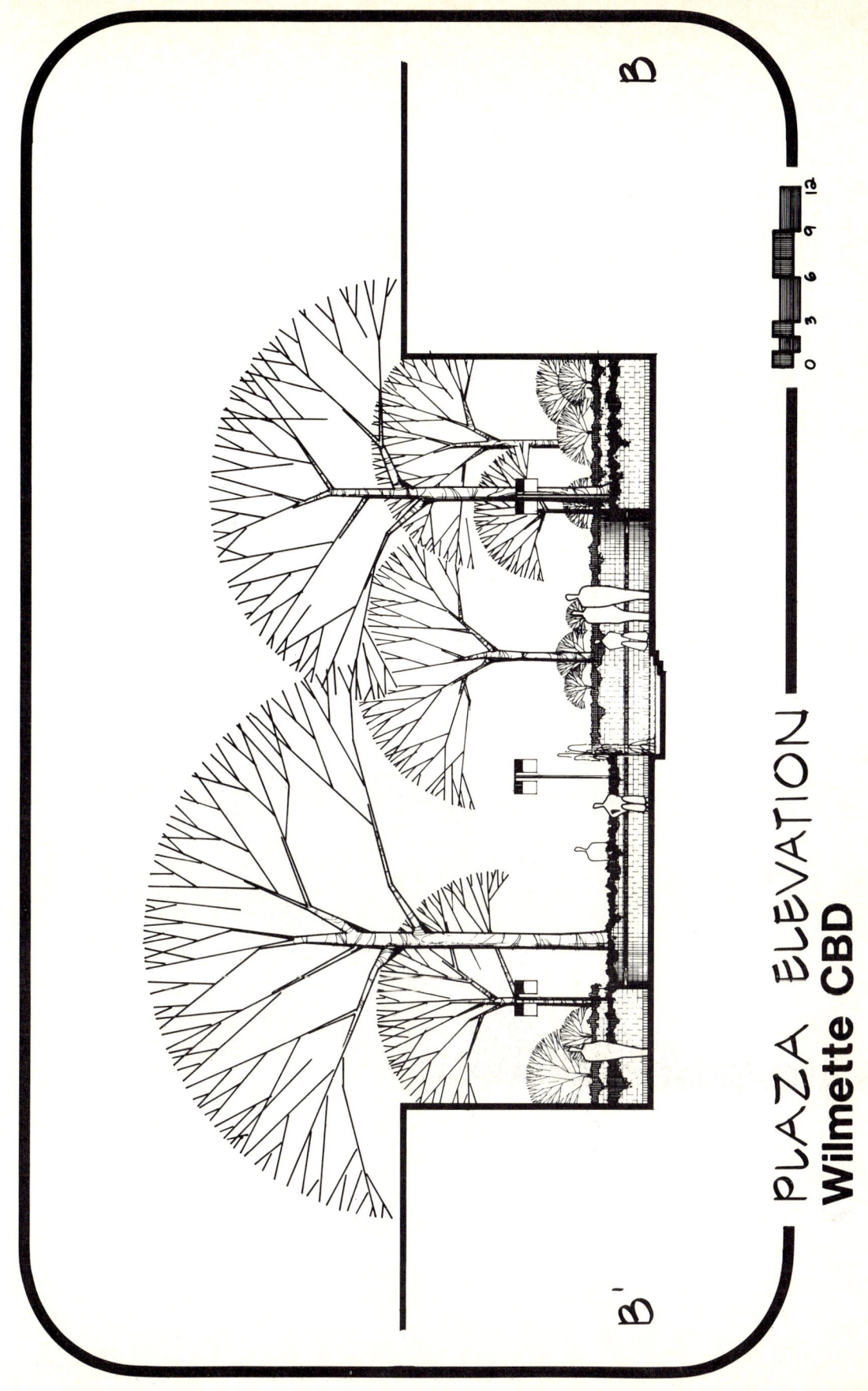

GRAPHICS IN GENERAL 19

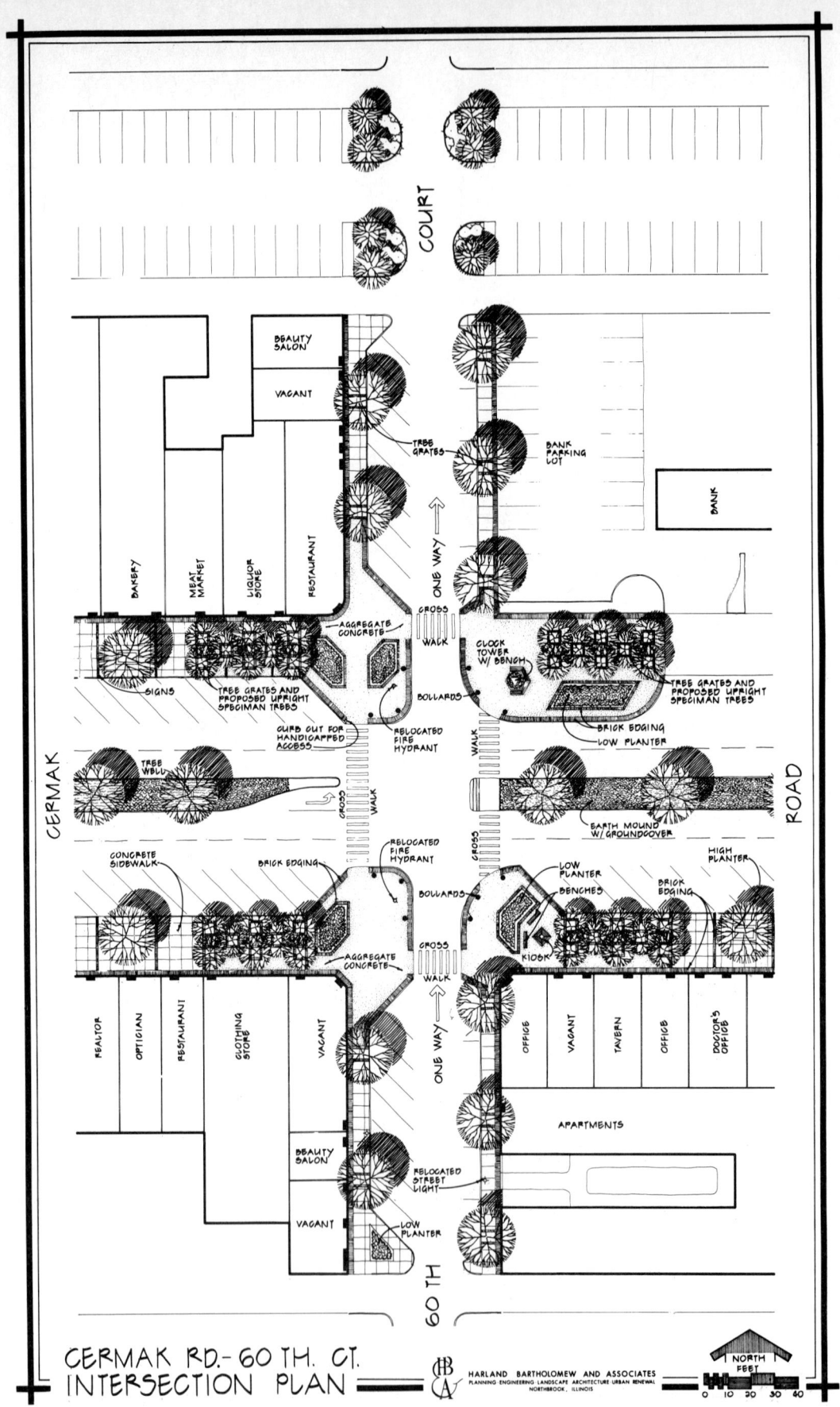

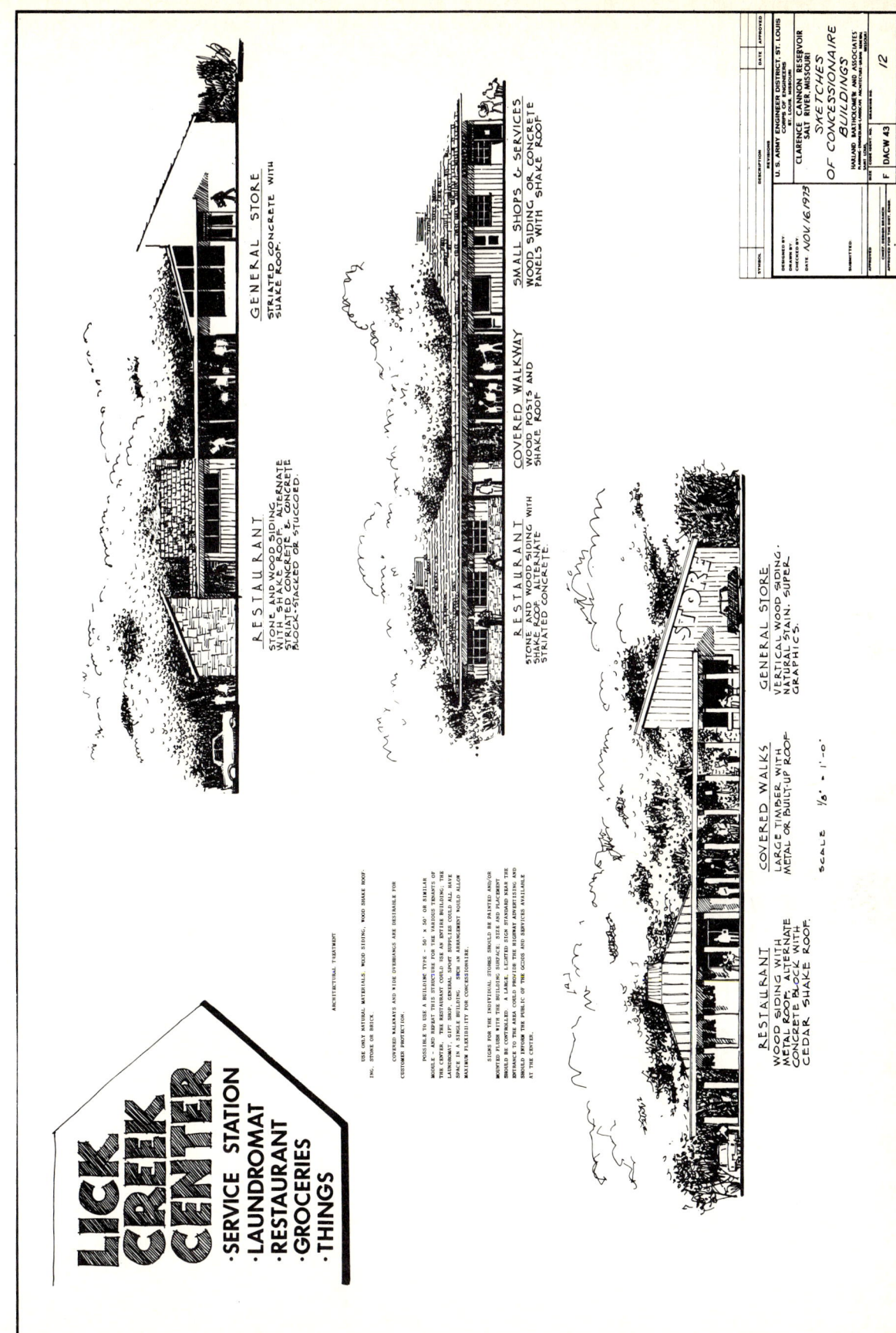

GRAPHICS IN GENERAL 21

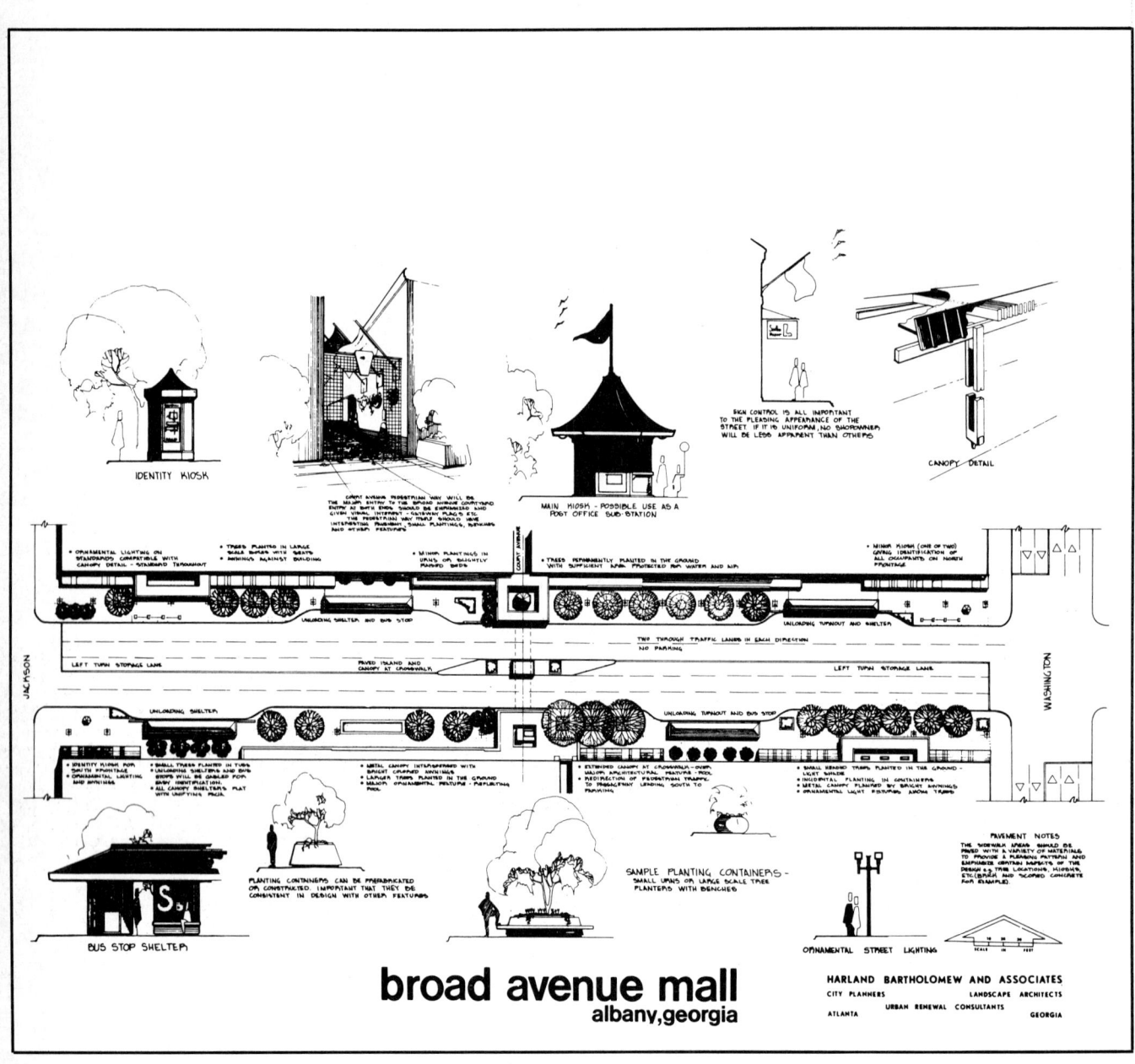

GRAPHICS IN GENERAL

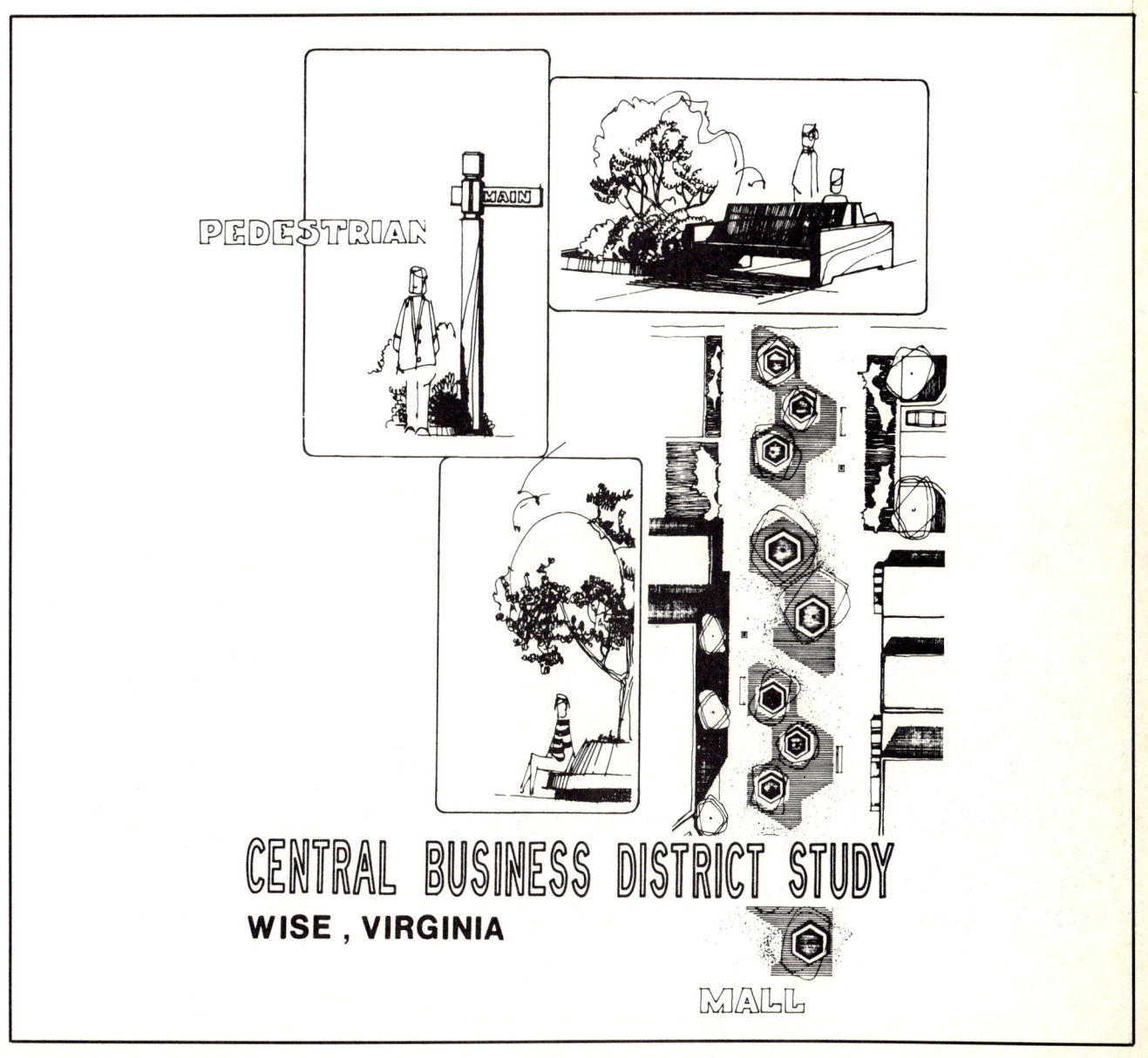

GRAPHICS IN GENERAL

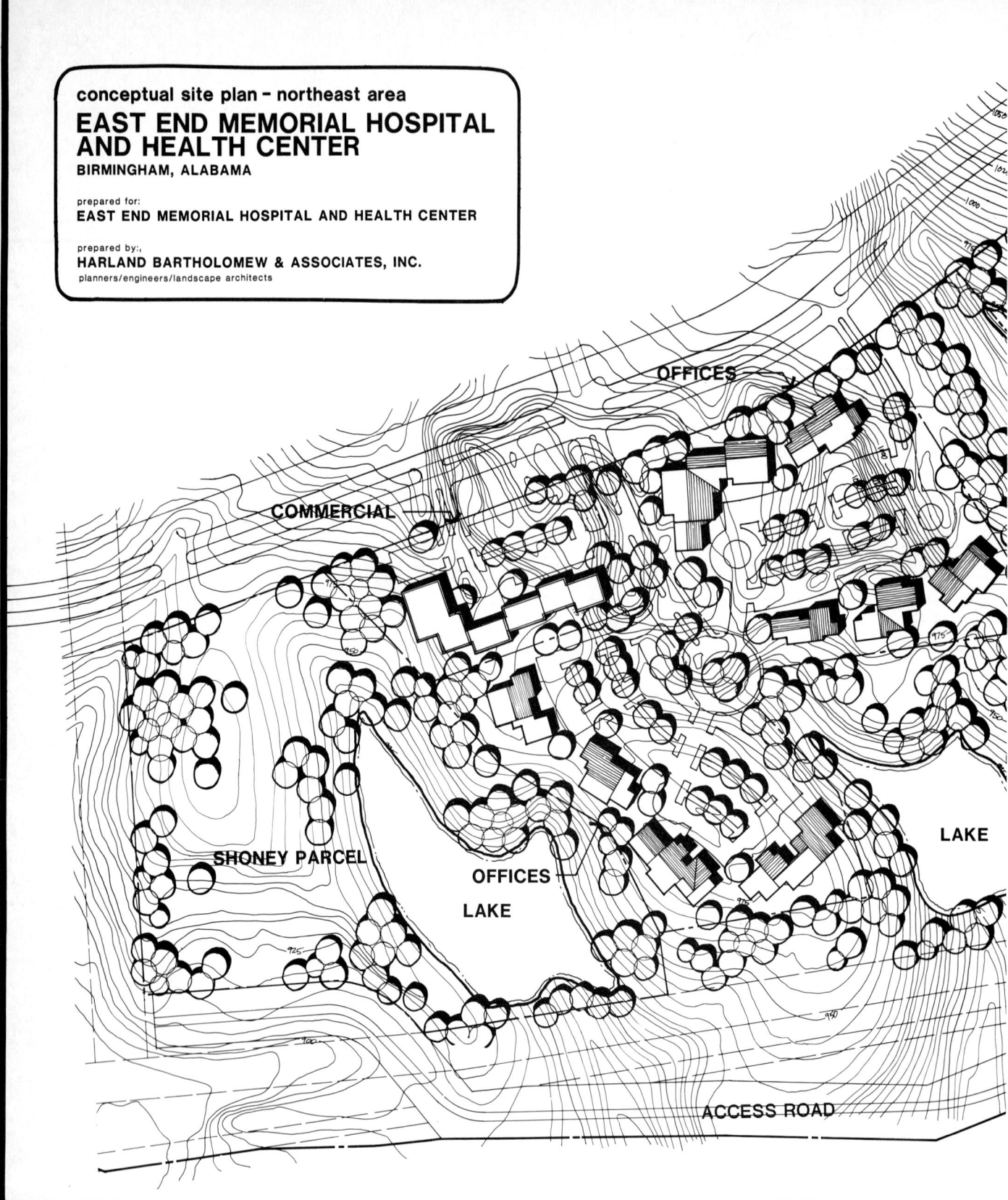

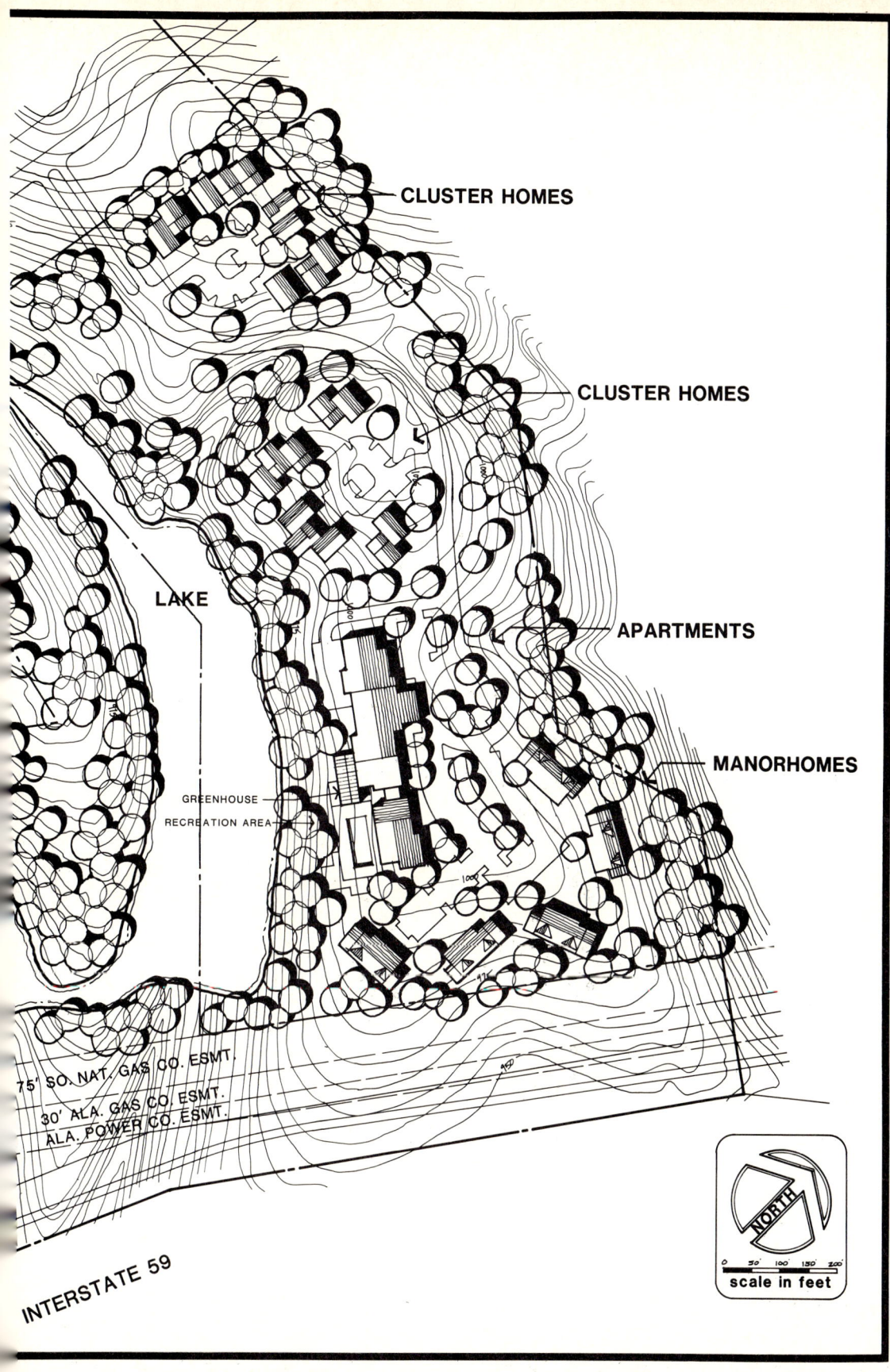

TWO
PLANTING PLAN

INTRODUCTION

As a minimum, a planting plan should show the type, quantity, and location of plants. Small lots may have the plants labeled directly on the plan. Larger projects usually number the plants, identify them by common and botanical names, and provide quantities and sizes on a separate list. Other information frequently required includes detail drawings and instructions for plant installation on decks, terraces, borders, and other areas.

The following planting plans illustrate two methods of handling planting for two different site conditions.

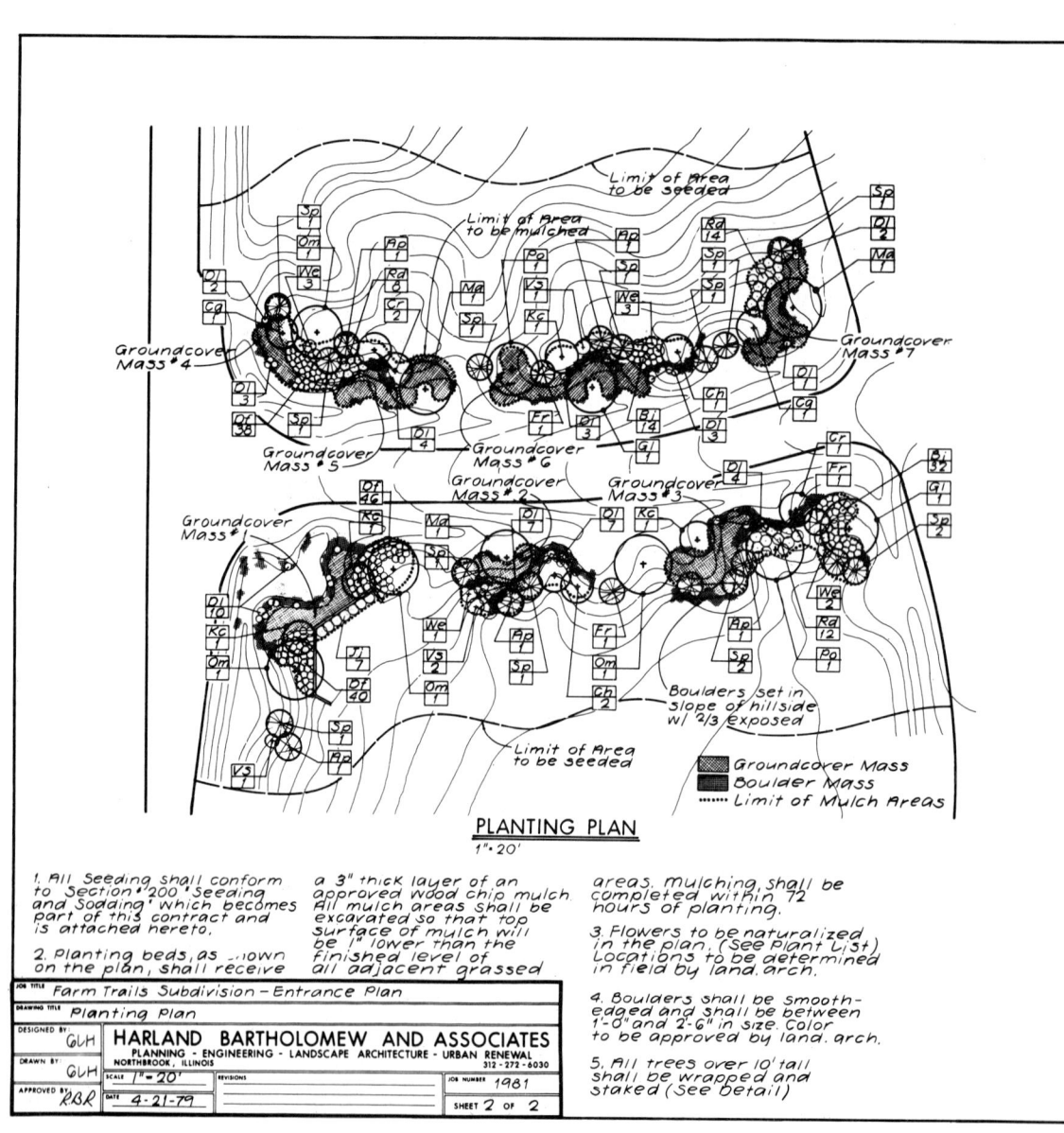

PLANTING PLAN

Key	Botanical Name	Common Name	Quan.	Size	Spacing	Remark
		Trees				
Ma	Fraxinus pennsylvanica "Marshall Seedless"	Marshall Seedless Ash	3	5" cal.	as shown	B&B
Sp	Pinus sylvestris	Scotch Pine	14	8' ht.		
Ap	Pinus nigra	Austrian Pine	5	8' ht.		
Fr	Pseudotsuga menziesii	Douglas Fir	3	8' ht.		
Gl	Tilia cordata Greenspire	Greenspire Linden	2	5" cal.		
Po	Quercus palustris	Pin Oak	2	5" cal.		
Om	Acer rubrum "October Glory"	October Glory Maple	4	4" cal.		
		Flowering Trees				
Cr	Malus zumi calocarpa	Japanese Zumi Crab	3	4" cal	as shown	low branched
Cg	Malus "Prince George"	Prince George Crab	4	4" cal.		low branched
Kc	Prunus kwanzan	Kwanzan Cherry	4	10' ht.		tree form
Ch	Crataegus crusgalli	Cockspur Hawthorn	3	10' ht.		low branched
		Shrubs				
We	Euonymus alatus	Winged Euonymus	9	6' ht.	as shown	B&B
Vs	Spirea van houtte	Van Houtte Spirea	4	6' ht.		
Bj	Rhototypos scandens	Black Jetbead	46	3' ht.	3' O.C.	
Rd	Cornus stolonifera bailey	Red Osier Dogwood	34	5' ht	4' O.C.	
Df	Forsythia viridissima "Bonxensis"	Dwarf Forsythia	124	2 gal.	3' O.C.	potted
Jj	Juniperus chinensis procumbens	Japgargen Juniper	7	5 gal.	4' O.C.	
Dl	Hemerocallis sp..	Daylilies	43	1½ gal.	as shown	mix colors
		Groundcover				
Mass 1	Ajuga reptans rubra	Bugleweed	1300	3" pot	8" O.C.	—
Mass 2	Hedra helix "Baltica"	Baltic Ivy	1050			—
Mass 3	Vinca minor	Periwinkle	1550			—
Mass 4	Ajuga reptans rubra	Bugleweed	640			—
Mass 5	Polygonum reynoutria	Dwarf Fleeceflower	1450			—
Mass 6	Vinca minor	Periwinkle	2000			—
Mass 7	Sedum acre	Acre Sedum	560	Qt.	12" O.C.	Yellow
		Flowers				
See Note Three	Narcissus mixture	Daffodils	500 Bulbs	—	—	mix to be approved
See Note Three	Rudbeckia hirta	Black eyed Susans	500	3" pots	—	

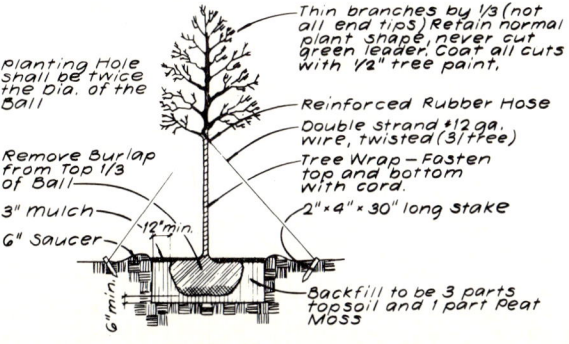

PLANTING PLAN

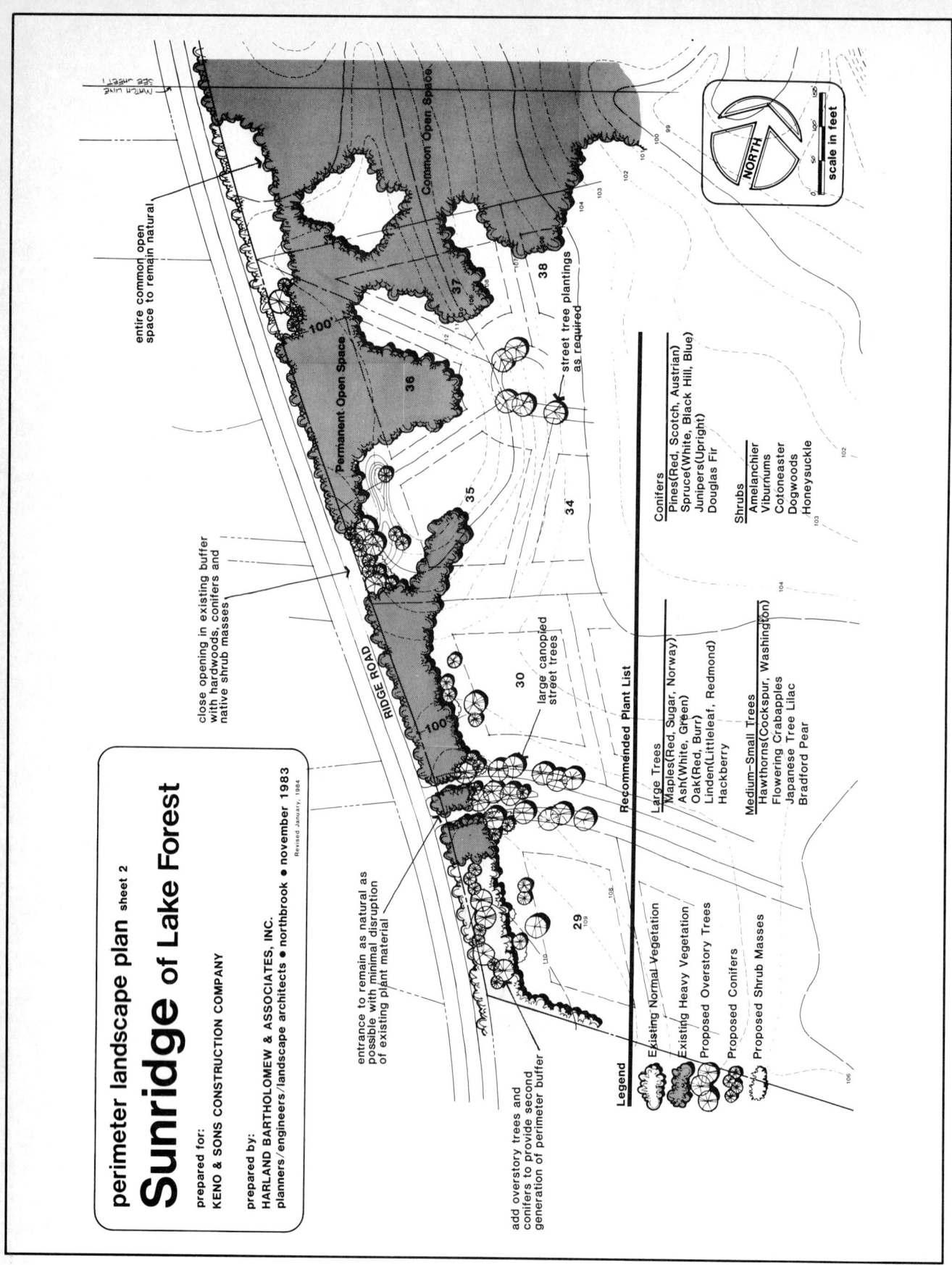

PLANTING PLAN

THREE
STREET FURNITURE

INTRODUCTION

Street furniture is an important element in the overall visual environment of the city. Typical elements include traffic lights, fire hydrants, directional signs and symbols, benches, drinking fountains, bollards to help control traffic, bicycle racks, trash receptacles, telephone booths, and accessories.

These elements should be designed to withstand weather and heavy usage and should be reasonably resistant to vandalism. Also, furniture and other street elements should be designed and positioned with the handicapped and children in mind, that is, drinking fountains should not be too high, elements should not be too close together to allow passage of wheelchairs, and so forth.

Planter/Bench

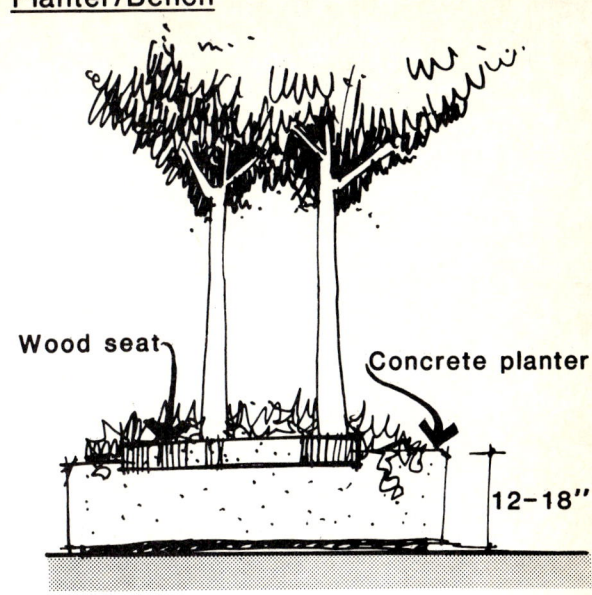

- Wood seat
- Concrete planter
- 12-18"

Free Standing Bench

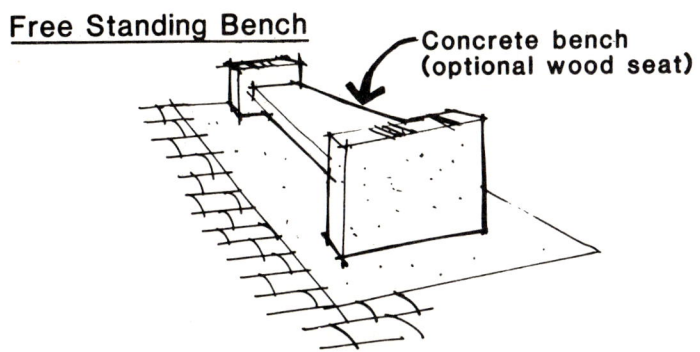

Concrete bench (optional wood seat)

Litter Receptacles

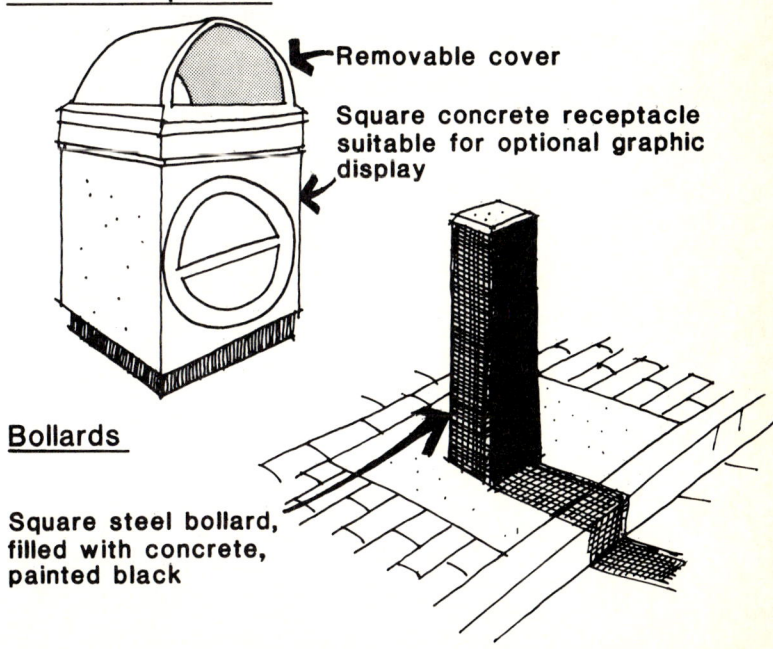

- Removable cover
- Square concrete receptacle suitable for optional graphic display

Bollards

Square steel bollard, filled with concrete, painted black

STREET FURNITURE

FOUR
SCHEMATIC SITE PLANS

INTRODUCTION

The schematic site plan is the refined next step after the conceptual plan is formed. Elements usually seen on the schematic site plan include layout of structures, showing the relationship of structures to each other and to the site as a whole; circulation; parking; site amenities such as play areas, tennis courts, swimming pools, and lakes; and other elements that influence function or appearance of site. Plantings are shown. An indication of grading and lighting may be shown. Generally speaking, the schematic site plan is a nontechnical plan used to illustrate the site plan at a glance.

The following are examples of schematic site plans.

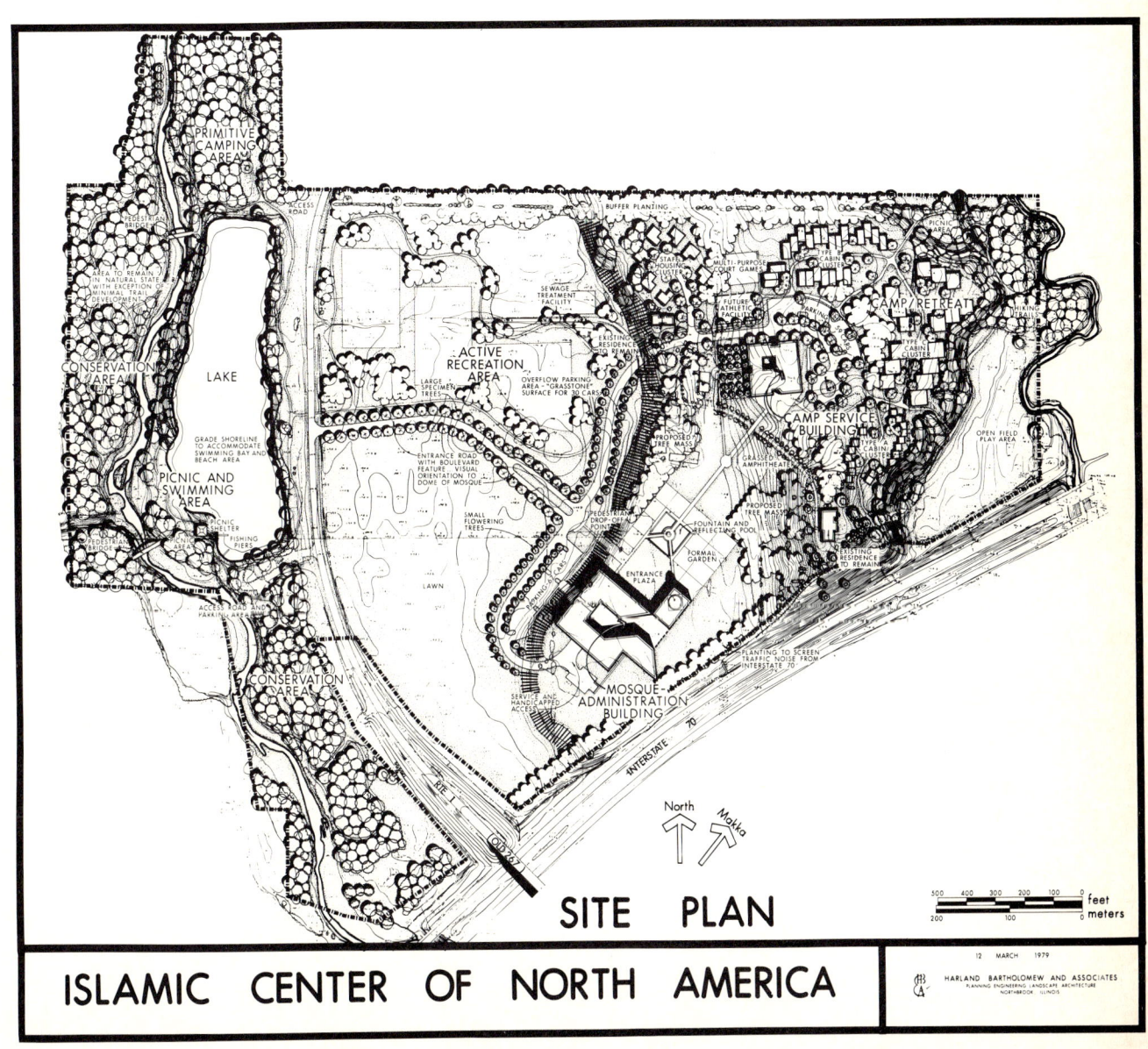

SCHEMATIC SITE PLAN

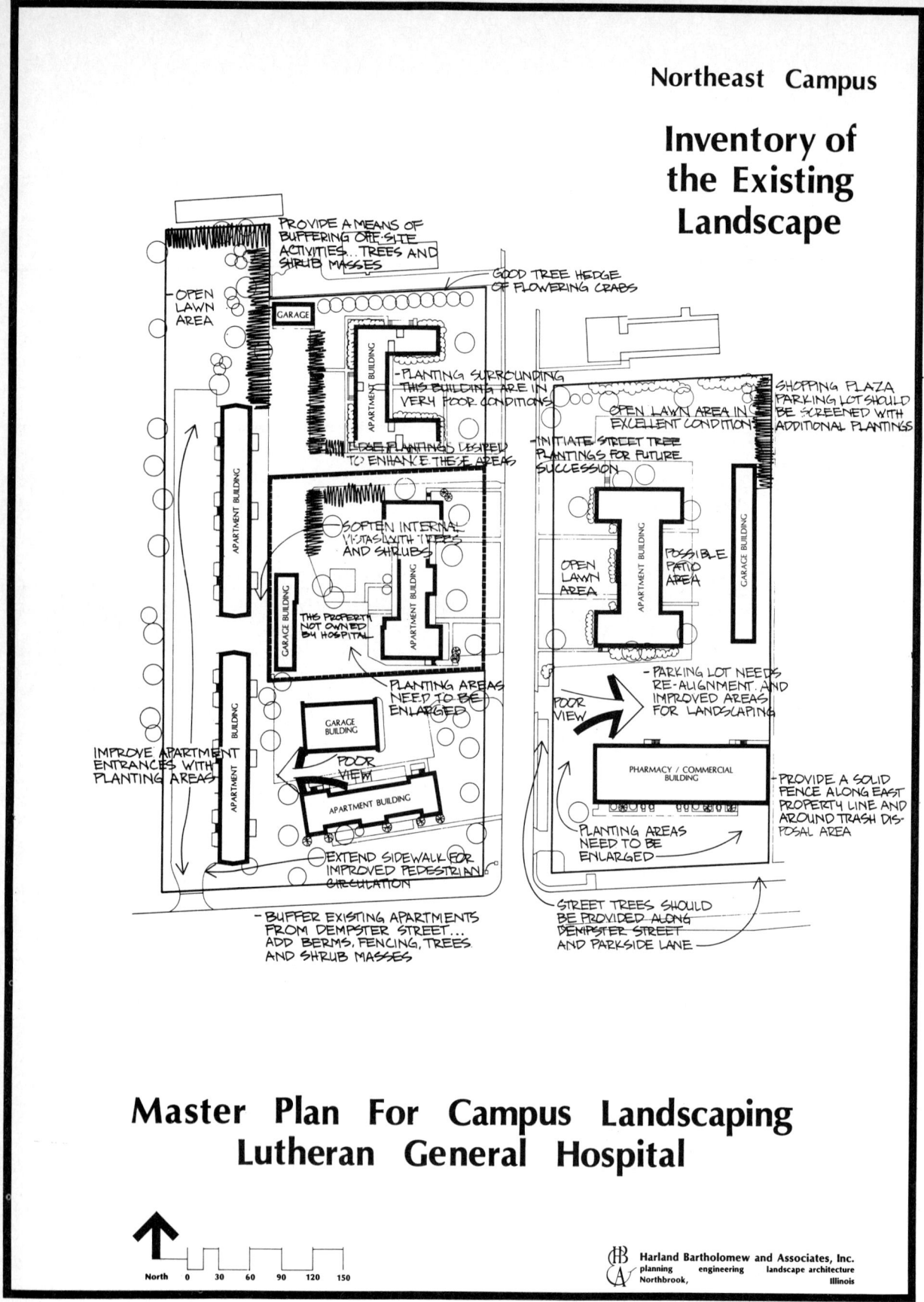

38 SCHEMATIC SITE PLAN

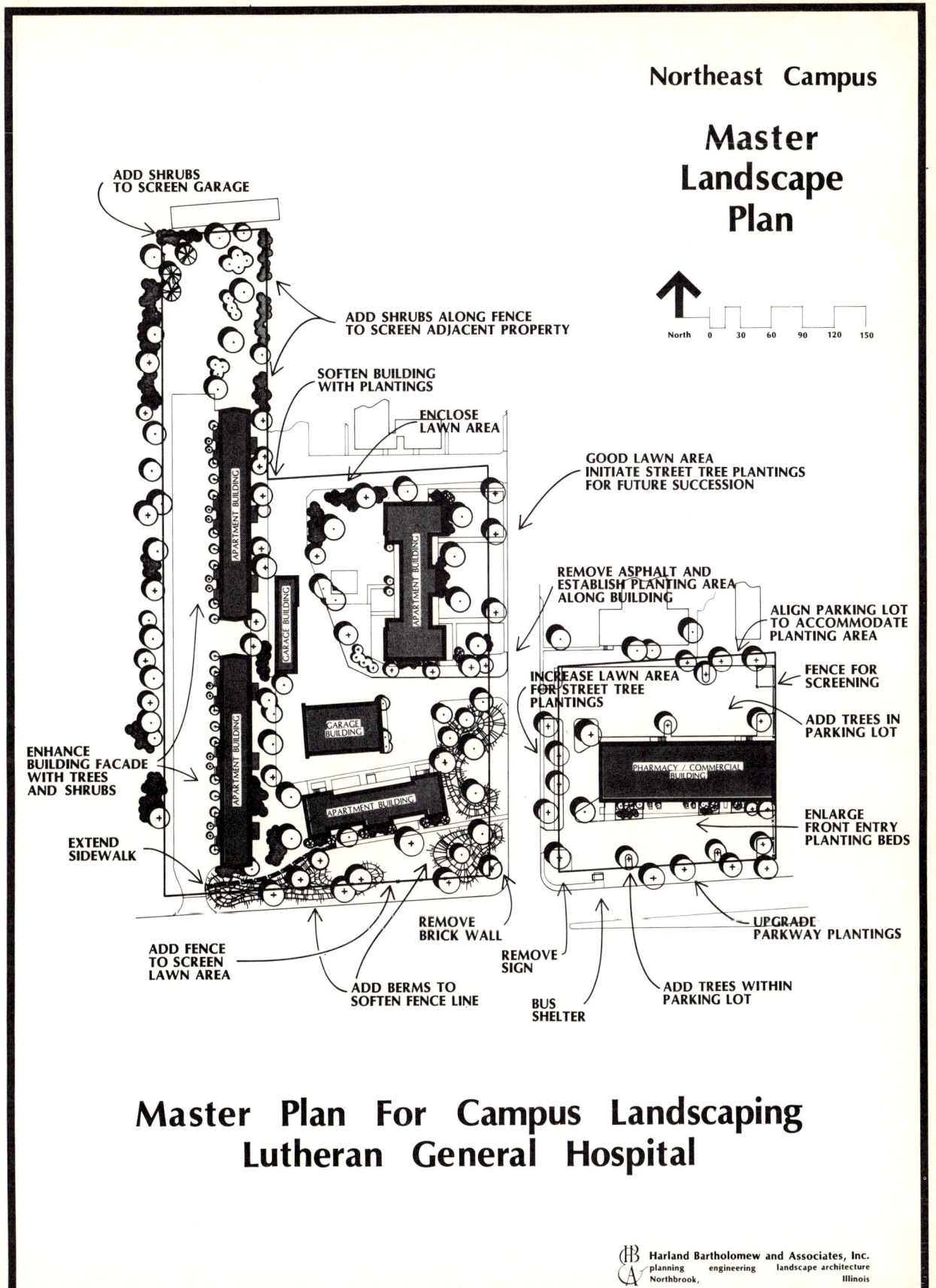

SCHEMATIC SITE PLAN 39

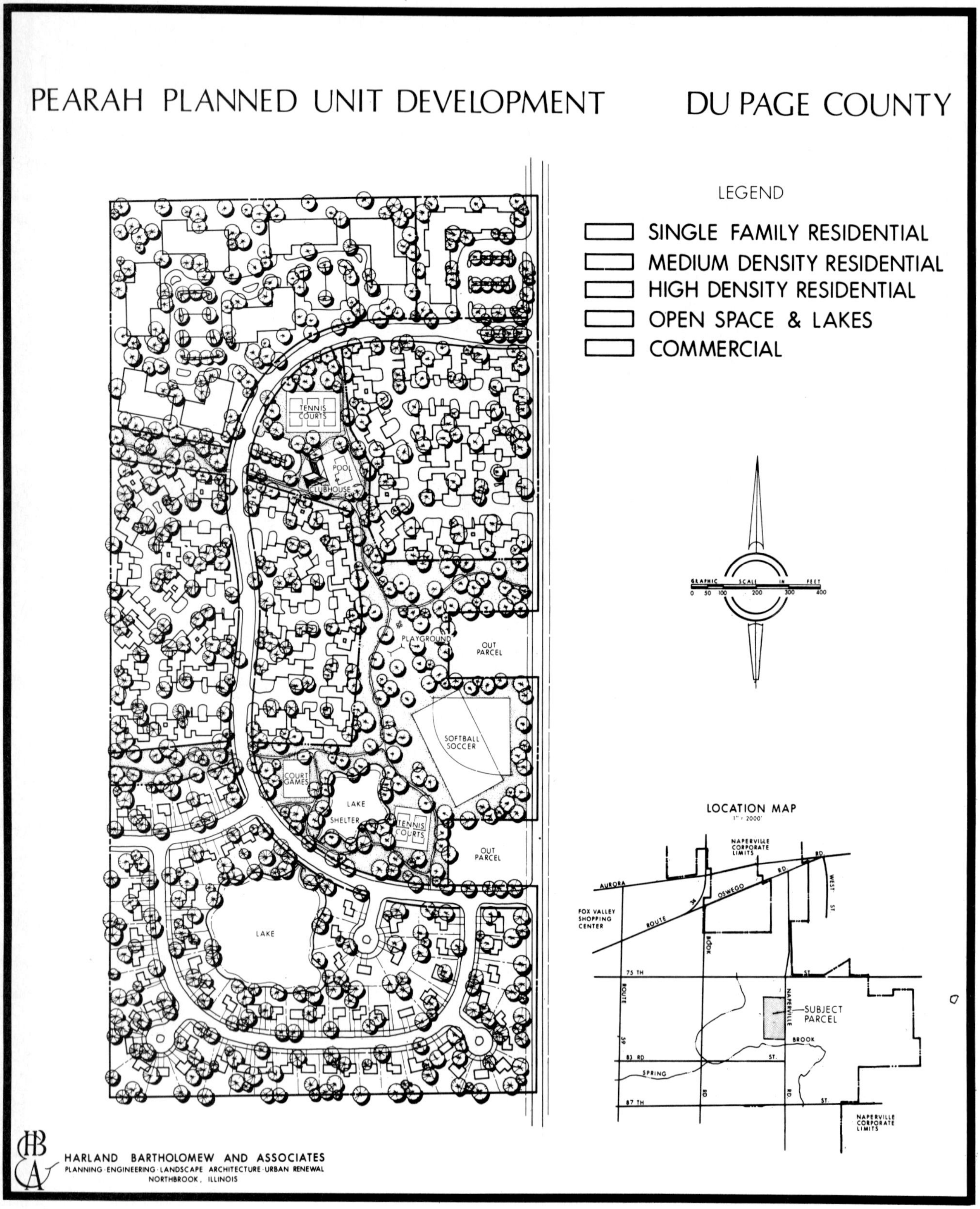

PEARAH PLANNED UNIT DEVELOPMENT   DU PAGE COUNTY

LEGEND
- SINGLE FAMILY RESIDENTIAL
- MEDIUM DENSITY RESIDENTIAL
- HIGH DENSITY RESIDENTIAL
- OPEN SPACE & LAKES
- COMMERCIAL

LOCATION MAP
1" = 2000'

HARLAND BARTHOLOMEW AND ASSOCIATES
PLANNING · ENGINEERING · LANDSCAPE ARCHITECTURE · URBAN RENEWAL
NORTHBROOK, ILLINOIS

40   SCHEMATIC SITE PLAN

GREGORY PLANNED UNIT DEVELOPMENT   DU PAGE COUNTY

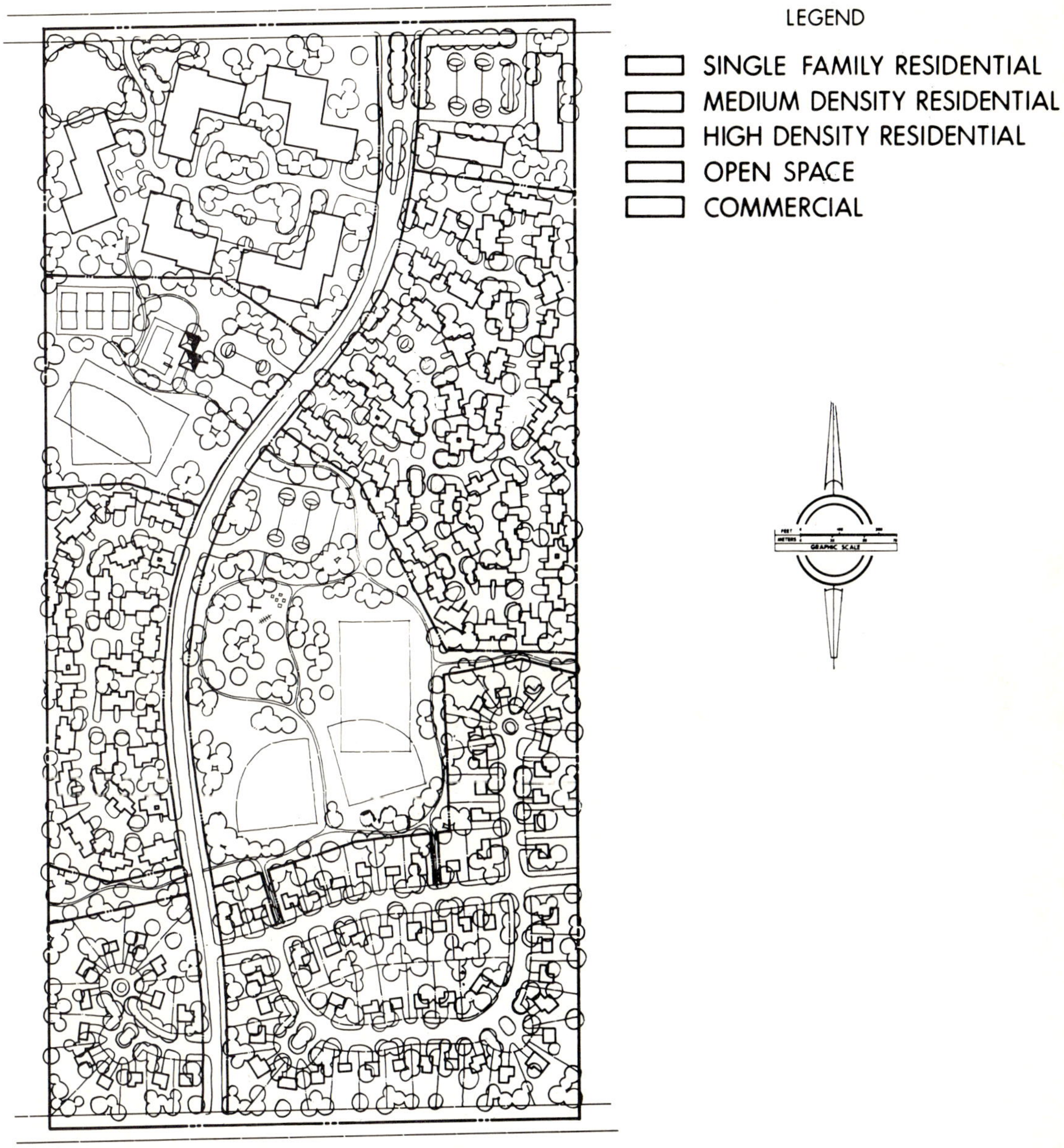

LEGEND
- SINGLE FAMILY RESIDENTIAL
- MEDIUM DENSITY RESIDENTIAL
- HIGH DENSITY RESIDENTIAL
- OPEN SPACE
- COMMERCIAL

HARLAND BARTHOLOMEW AND ASSOCIATES
PLANNING·ENGINEERING·LANDSCAPE ARCHITECTURE·URBAN RENEWAL
NORTHBROOK, ILLINOIS

SCHEMATIC SITE PLAN

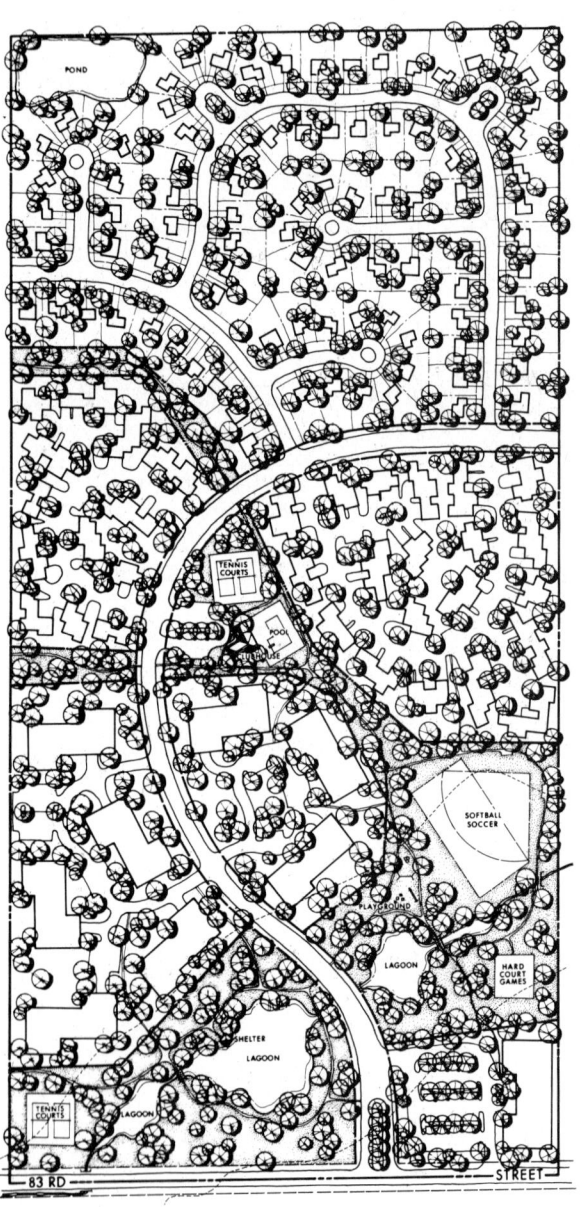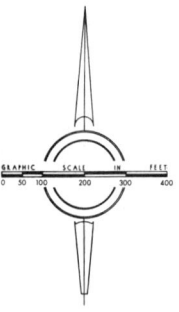

42 SCHEMATIC SITE PLAN

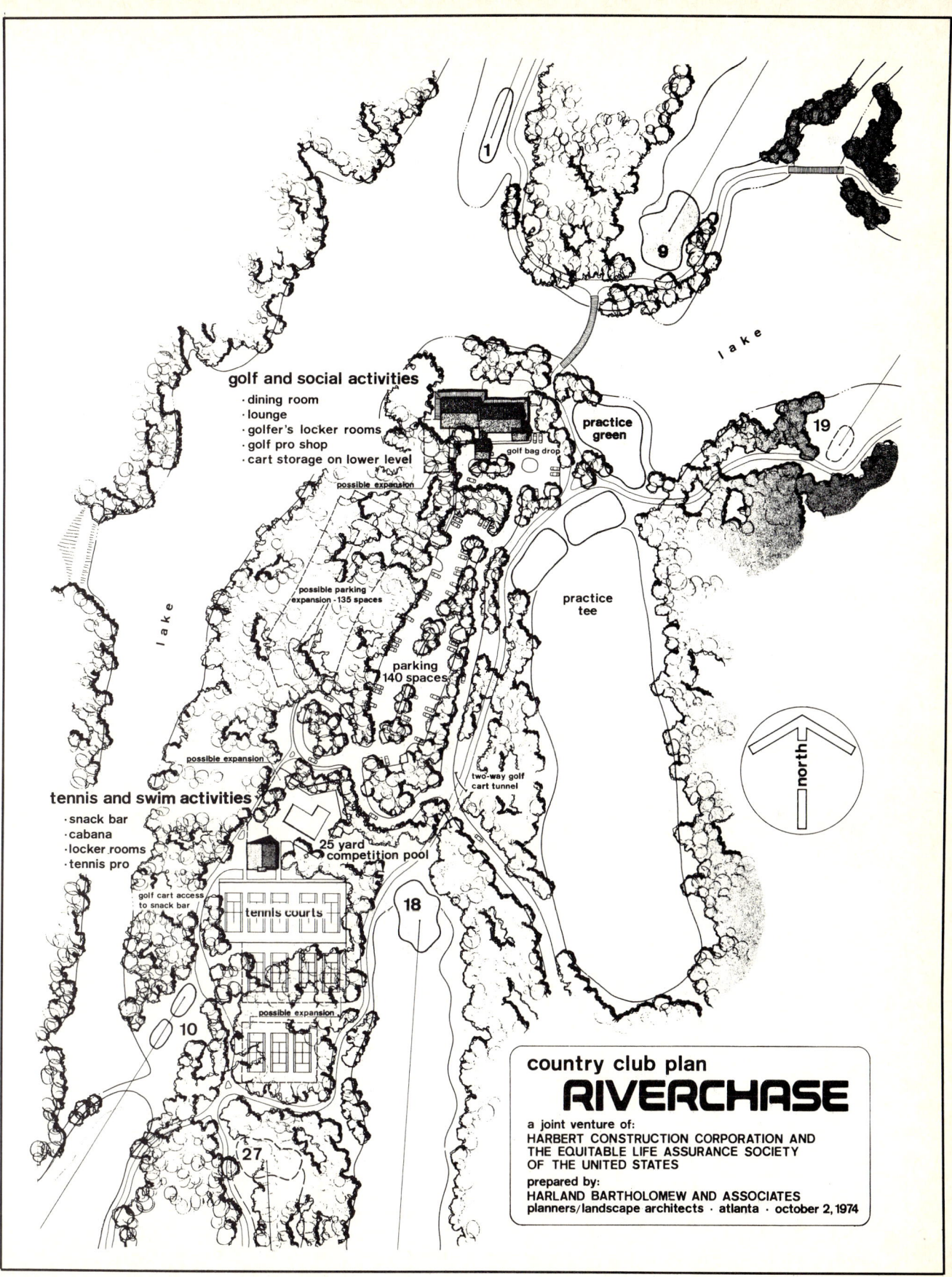

SCHEMATIC SITE PLAN   43

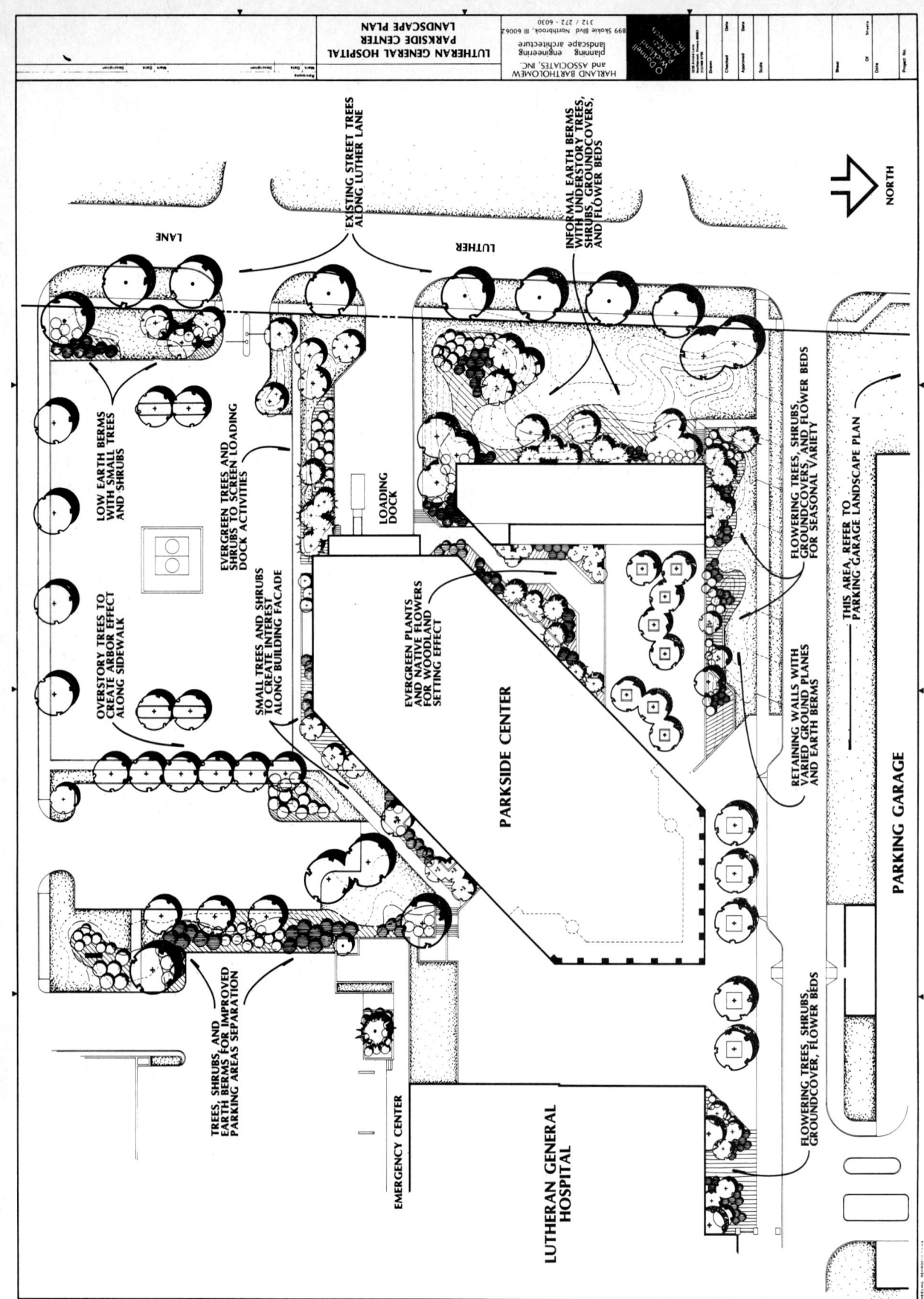

44 SCHEMATIC SITE PLAN

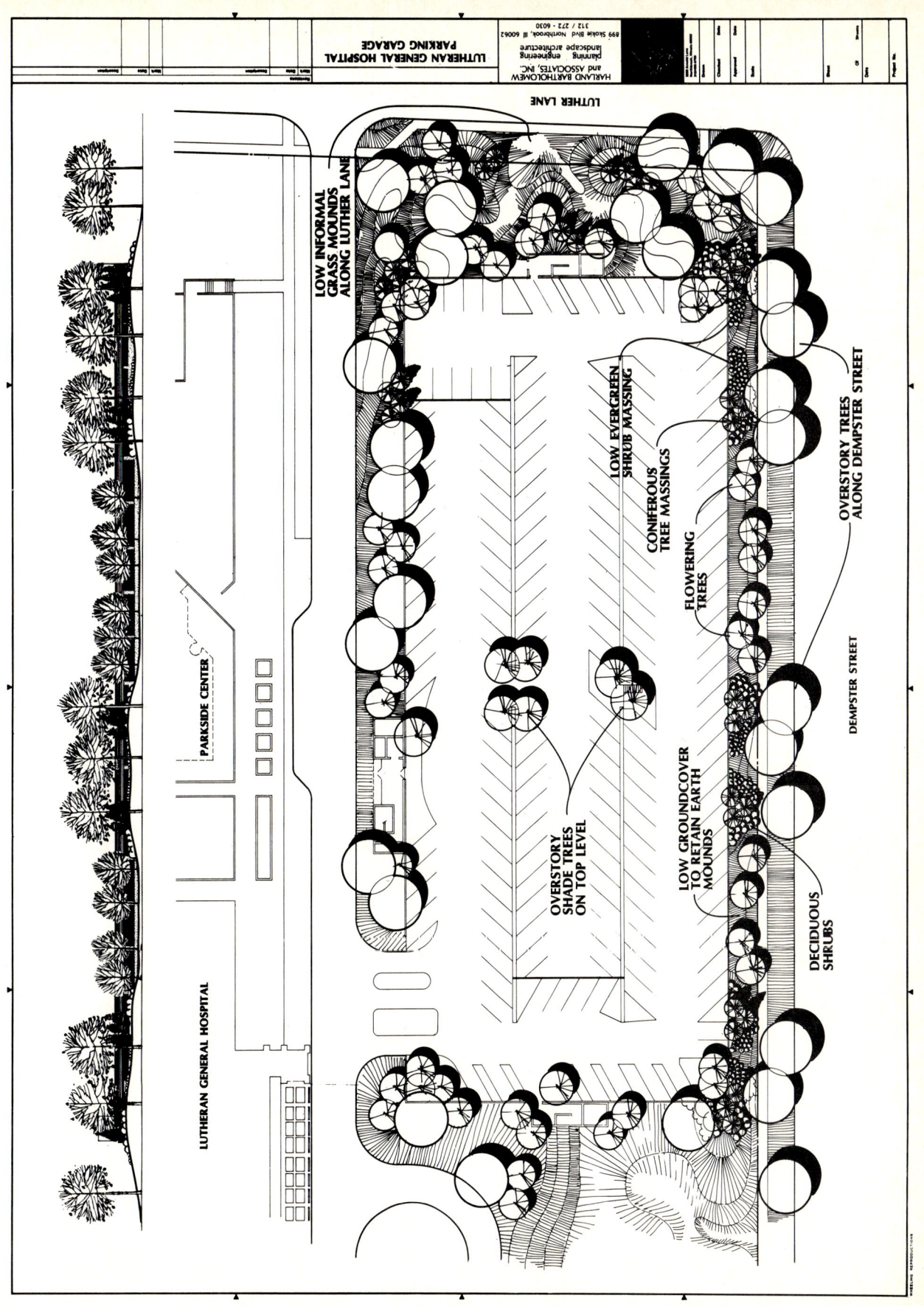

SCHEMATIC SITE PLAN 45

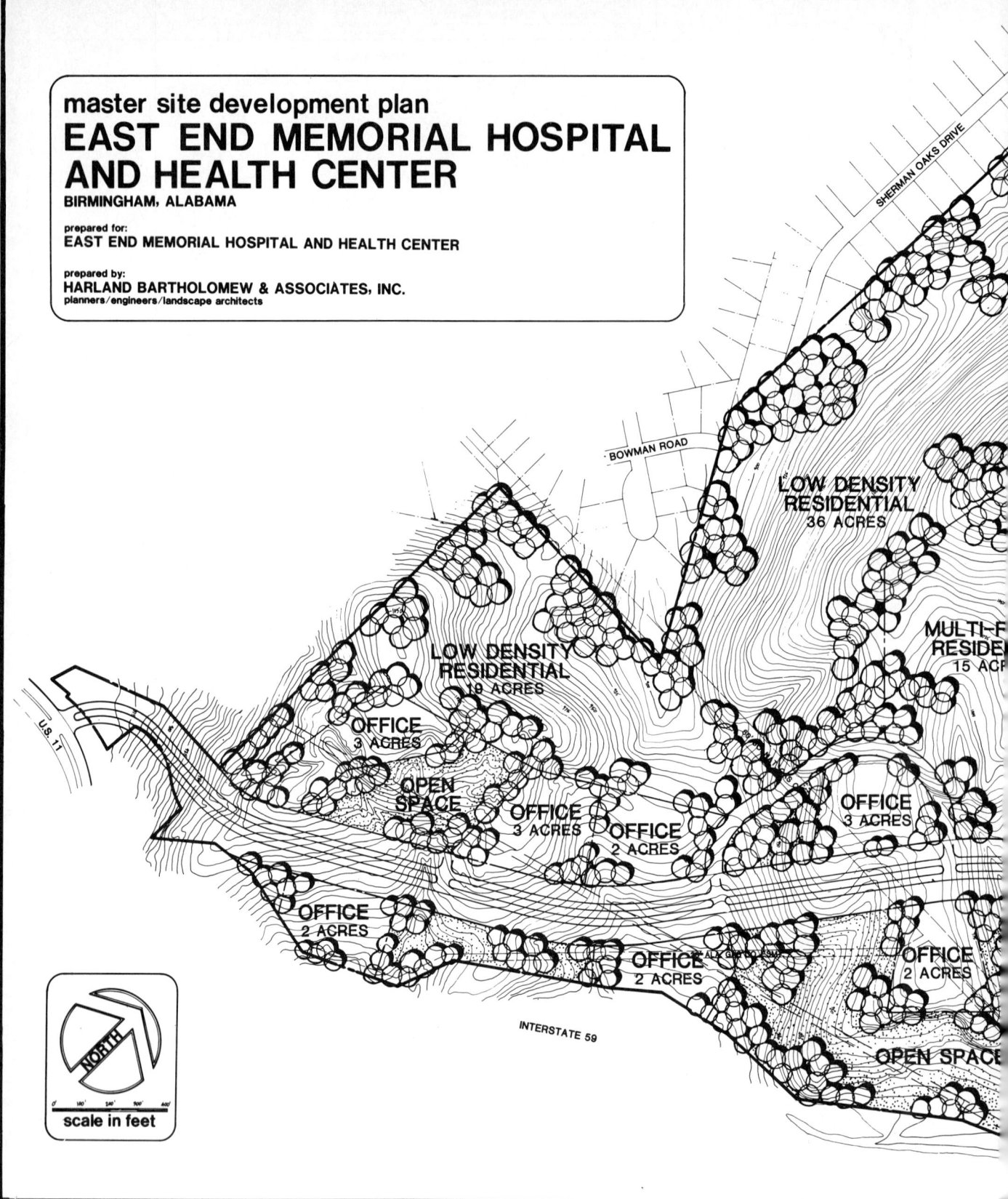

46 SCHEMATIC SITE PLAN

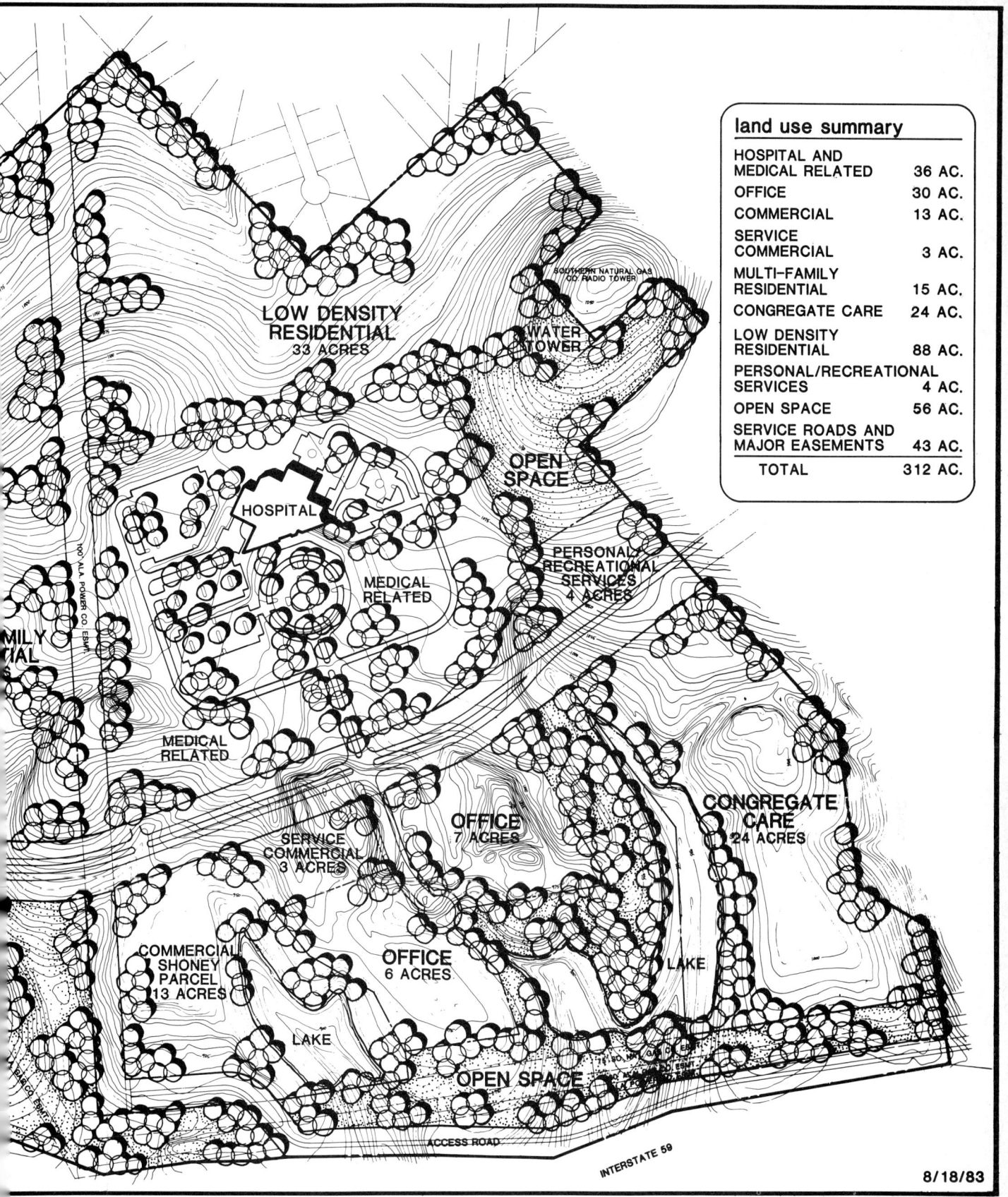

SCHEMATIC SITE PLAN

FIVE
SUBDIVISIONS

INTRODUCTION

Subdividing raw land is inherent in almost all development—particularly land that is to be used for residential purposes. Residential use is the largest land area use in any community. Simply put, subdivision is the process of dividing a large tract of land into smaller parts of particular size and form that accommodate individual parcel use and that function well within the whole of the development.

The process often begins by designing streets through the land in such a manner that they function well within the development and are relative to the surrounding area or community. In some cases, land is set aside for parks and recreational uses, schools, commercial areas, and other uses; in any case, the development is studied relative to its total needs, whether those needs are met on the site or in the immediate vicinity.

Designers are subject to land-use intensity standards, zoning, and other authority standards. Such standards generally determine where the various types of structures may be placed, maximal and minimal floor space required, parking required, open space, size and type of streets, and other working parameters. The developer must be concerned with the number of income-producing units (number of houses, offices, and so forth) that may be placed on the land—for obvious reasons.

It is good planning and good architecture that resolve the various interests to produce harmonious development plans. The subdivision plat is the typical format for describing land use within the development. The following plats illustrate several types of developments and layouts.

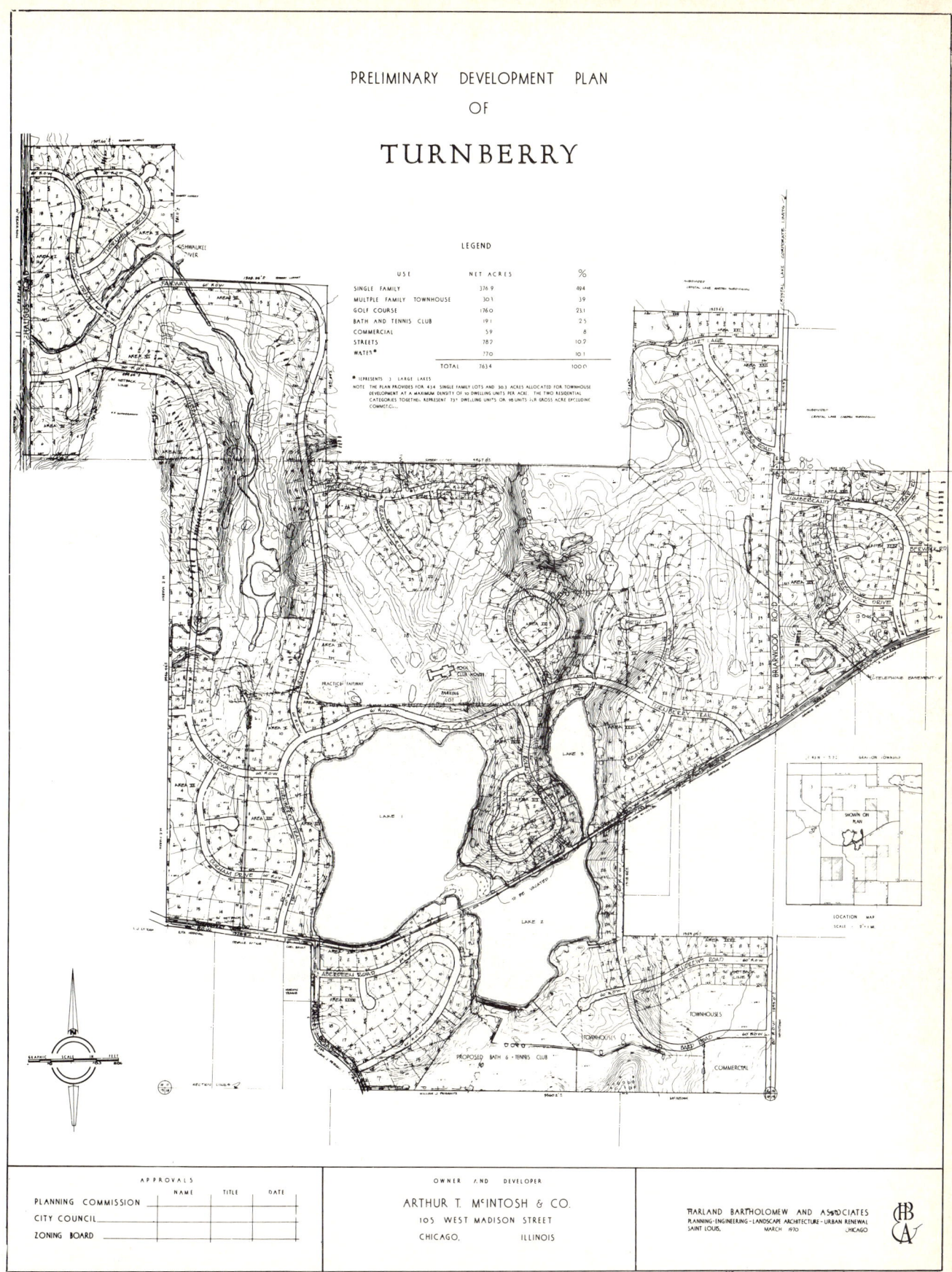

SUBDIVISIONS

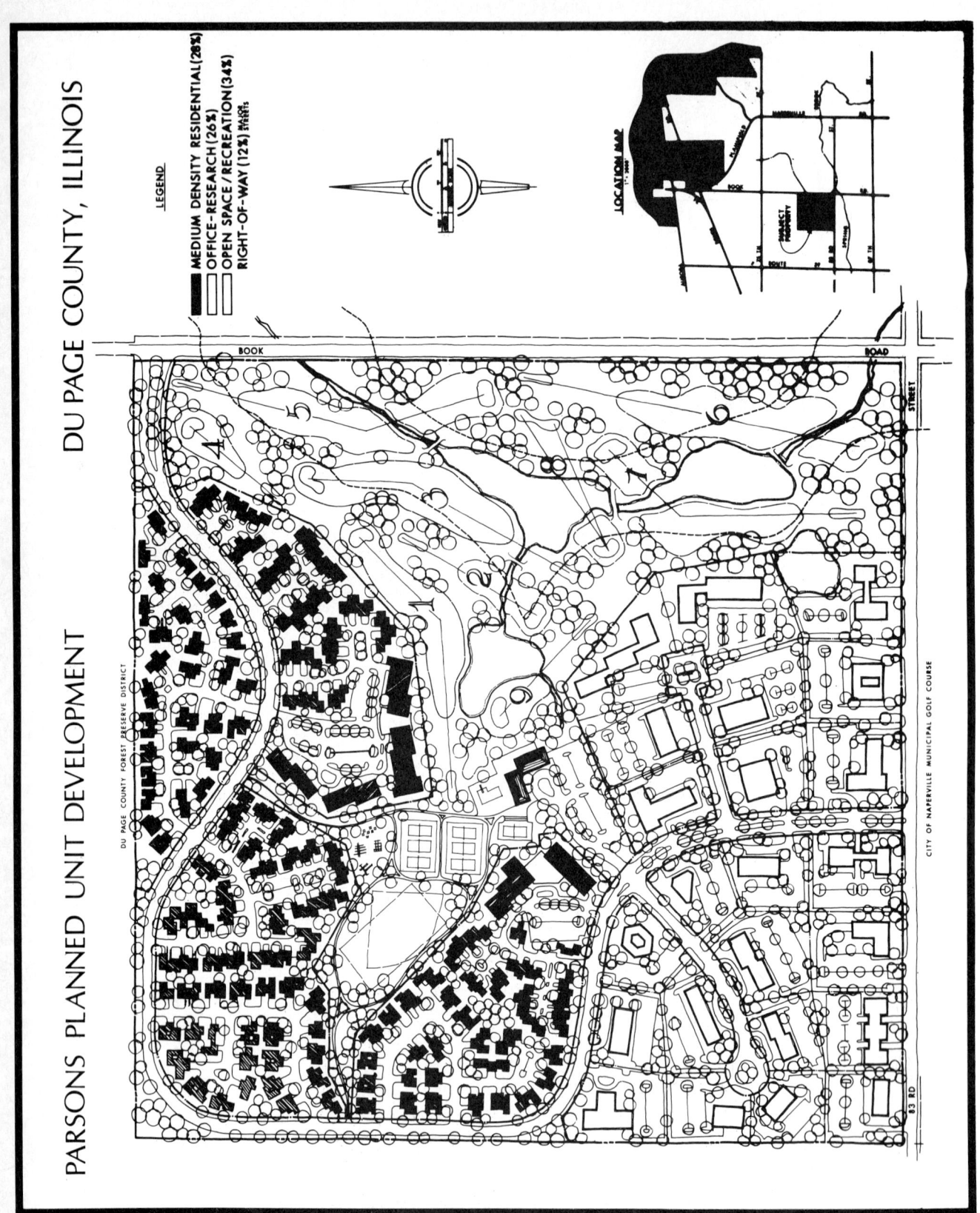

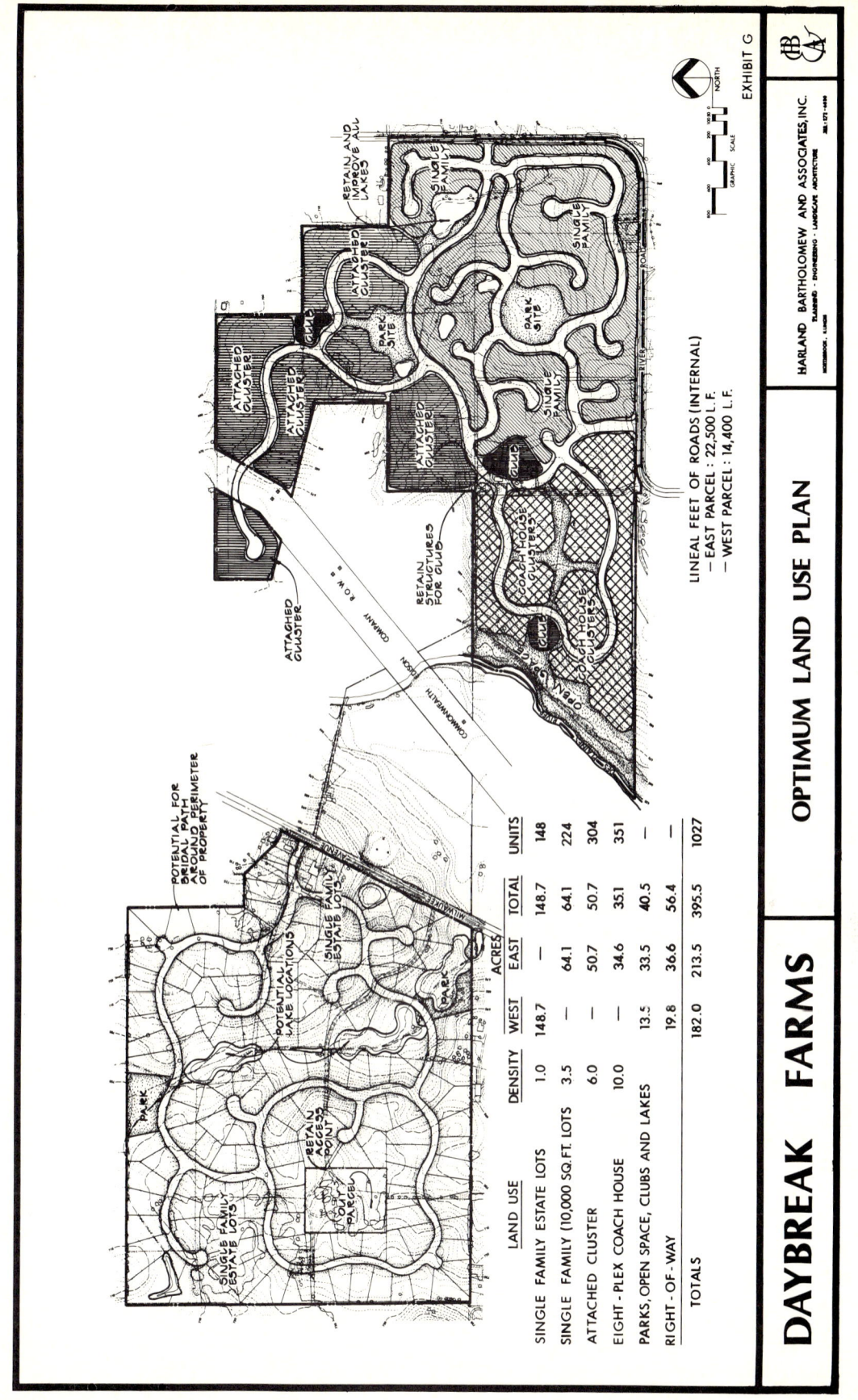

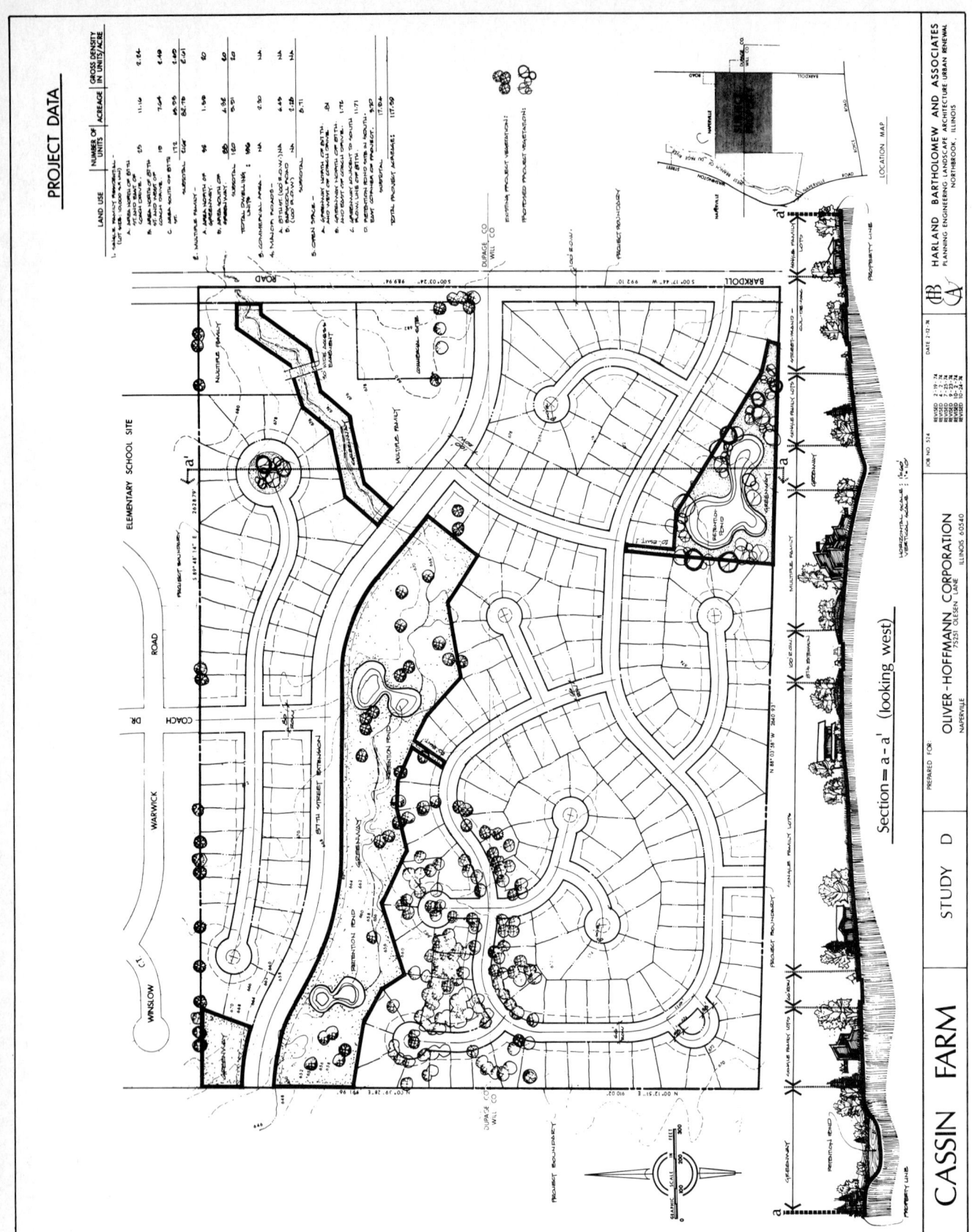

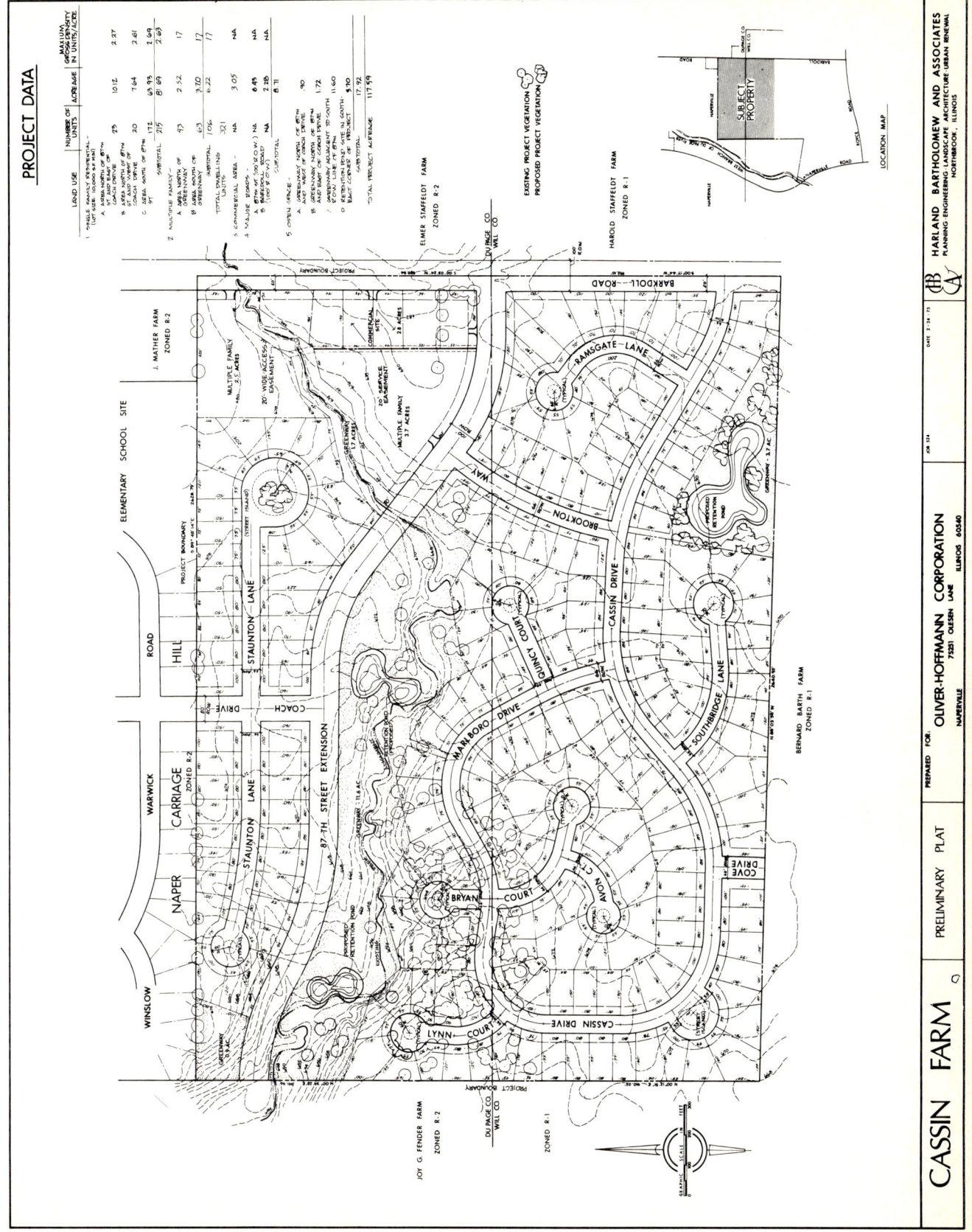

SUBDIVISIONS 55

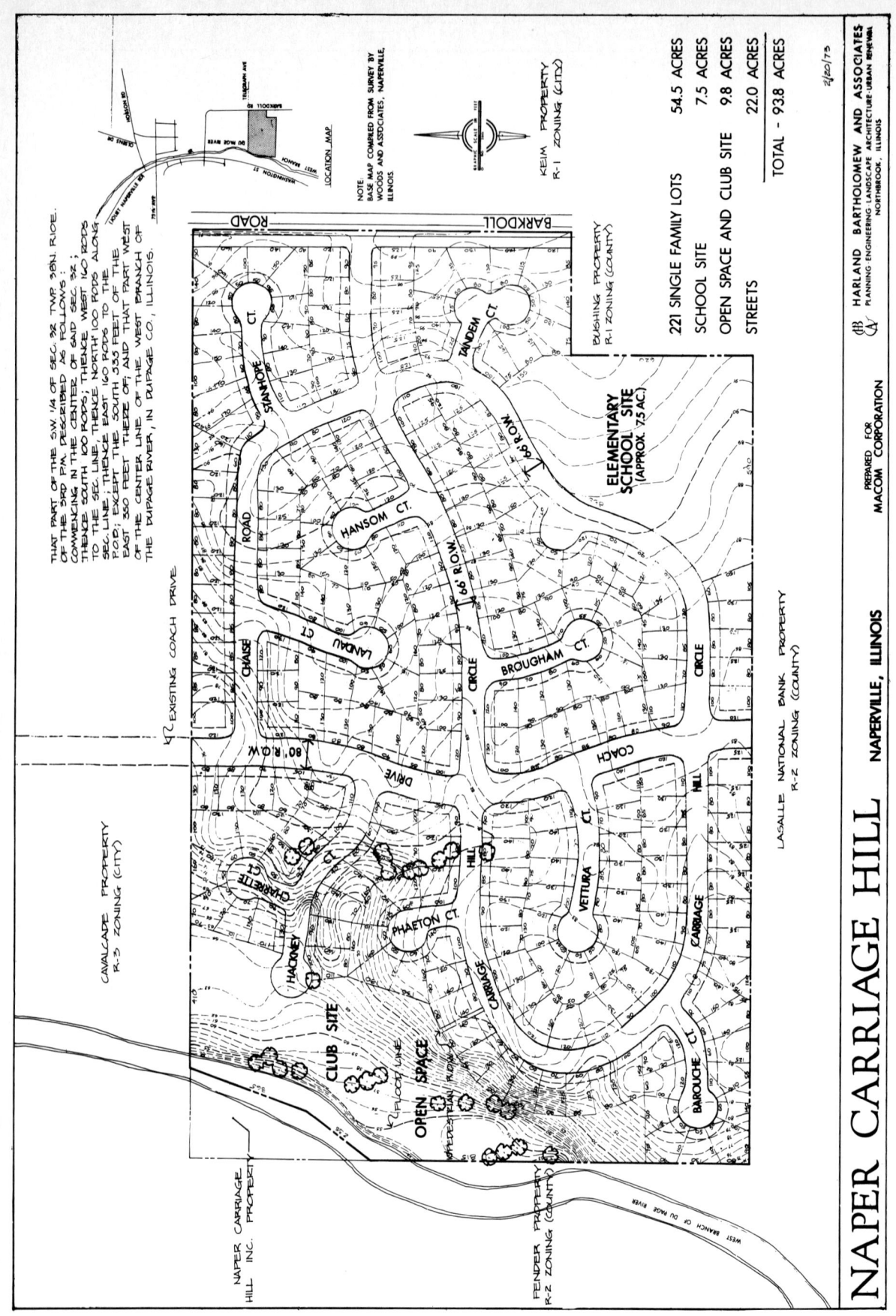

56 SUBDIVISIONS

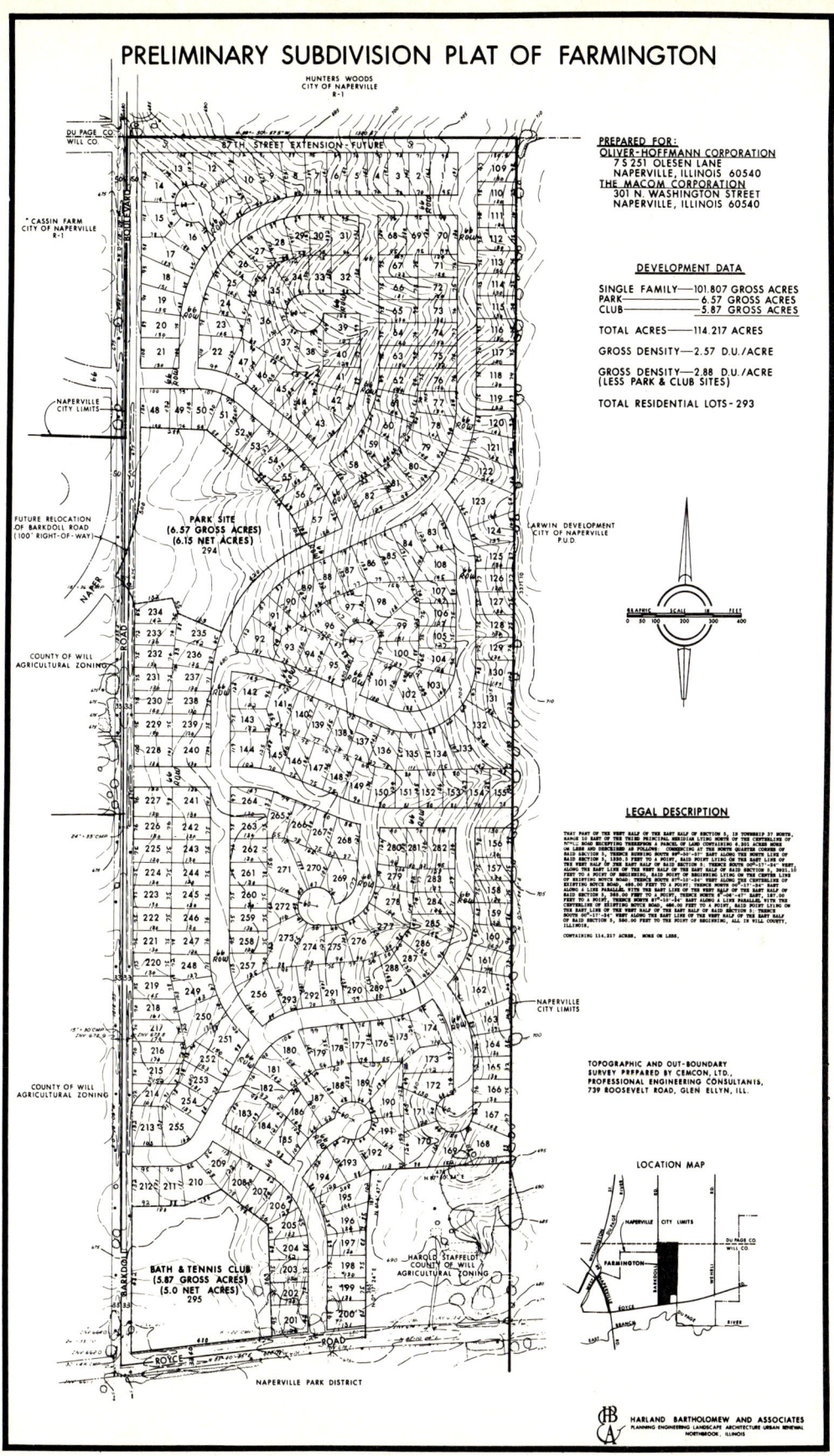

SIX
COMPREHENSIVE PLANS

ILLINOIS AND MICHIGAN CANAL COMPREHENSIVE DEVELOPMENT AND MANAGEMENT PLAN
Joliet to LaSalle, Illinois

Built between 1836 and 1850, the Illinois and Michigan Canal, known generally as the I&M, was designed to link Chicago to the Mississippi River and the South. The Canal was a major factor in the rapid development of Chicago and its eventual dominance of Midwest agricultural markets. Commercial use of the waterway ended in 1933, and it was largely abandoned. The locks, aqueducts, spillways, culverts, and lock-keepers' houses along the Canal, all of which constitute an outstanding example of early American engineering expertise, were allowed to fall into disrepair.

In 1971, the Secretary of the Illinois Department of Transportation appointed a task force to develop a plan for the future of the Canal. Harland Bartholomew & Associates, Inc., was asked to serve as staff to the task force and to prepare both an assessment of the current conditions of the Canal and a master plan for the restoration and rehabilitation of a 61-mile stretch.

The Canal Plan, published in 1974, emphasized both the historical and educational values of the Canal and its potential as a linear recreational resource. The plan provided for 60 miles of bicycle and hiking trails and several Canal access points for canoeing. Overall development along the Canal was kept to a minimum, with emphasis on linear mobility.

A special historic district was proposed for one section of the Canal that offered extraordinary opportunities to demonstrate the rural settlements served by the Canal. Historic buildings, lock demonstrations, aqueducts, and relatively unspoiled countryside are being preserved.

In addition, a Canal boat concession was proposed so that visitors could experience travel in a canal boat pulled by mules. An extensive self-instructive sign system throughout the trails and facilities completes the interpretive focus of the Canal and its lands.

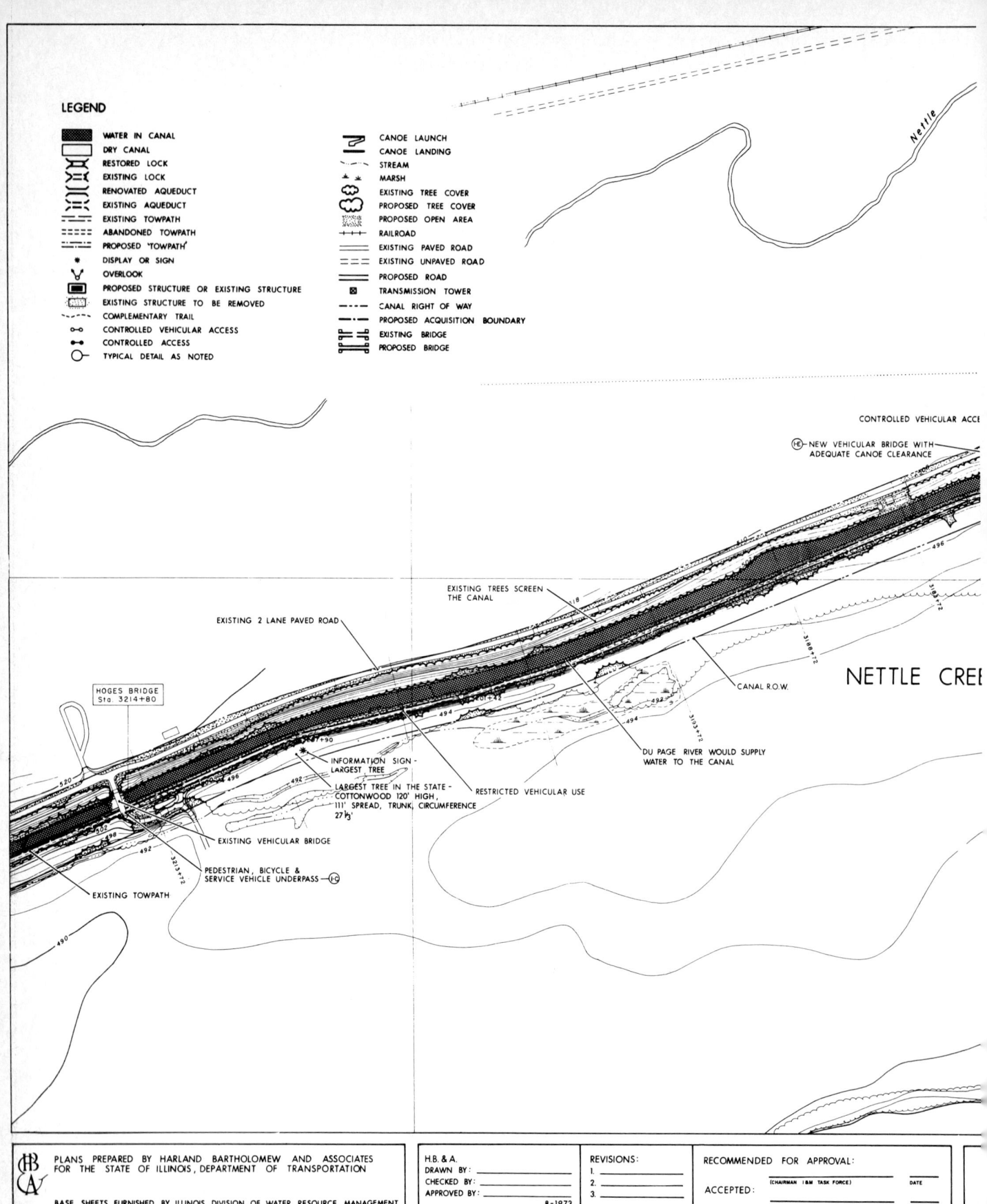

62 COMPREHENSIVE PLANS

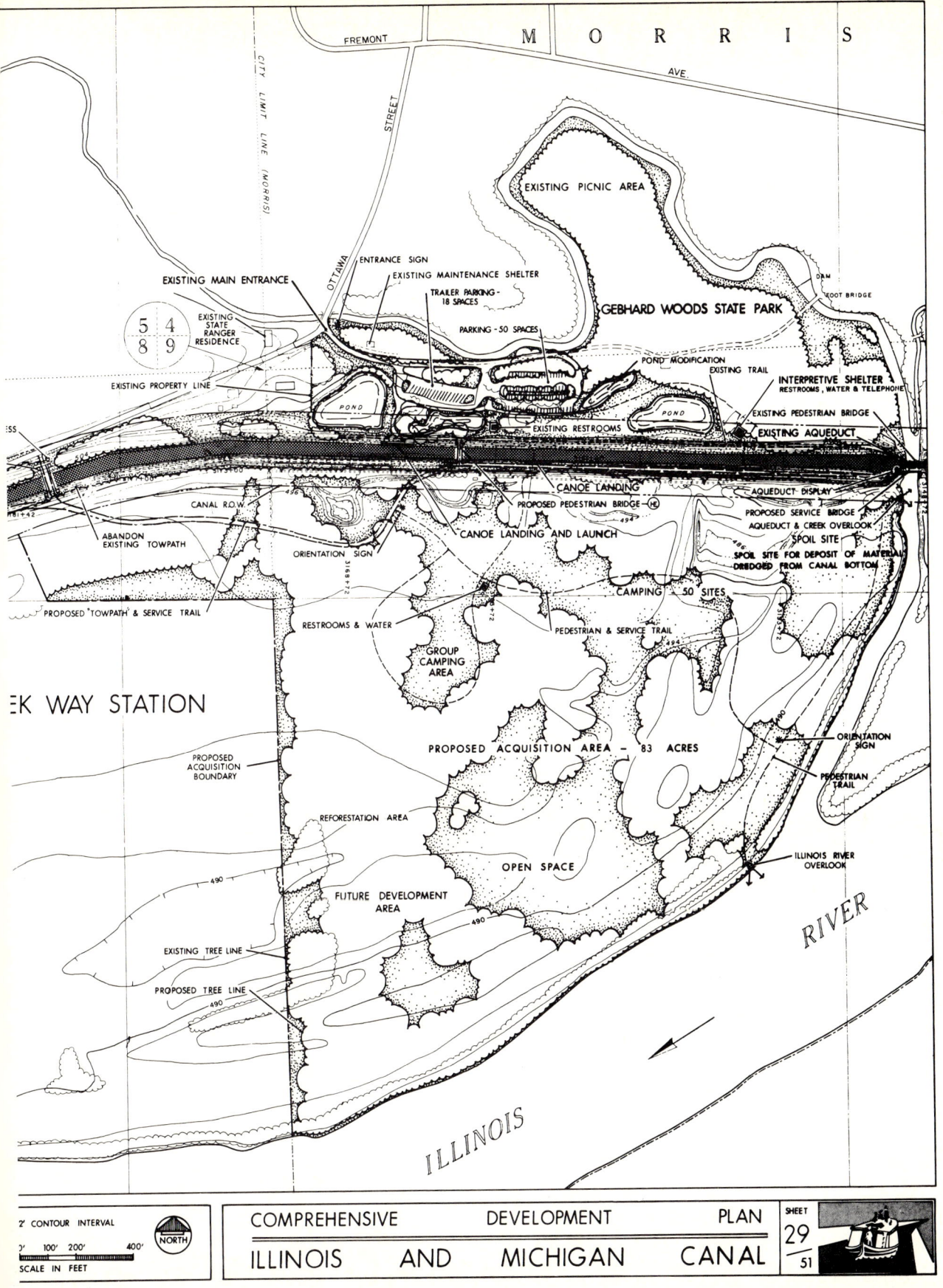

COMPREHENSIVE PLANS 63

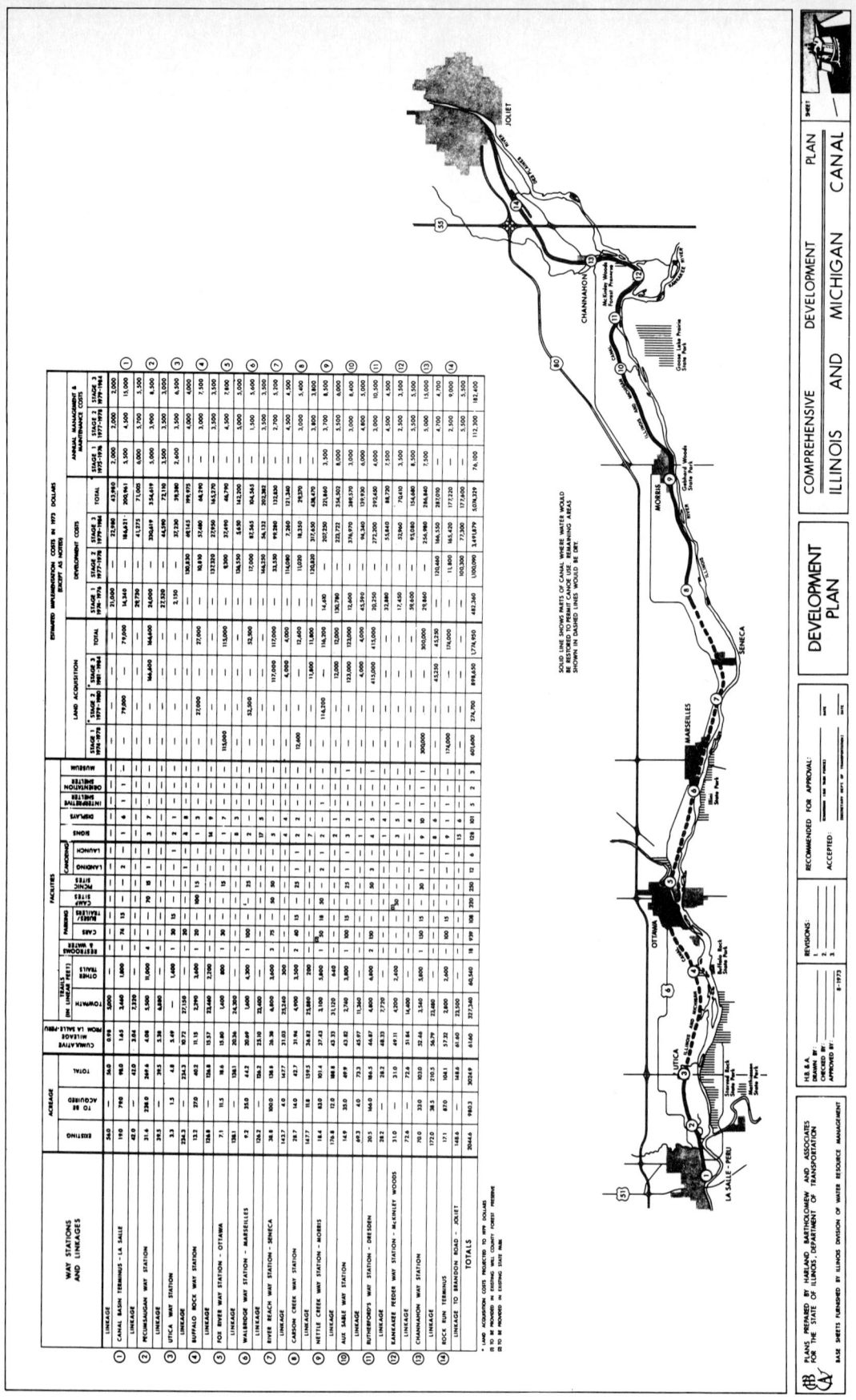

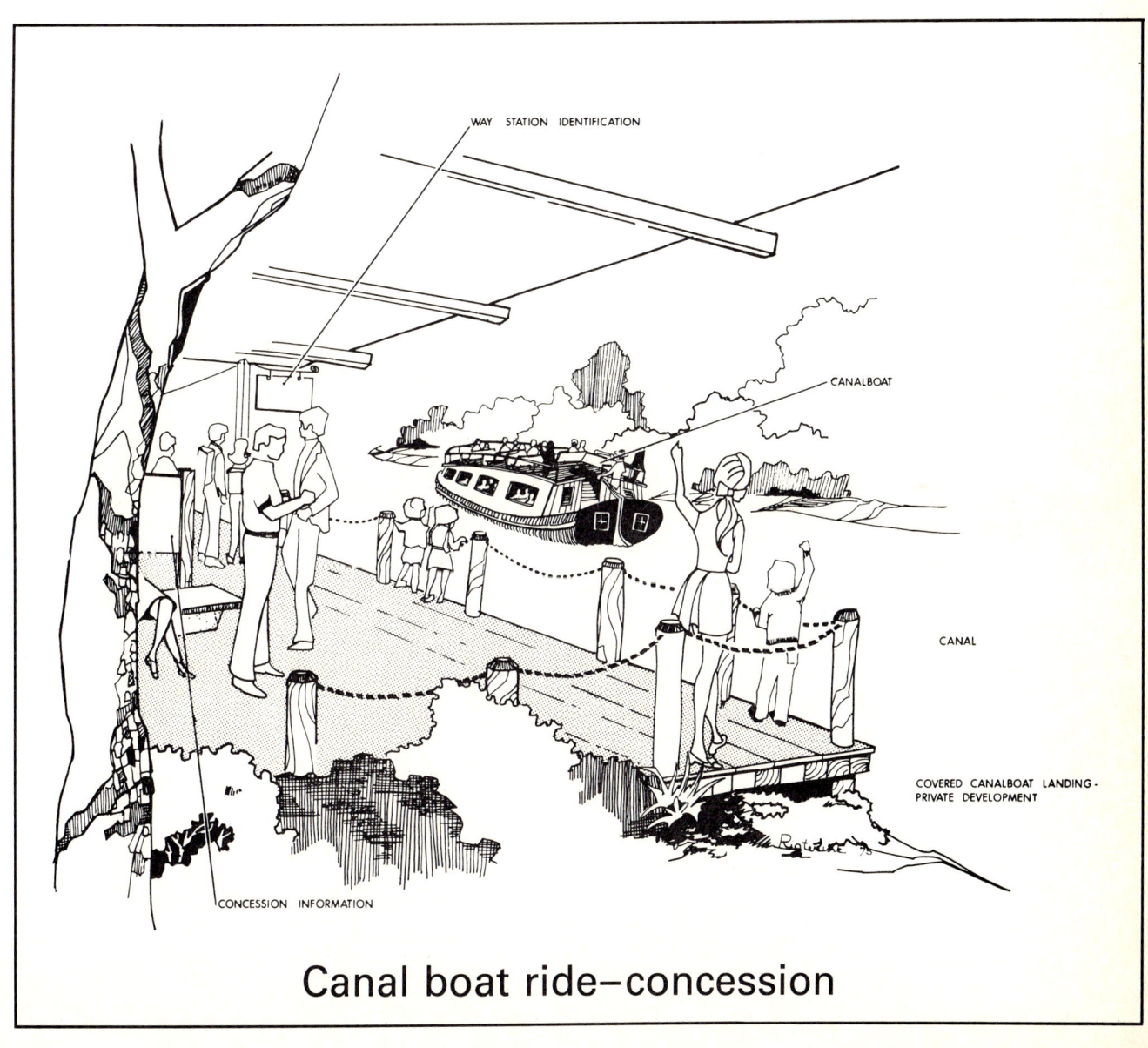

Canal boot ride–concession

COMPREHENSIVE PLANS

COMPREHENSIVE PLAN
St. Charles, Illinois

As growth pressures increased from the Chicago metropolitan area, the city of St. Charles engaged in a planning program in 1972. The overall objective of the program was to ensure the perpetuation of the high-quality residential environment and the preservation of the unique and beautiful environment of the Fox River Valley of which the city is a part.

Various environmental features, including wetlands, watershed areas, water-recharge areas, and unique habitats, are safeguarded by spelling out specific development limitations in these areas. In fact, every area of the city and the township have maximal density limitations attuned to the carrying capacity of the land. A "Land-Use Assignments" map was prepared as part of the overall plan to delineate various land-use types and intensities. Each land-use assignment is accompanied with total acreage, maximum density, permitted number of dwelling units, and population equivalent.

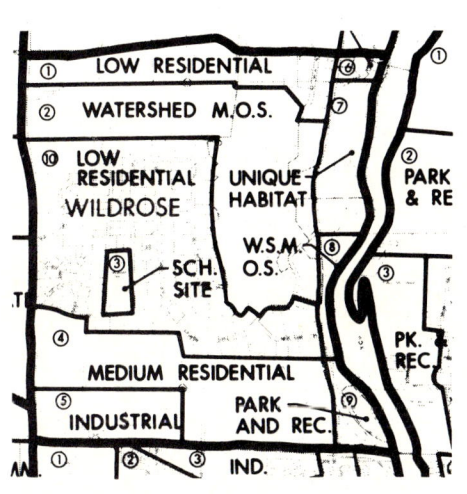 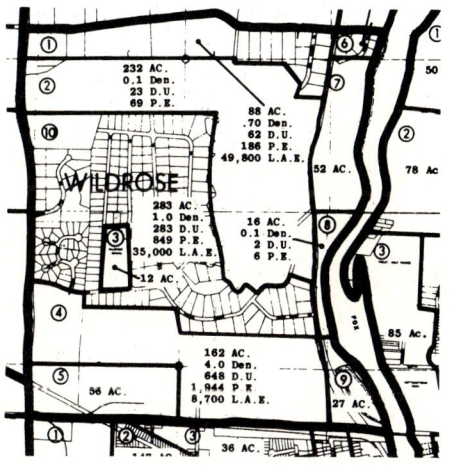

LAND USE ASSIGNMENTS

RESIDENTIAL EQUIVALENTS 1990

▬▬▬ PLANNING COMPONENTS BOUNDARY
─── SUB - COMPONENTS BOUNDARY
① SUB - COMPONENTS NUMBER
ESTATE RESIDENTIAL LAND USE ASSIGNMENT

100 A.C. — TOTAL ACRES
3.0 DEN. — GROSS DENSITY – MAXIMUM DWELLING UNITS PER ACRE
300 D.U. — TOTAL NUMBER DWELLING UNITS
900 P.E. — POPULATION EQUIVALENTS AT 3 PERSONS PER DWELLING UNIT
11,600 L.A.E. — LOT AREA EQUIVALENTS – IF ALL LOTS OF UNIFORM SIZE

COMPREHENSIVE PLANS

THE COMPREHENSIVE PLAN
Cape Girardeau, Missouri

The comprehensive plan for Cape Girardeau is initially concerned with the arrangement of public physical facilities such as parks, schools, utilities, streets, and public buildings. Recommendations for land-use arrangements—residential, commercial, industrial, and public—are suggested relative to the various physical facilities. Regulatory measures, such as zoning and subdivision regulations, are suggested to maintain development within the desired land-use patterns. Finally, the plan includes a capital improvement program of specific development activities for accomplishing the purposes of the plan.

Street improvements were recommended to get traffic to and from the central business district (CBD) smoothly; street improvements within the CBD were also recommended, moving the traffic around the CBD, rather than through it.

A mall was proposed to improve both the appearance and convenience of a portion of the district. The mall was planned to be attractively landscaped and improved for the comforts and convenience of the shoppers, yet provide access for emergency vehicles and other utilitarian needs. Underground wiring, better lighting, stricter control of signs and advertising material, and street trees also were among the suggestions.

The comprehensive plan, however, is not intended to be a rigid set of rules that the community must obey. Rather, it is intended to serve as a guide for the future physical growth of the city of Cape Girardeau. The building of a city is a gradual process of growth, stimulated and fostered by numerous individuals and public agencies. Cape Girardeau is in the enviable position of being able to direct a significant amount of its projected future growth. It is hoped that the comprehensive plan will serve as a functional, working instrument to help guide that growth.

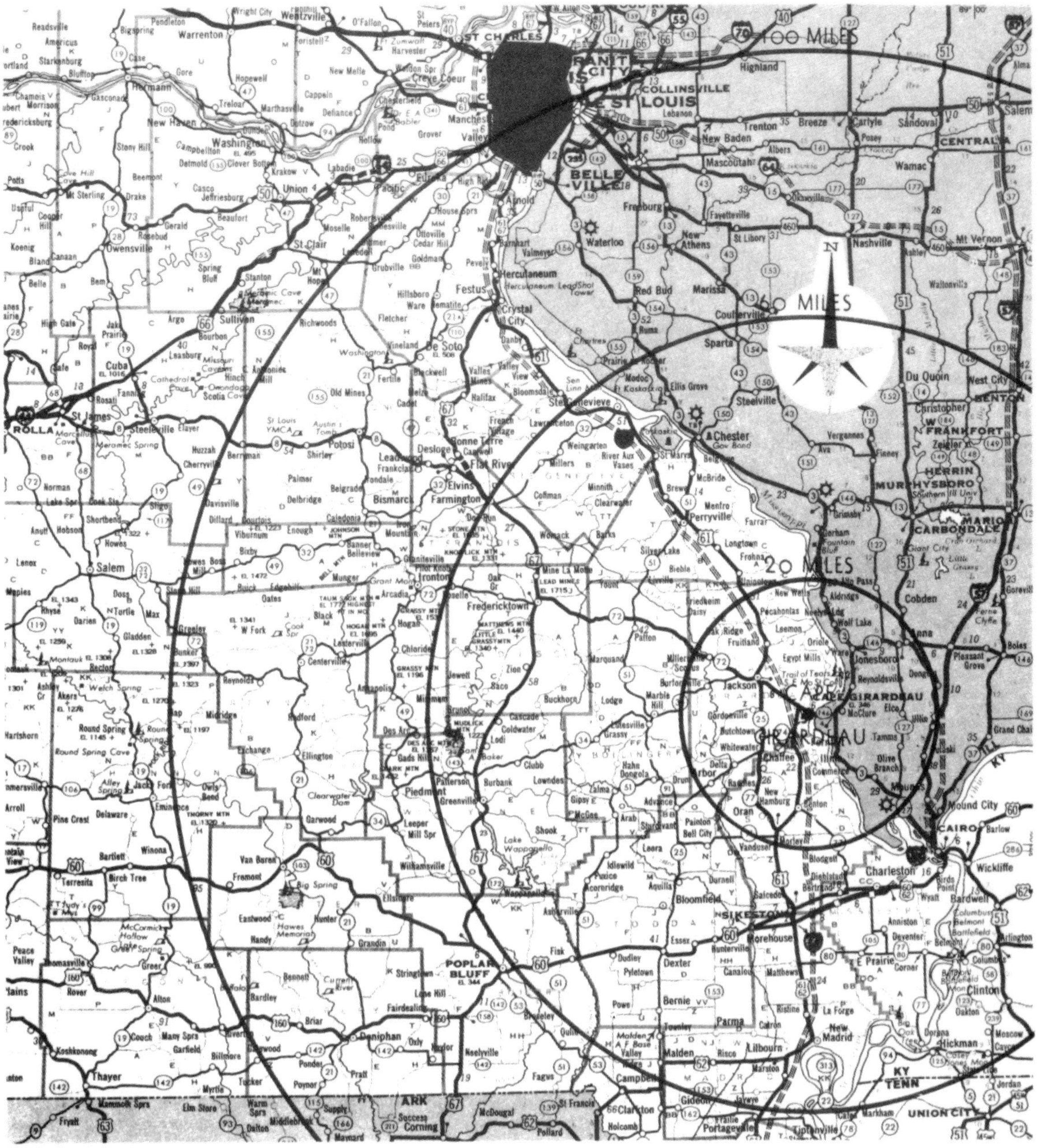

REGIONAL LOCATION

THE PREPARATION OF THIS MAP WAS FINANCIALLY AIDED THROUGH A FEDERAL GRANT FROM THE DEPARTMENT OF HOUSING AND URBAN DEVELOPMENT UNDER THE URBAN PLANNING ASSISTANCE PROGRAM AUTHORIZED BY SECTION 701 OF THE HOUSING ACT OF 1954, AS AMENDED.

HARLAND BARTHOLOMEW AND ASSOCIATES
CITY PLANNERS, CIVIL ENGINEERS, LANDSCAPE ARCHITECTS
SAINT LOUIS, FEBRUARY, 1968 MISSOURI

COMPREHENSIVE PLANS 69

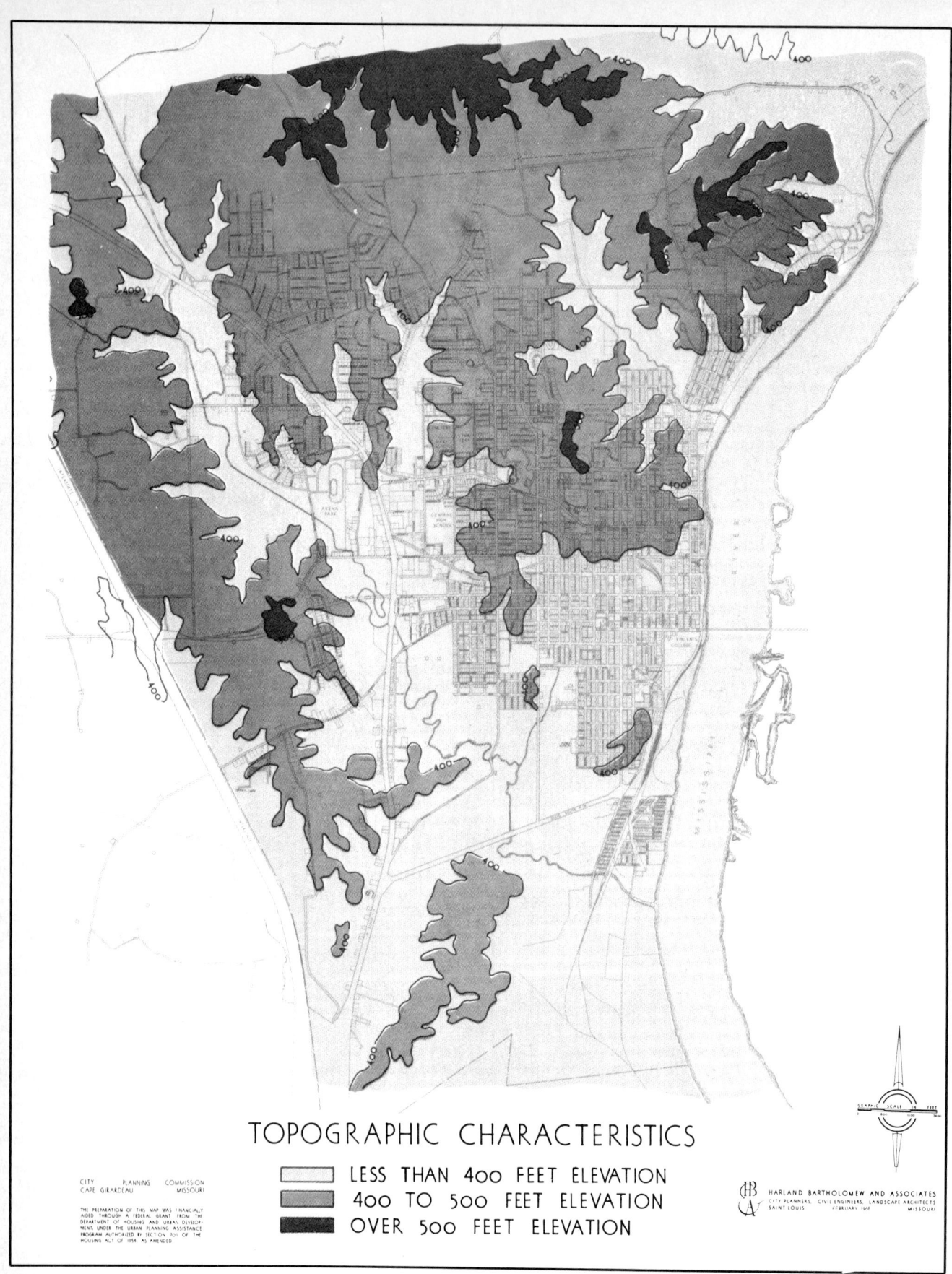

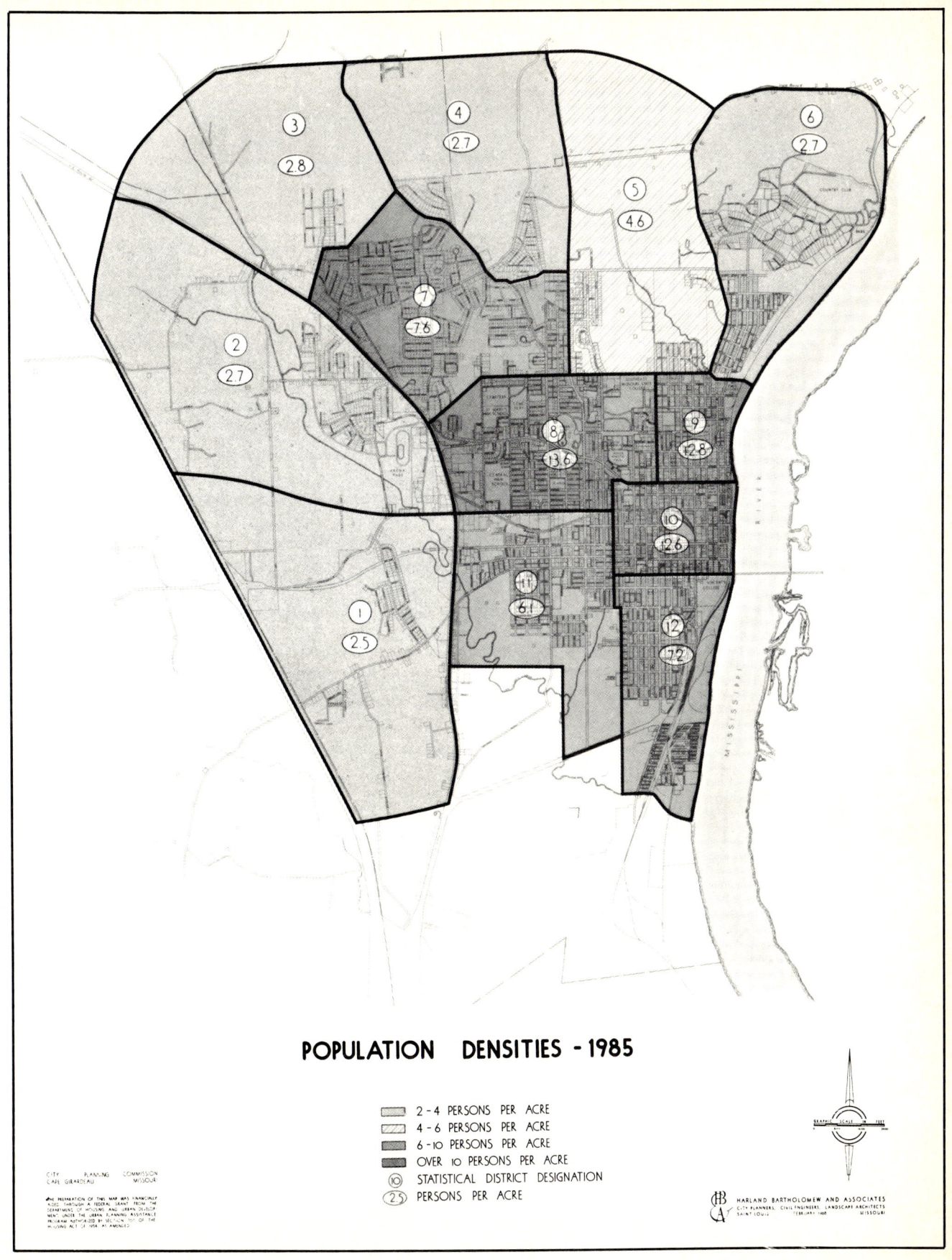

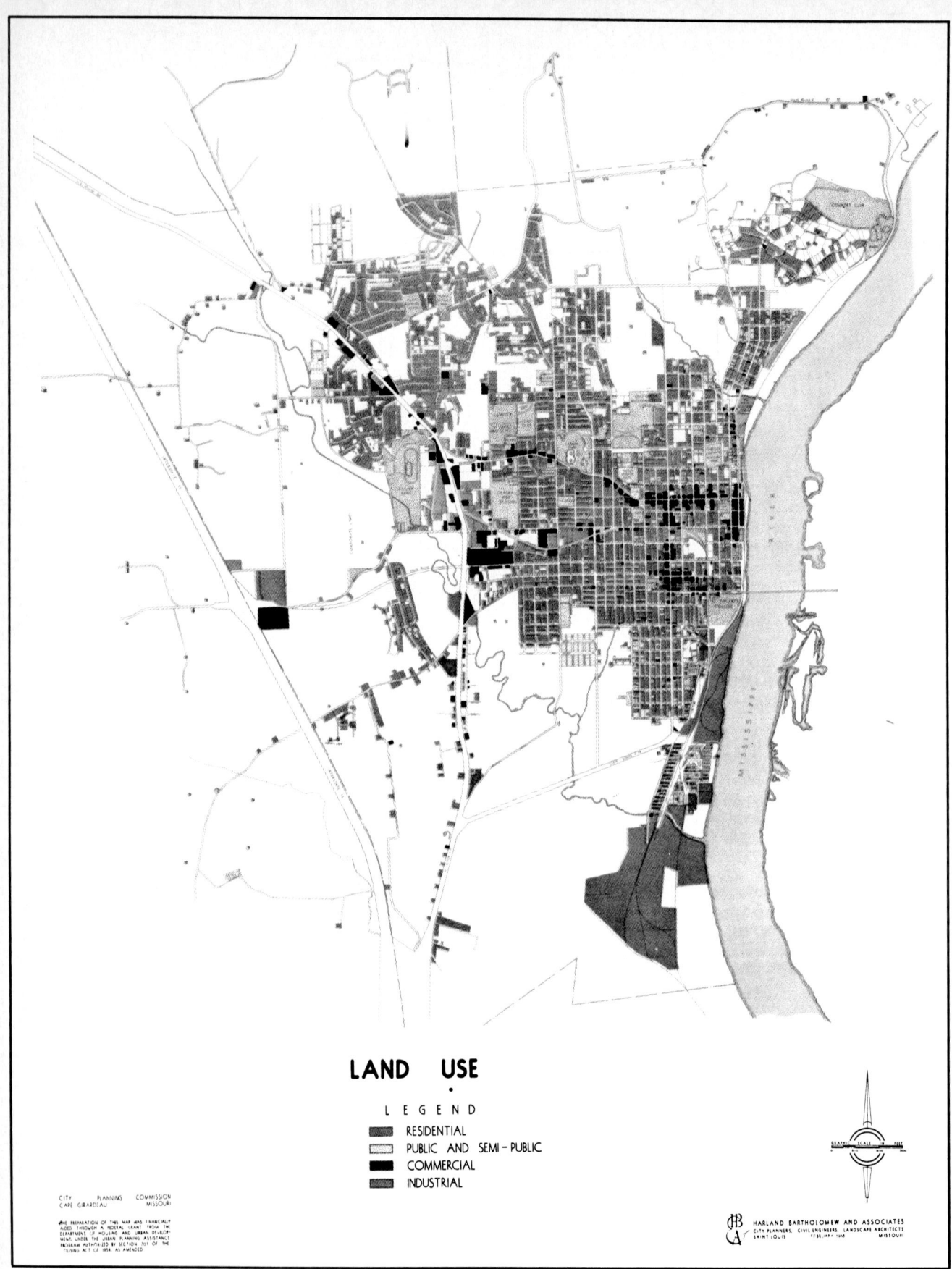

72 COMPREHENSIVE PLANS

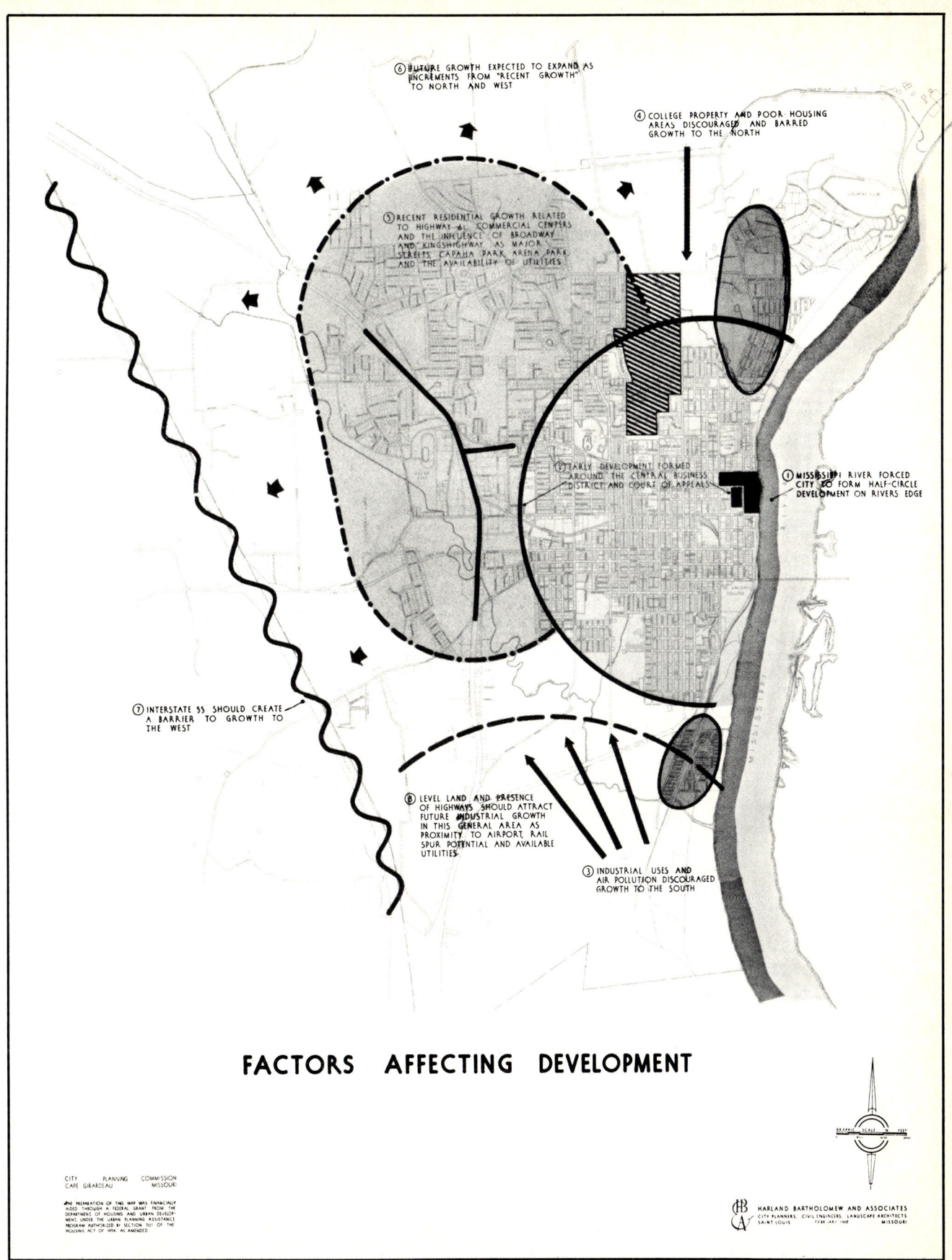

FACTORS AFFECTING DEVELOPMENT

COMPREHENSIVE PLANS

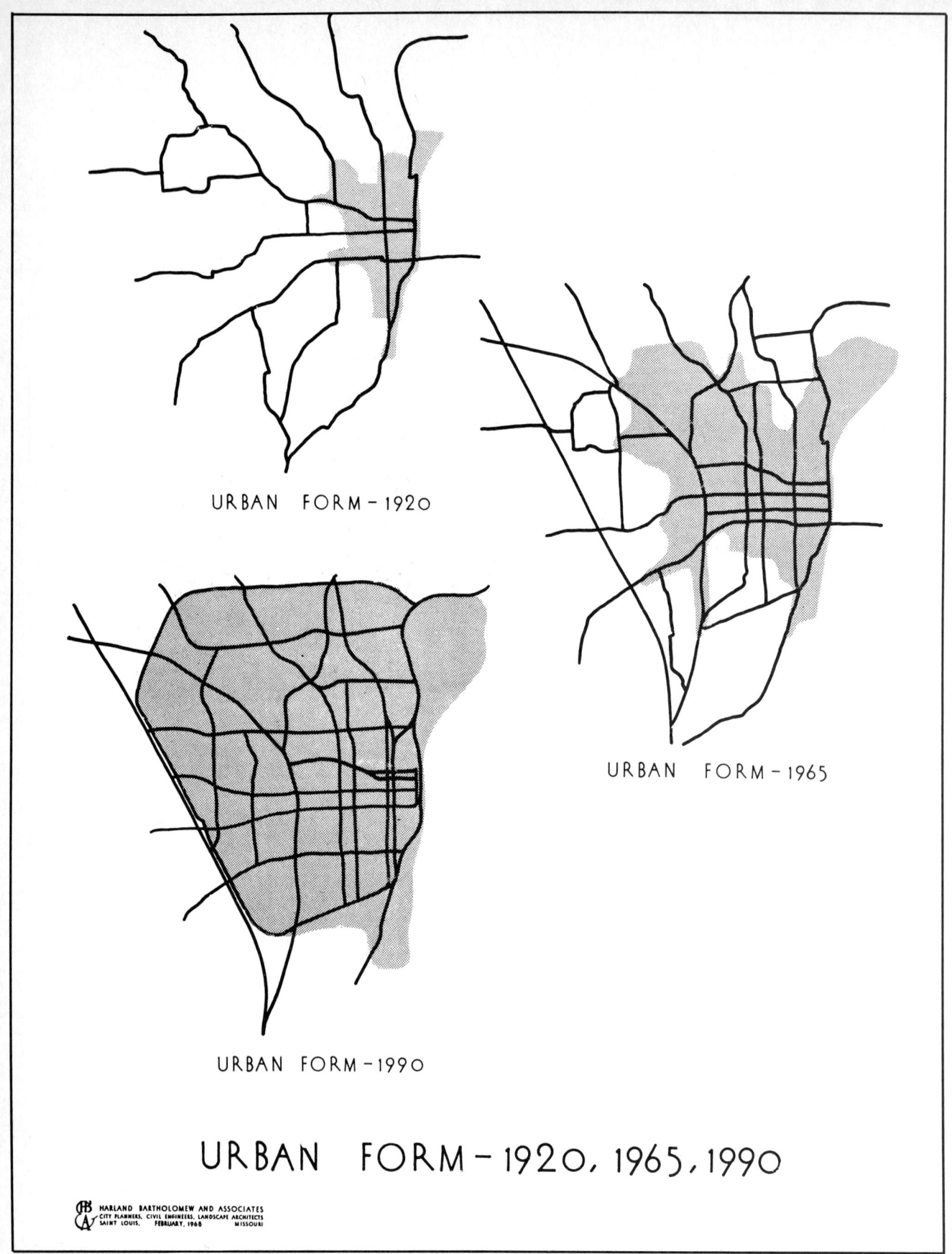

URBAN FORM – 1920, 1965, 1990

74 COMPREHENSIVE PLANS

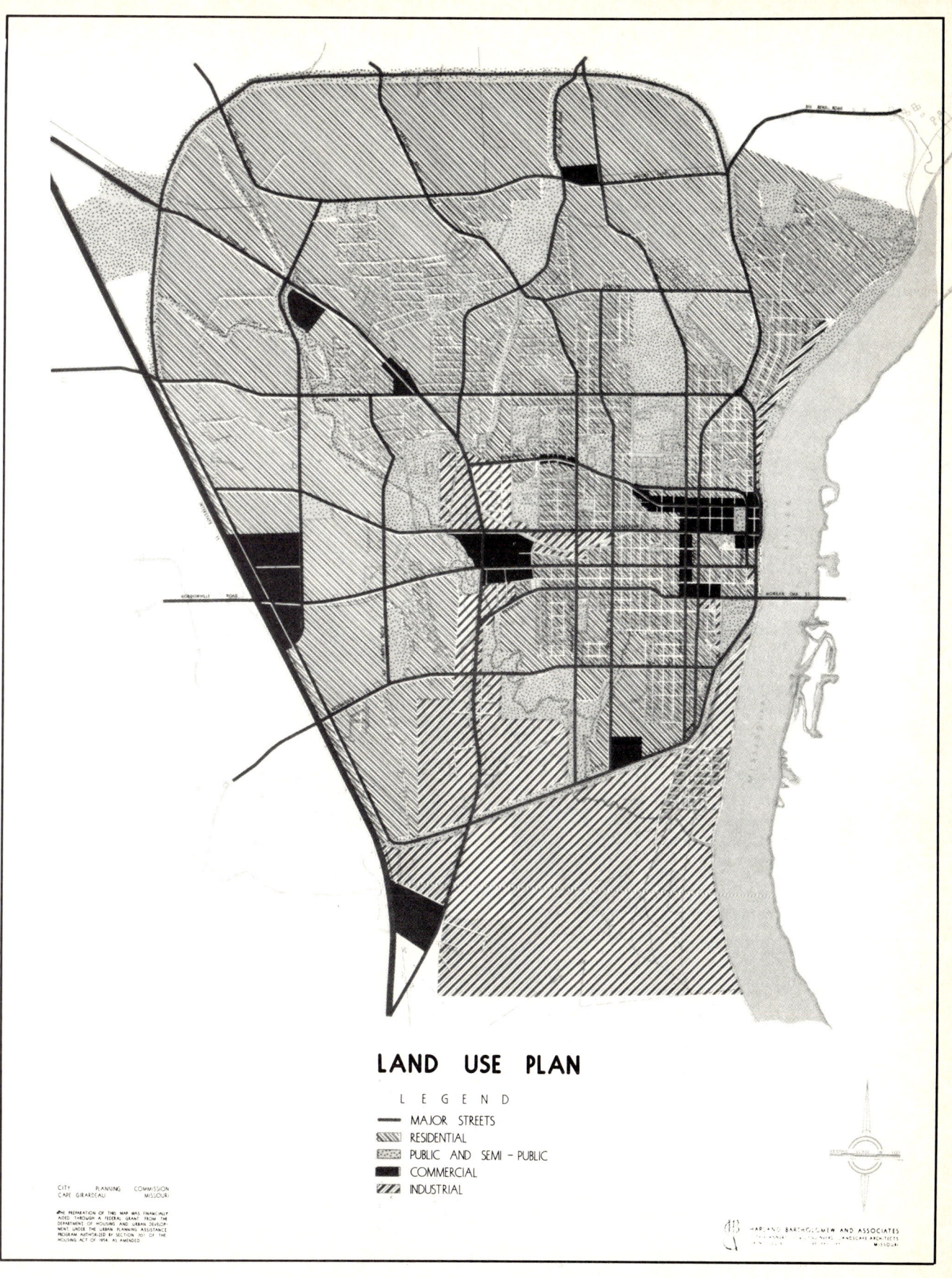

COMPREHENSIVE PLANS 75

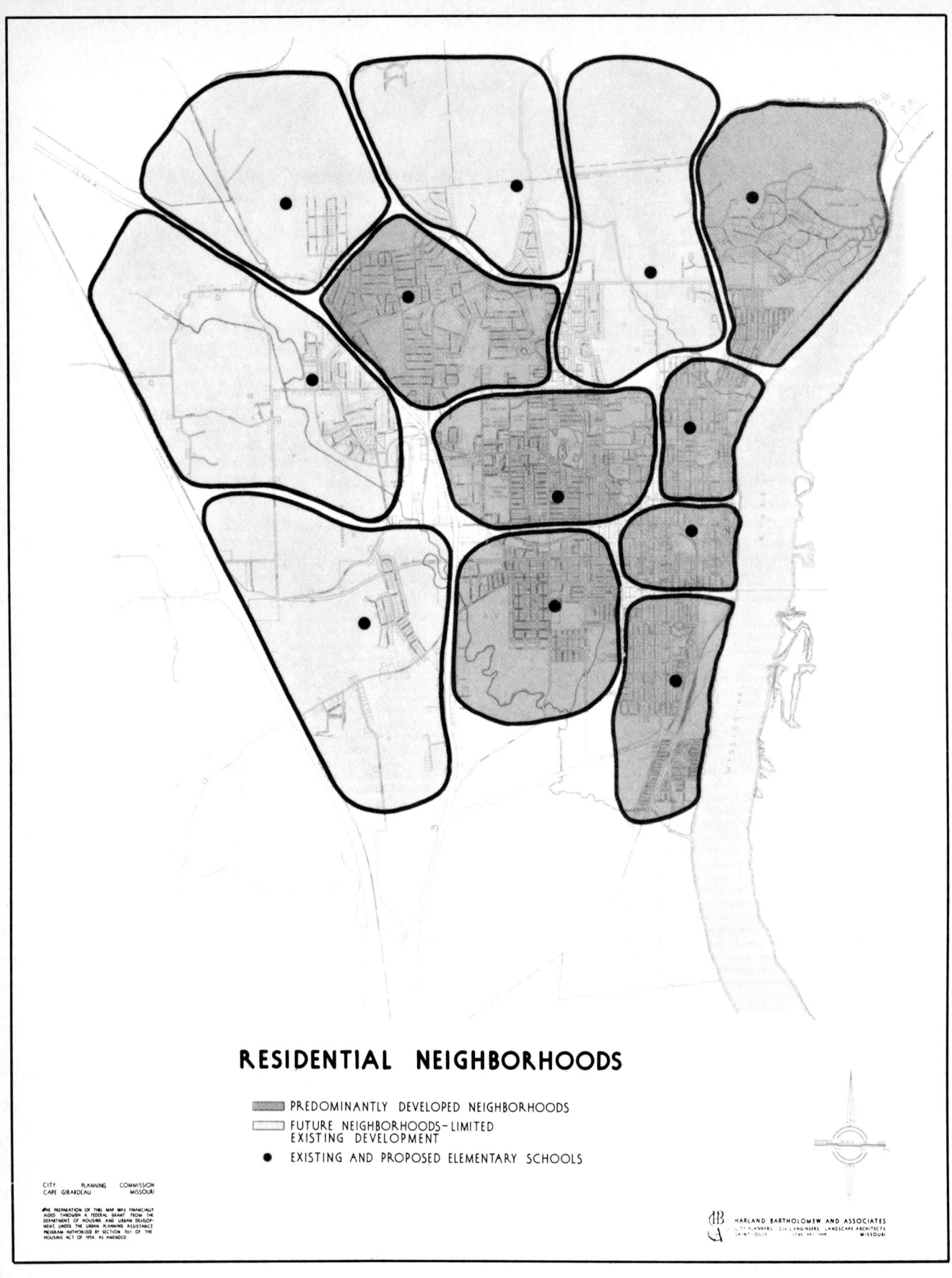

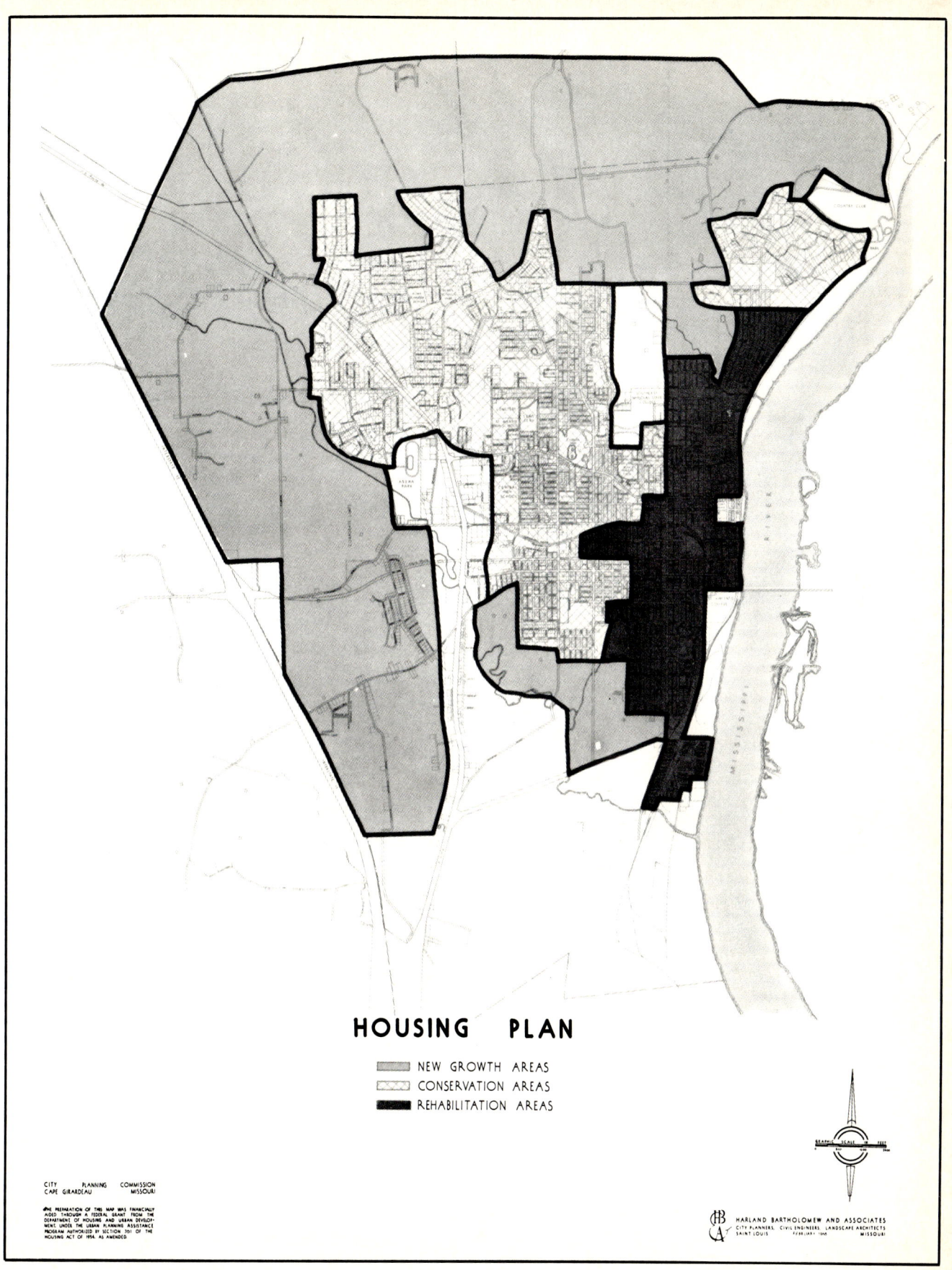

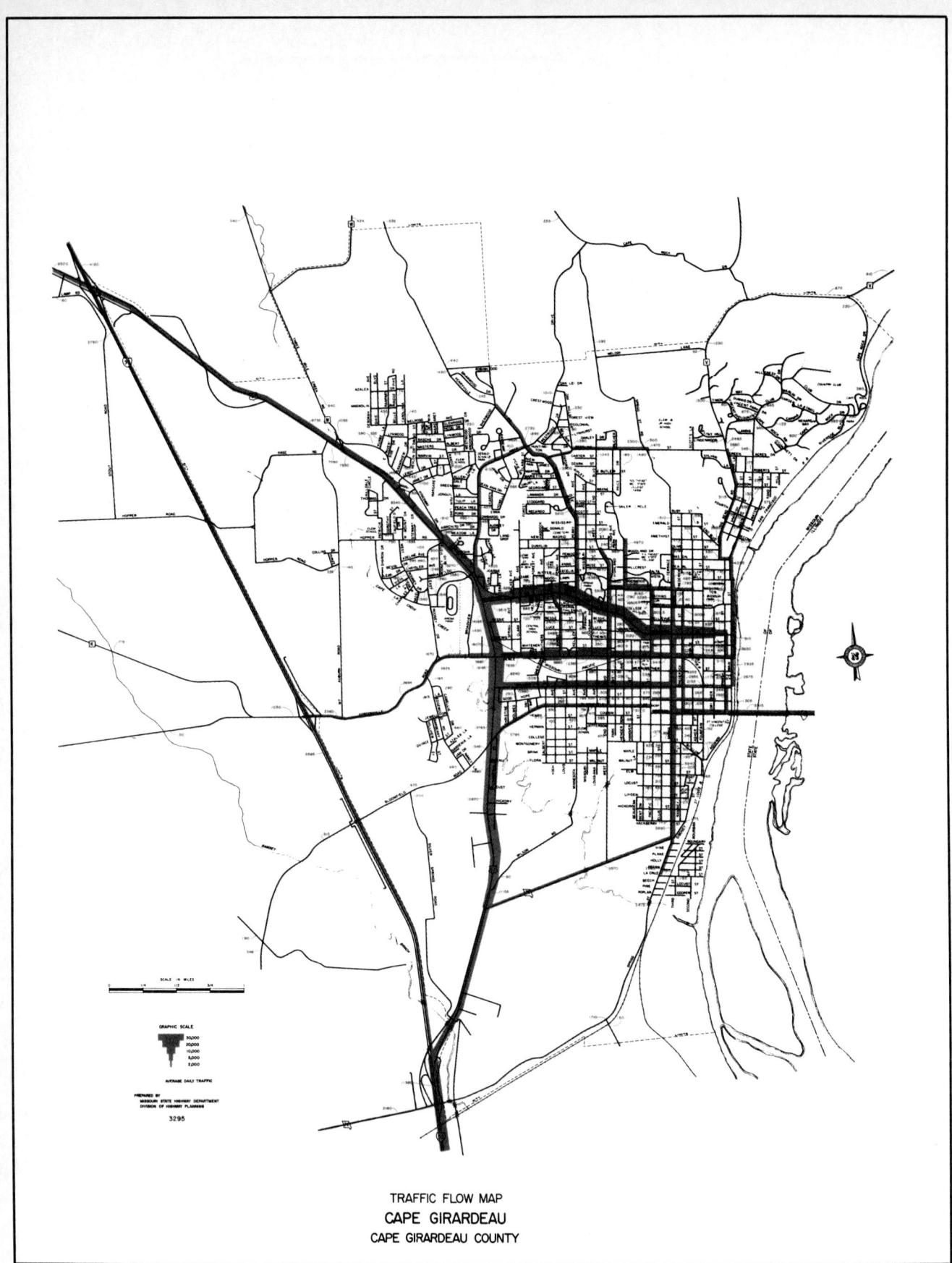

TRAFFIC FLOW MAP
CAPE GIRARDEAU
CAPE GIRARDEAU COUNTY

78 COMPREHENSIVE PLANS

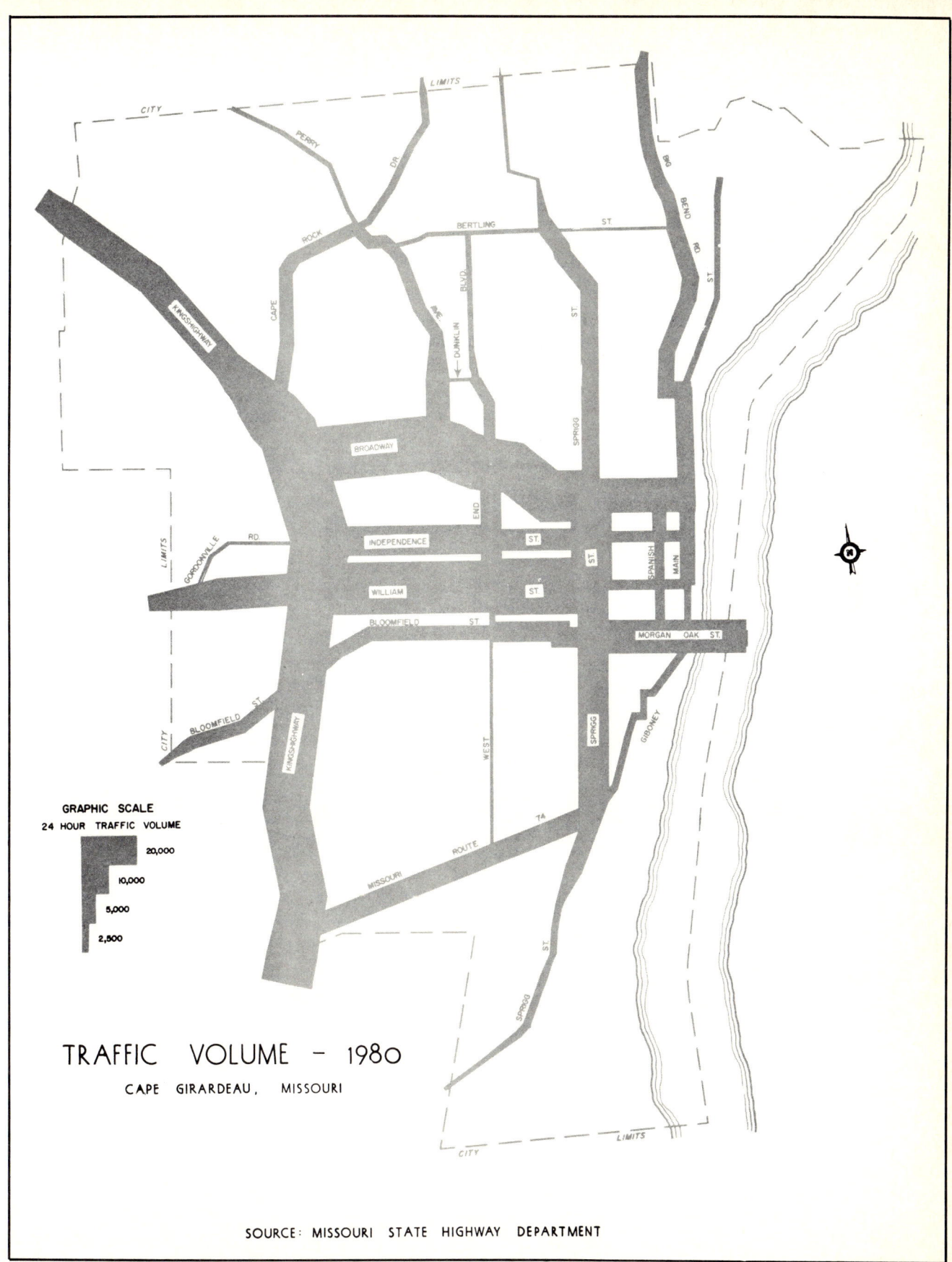

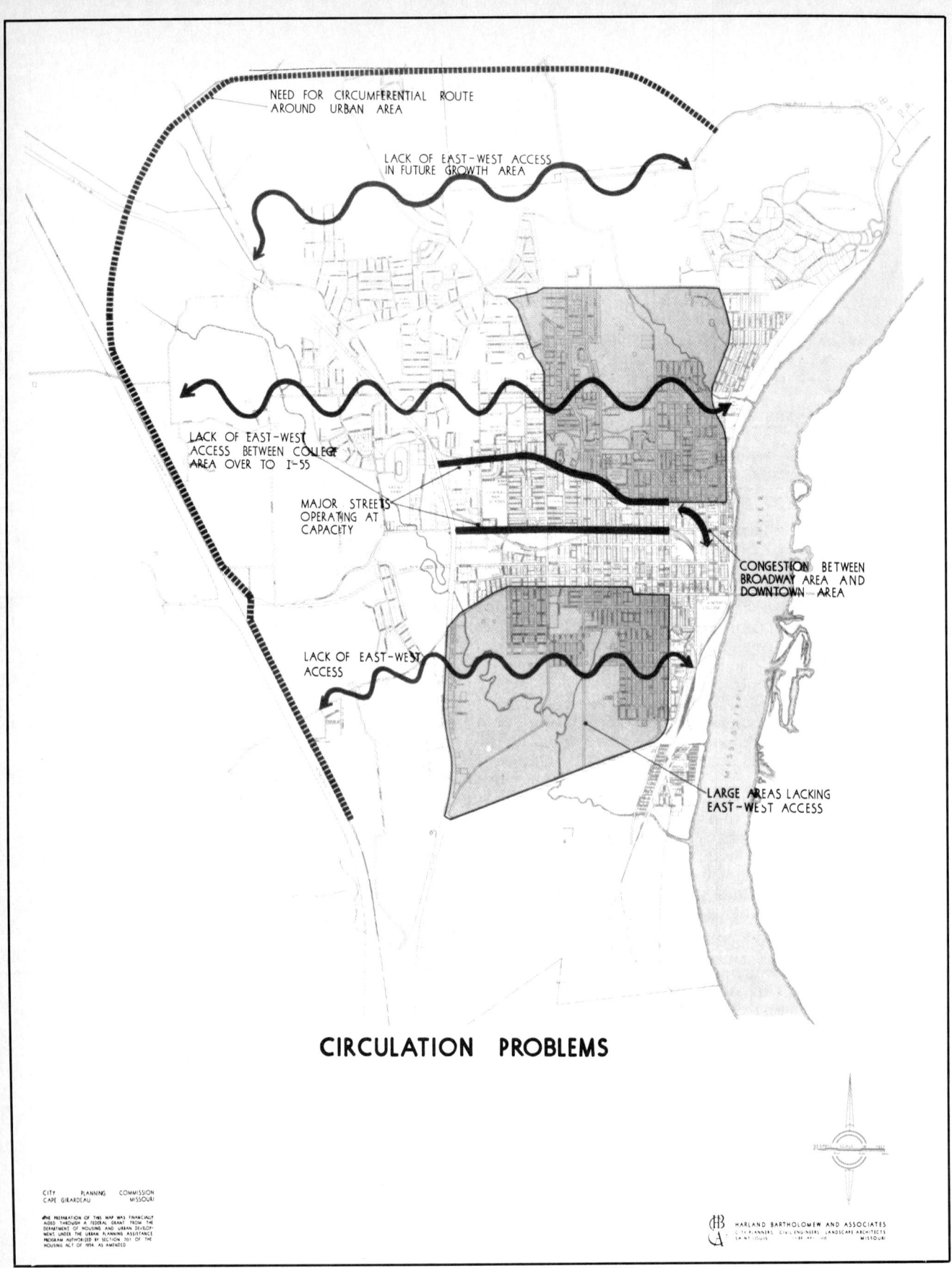

80 COMPREHENSIVE PLANS

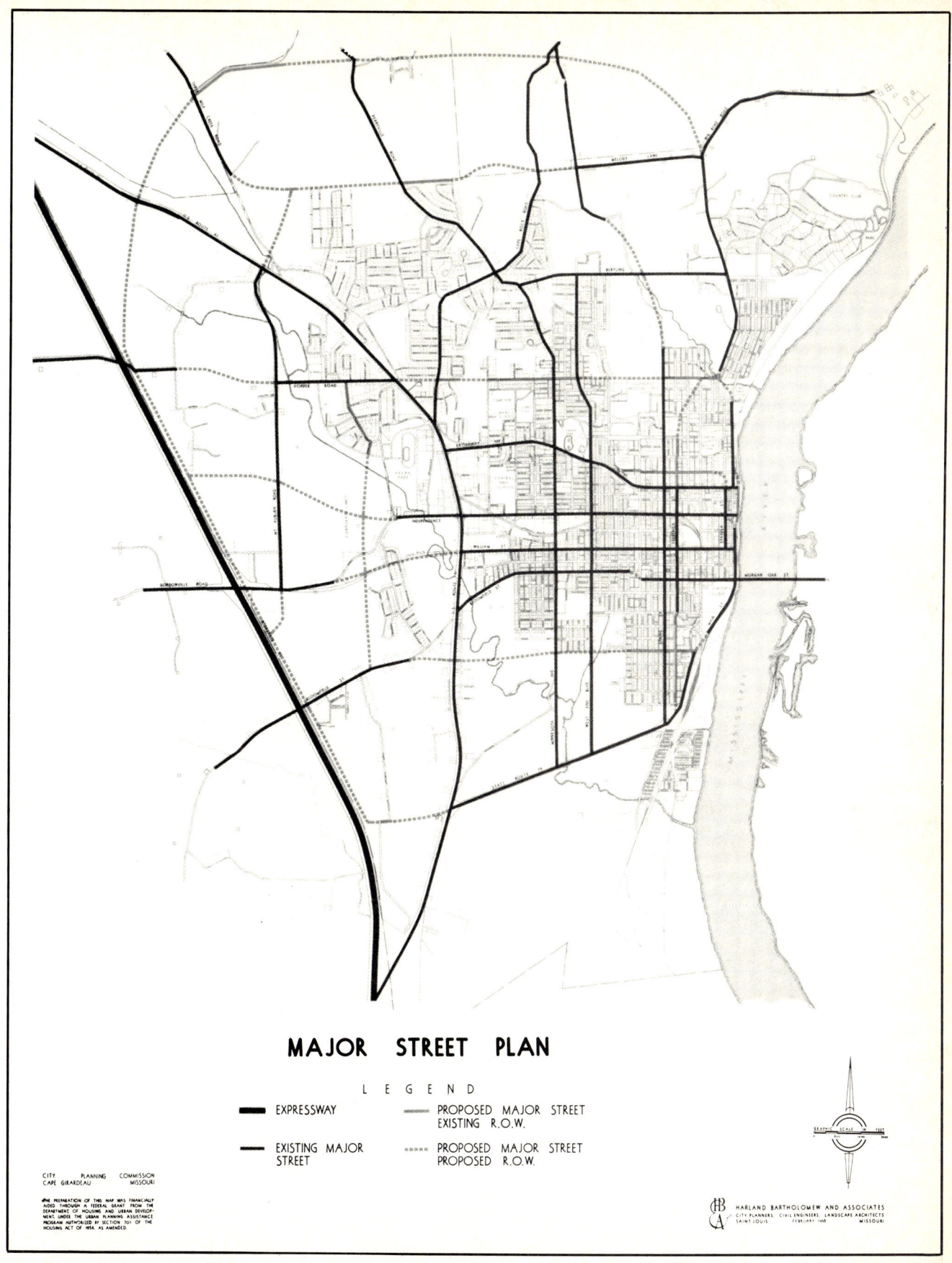

MAJOR STREET PLAN

COMPREHENSIVE PLANS 81

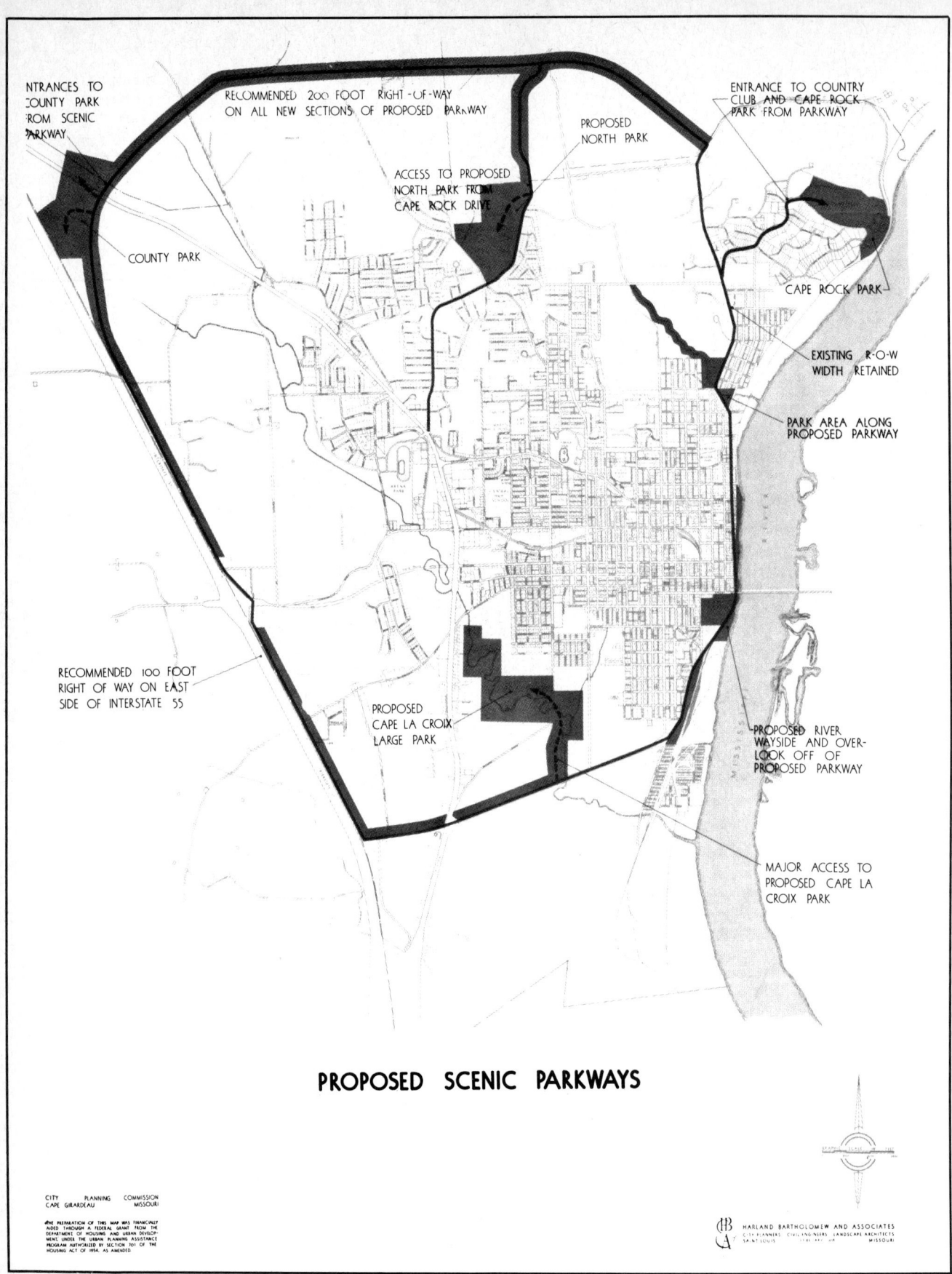

PROPOSED SCENIC PARKWAYS

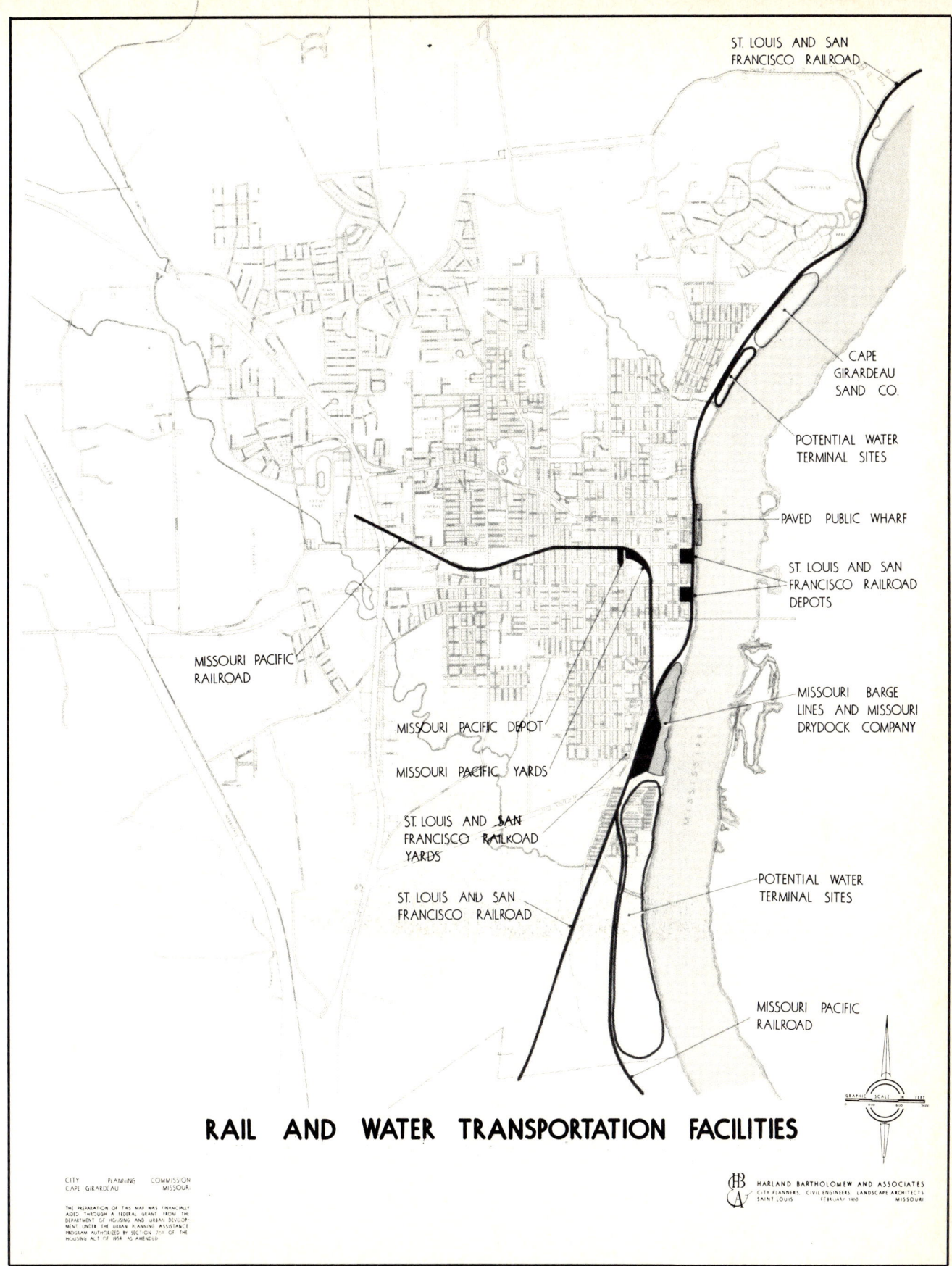

RAIL AND WATER TRANSPORTATION FACILITIES

COMPREHENSIVE PLANS 83

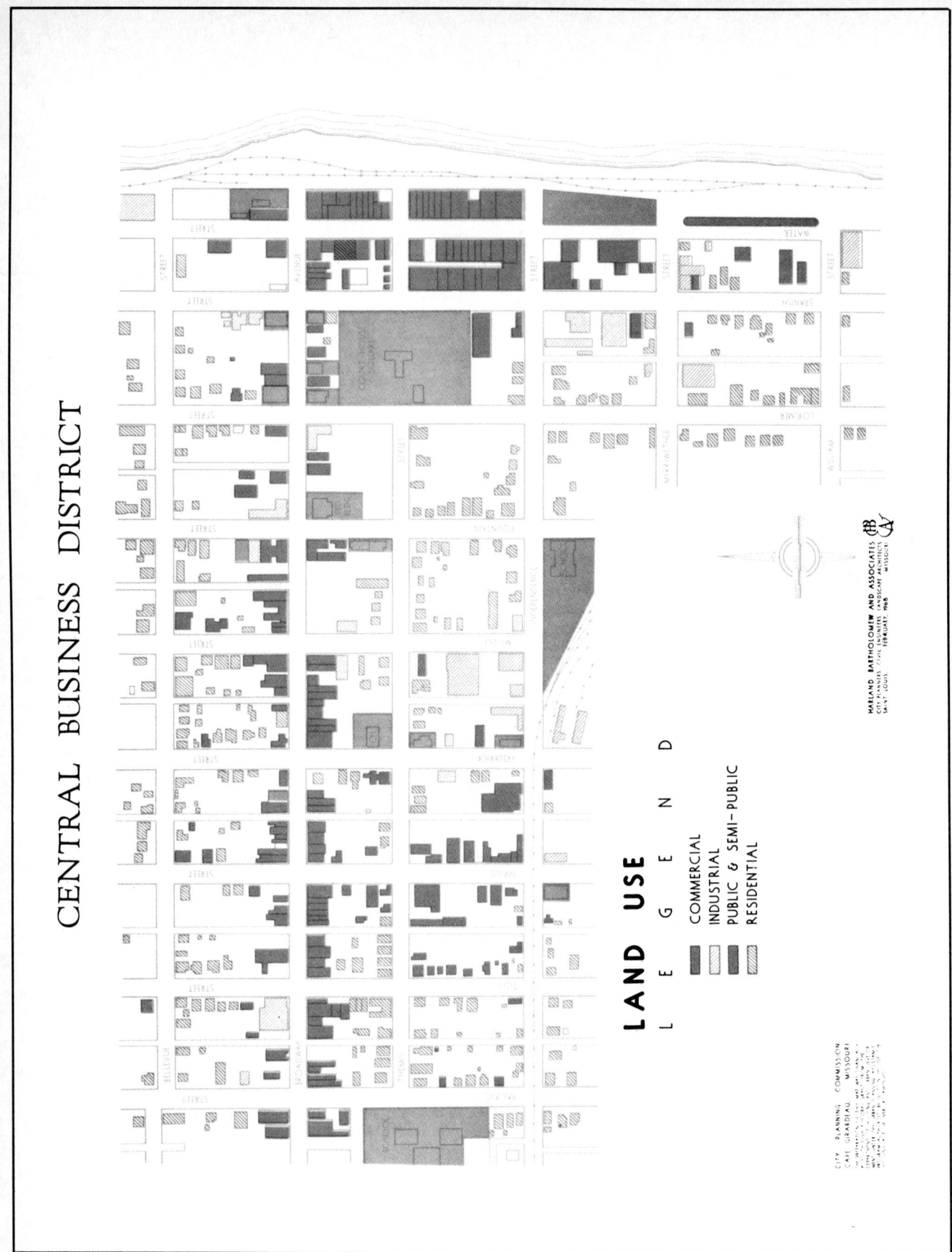

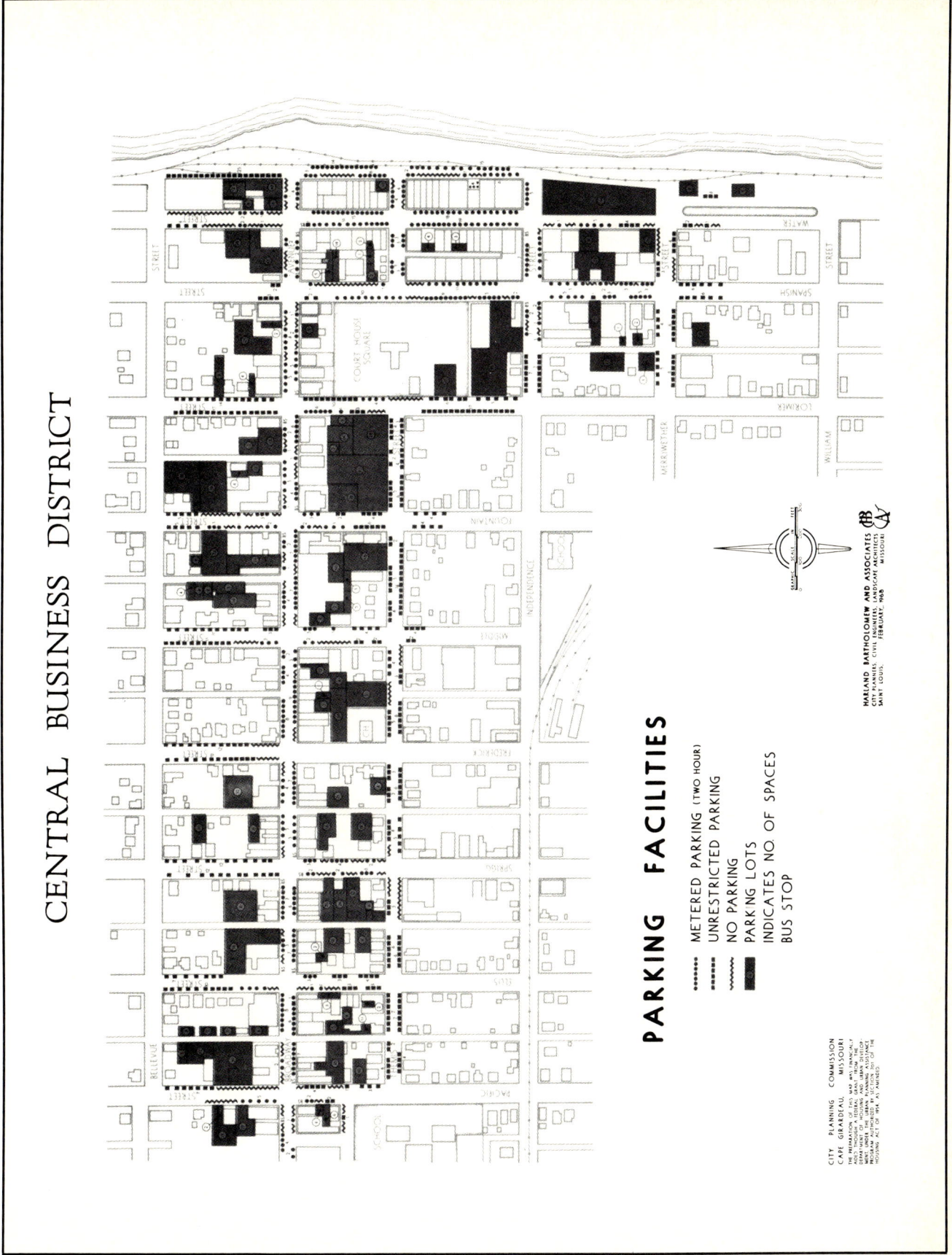

COMPREHENSIVE PLANS 85

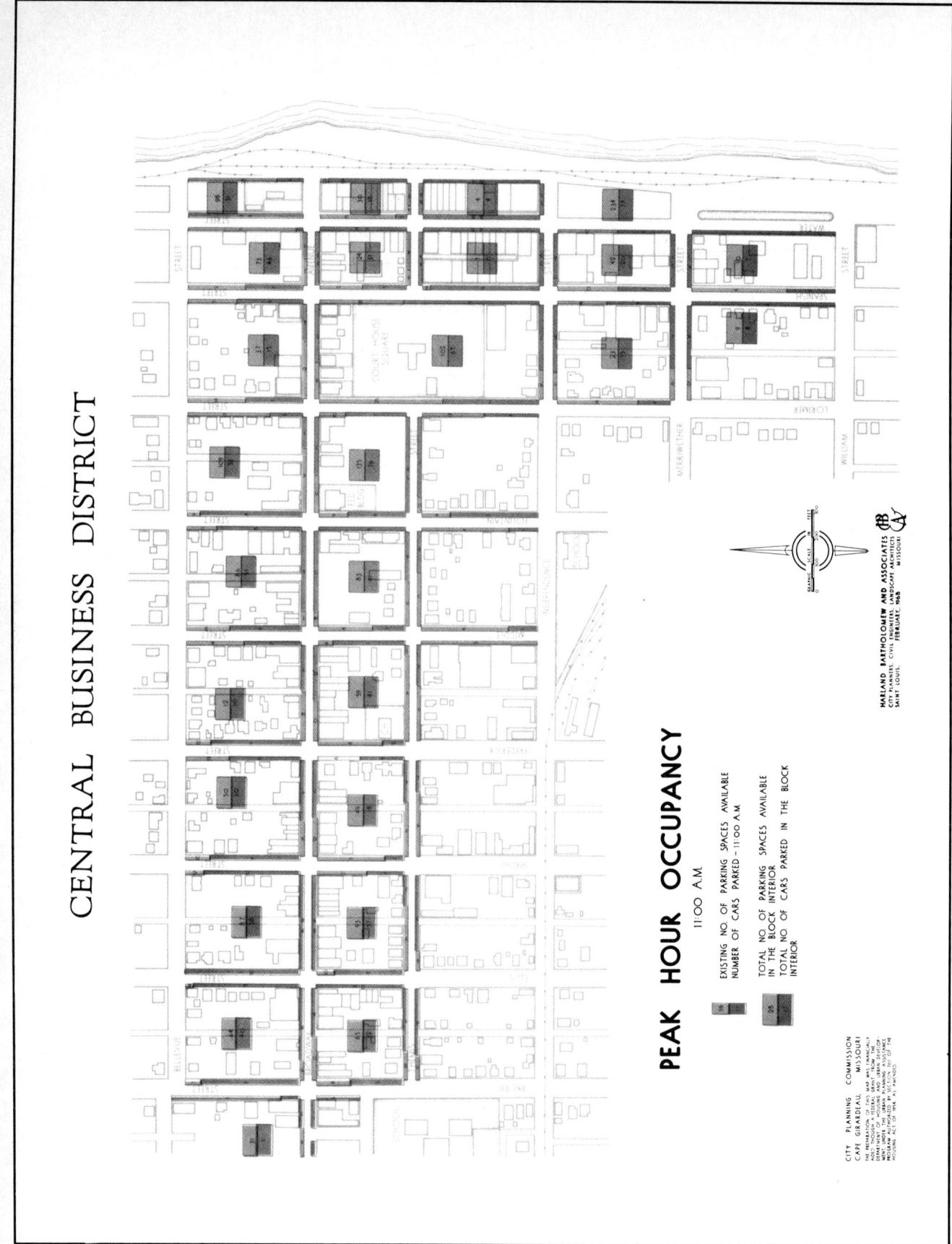

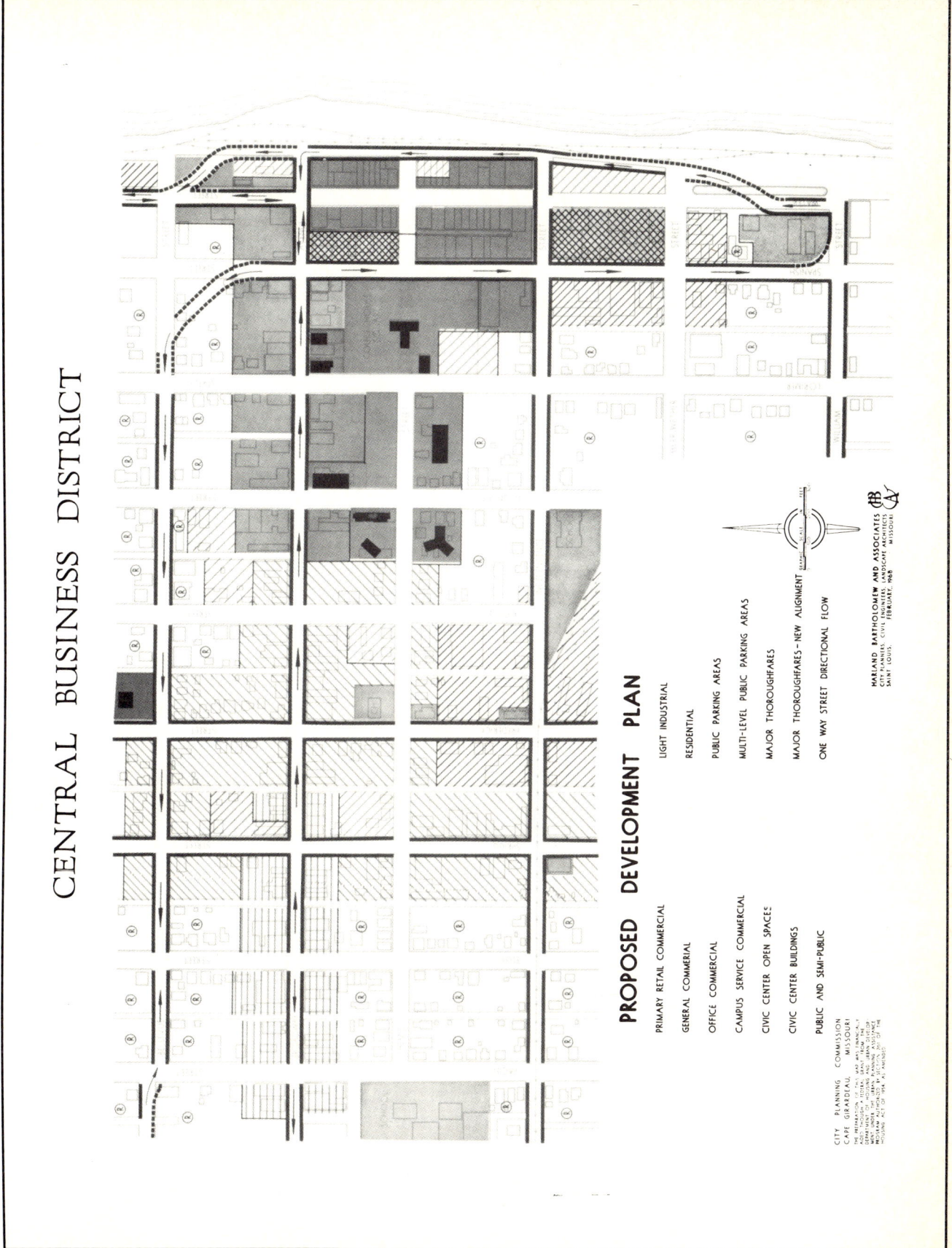

COMPREHENSIVE PLANS 87

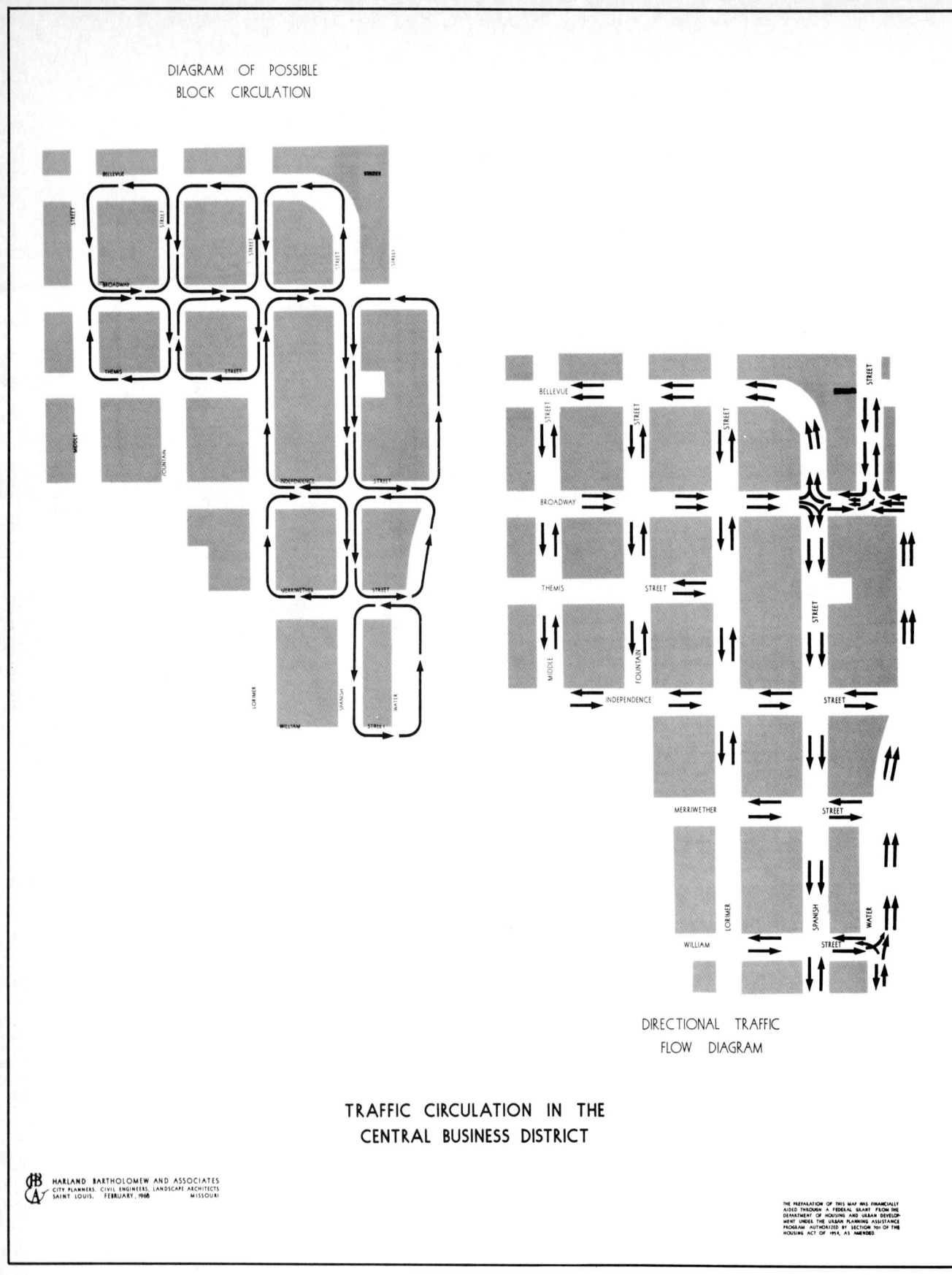

TRAFFIC CIRCULATION IN THE
CENTRAL BUSINESS DISTRICT

88 COMPREHENSIVE PLANS

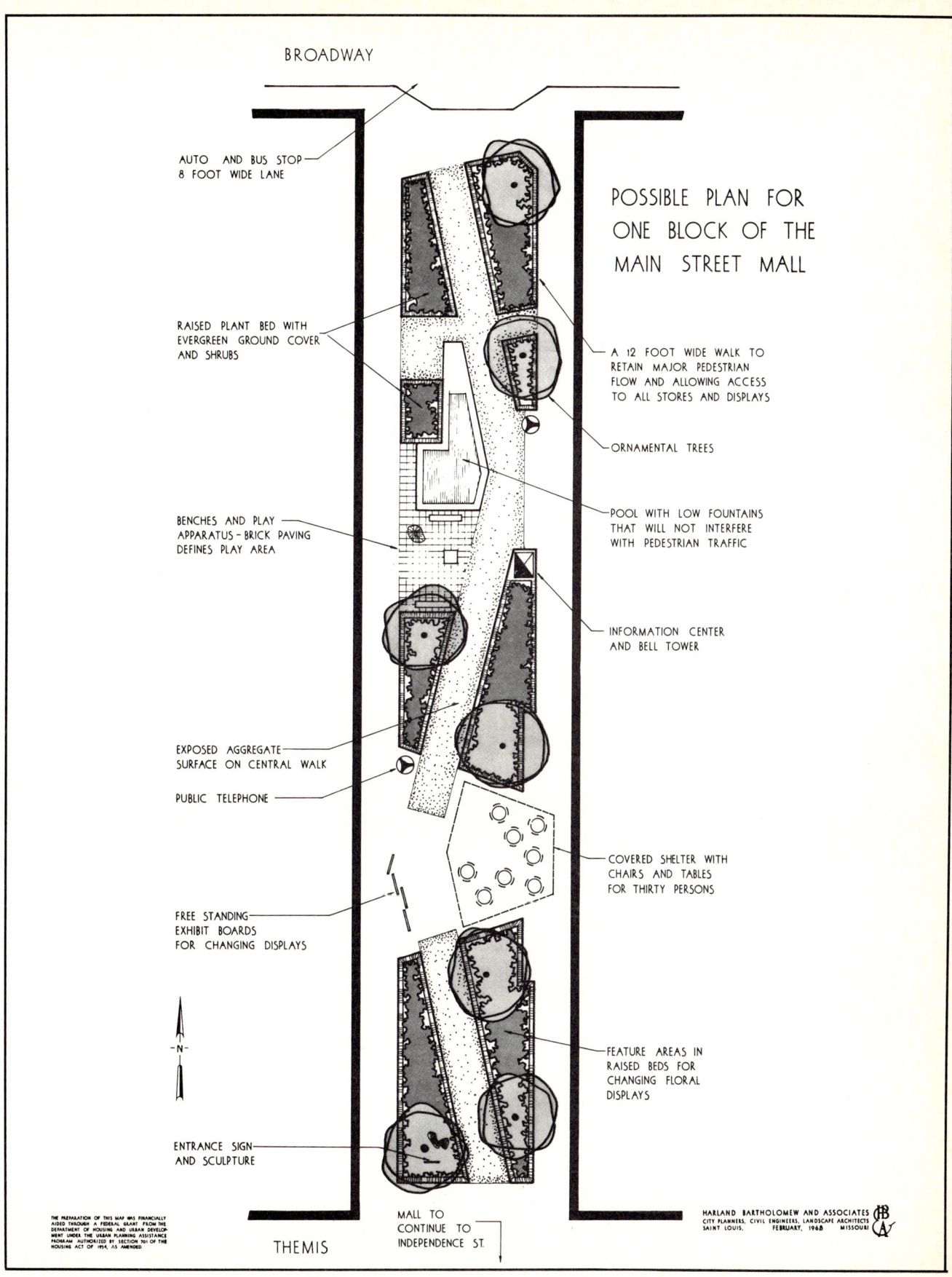

COMPREHENSIVE PLANS 89

MAIN STREET
LOOKING NORTH
BETWEEN
INDEPENDENCE
AND
THEMIS STREETS

PROPOSED MALL

MAIN STREET MALL VIEW

HARLAND BARTHOLOMEW AND ASSOCIATES
CITY PLANNERS, CIVIL ENGINEERS, LANDSCAPE ARCHITECTS
SAINT LOUIS, FEBRUARY, 1968 MISSOURI

COMPREHENSIVE PLANS

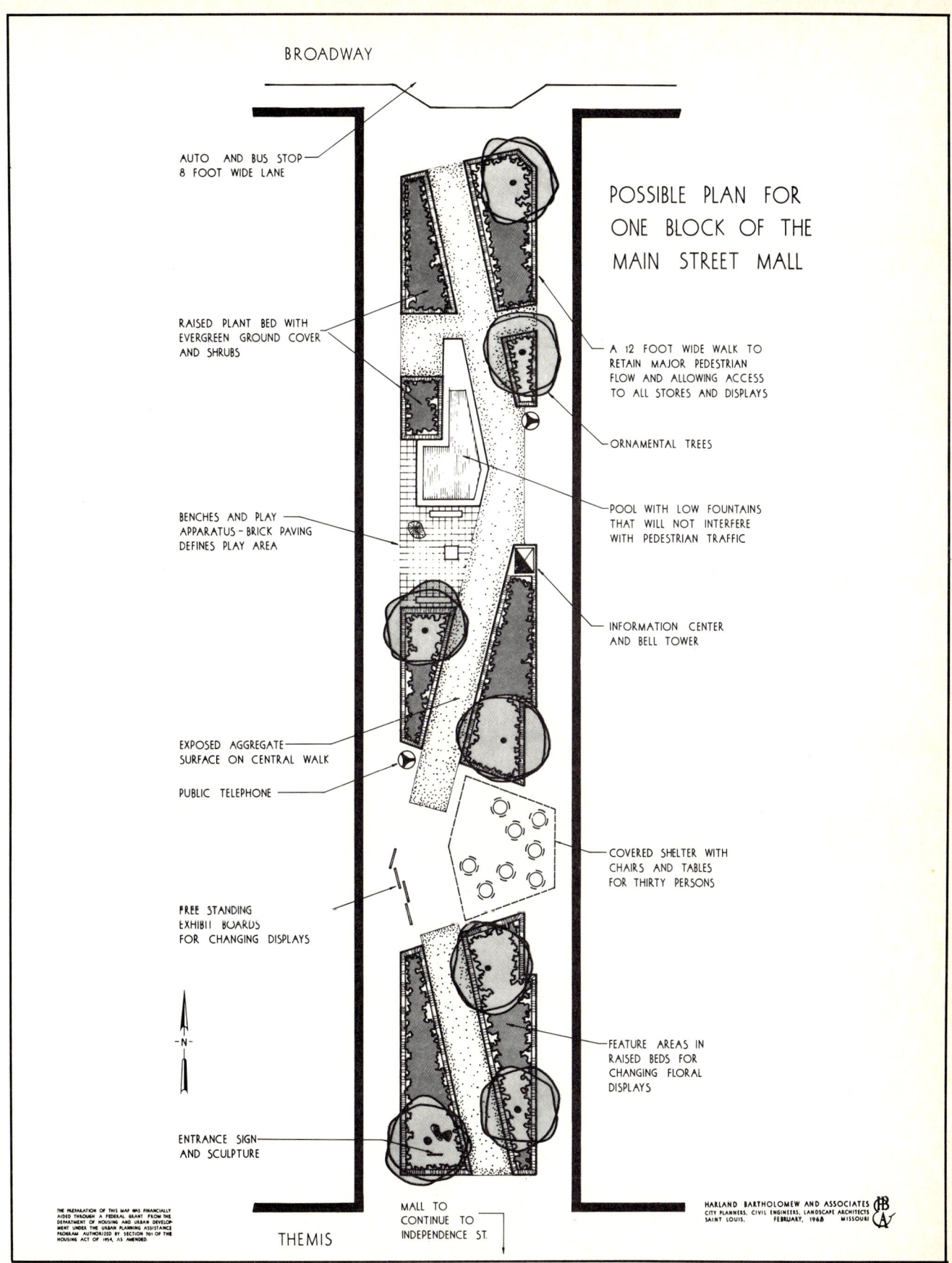

COMPREHENSIVE PLANS 89

MAIN STREET
LOOKING NORTH
BETWEEN
INDEPENDENCE
AND
THEMIS STREETS

PROPOSED MALL

MAIN STREET MALL VIEW

HARLAND BARTHOLOMEW AND ASSOCIATES
CITY PLANNERS, CIVIL ENGINEERS, LANDSCAPE ARCHITECTS
SAINT LOUIS.   FEBRUARY, 1968   MISSOURI

MIDTOWN BUSINESS DISTRICT

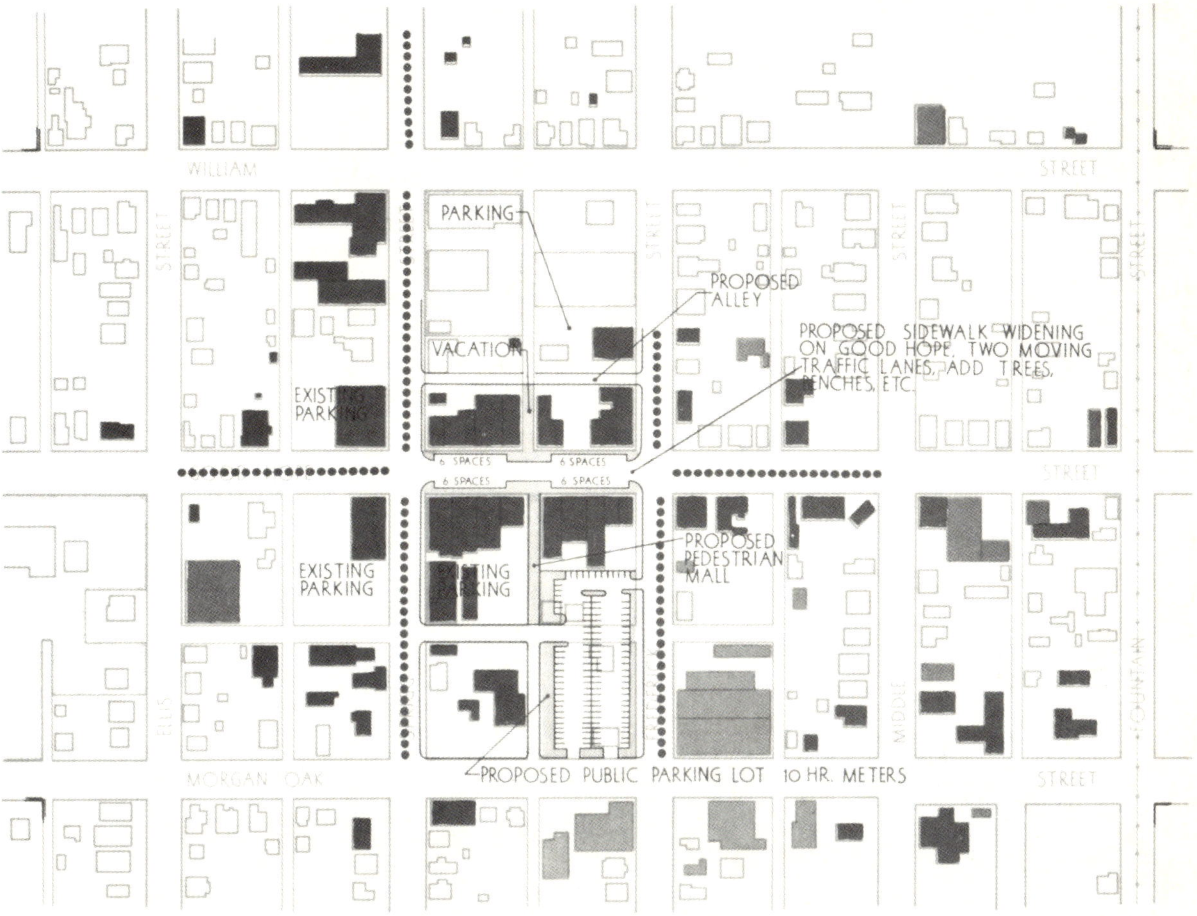

DEVELOPMENT PLAN

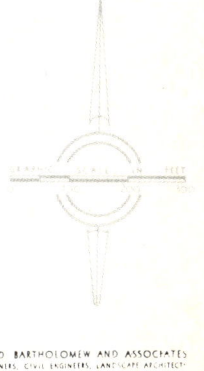

- COMMERCIAL USES
- INDUSTRIAL USES
- RESIDENTIAL–PUBLIC USES
- PROPOSED PEDESTRIAN MALLS
- PROPOSED PUBLIC PARKING
- EXISTING AND PROPOSED 2 HOUR CURB METERS

CITY PLANNING COMMISSION
CAPE GIRARDEAU, MISSOURI

THE PREPARATION OF THIS MAP WAS FINANCIALLY AIDED THROUGH A FEDERAL GRANT FROM THE DEPARTMENT OF HOUSING AND URBAN DEVELOPMENT, UNDER THE URBAN PLANNING ASSISTANCE PROGRAM AUTHORIZED BY SECTION 701 OF THE HOUSING ACT OF 1954, AS AMENDED.

HARLAND BARTHOLOMEW AND ASSOCIATES
CITY PLANNERS, CIVIL ENGINEERS, LANDSCAPE ARCHITECTS
SAINT LOUIS, FEBRUARY, 1968 MISSOURI

COMPREHENSIVE PLANS

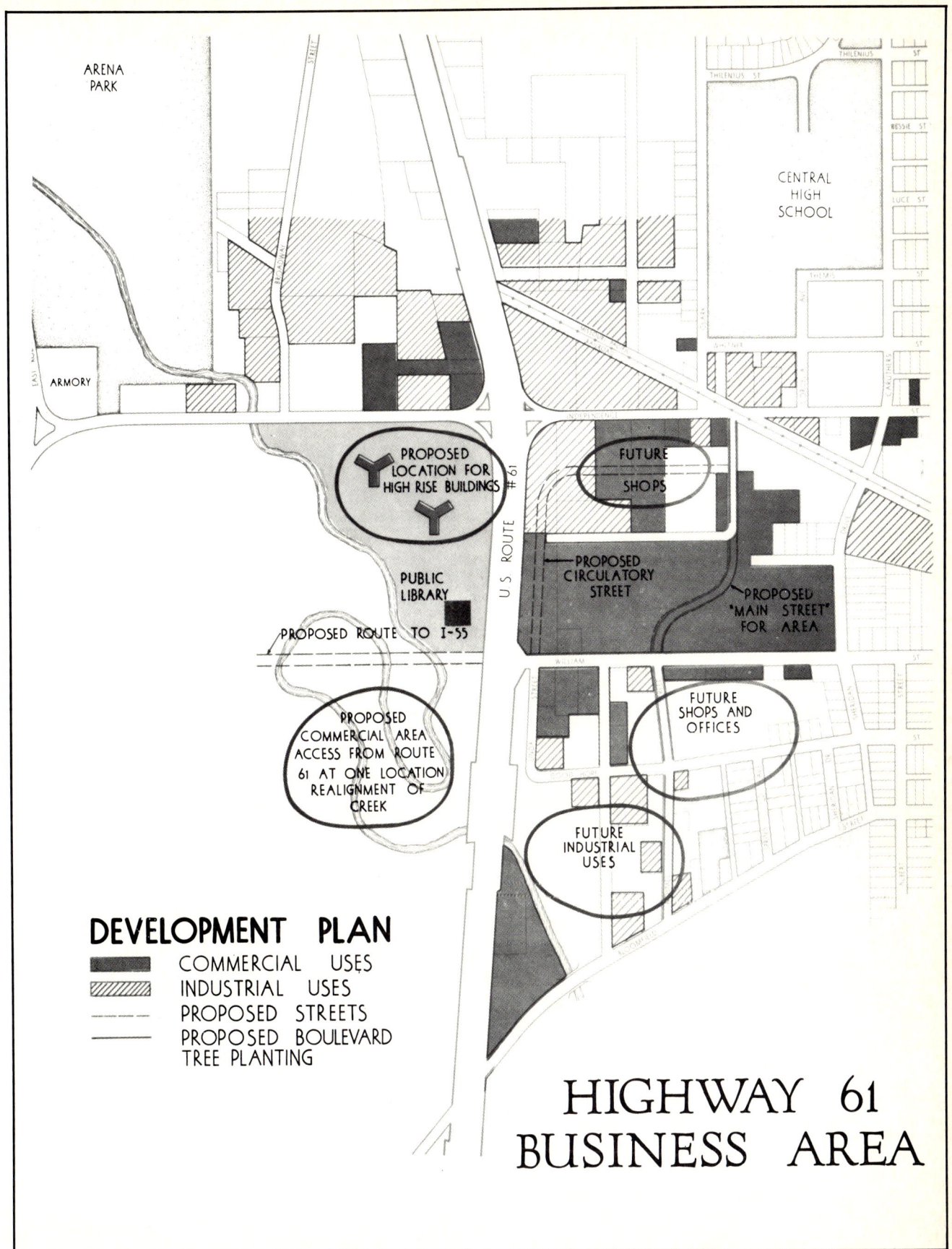

COMPREHENSIVE PLANS 93

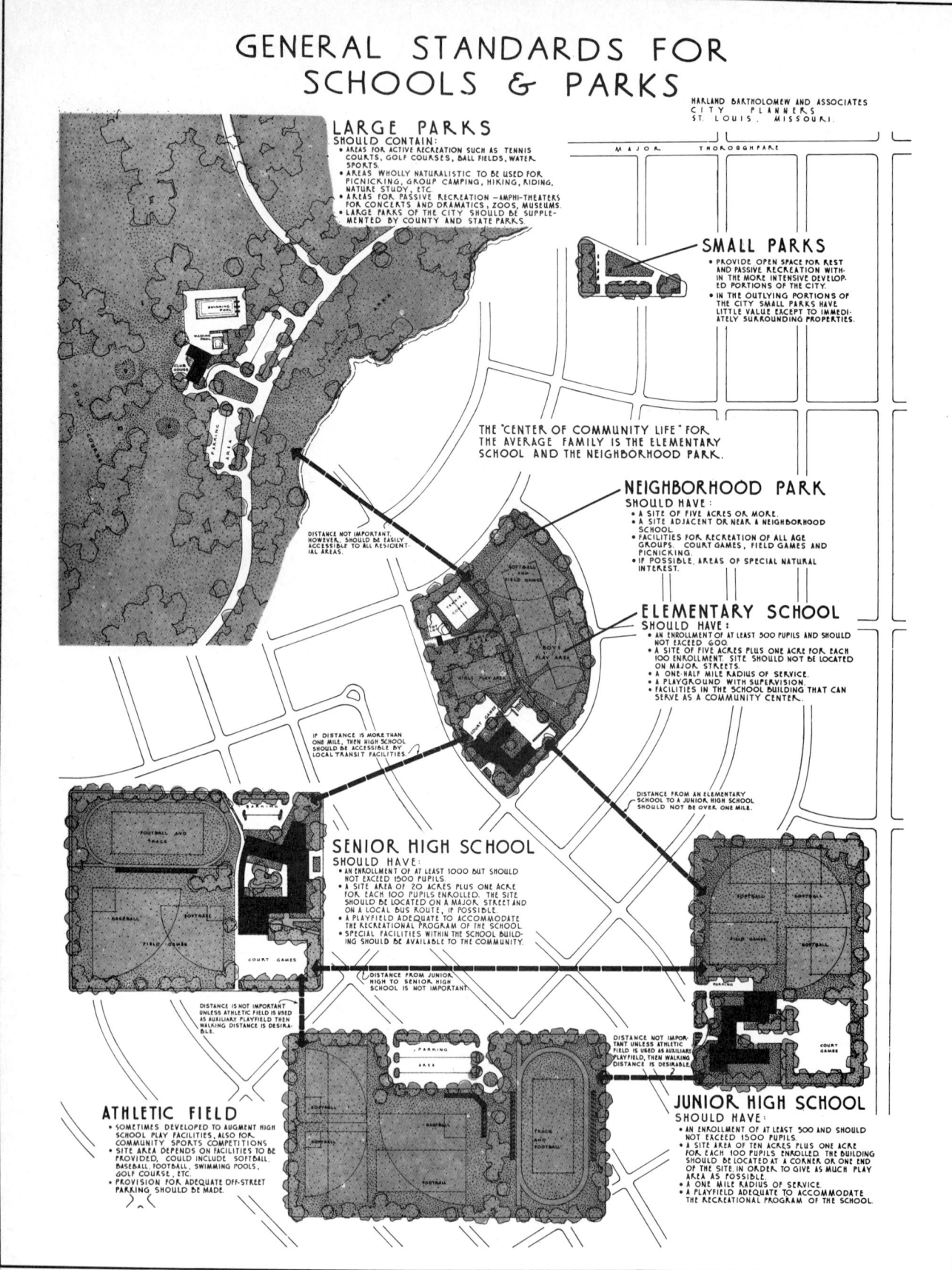

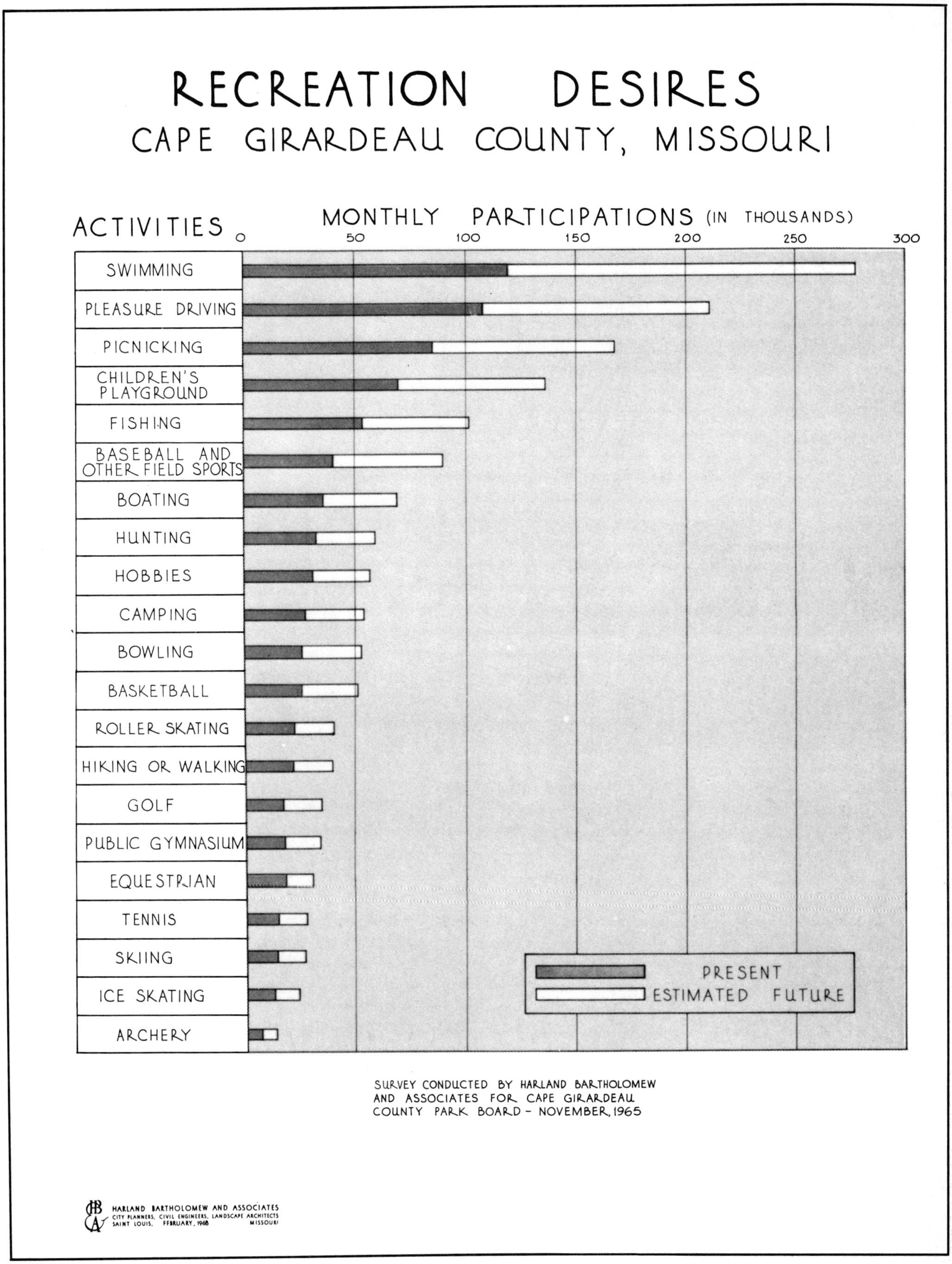

RECREATION DESIRES
CAPE GIRARDEAU COUNTY, MISSOURI

ACTIVITIES — MONTHLY PARTICIPATIONS (IN THOUSANDS)

- SWIMMING
- PLEASURE DRIVING
- PICNICKING
- CHILDREN'S PLAYGROUND
- FISHING
- BASEBALL AND OTHER FIELD SPORTS
- BOATING
- HUNTING
- HOBBIES
- CAMPING
- BOWLING
- BASKETBALL
- ROLLER SKATING
- HIKING OR WALKING
- GOLF
- PUBLIC GYMNASIUM
- EQUESTRIAN
- TENNIS
- SKIING
- ICE SKATING
- ARCHERY

■ PRESENT
□ ESTIMATED FUTURE

SURVEY CONDUCTED BY HARLAND BARTHOLOMEW AND ASSOCIATES FOR CAPE GIRARDEAU COUNTY PARK BOARD – NOVEMBER, 1965

HARLAND BARTHOLOMEW AND ASSOCIATES
CITY PLANNERS, CIVIL ENGINEERS, LANDSCAPE ARCHITECTS
SAINT LOUIS, FEBRUARY, 1968   MISSOURI

COMPREHENSIVE PLANS

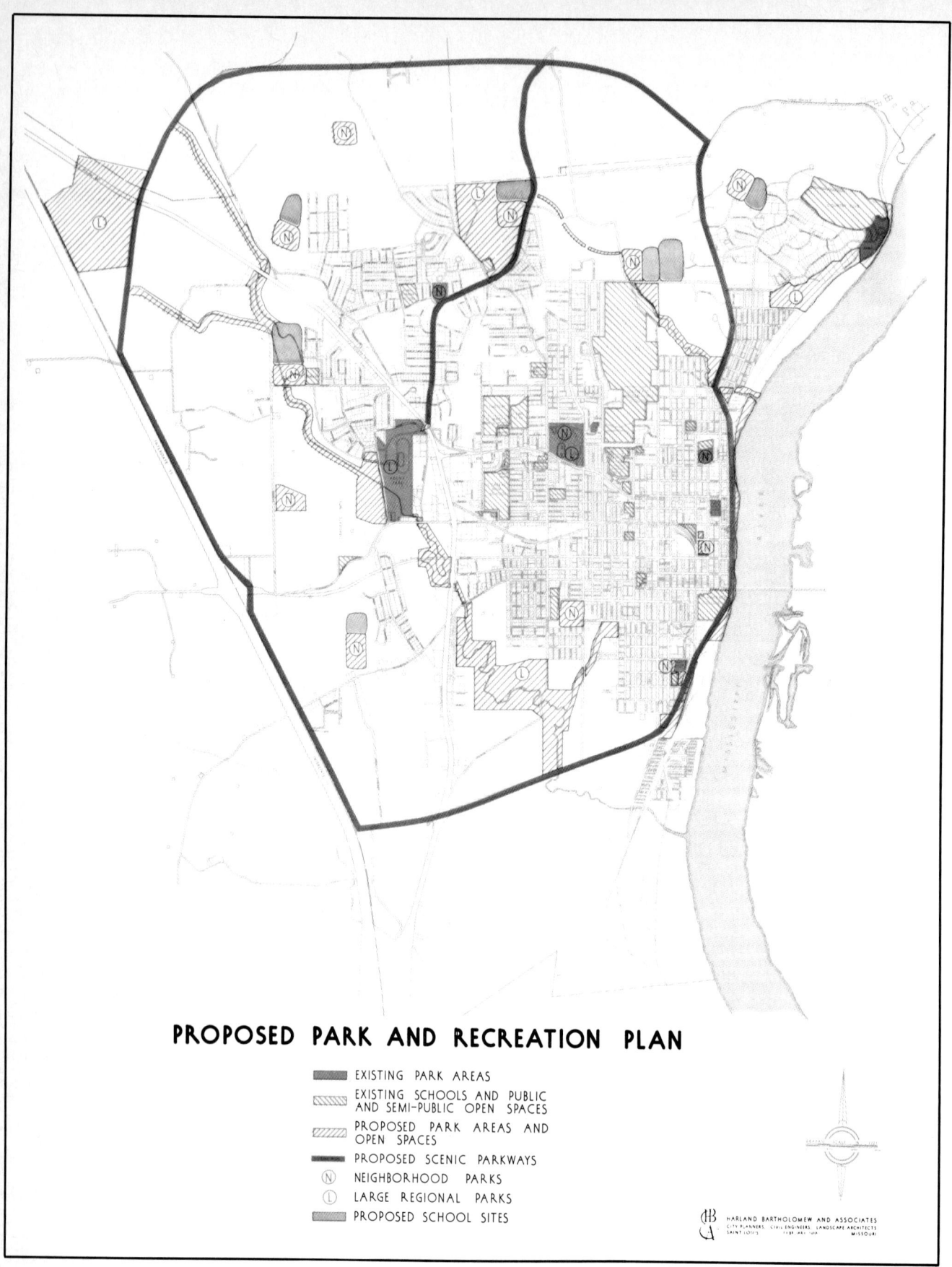

PROPOSED PARK AND RECREATION PLAN

- EXISTING PARK AREAS
- EXISTING SCHOOLS AND PUBLIC AND SEMI-PUBLIC OPEN SPACES
- PROPOSED PARK AREAS AND OPEN SPACES
- PROPOSED SCENIC PARKWAYS
- Ⓝ NEIGHBORHOOD PARKS
- Ⓛ LARGE REGIONAL PARKS
- PROPOSED SCHOOL SITES

COMPREHENSIVE PLANS

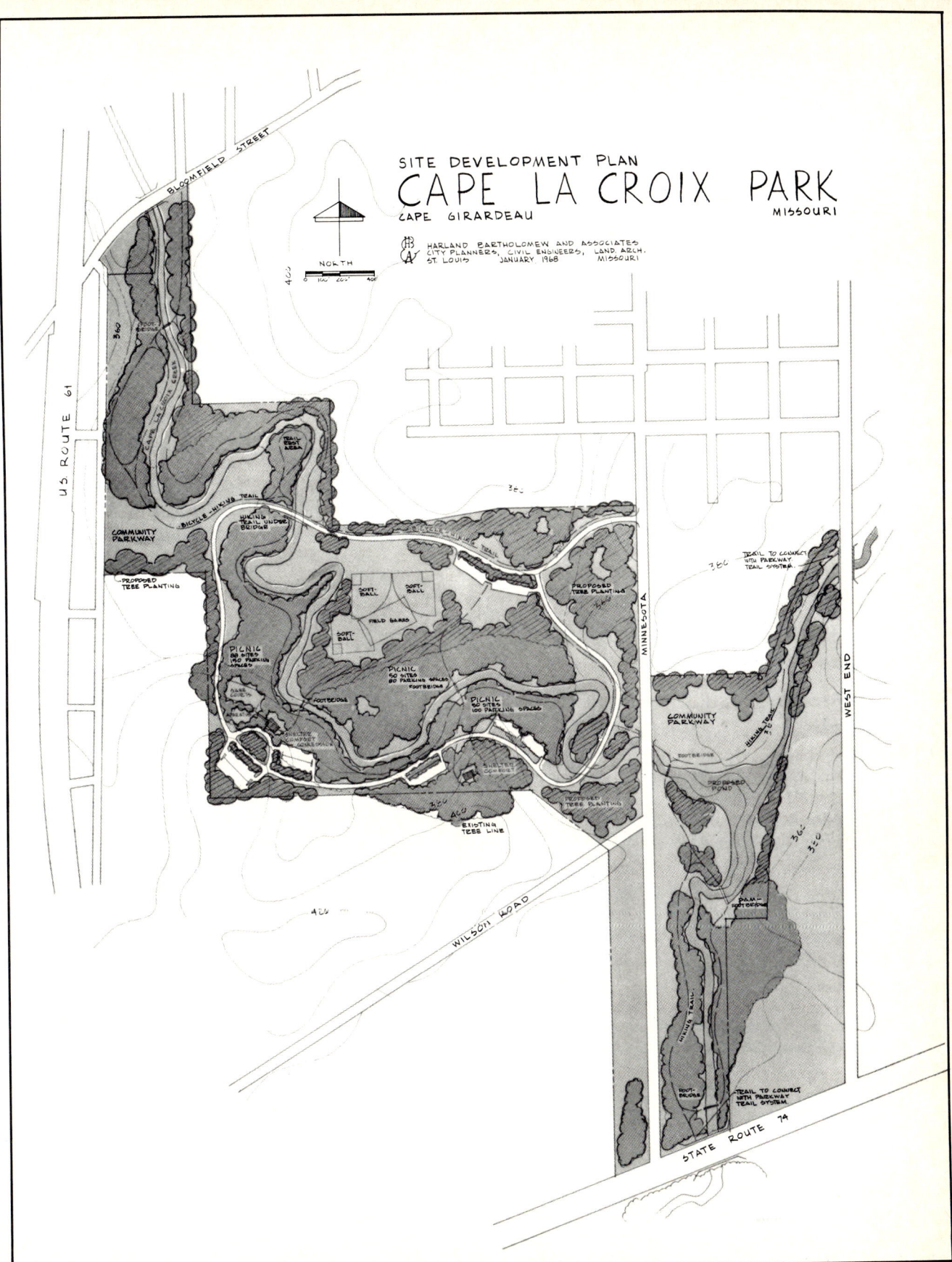

COMPREHENSIVE PLANS

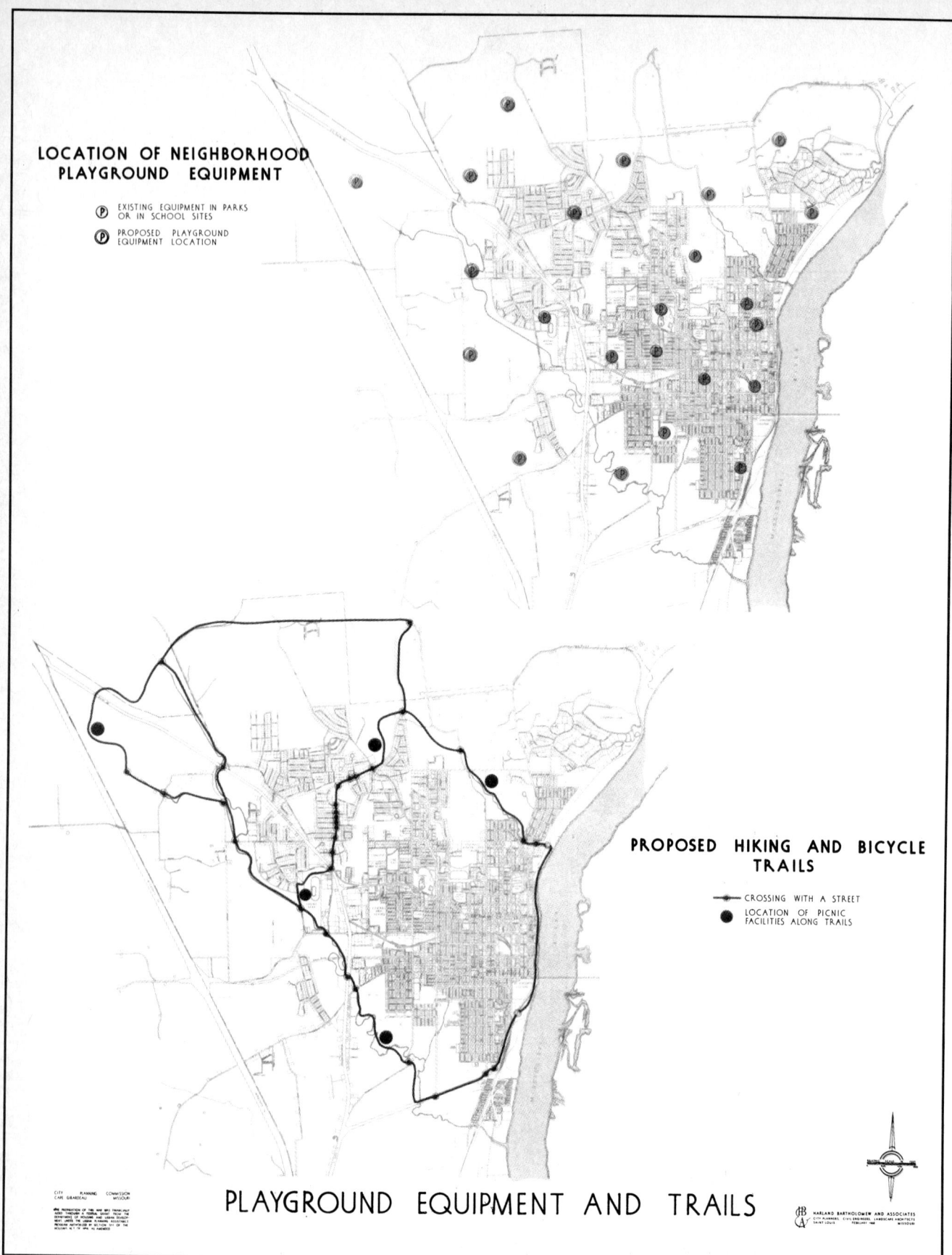

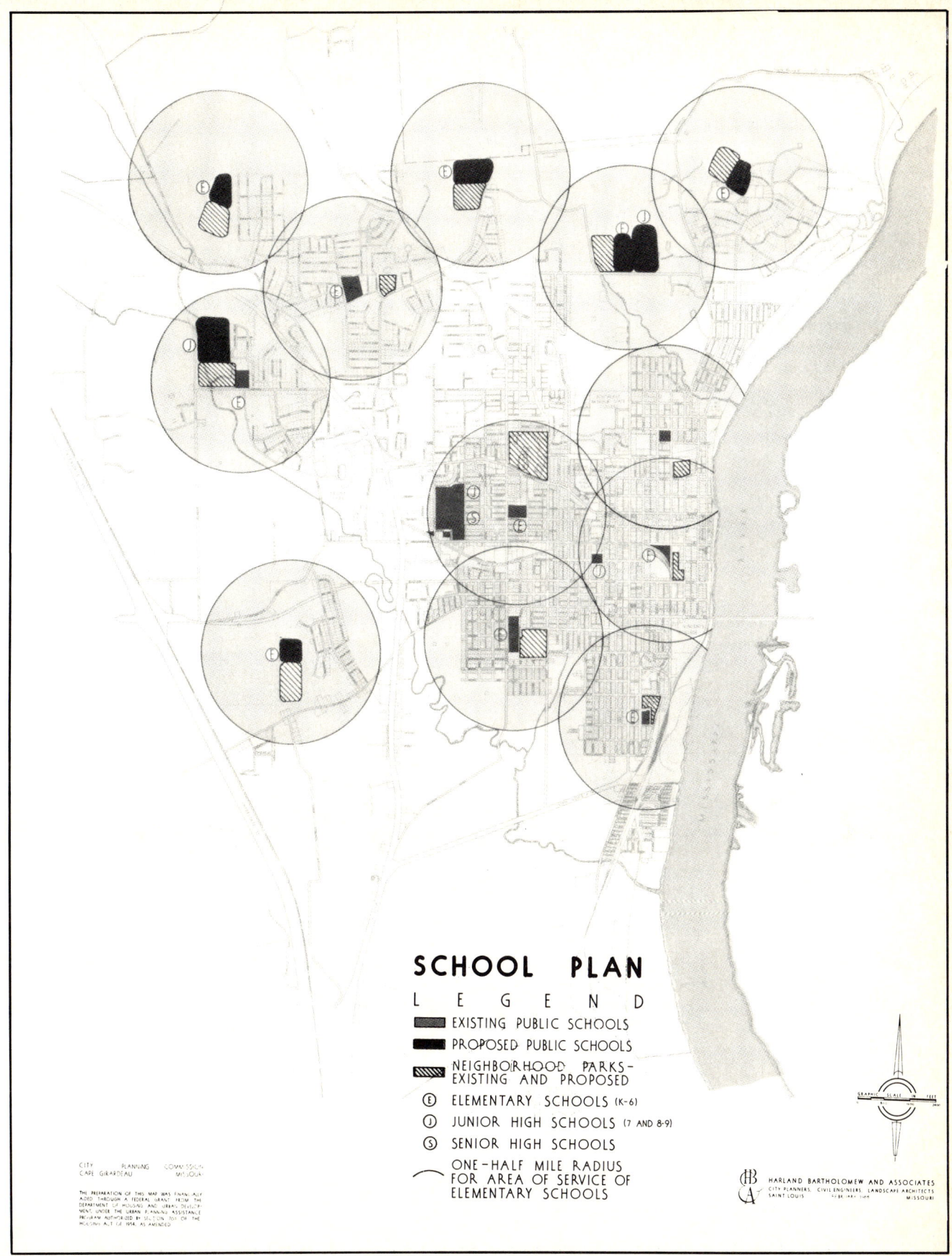

COMPREHENSIVE PLANS 99

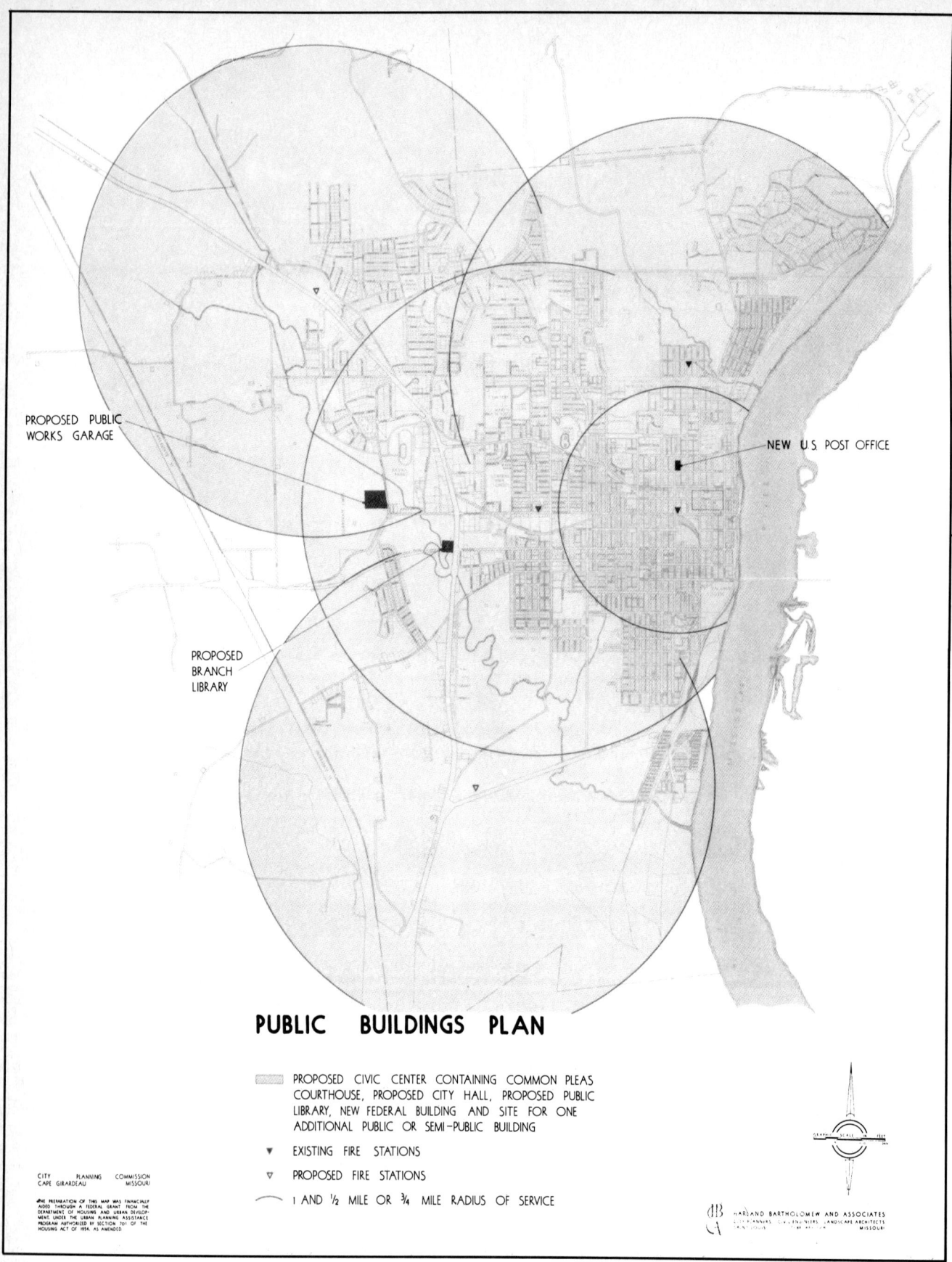

100 COMPREHENSIVE PLANS

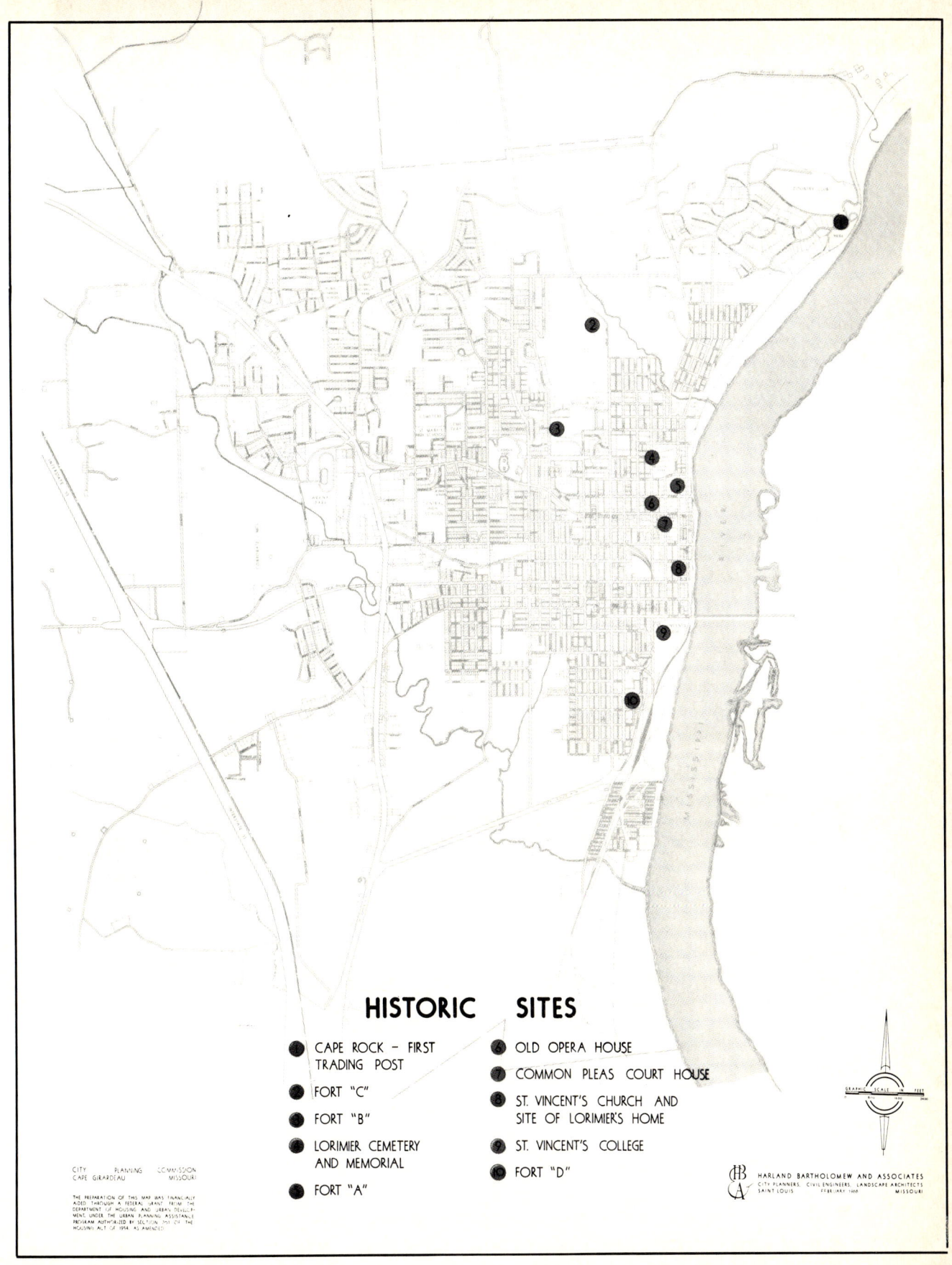

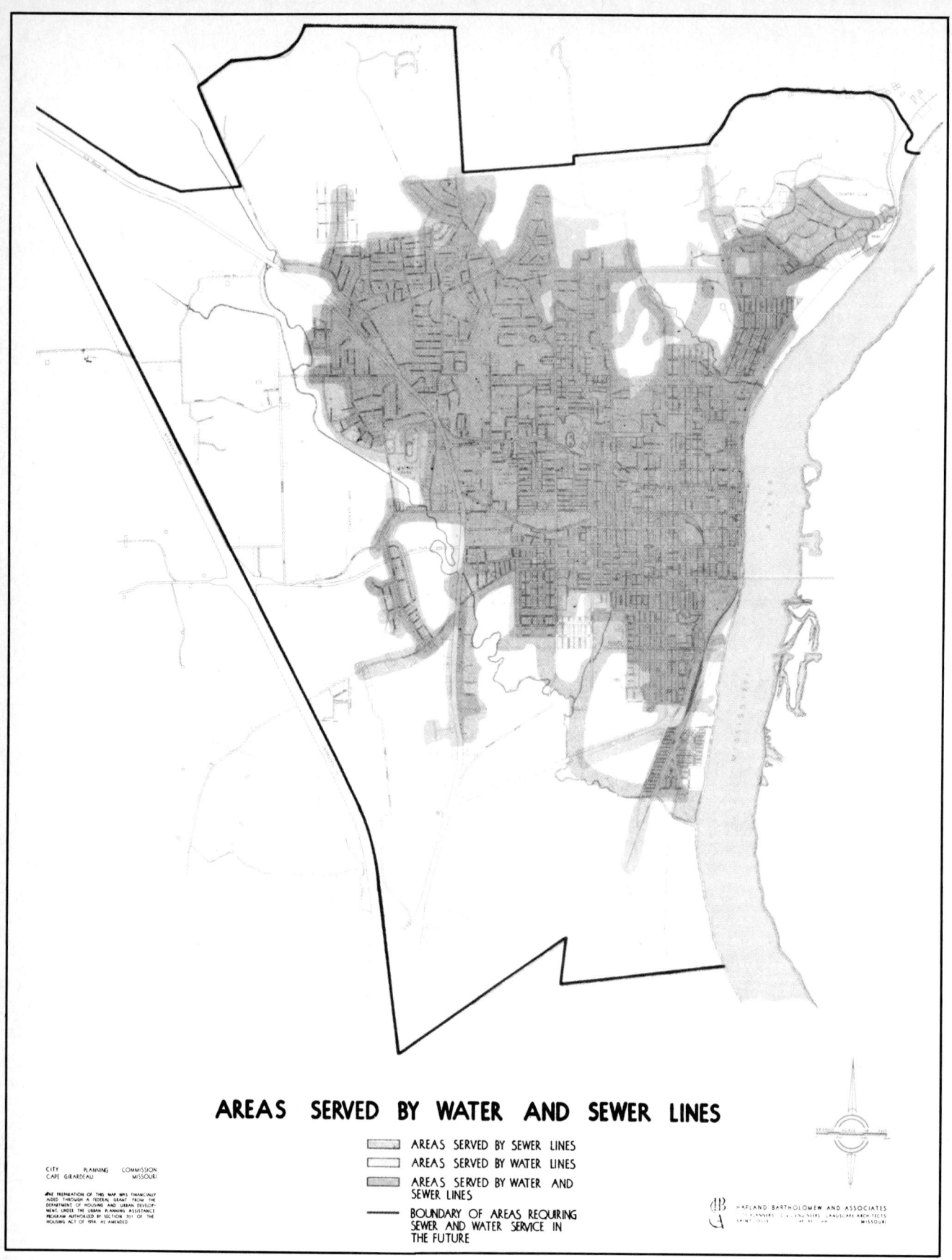

AREAS SERVED BY WATER AND SEWER LINES

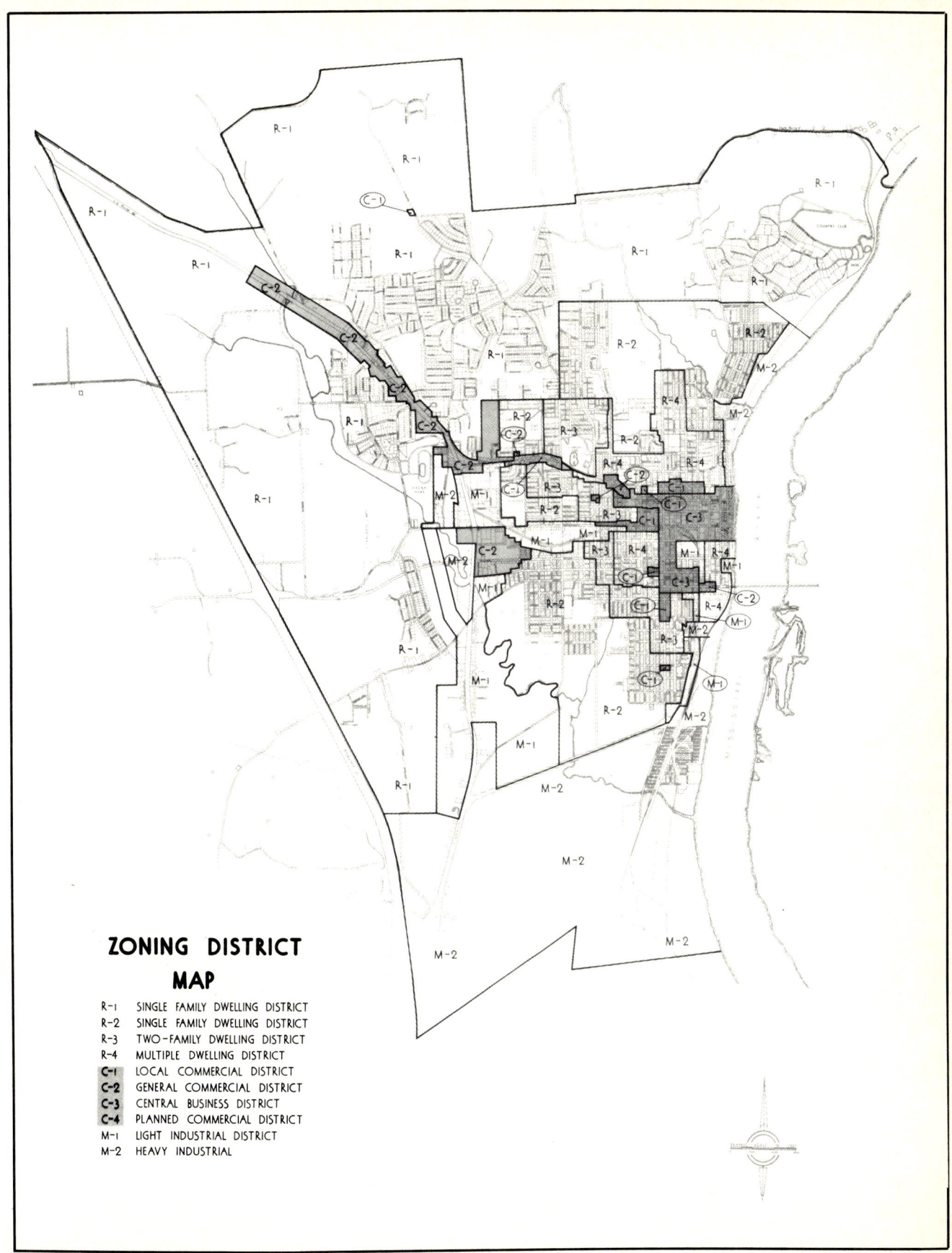

COMPREHENSIVE PLANS 103

SUBDIVISION DESIGN PRINCIPLES

1 EXISTING CONDITIONS

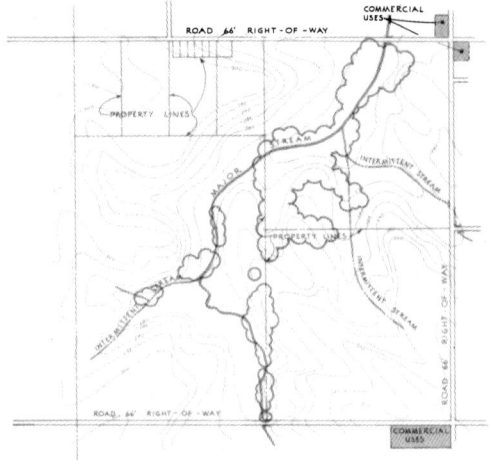

2 PROPOSALS OF THE COMPREHENSIVE PLAN

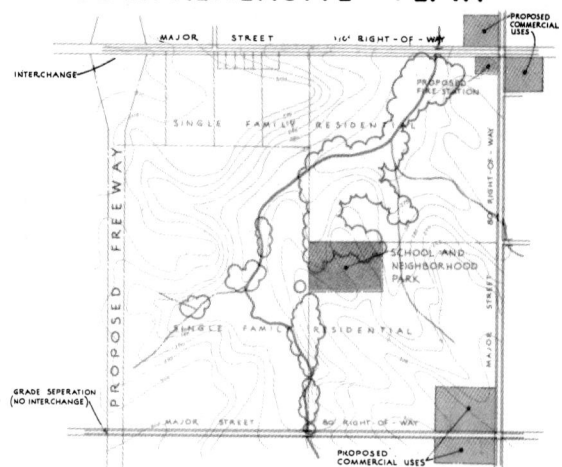

3 NEIGHBORHOOD UNIT PLAN

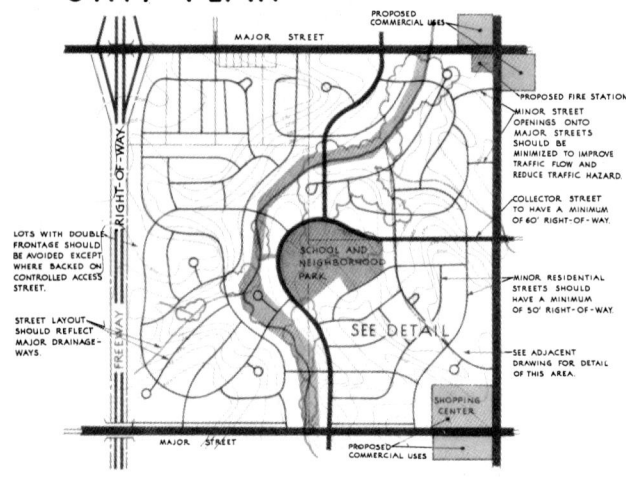

NOTE:
THIS DESIGN ILLUSTRATES PLANNING PRINCIPLES APPLYING TO TYPICAL NEW RESIDENTIAL NEIGHBORHOODS. IT DOES NOT ILLUSTRATE PLANNED INTERMIXTURES OF RESIDENTIAL LAND USES. IT HAS NOT BEEN ADJUSTED TO SIGNIFICANT LOCAL CONDITIONS OF RAINFALL, MICROCLIMATOLOGY OR WIND DIRECTION. WHILE IT SHOWS SOME PEDESTRIAN CIRCULATION ROUTES IT DOES NOT CALL FOR A COMPLETE SYSTEM OF SEPARATED PEDESTRIAN ROUTES BECAUSE THESE REQUIRE A SINGLE OWNER OF THE ENTIRE DEVELOPMENT. THIS PLAN IS BASED UPON CREATION OF A SATISFACTORY NEIGHBORHOOD THROUGH COOPERATIVE ACTION BY SEVERAL OWNERS.

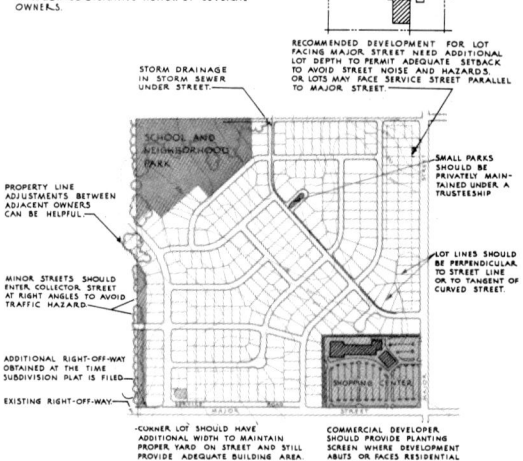

HARLAND BARTHOLOMEW AND ASSOCIATES
PLANNERS, ENGINEERS, LANDSCAPE ARCHITECTS

SEVEN
CENTRAL BUSINESS DISTRICTS

CENTRAL AREA REVITALIZATION PLAN
Village of Lemont, Illinois

The Village of Lemont has a unique physical setting along the Illinois and Michigan Canal. The Central Area Revitalization Plan called for restoration of the Central Area as a focal point of activity for the local community, in coordination with the renovation of the Canal.

The banks of the Canal, within the 300-foot-wide right-of-way owned by the Village, would become pedestrian walkways with appropriate lighting, landscaping, and other activities. Ultimately, an amphitheater for community events would be located on the south bank, and pedestrian bridges would span the Canal connecting to a series of pedestrian ways linking other parts of the Central Area. Specific locations for new commercial and supporting facilities were also identified.

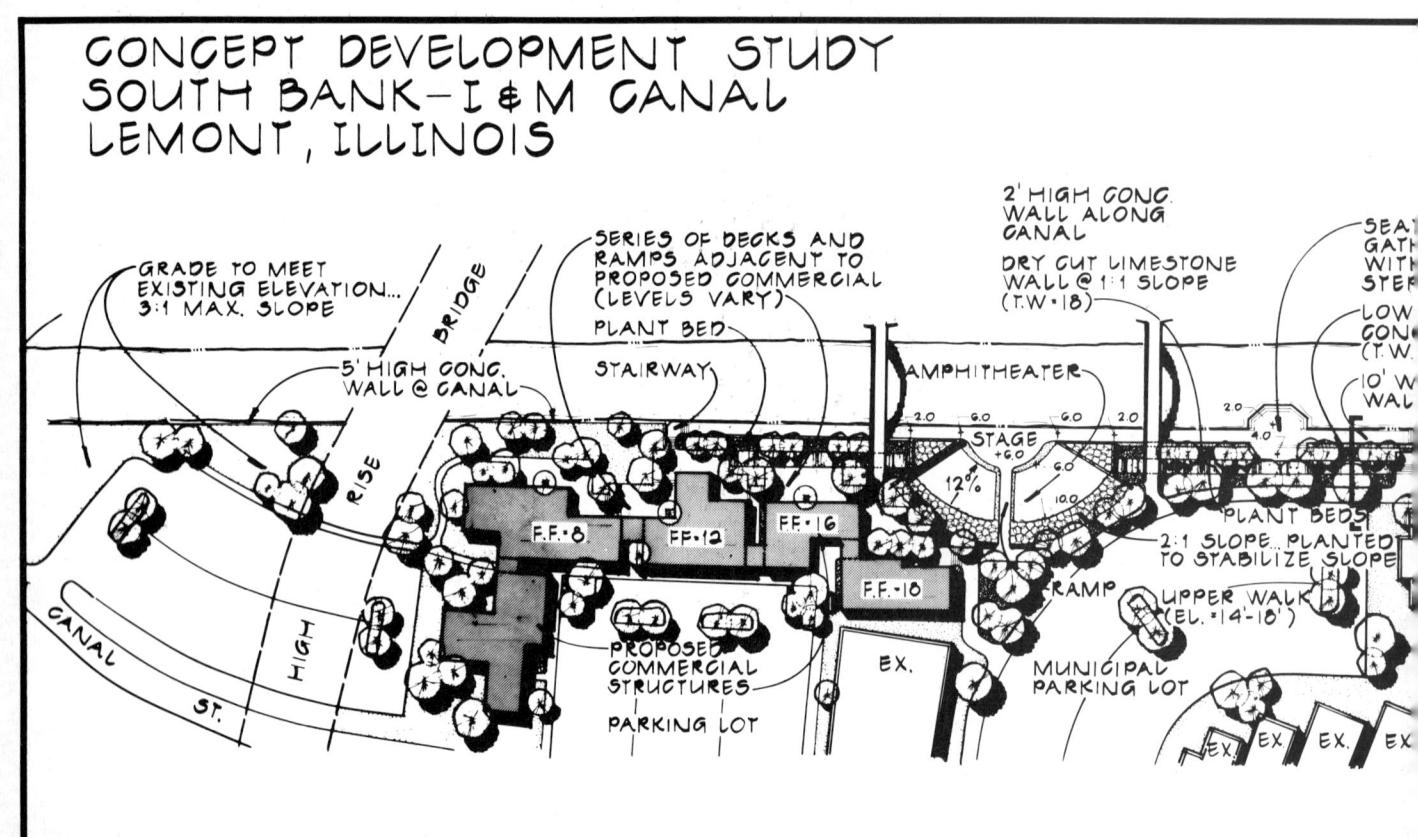

106   CENTRAL BUSINESS DISTRICTS

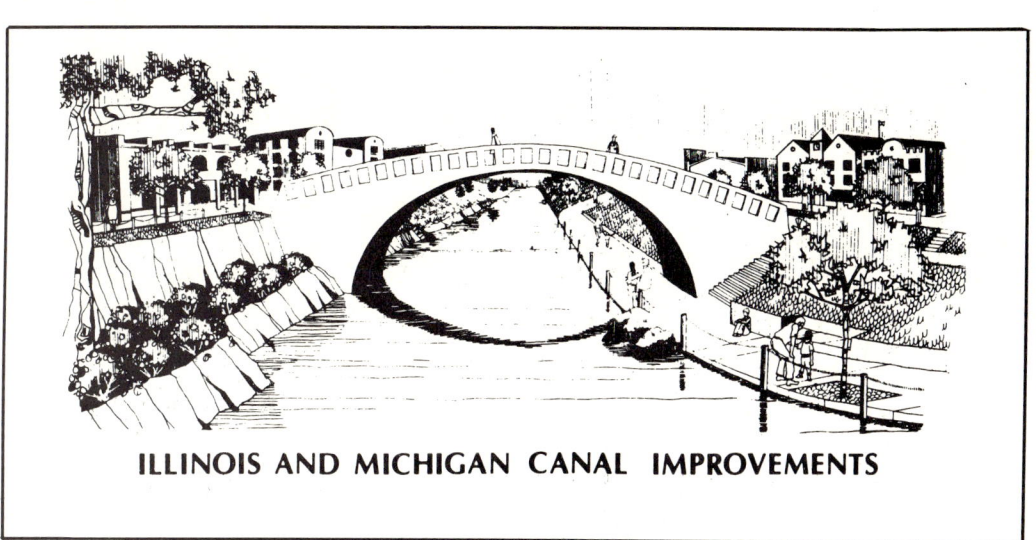

ILLINOIS AND MICHIGAN CANAL IMPROVEMENTS

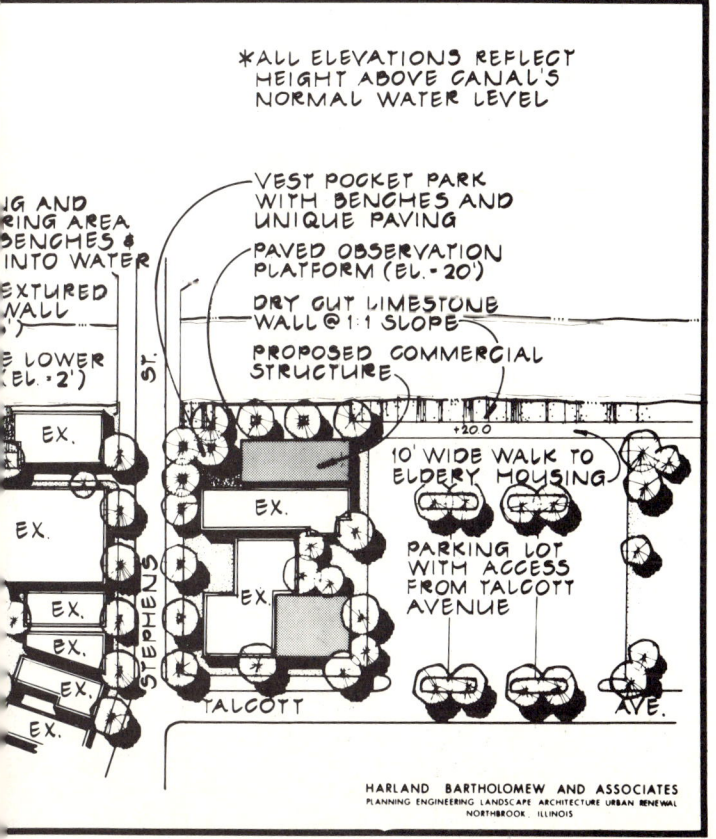

CENTRAL BUSINESS DISTRICTS   107

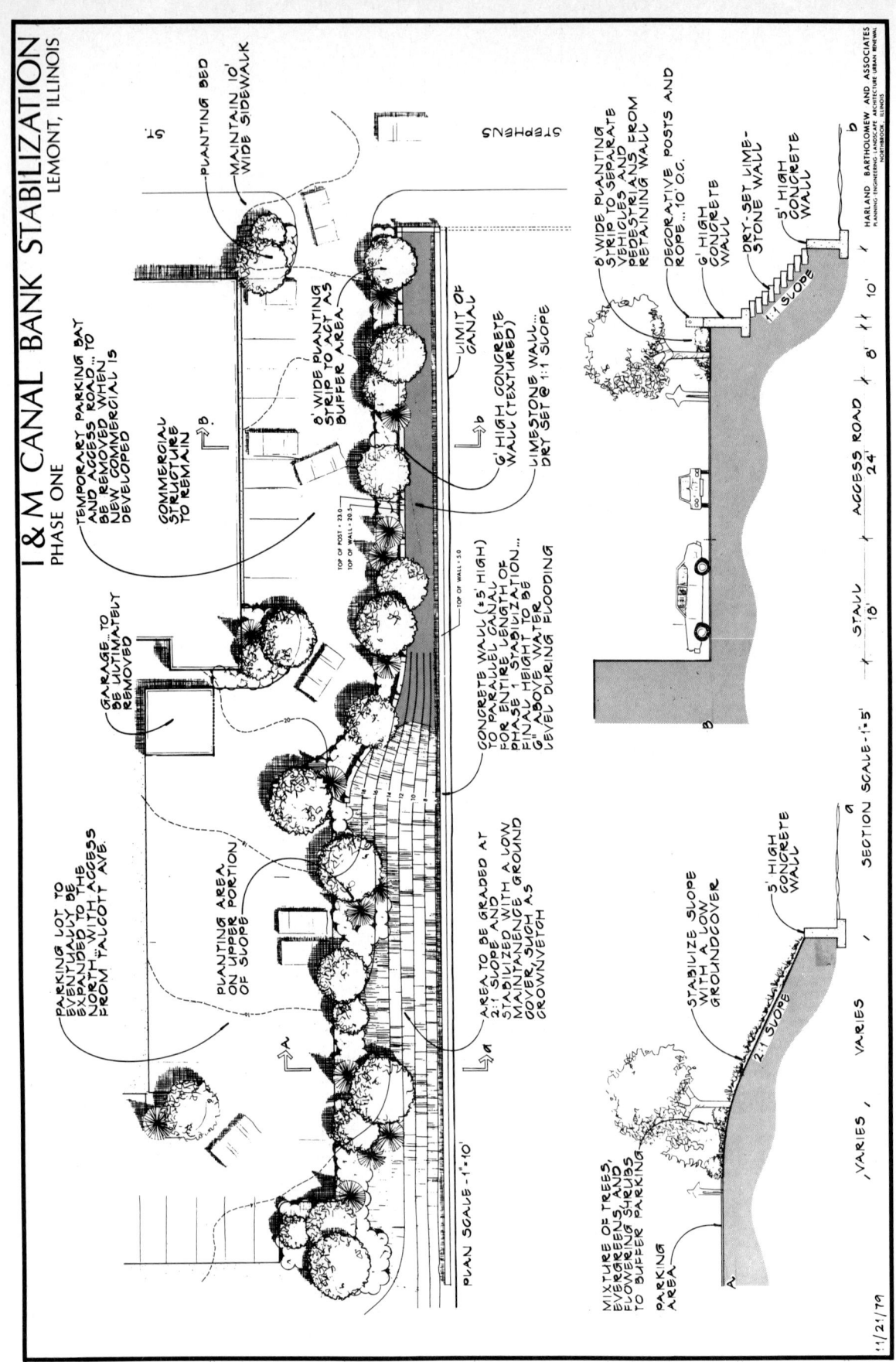

108 CENTRAL BUSINESS DISTRICTS

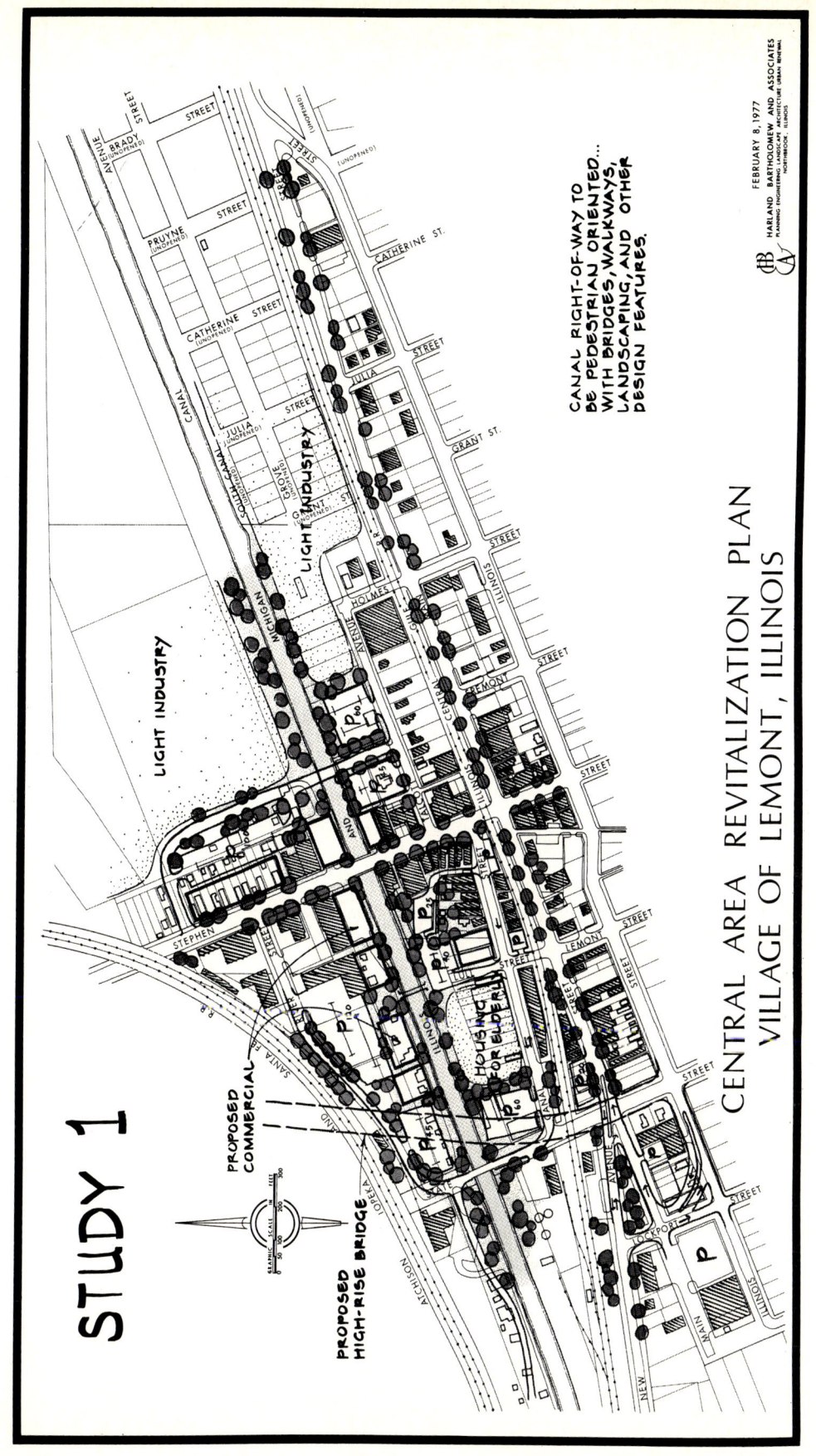

CENTRAL BUSINESS DISTRICTS

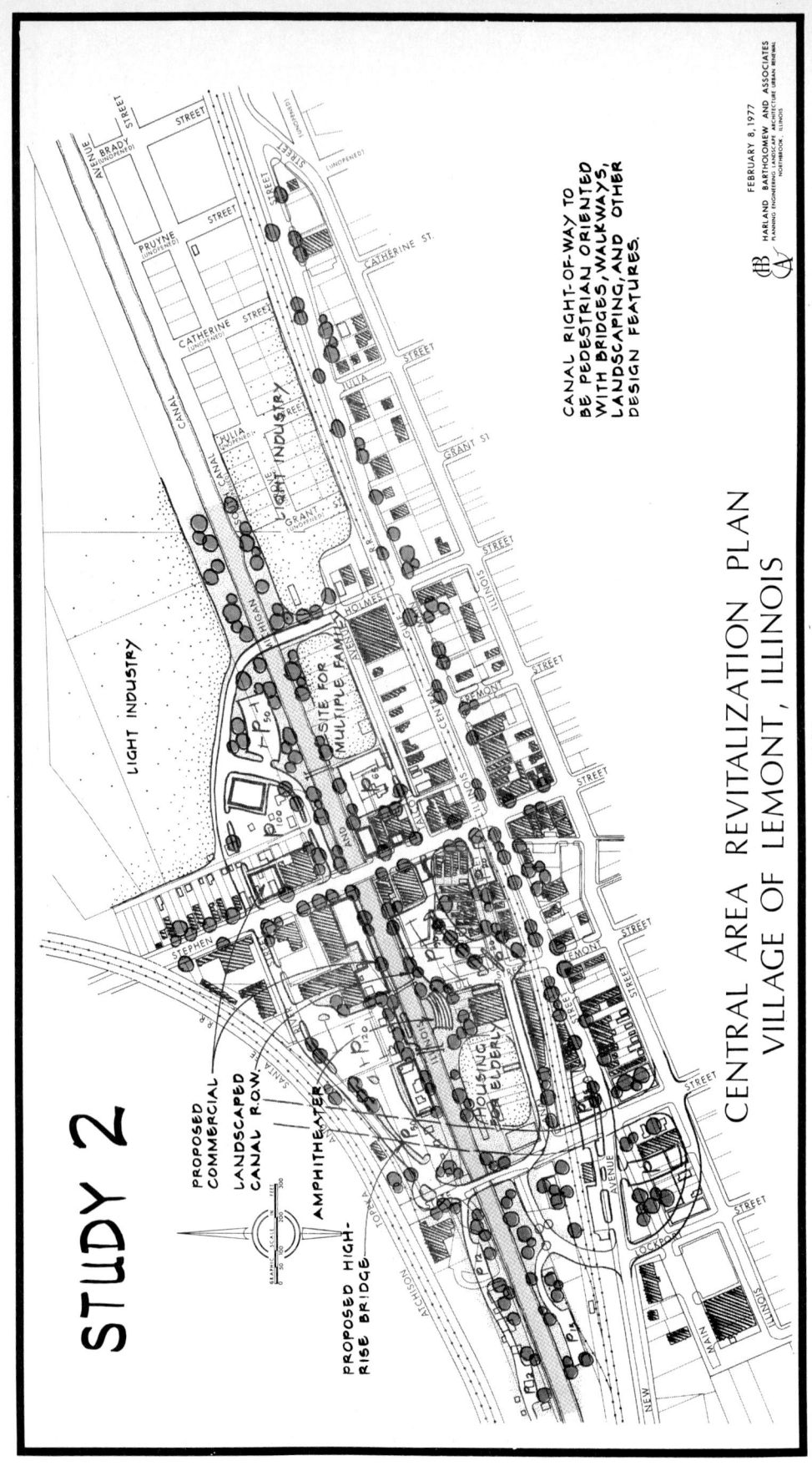

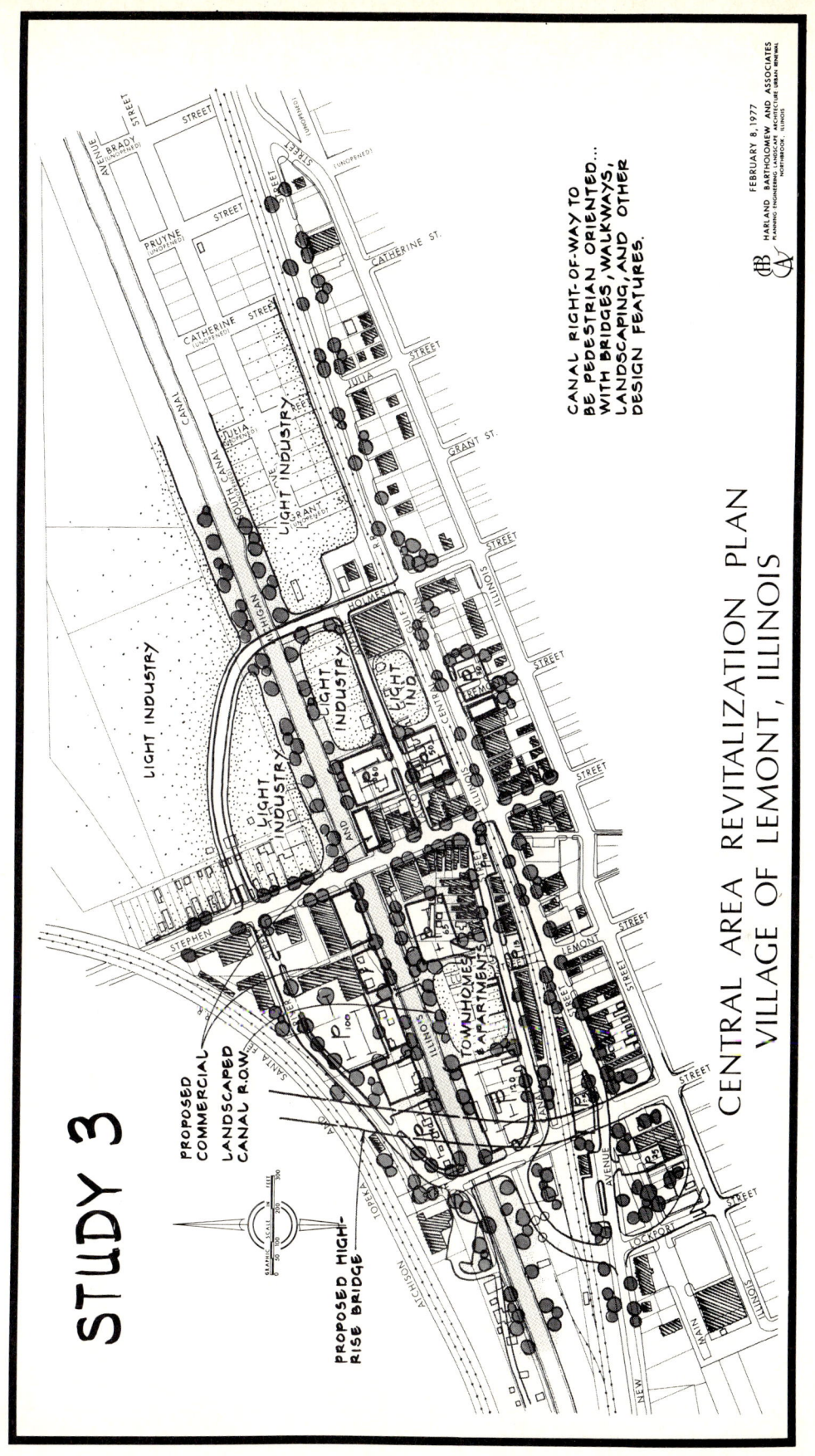

CENTRAL BUSINESS DISTRICTS 111

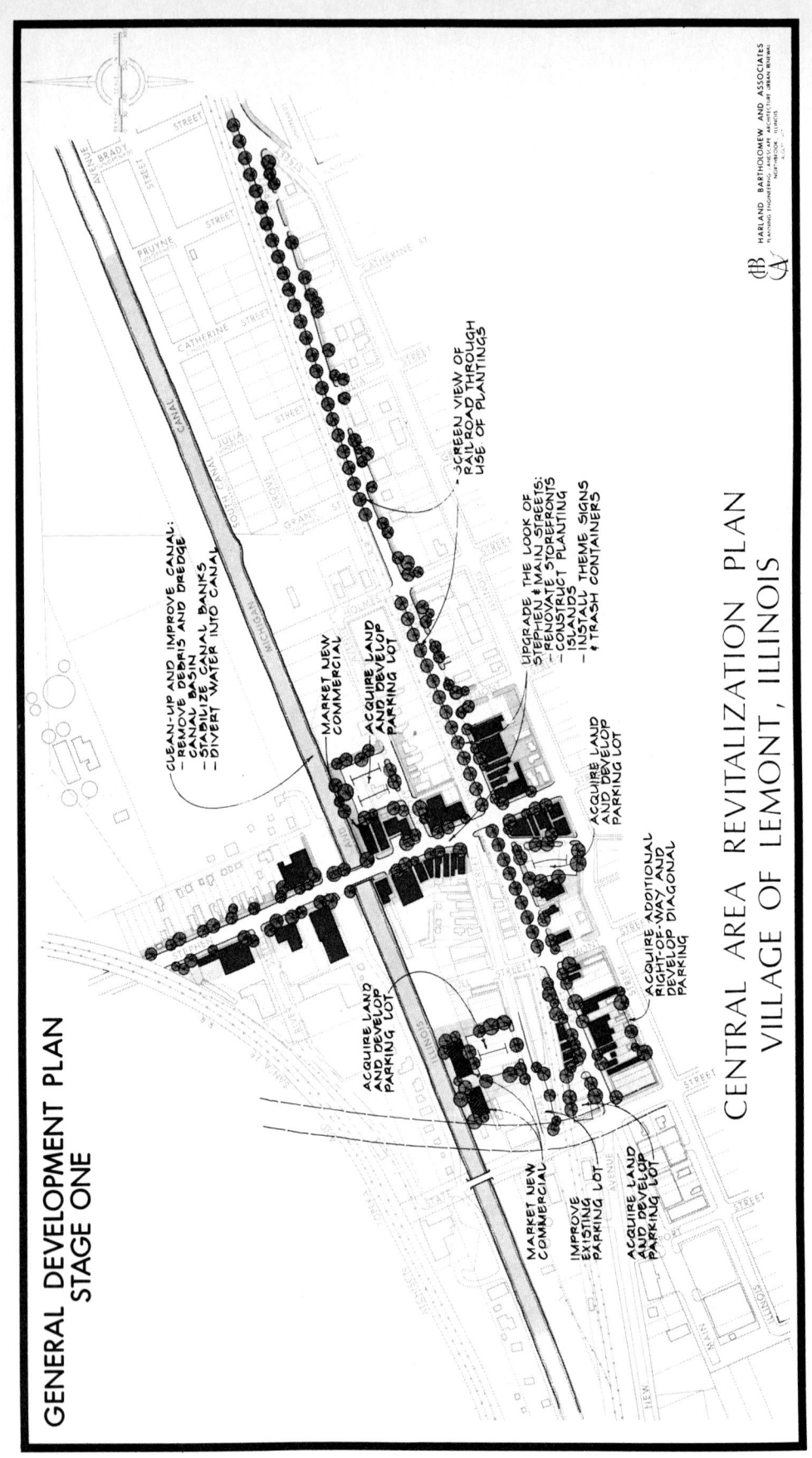

112 CENTRAL BUSINESS DISTRICTS

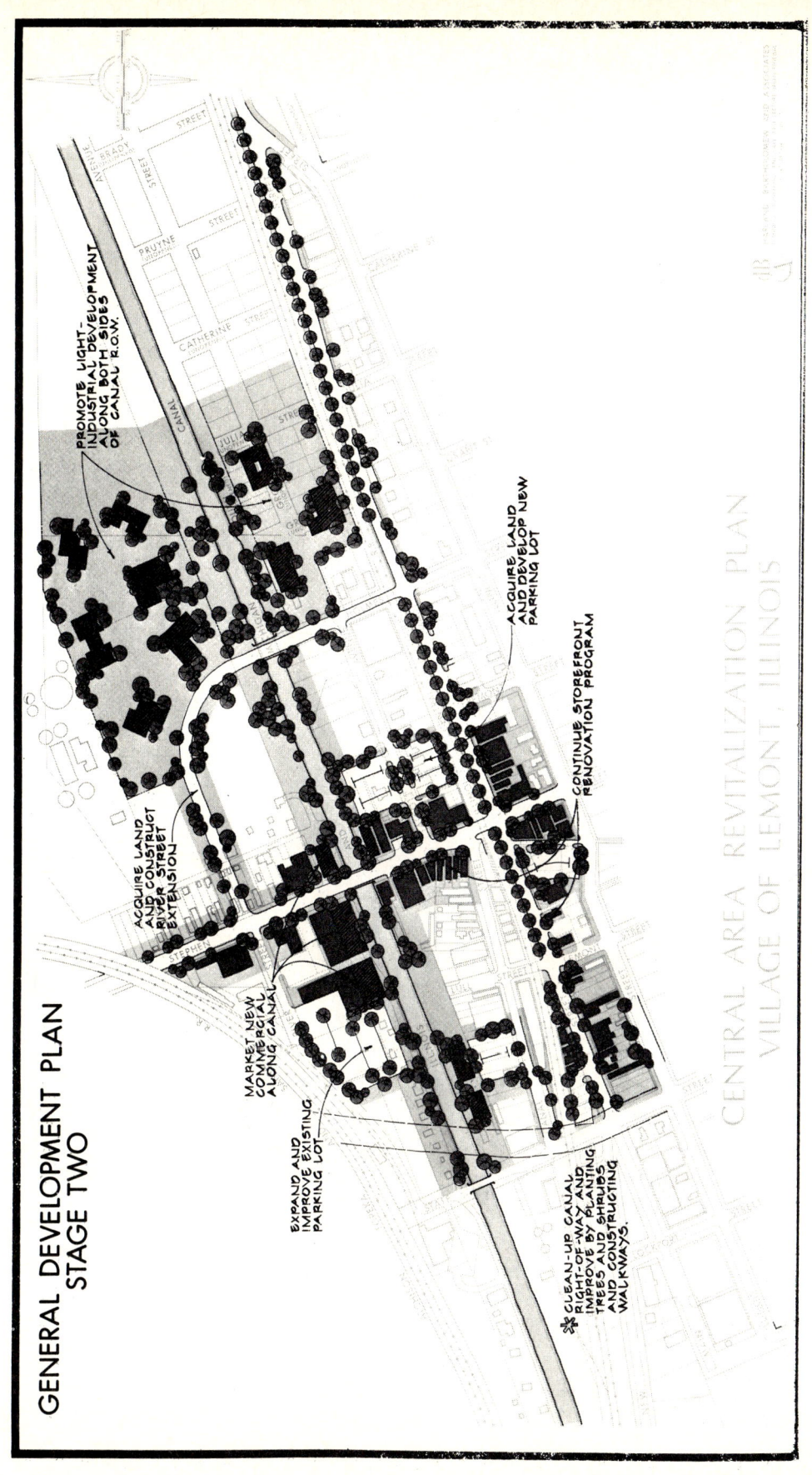

CENTRAL BUSINESS DISTRICTS

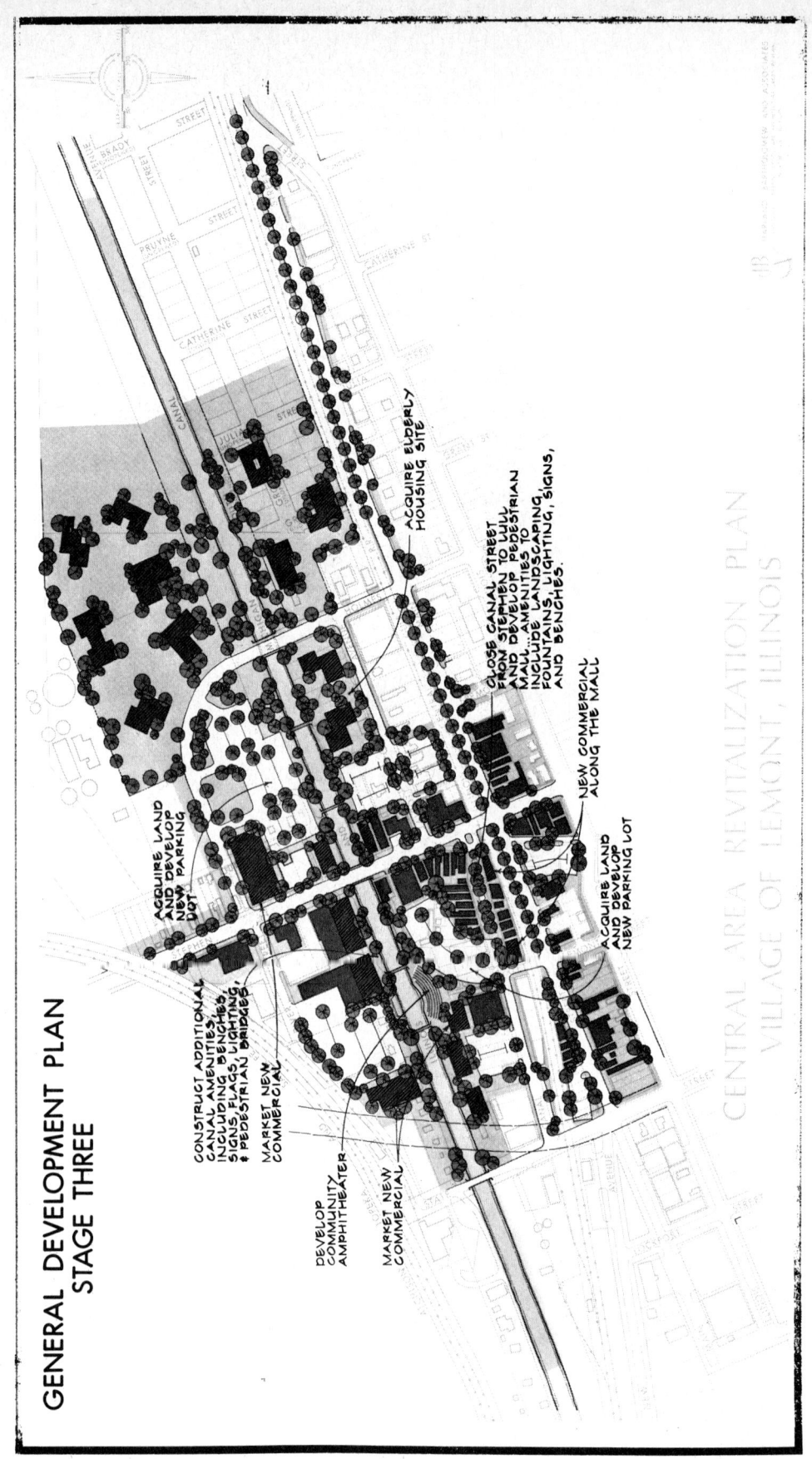

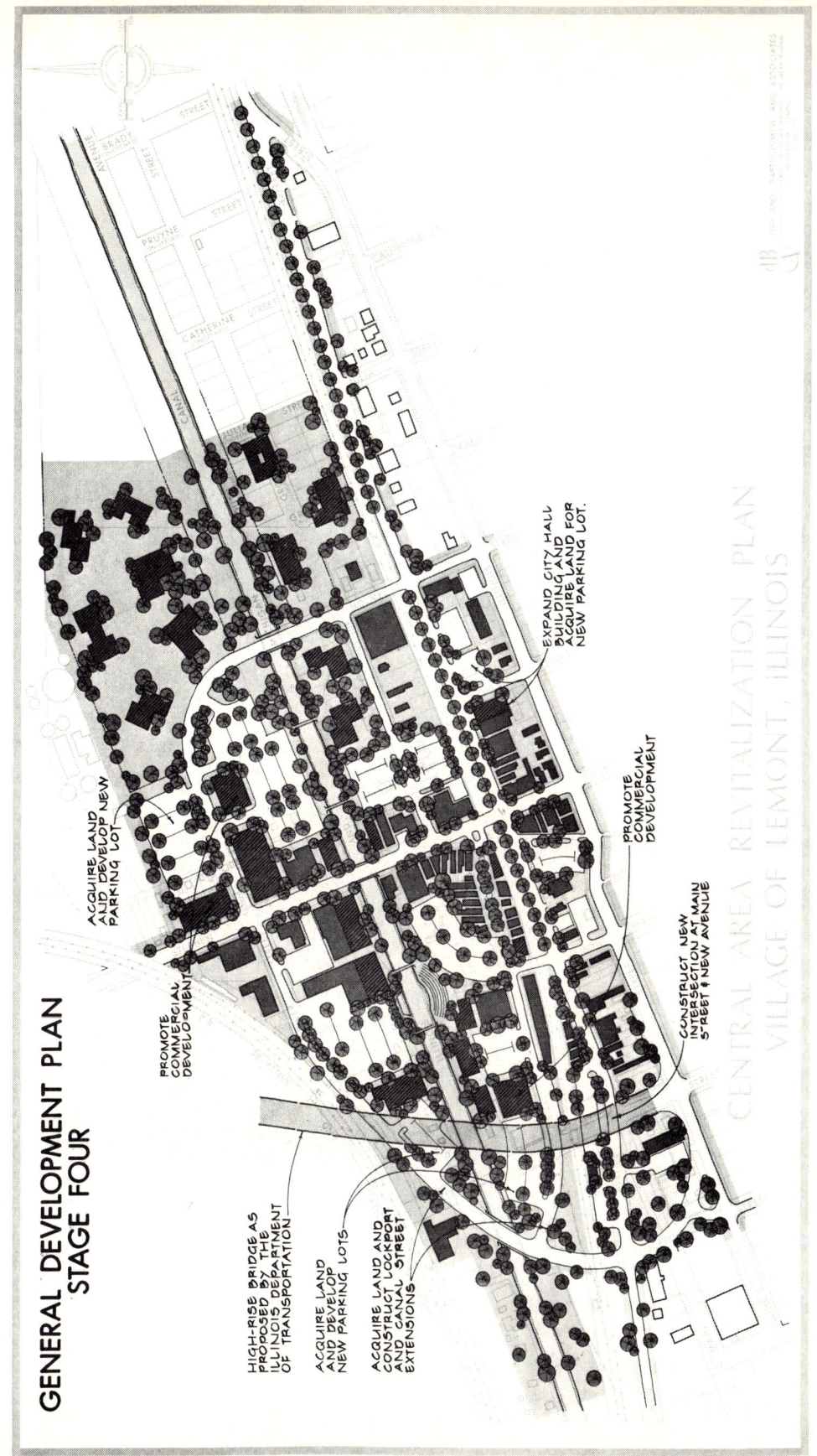

CENTRAL BUSINESS DISTRICTS 115

ST. CLOUD CENTRAL BUSINESS DISTRICT PLAN
St. Cloud, Minnesota

Based on a market analysis, Harland Bartholomew & Associates prepared a plan for the St. Cloud central business district (CBD) in 1980. The plan focused on identifying the best sites for residential/office development, a new civic center complex, and a river-front plaza.

Faced with stiff competition from outlying commercial centers, the proposals for the CBD were designed to emphasize the CBD's role as the activity center of the city. As part of the overall plan, recommendations concerning access and parking areas were made. Specific proposals were made to improve the existing loop road system now serving the CBD.

SPACE REQUIREMENTS FOR NEW USES St. Cloud CBD			
Use	Building Requirements	Parking Requirements	Land Area
Motel Expansion	100 Units or 30,000 sq.ft.	1 space per unit 100 spaces	±1.5 acres
Offices	240,000 sq.ft. 5 levels (base ± 50,000 sq.ft.)	1 space per 400 sq.ft. 625 spaces	5-10 acres (varies)
Residential	410 units @ 20/acre 410 units @ 30/acre	615 spaces 615 spaces	20 acres 14 acres
Auditorium	50,000 sq.ft. 3,000 seats	1 space/4 seats 750 spaces	2 acres
Government Offices	30,000 sq.ft. (replacement)	1 space/150 sq.ft.	4 acres
			26 acres minimum

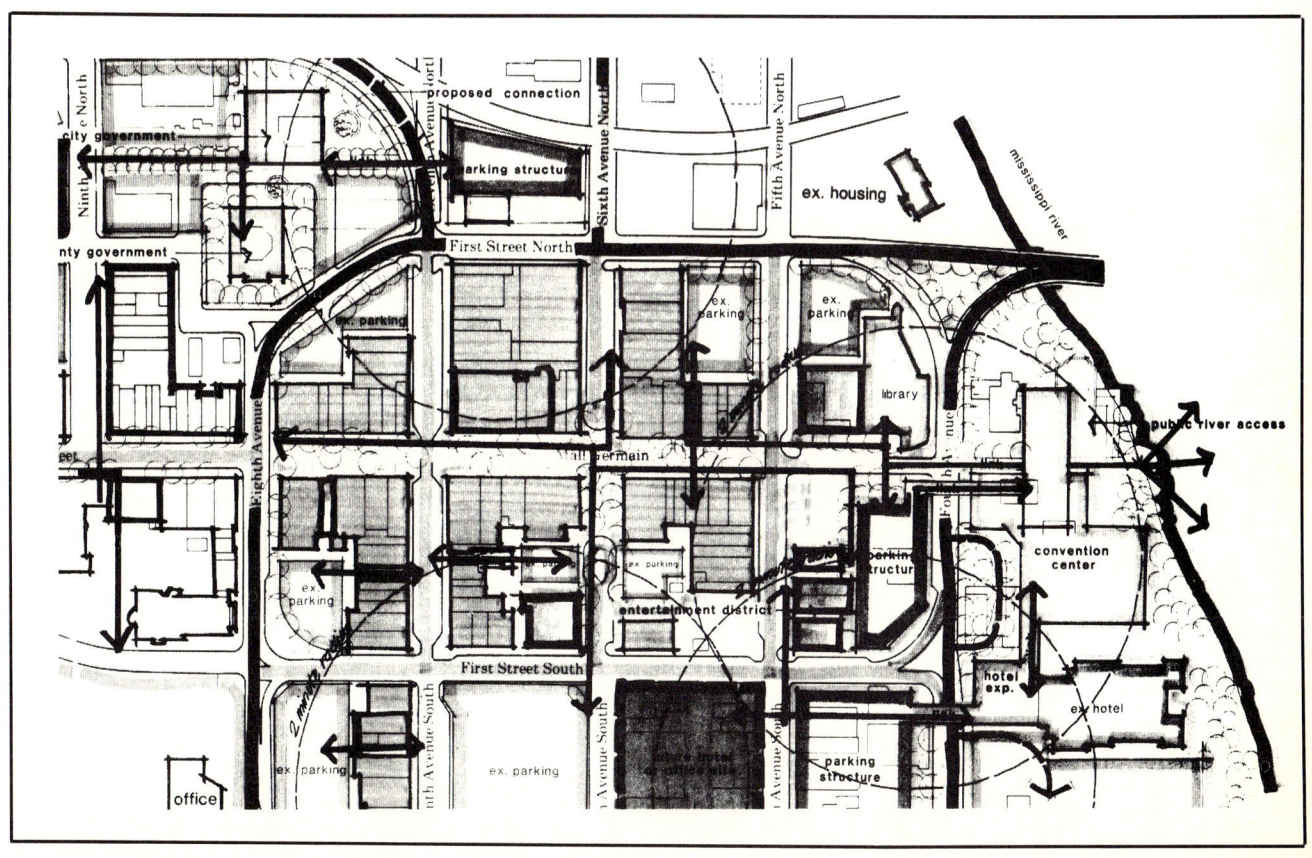

CENTRAL BUSINESS DISTRICTS 117

DEVELOPMENT PLAN FOR DOWNTOWN ST. CHARLES
St. Charles, Missouri

The overall goal of the development plan for the St. Charles central business district was to strengthen the position of the city center of the St. Charles County area, capitalize on its unique historical characteristics, and provide a mix of retail, service, and office uses with good access, circulation, and parking. This goal provided the focus of the overall plan and design details for parking lots, pedestrian walks, streets, crosswalks, landscaping, and signing.

Gladstone Associates helped prepare a market analysis that assessed future development potentials. Based on this demand, redevelopment sites were identified and schematic site plans and proforma analysis were carried out for selected projects.

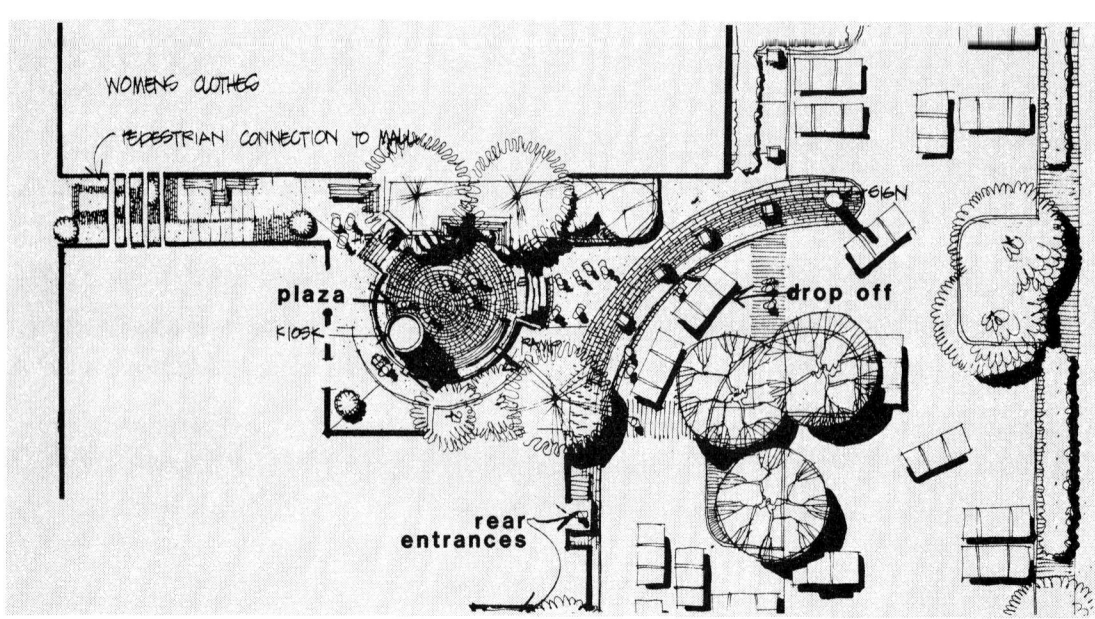

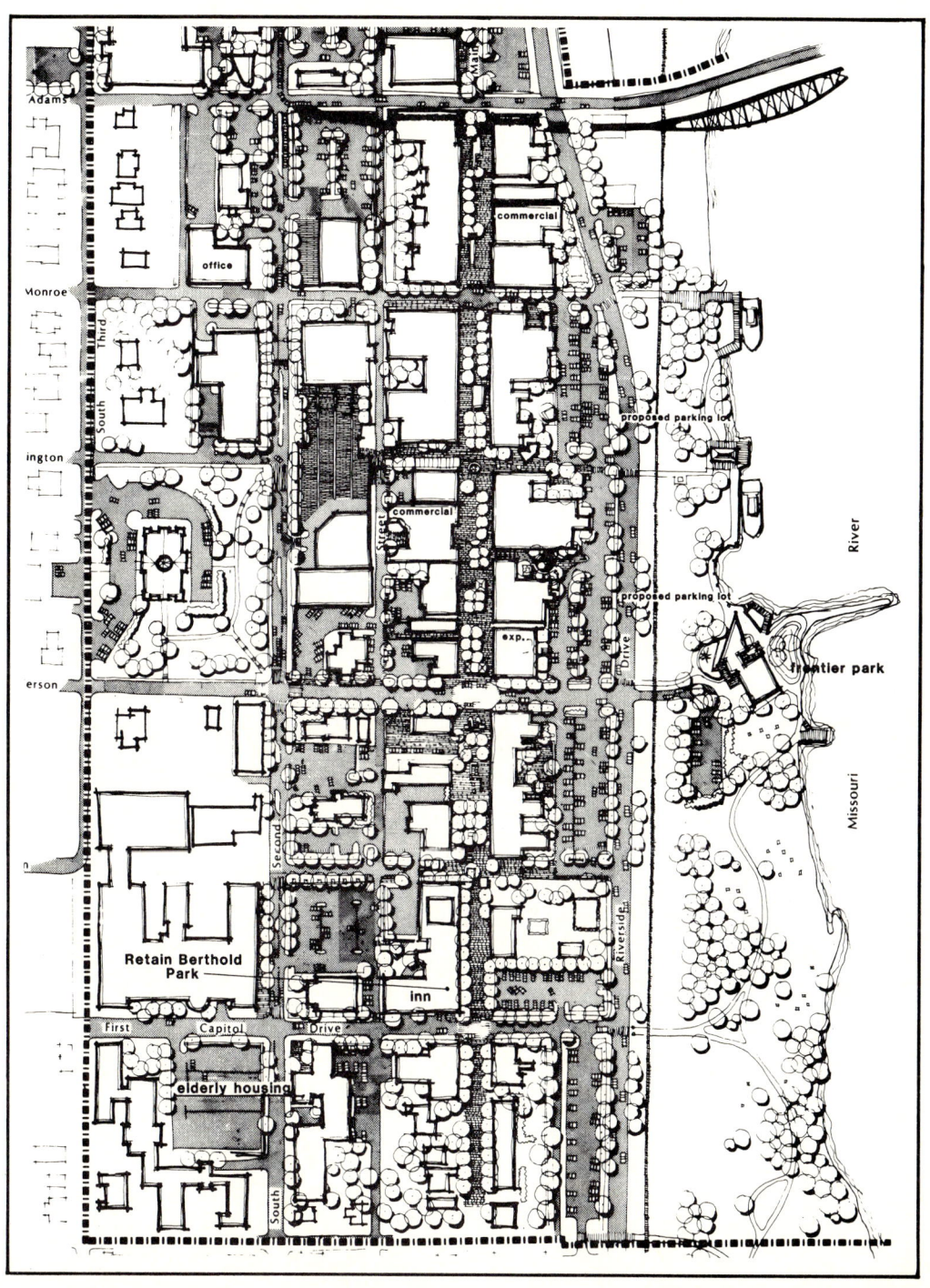

CENTRAL BUSINESS DISTRICTS 119

PLAN FOR DOWNTOWN ST. LOUIS
St. Louis, Missouri

The plan for downtown St. Louis was a major undertaking for the planning staff of the city's Community Development Agency. A concerted effort was made to involve the downtown business community, the development community, the public sector, historical preservation interests, and daytime and nighttime residents of the central business district. A Plan Review Committee was formed to direct the planning efforts. The Harland Bartholomew & Associates firm played a major supportive role during the two-year planning process.

The firm provided technical assistance as required by the Community Development Agency. The technical assistance involved reviewing and critiquing the city's plan review process, research methodology, technical reports, and drafts of the plan. Assistance was also provided to the city staff and the Plan Review Committee on public workshops, hearings, and presentations to Downtown St. Louis, Inc., (the CBD business group), and the Mayor's Development Committee.

The city's planning staff utilized consultants for portions of the plan that dealt with expertise beyond their capabilities. Harland Bartholomew & Associates analyzed urban design alternatives for specific areas of downtown. Also, the firm performed significant analysis of transportation alternatives. Factors such as project costs, environmental impacts, and economic benefits were examined for selected alternatives. For example, in-depth studies were completed on parking demand, traffic circulation, a bus-shuttle system, and an underground light rail system using an existing railroad tunnel.

The firm also performed a major analysis of historic buildings. Factors considered were historical significance, architectural condition, marketing and financing, planning and development, public policy, and transportation.

Harland Bartholomew's support services were utilized in drafting maps and diagrams for the plan, in preparing the Executive Summary, in editing the plan, and in preparing and printing both the final plan and a summary poster.

CENTRAL BUSINESS DISTRICTS   121

CENTRAL BUSINESS DISTRICT
Des Moines, Iowa

Downtown development was planned with four major objectives in mind.

Downtown should be a major attraction. It should be a lively area, an interesting area, a colorful area, a place where things are going on, where there is activity and excitement. Appearance is an important part of attraction. Functional attractions include competitive prices for merchandise, office space, retail space, and services.

Downtown should be a "one-stop" area. The downtown should be arranged so that it can be reached by public transit or by driving. There should be adequate parking. And, when a person arrives, he or she should be able to visit all the major downtown destinations by walking. In this respect, the practical conveniences of the modern shopping center should be introduced in the central business district.

Downtown must be an efficient office area. This objective requires good office space at reasonable rentals and shopping and dining places near the offices. To achieve this objective, the city must grow vertically, not horizontally.

Good access must be provided. The transit system must be maintained to achieve this goal. Also, good streets, highways, and expressways must be provided.

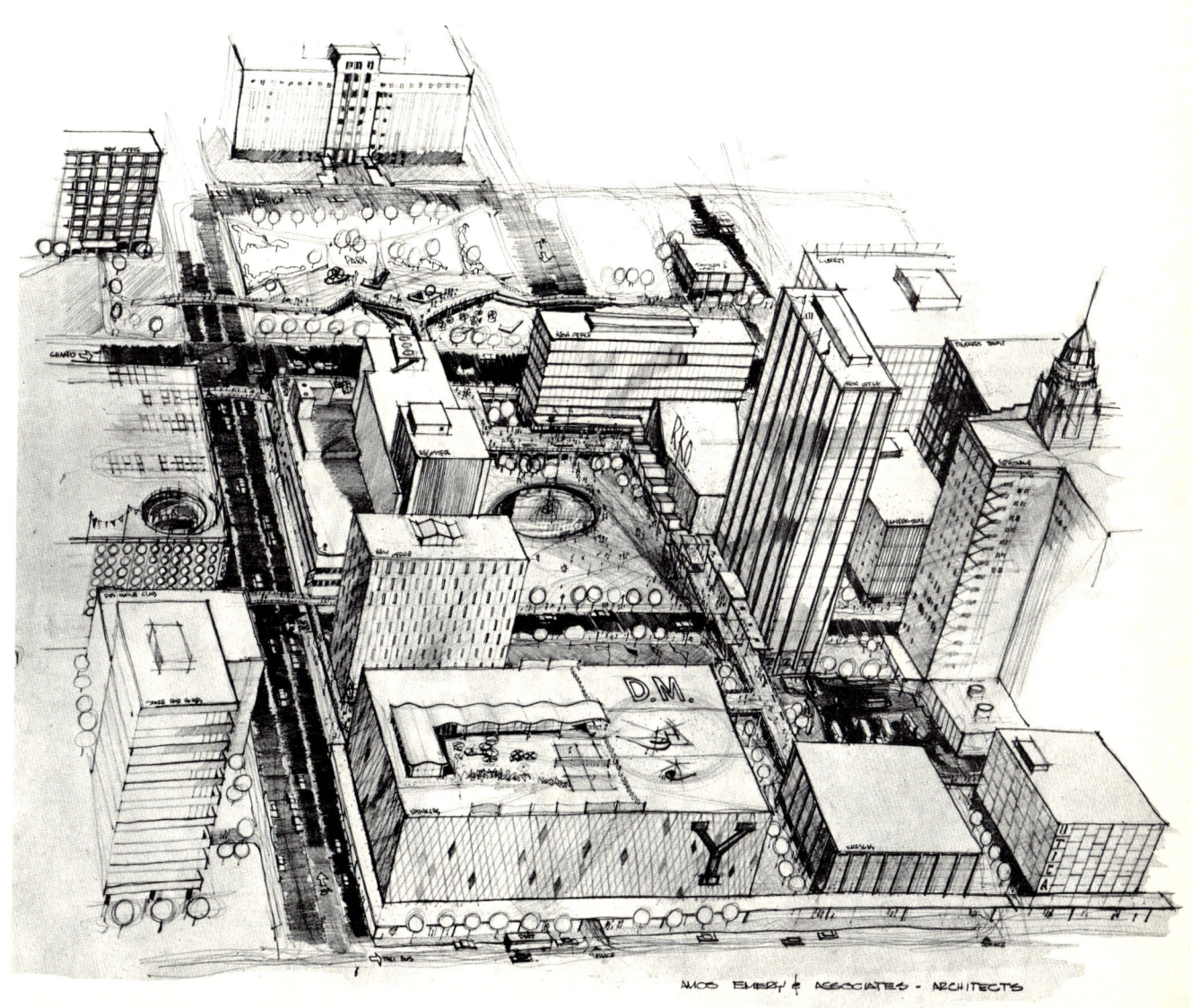

AMOS EMERY & ASSOCIATES - ARCHITECTS

CENTRAL BUSINESS DISTRICTS 123

LOOKING NORTHWEST FROM 5TH AND COURT   RUSSELL AND LYNCH ARCHITECTS

LOOKING NORTH FROM 5TH AND CHERRY   RUSSELL AND LYNCH ARCHITECTS

124   CENTRAL BUSINESS DISTRICTS

CENTRAL BUSINESS DISTRICTS 125

126 CENTRAL BUSINESS DISTRICTS

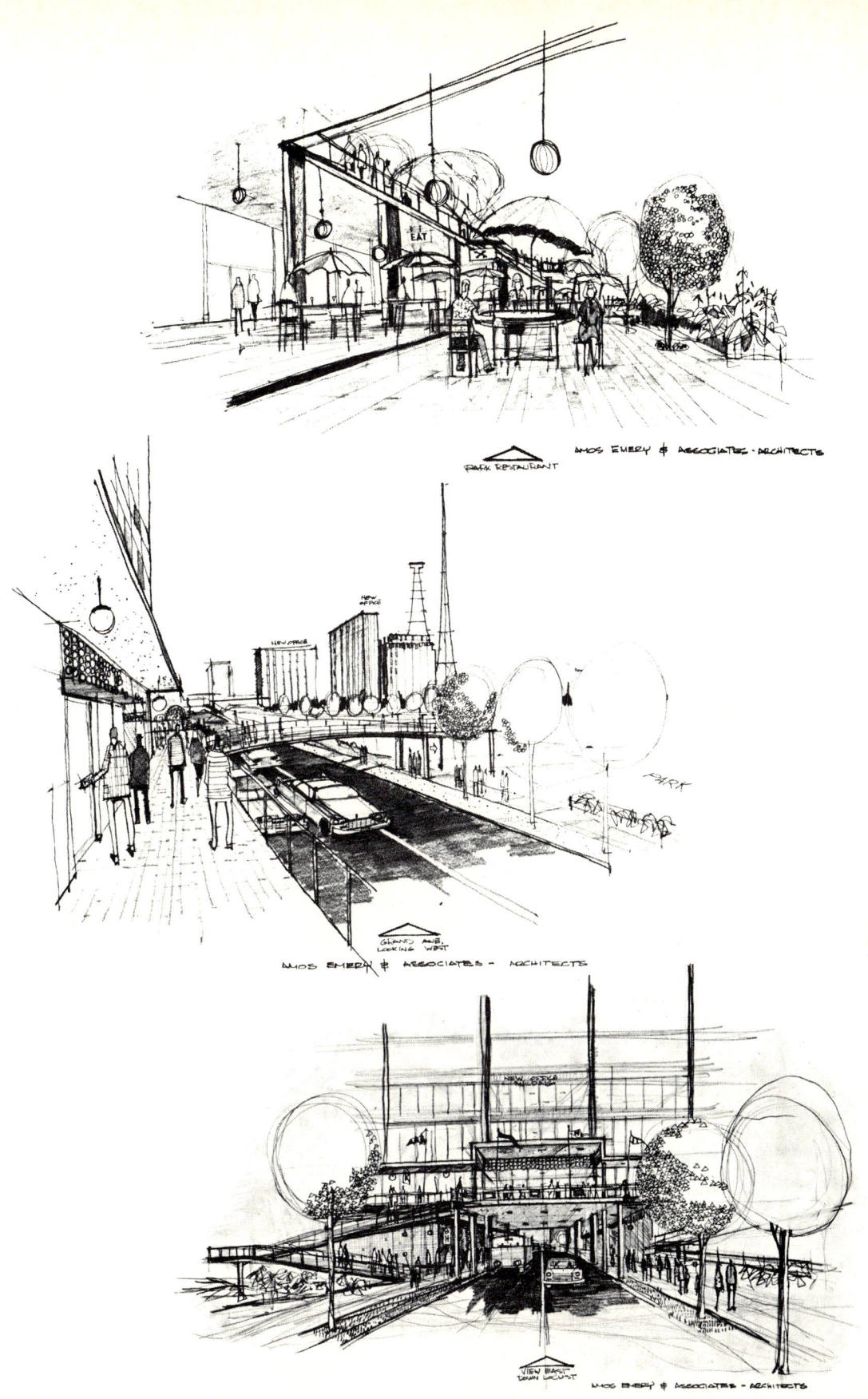

CENTRAL BUSINESS DISTRICTS 127

128 CENTRAL BUSINESS DISTRICTS

CENTRAL BUSINESS DISTRICT
Thomson, Georgia

Thomson is the county seat of McDuffie County, Georgia, located 3 miles south of Interstate Route 20 and 35 miles west of Augusta and the South Carolina state line. Changes in basic site requirements by business activity and lack of modernization to provide for current requirements resulted in deterioration of the attractiveness and shopper appeal of the downtown area.

Harland Bartholomew's specific recommendations included:

- Preserve brickwork of existing buildings
- Remove clutter, signs, and so forth, from building façades
- Use awnings to provide sidewalk shelter, add color, and unify façades
- Provide traditional street furniture and lighting fixtures in keeping with existing style of architecture
- Provide new landscaping
- Install overhead wiring underground

130   CENTRAL BUSINESS DISTRICTS

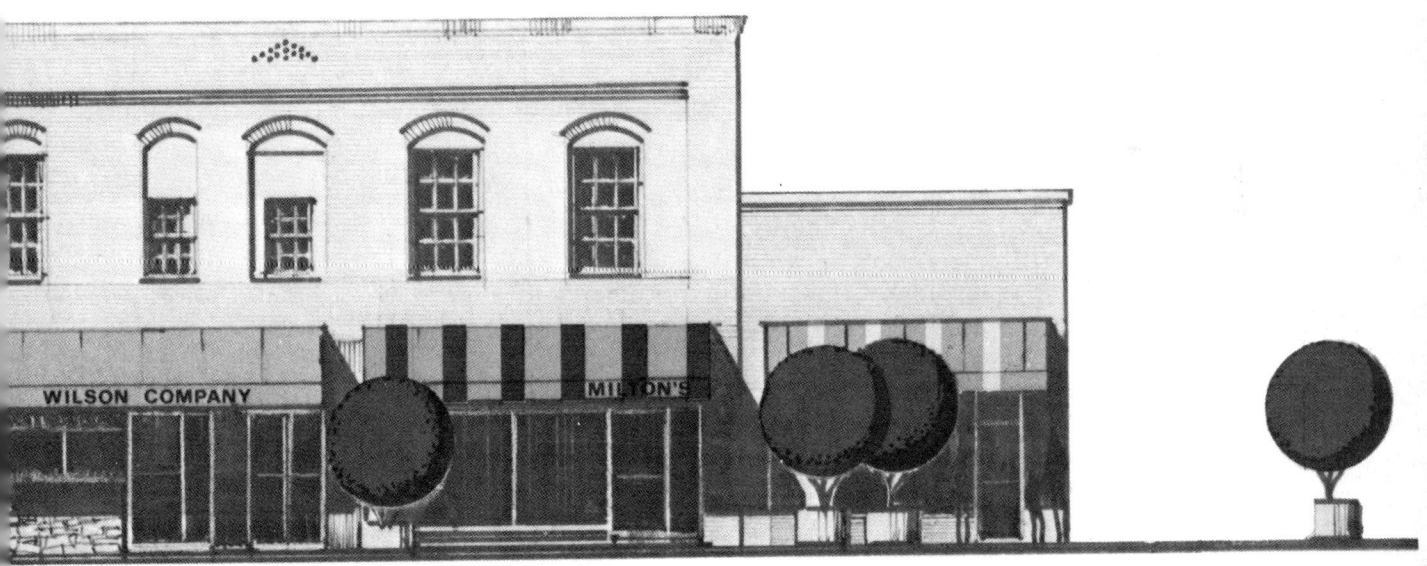

MAIN STREET - WEST FACADE

CENTRAL BUSINESS DISTRICTS

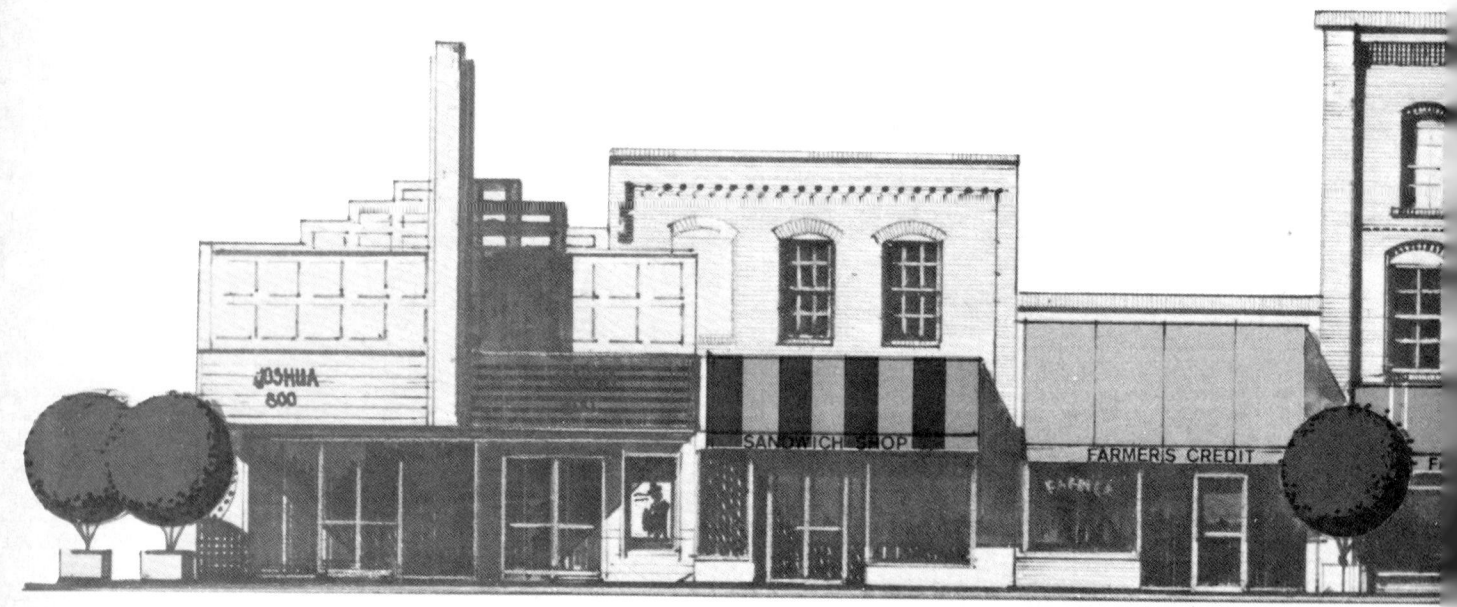

MAIN STREET - WEST FACADE

132 CENTRAL BUSINESS DISTRICTS

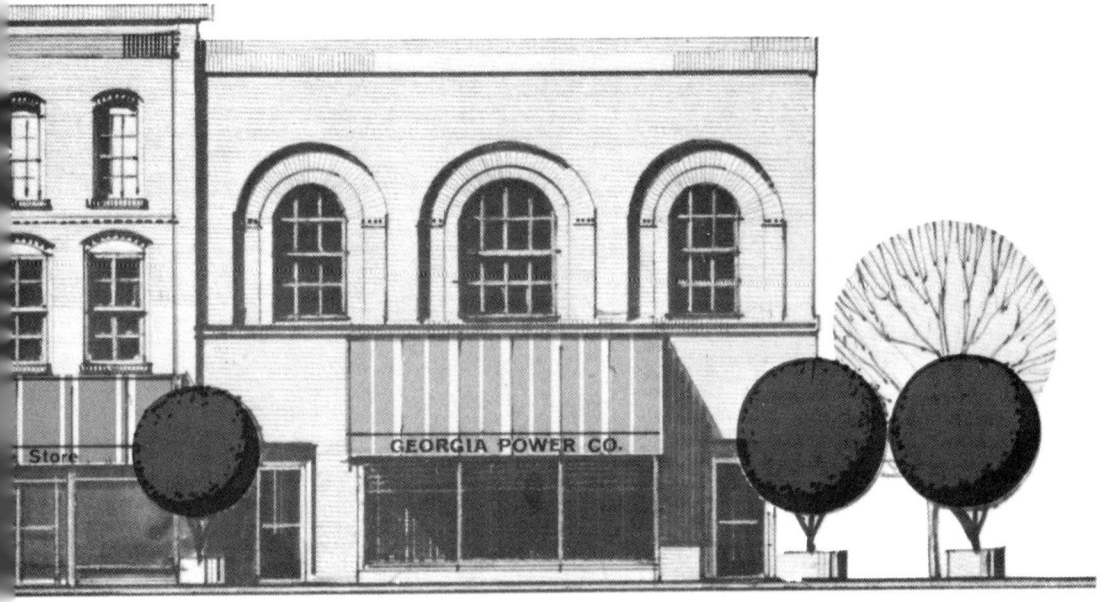

CENTRAL BUSINESS DISTRICTS 133

CENTRAL BUSINESS DISTRICT
Jackson, Tennessee

The Jackson CBD (central business district) was located at a disadvantage to the new shopping centers because the CBD was near the southern edge of the residential area and the center of population was moving northward. Newer homes were being built toward the north, away from the CBD, and the shopping centers positioned themselves in the most favorable location to draw customers from the higher-income areas and new housing. Thus, the immediate surroundings of the CBD were the major blighted areas of the city.

An important element of the developed CBD plan was the creation of a shopping environment free of pedestrian-vehicular conflict and generally oriented toward shopper convenience and enjoyment by way of the following recommendations:

1. Provide free flow of traffic and larger blocks of land for commercial development by widening some streets and closing others.

2. Provide pedestrian amenities such as:

    a. Canopied sidewalks

    b. Shade trees

    c. Benches

    d. Drinking fountains

    e. Play equipment for children

    f. Aesthetic quality in architecture and decoration, art, sculpture, plantings, and water features

RESTAURANT SKETCH

CENTRAL BUSINESS DISTRICTS 135

RESTAURANT SKETCH

136   CENTRAL BUSINESS DISTRICTS

RESTAURANT SKETCH

CENTRAL BUSINESS DISTRICTS 137

CENTRAL CITY PLAN
Corpus Christi, Texas

In Corpus Christi, as in many cities, the central business district has been faced with competition from suburban shopping centers over the years. Highway improvements have displaced commercial and residential activities. Traffic patterns have been altered, and established commercial areas around the retail core have declined in importance. These and other factors have resulted in deterioration and decline and loss of production.

Specific goals and objectives were established to guide the development of the central city plan. One of the important objectives of the plan was to provide adequate facilities for pedestrian circulation throughout the uptown and downtown areas by establishing malls, walkways, and concourses that satisfy requirements for both vertical and horizontal pedestrian movements.

CENTRAL BUSINESS DISTRICTS 139

CENTRAL AVENUE IMPROVEMENT
Highland Park, Illinois

The Central Avenue improvement was designed to provide a more pleasing appearance and pedestrian amenities for a major shopping street while maintaining the necessary on-street parking and traffic flow. Development of a landscaped median, along with redesign of existing curbside plantings, provides a tree canopy and opportunities for seasonal plantings, while allowing for separation of opposing traffic. Additional landscaping, paving, and street furnishings were planned for a highly visible corner as a pedestrian "oasis." Lighting and irrigation were planned as an integral part of the improvement.

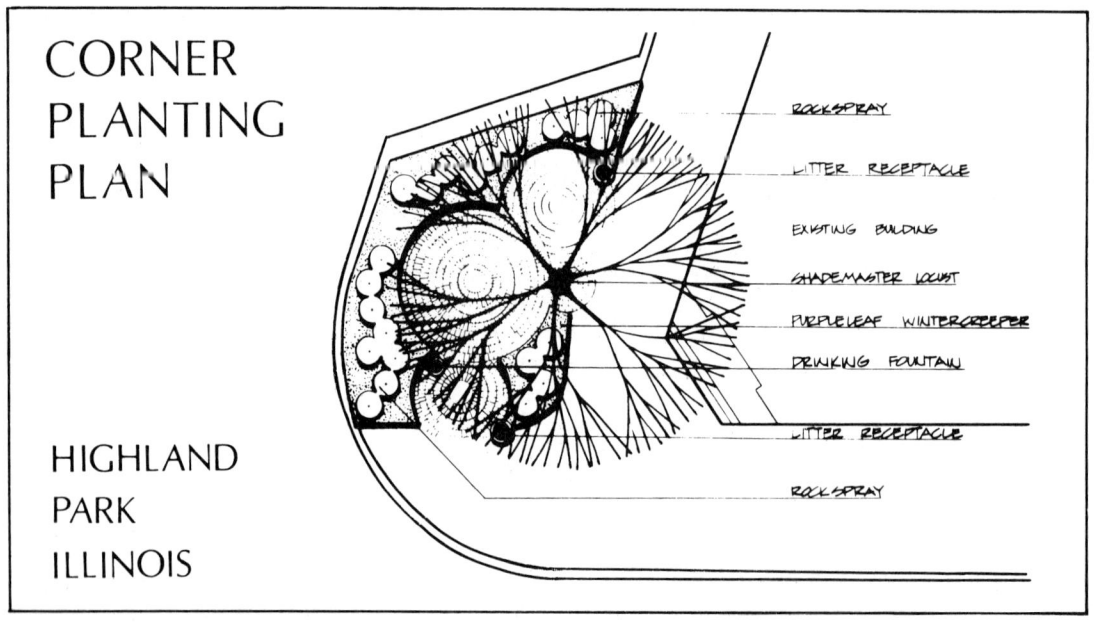

CENTRAL BUSINESS DISTRICT
Wheeling, Illinois

The core area of Wheeling contains the highest intensity of existing development in the business area, as well as several potential development areas. Due to the importance of the core as a focal point for development, a detailed design plan was prepared for the major street frontage in that area. Recommendations included moving wires from overhead to underground installations, stricter controls for street signs and advertising, and improved signage. Improved parking, pedestrian circulation, and landscaping also were advised.

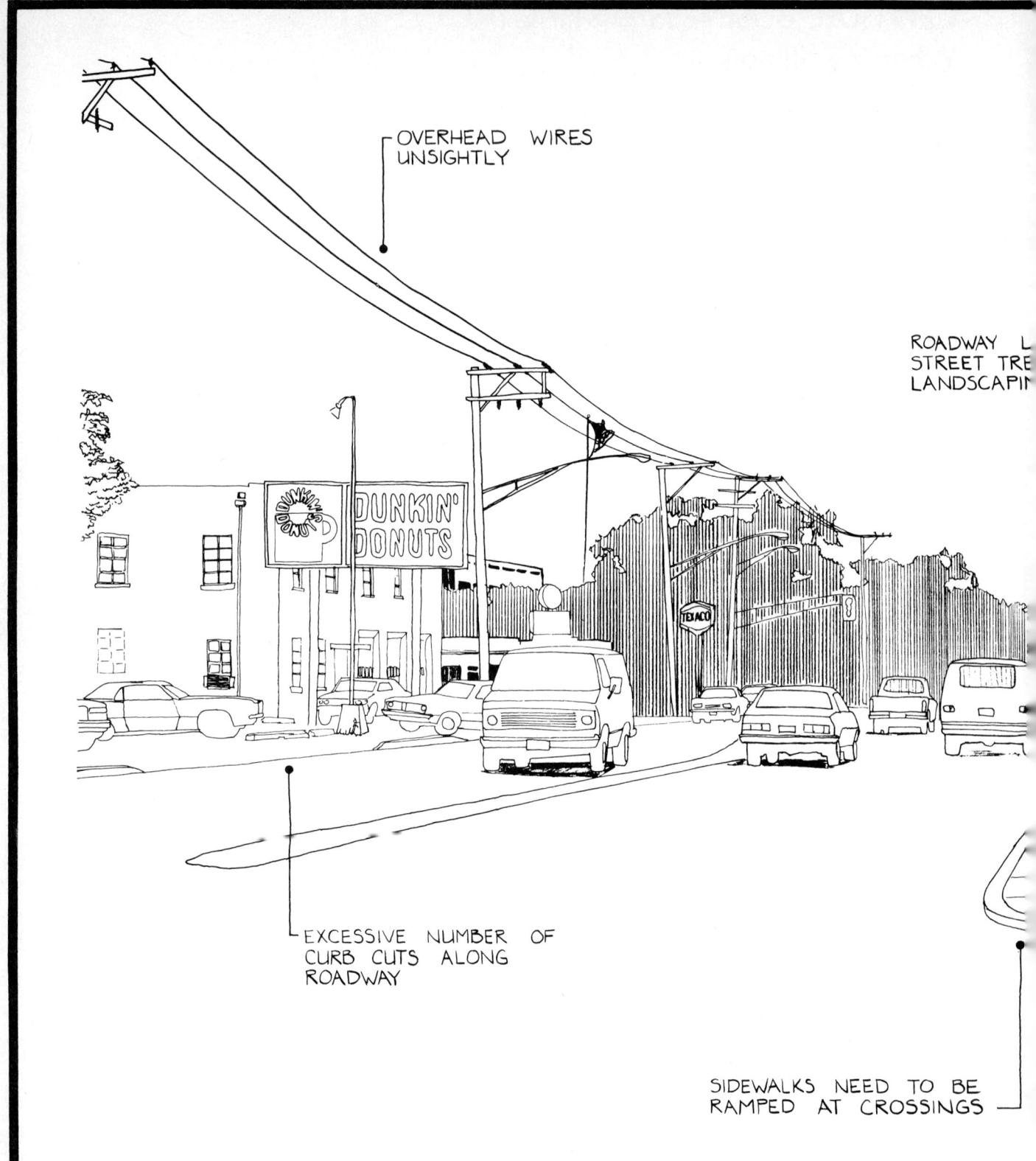

142 CENTRAL BUSINESS DISTRICTS

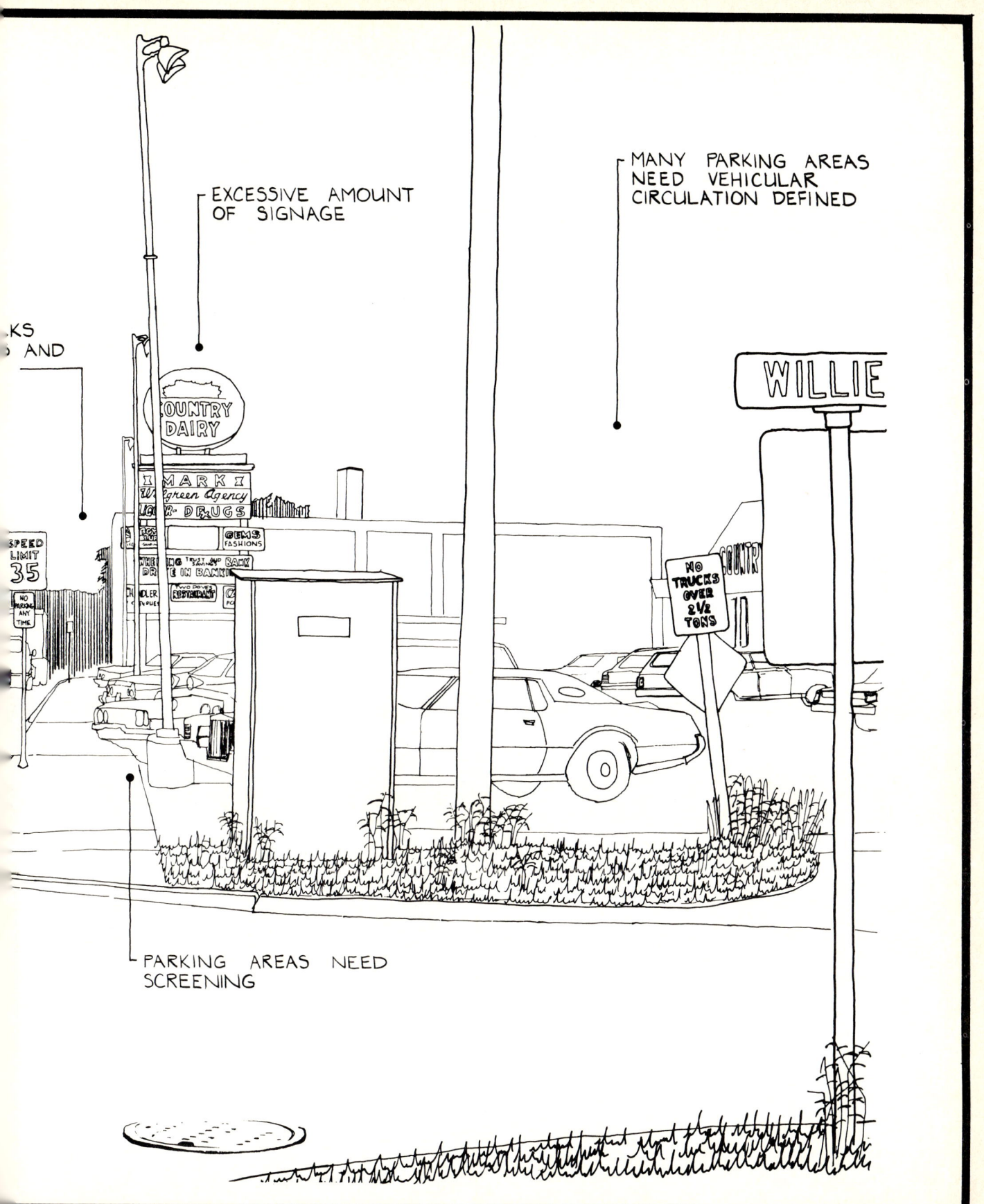

CENTRAL BUSINESS DISTRICTS 143

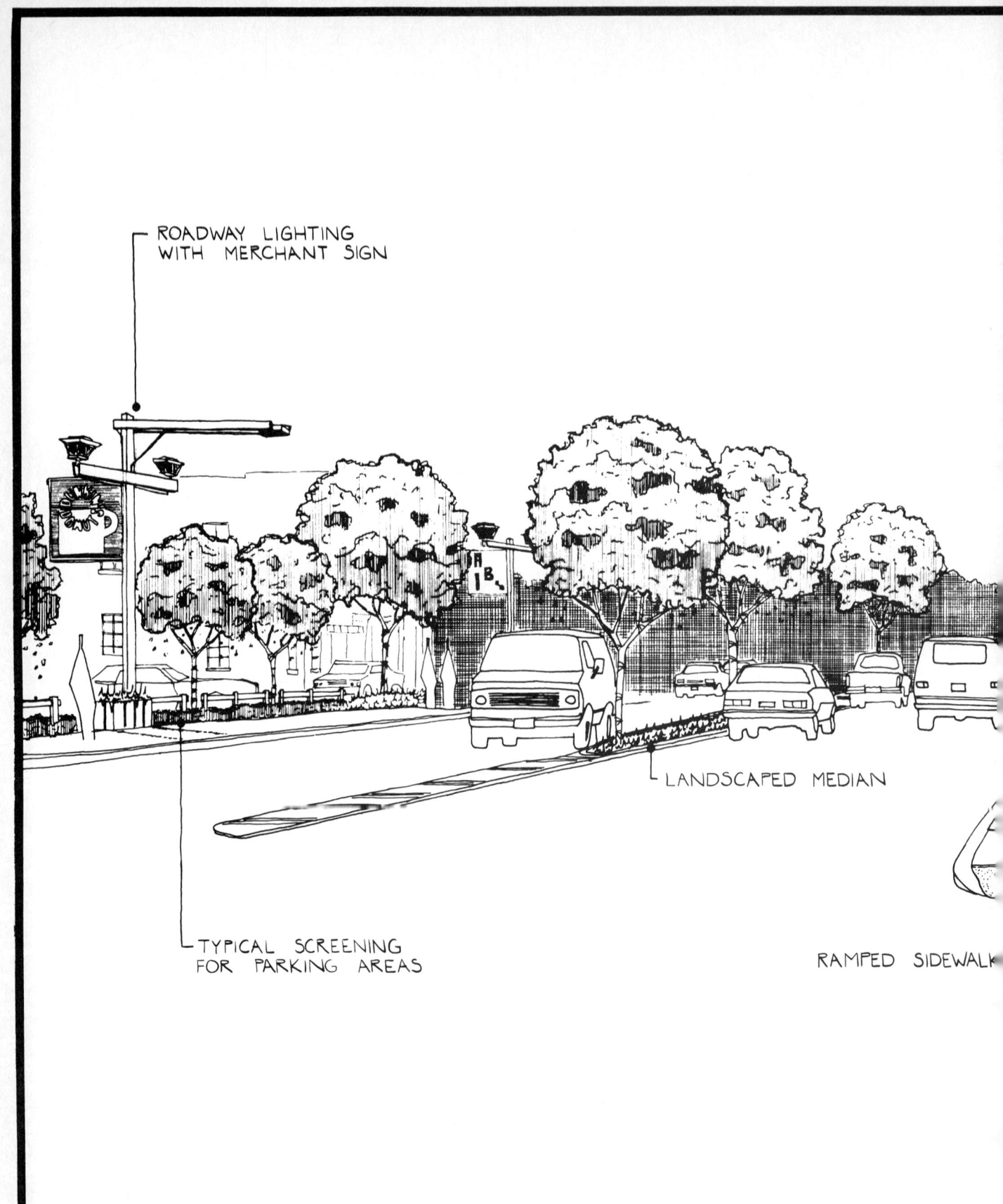

144 CENTRAL BUSINESS DISTRICTS

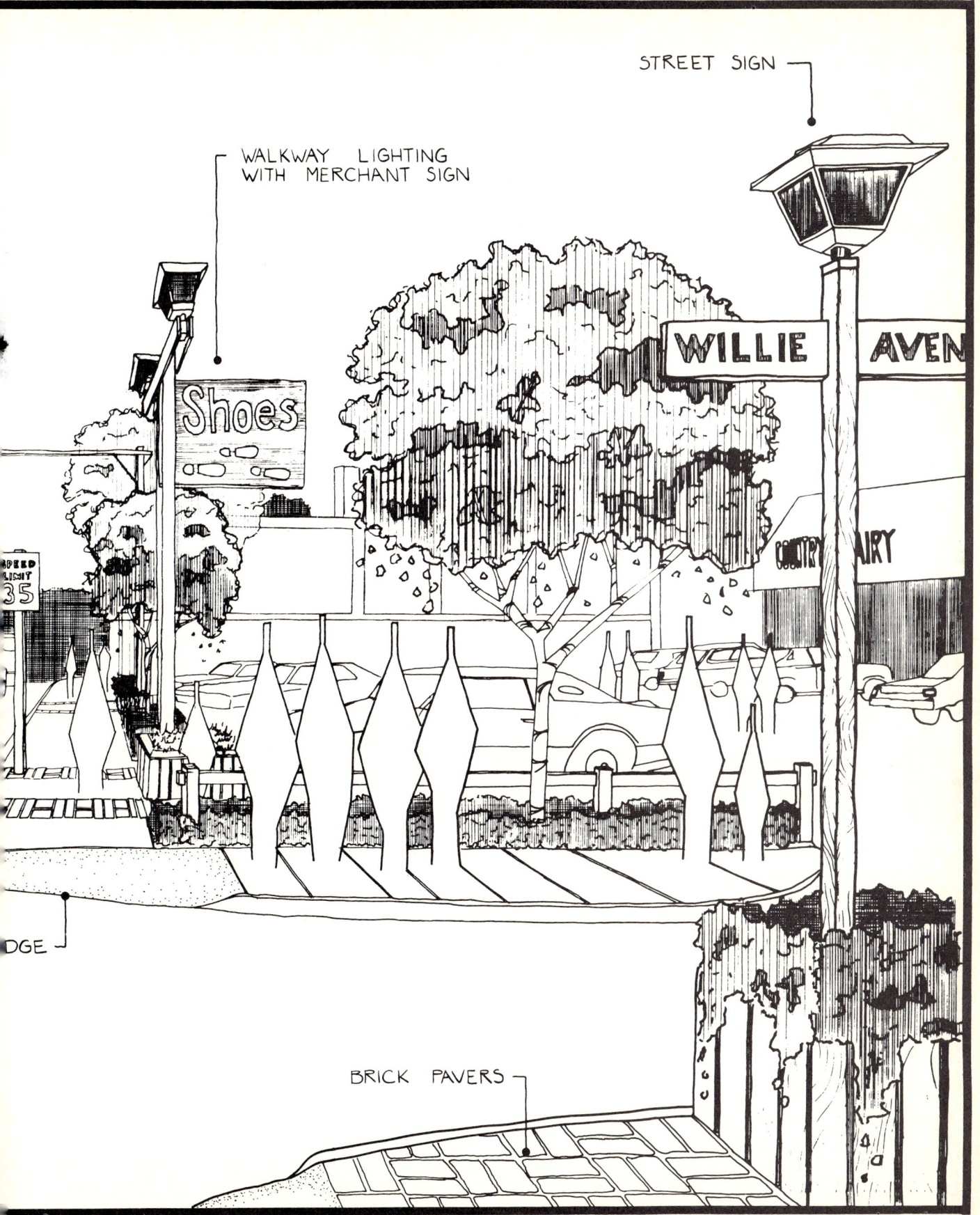

CENTRAL BUSINESS DISTRICTS   145

CENTRAL BUSINESS DISTRICT
Wise, Virginia

The town of Wise, Virginia, is the county seat of Wise County. At the time of the study, the central business district was suffering from obsolescence and attendant problems. The study identified the problems, assets, and opportunities and included a plan for redevelopment that overcomes the physical deficiencies of the district. In addition to recommendations for improved vehicular circulation and off-street parking, the plan provided renovation concepts and a plan for a pedestrian mall.

EXISTING VIEW OF MAIN STREET

VIEW LOOKING NORTHWEST ACROSS MAIN STREET MALL FROM NEW JAILHOUSE

CENTRAL BUSINESS DISTRICTS

EXISTING VIEW OF REAR OF COMMERCIAL STORES

VIEW FROM PARKING AREA LOOKING TOWARD REAR OF REHABILITATED COMMERCIAL STORES

CENTRAL BUSINESS DISTRICTS

CENTRAL BUSINESS DISTRICT
Dalton, Georgia

Dalton is the county seat of Whitfield County, located in northwest Georgia, 15 miles south of the Tennessee state line, 88 miles northwest of Atlanta, and 31 miles southeast of Chattanooga.

Dalton was a rural community with a population of just over 8000 in 1930. By 1969, the city population had grown to approximately 21,000 and the county to 52,800. This growth was due largely to Dalton's success in the textile industry. As the town grew outward, the CBD was weakened.

The purpose of the CBD plan was threefold:

1. To identify optimal economic parameters of future function and development

2. To seek out ways in which this optimal future function and development could be advanced

3. To prepare a long-range plan for development

The restoration of Dalton's CBD was an important element in the plan. Renovation of existing structures and a pedestrian mall were tools in stimulating the planned objectives.

LIBRARY – CHURCH PLAZA

MALL VIEW

CENTRAL BUSINESS DISTRICTS 151

CENTRAL BUSINESS AREA
Village of Northfield, Illinois

After completion of the Northfield Township Comprehensive Plan, which set guidelines for future development, the need was recognized for a more detailed study of the Village's Central Business Area. The purpose of the study was not only to recommend specific patterns of future development but also to recommend a realistic implementation program for both public and private action.

Northfield is a suburban community with a population of 5000 (at time of study). Key recommendations for future development included concentration of prime retail functions in the southern half of the area, along with an expansion of public facilities; expansion of existing office development in the northern half of the area; development of additional apartments and condominiums in key locations; and construction of a local access route bypassing Willow Road, a major regional artery.

Beautification programs to complement new development in the central area included landscape planting for major streets and public facilities, a Village signing system, and development of small parks in the center of the business area.

ASSETS, LIABILITIES AND POTENTIALS
NORTHFIELD, ILLINOIS

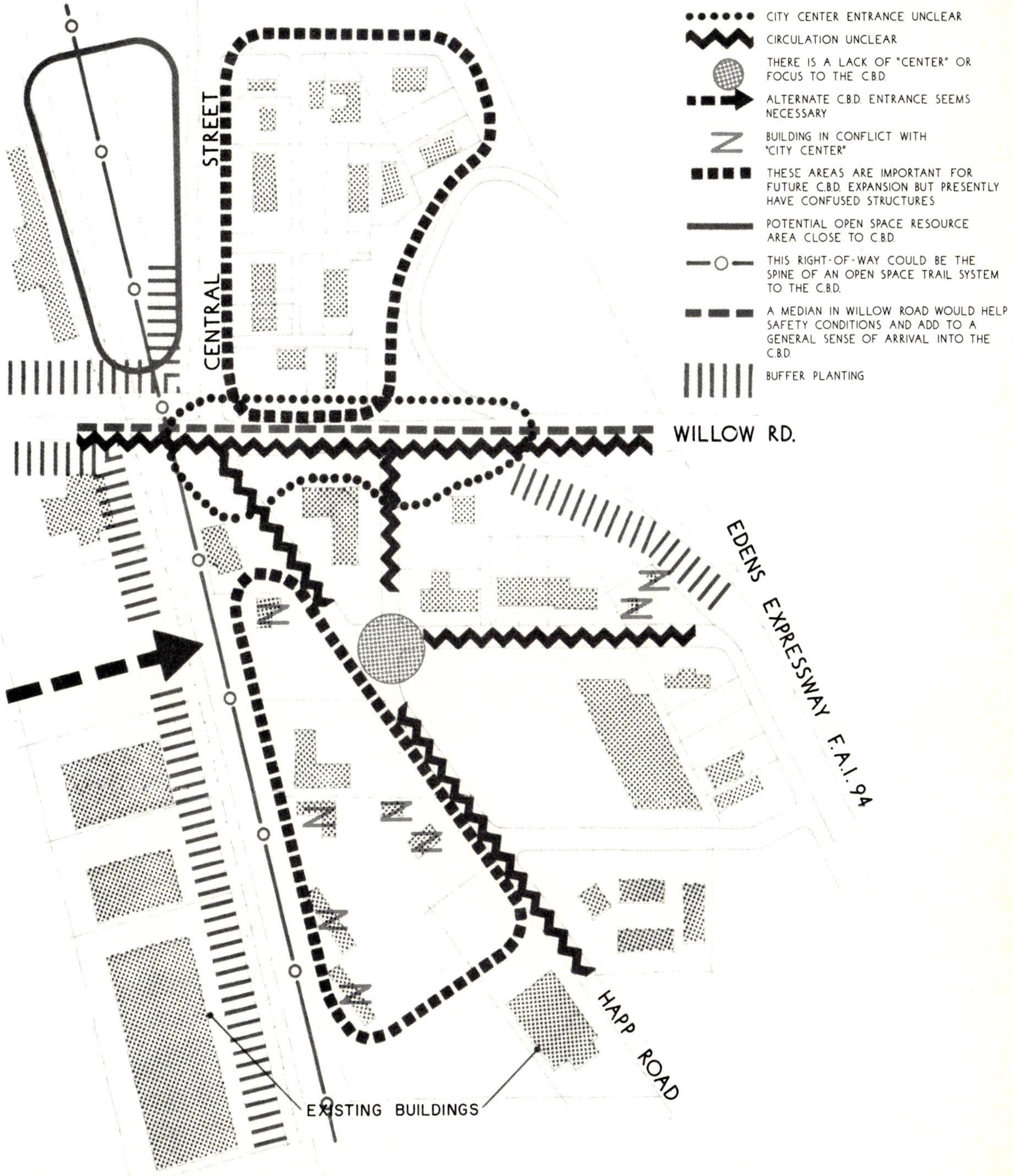

- •••••• CITY CENTER ENTRANCE UNCLEAR
- ⋙⋙ CIRCULATION UNCLEAR
- ● THERE IS A LACK OF "CENTER" OR FOCUS TO THE C.B.D.
- ▪▪▪▶ ALTERNATE C.B.D. ENTRANCE SEEMS NECESSARY
- N BUILDING IN CONFLICT WITH "CITY CENTER"
- ■■■■ THESE AREAS ARE IMPORTANT FOR FUTURE C.B.D. EXPANSION BUT PRESENTLY HAVE CONFUSED STRUCTURES
- ▬▬▬ POTENTIAL OPEN SPACE RESOURCE AREA CLOSE TO C.B.D.
- —O— THIS RIGHT-OF-WAY COULD BE THE SPINE OF AN OPEN SPACE TRAIL SYSTEM TO THE C.B.D.
- ▬ ▬ ▬ A MEDIAN IN WILLOW ROAD WOULD HELP SAFETY CONDITIONS AND ADD TO A GENERAL SENSE OF ARRIVAL INTO THE C.B.D.
- ||||| BUFFER PLANTING

WILLOW RD.

EDENS EXPRESSWAY F.A.I. 94

HAPP ROAD

CENTRAL STREET

EXISTING BUILDINGS

CENTRAL BUSINESS DISTRICTS 153

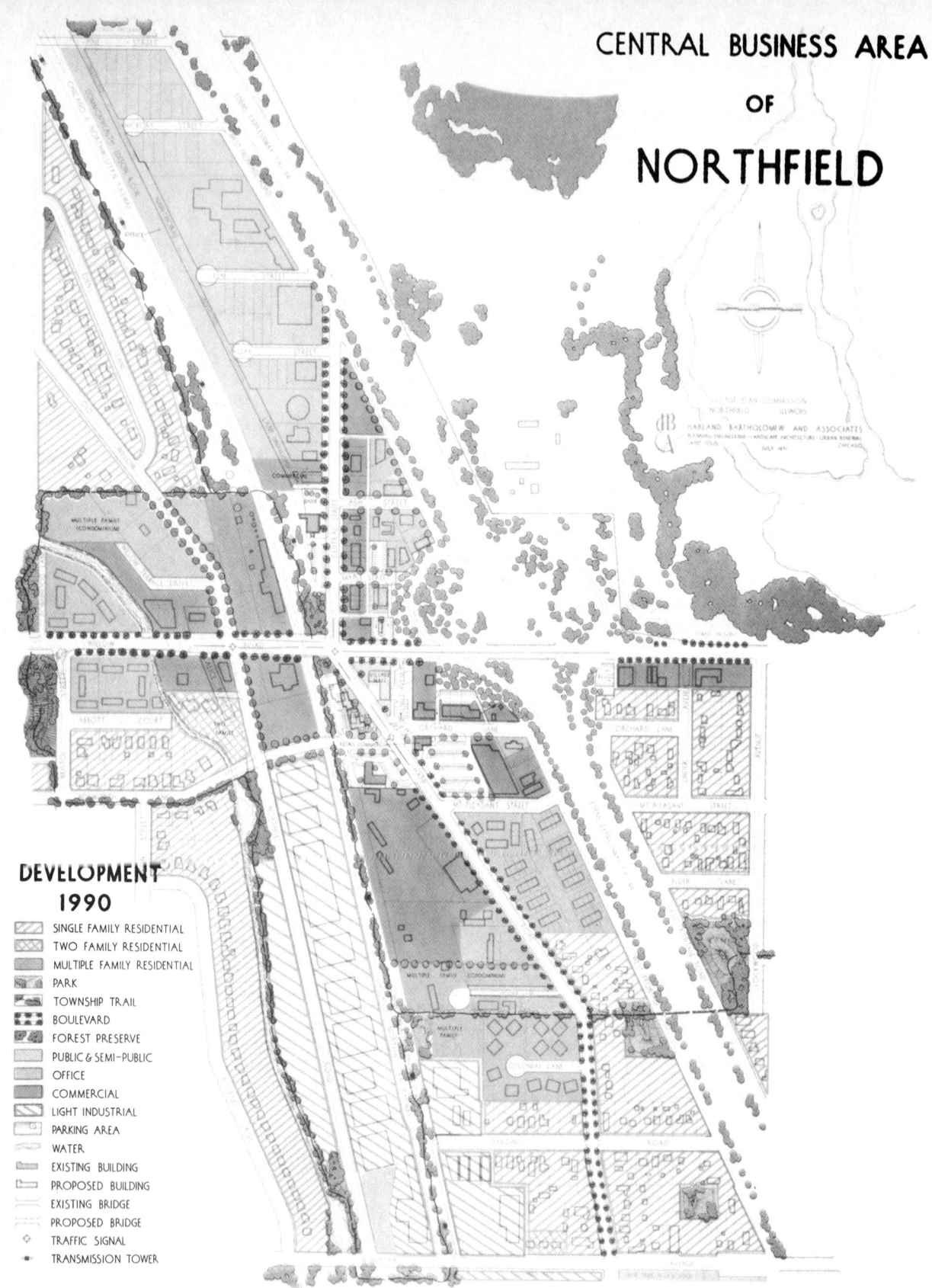

154 CENTRAL BUSINESS DISTRICTS

CENTRAL BUSINESS DISTRICTS 155

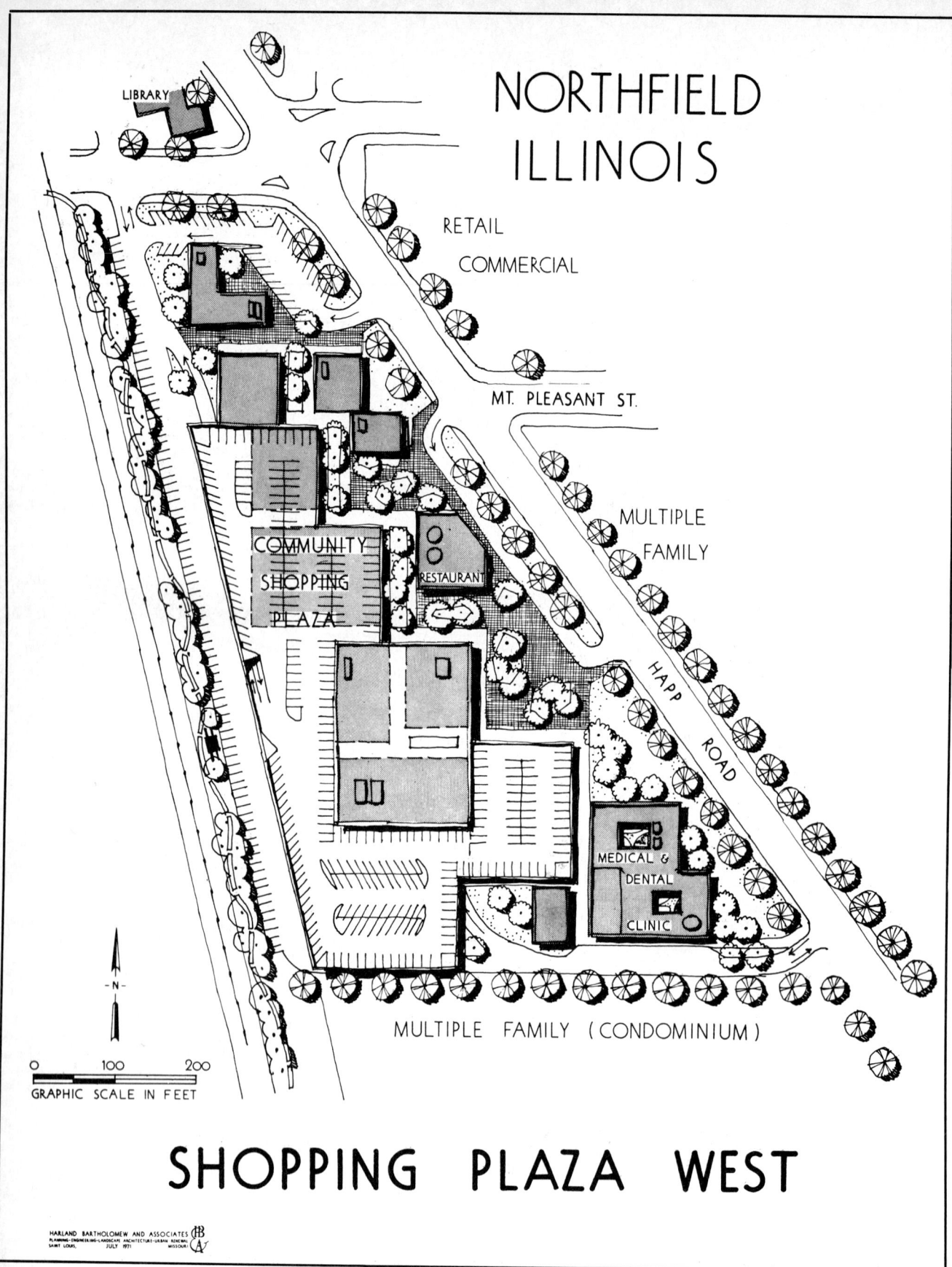

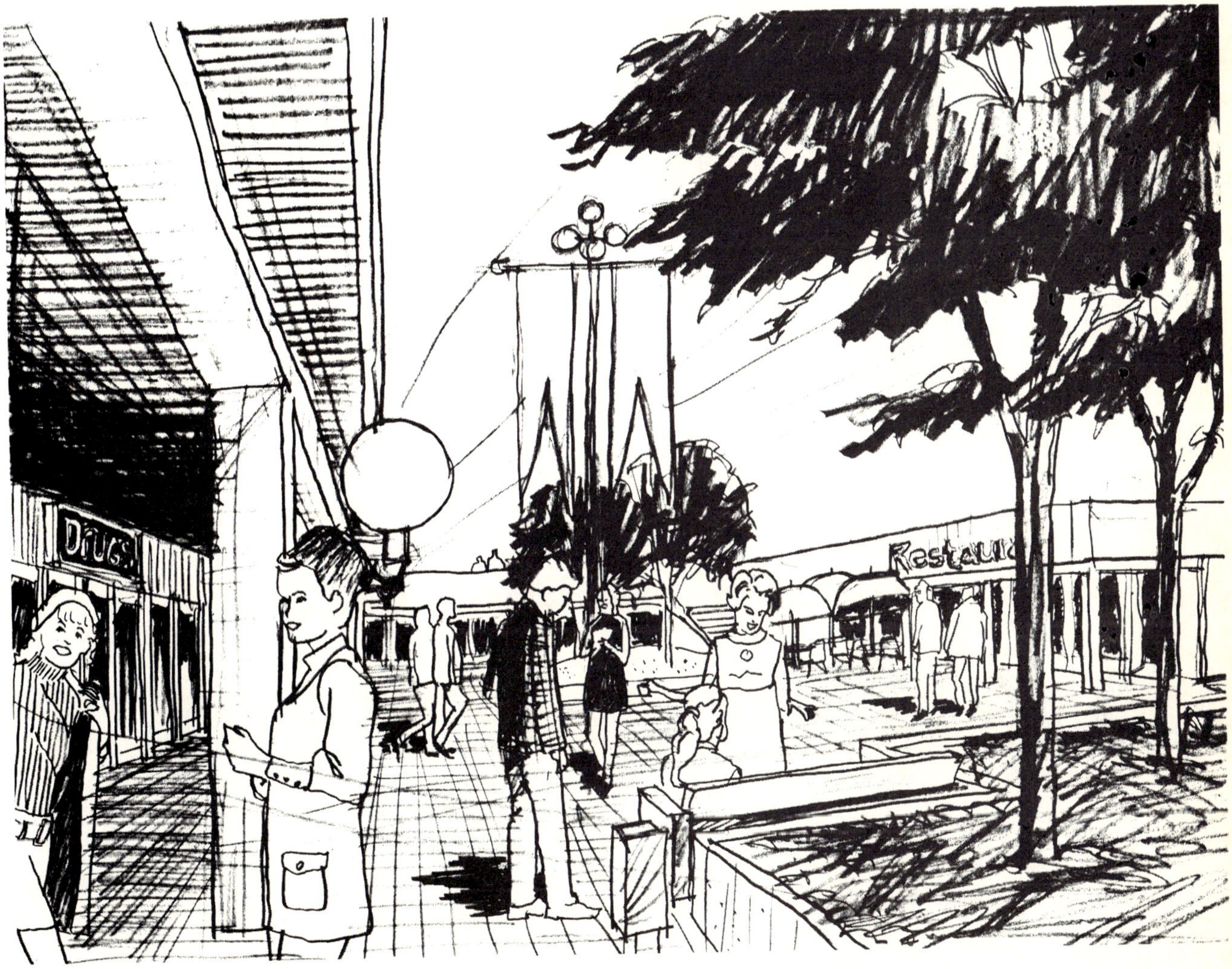

SHOPPING PLAZA WEST MALL

NORTHFIELD, ILLINOIS

TOWNSHIP TRAIL AT ROBINHOOD LANE

NORTHFIELD, ILLINOIS

RURAL VILLAGE

NORTHFIELD, ILLINOIS

CENTRAL BUSINESS DISTRICTS 159

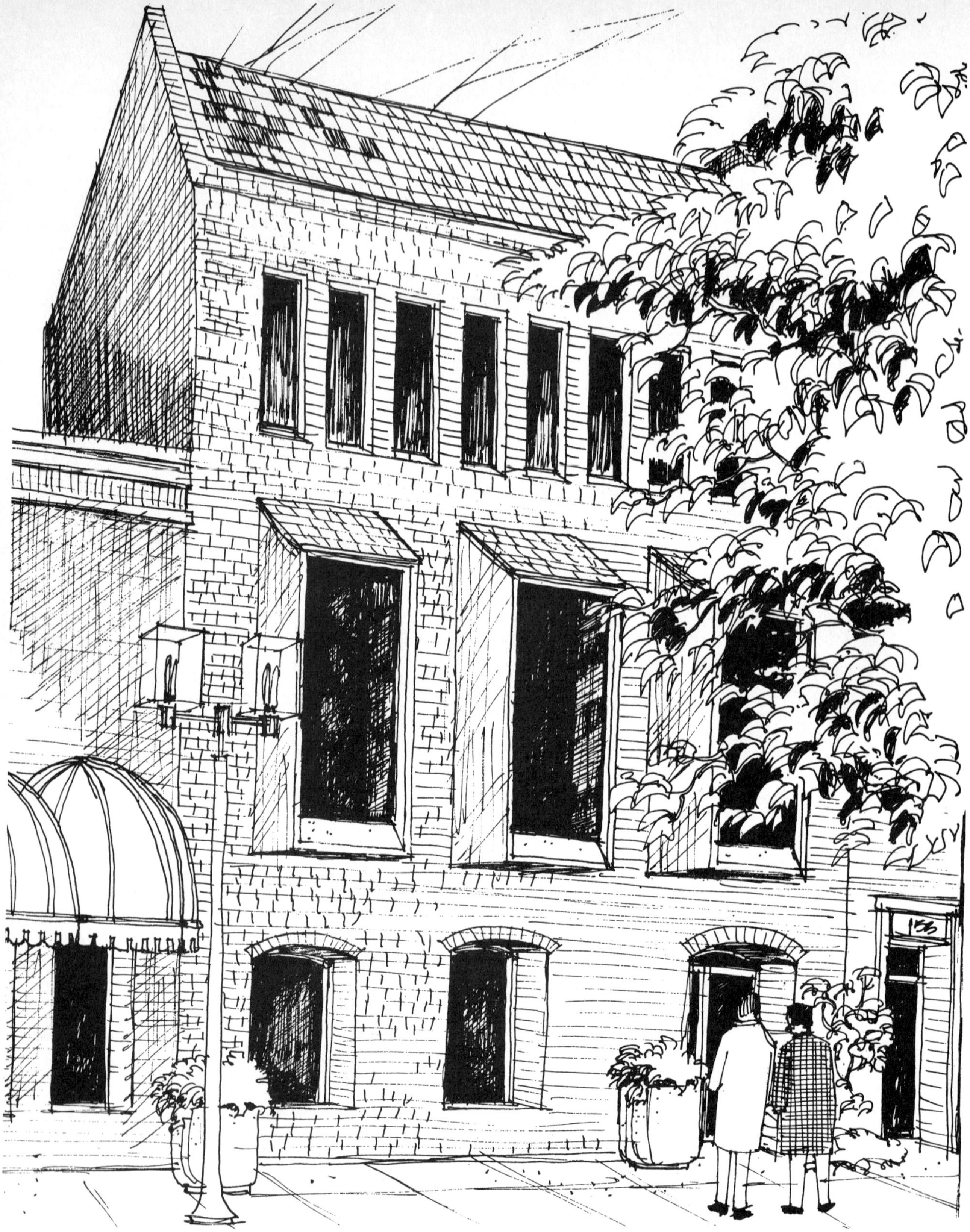

CONTEMPORARY SUBURBAN
NORTHFIELD, ILLINOIS

NORTHFIELD, ILLINOIS

STREET SCAPE VARIATIONS

CENTRAL BUSINESS DISTRICTS

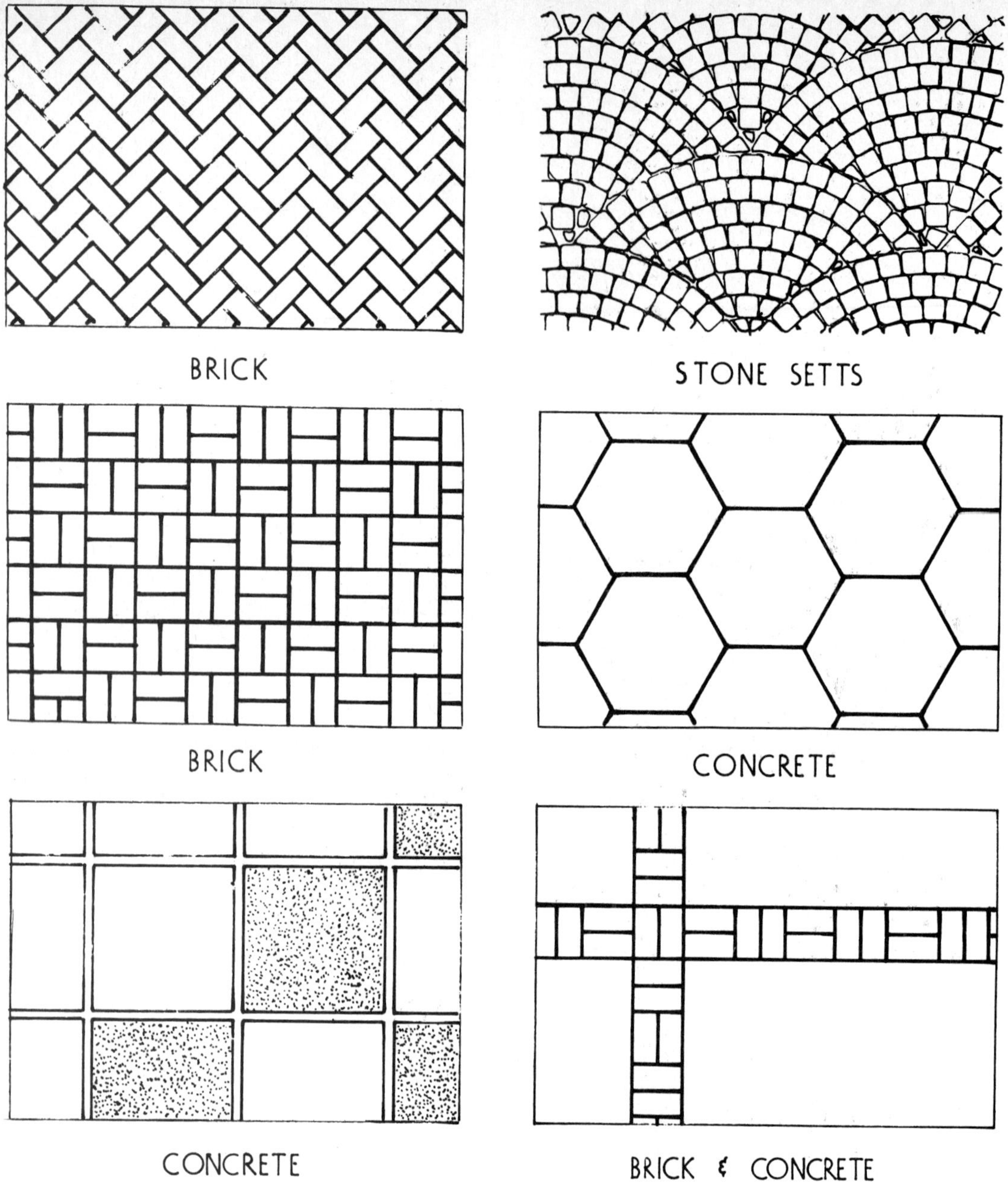
BRICK
STONE SETTS
BRICK
CONCRETE
CONCRETE
BRICK & CONCRETE

SUGGESTED PAVEMENT FOR THE CENTRAL BUSINESS DISTRICT

HARLAND BARTHOLOMEW AND ASSOCIATES
PLANNING-ENGINEERING-LANDSCAPE ARCHITECTURE-URBAN RENEWAL
SAINT LOUIS, JUNE 1971 MISSOURI

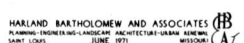

ORCHARD LANE SHOPS

NORTHFIELD, ILLINOIS

ORCHARD LANE KIOSK

URBAN DESIGN STUDY
Duluth, Minnesota

The Central Renewal Area of Duluth is a predominantly low-density housing area and, with the study concepts, should remain so. The northerly sections would be rehabilitated low-density housing areas, with new units of like housing interspersed on vacant or clearance lots. Low-density housing is considered to be largely single-family residences, with some two-family homes or townhouses on large lots.

This study is not an official document. Rather, it presents a set of guidelines, "design criteria" for the redevelopment of an important area of the city, blending new housing, commercial uses, and community facilities with the existing elements of the central neighborhoods.

TYPICAL REHABILITATED HOUSING

TYPICAL REHABILITATED HOUSING

CBD PLAN UPDATE
Harrisonburg, Virginia

Harland Bartholomew & Associates worked with the city of Harrisonburg and the Harrisonburg Redevelopment and Housing Authority to provide services in housing, marketing, community planning, urban design, community development, and engineering design/construction. Included in the project were a citywide community center and a 62-unit housing development for the elderly.

Harland Bartholomew & Associates assisted local officials in the preparation of applications for Community Development Block Grant funds and continued to serve the city by providing services targeted toward neighborhood stabilization, including the development of a residential rehabilitation program to be used in an area adjacent to the Harrisonburg central business district.

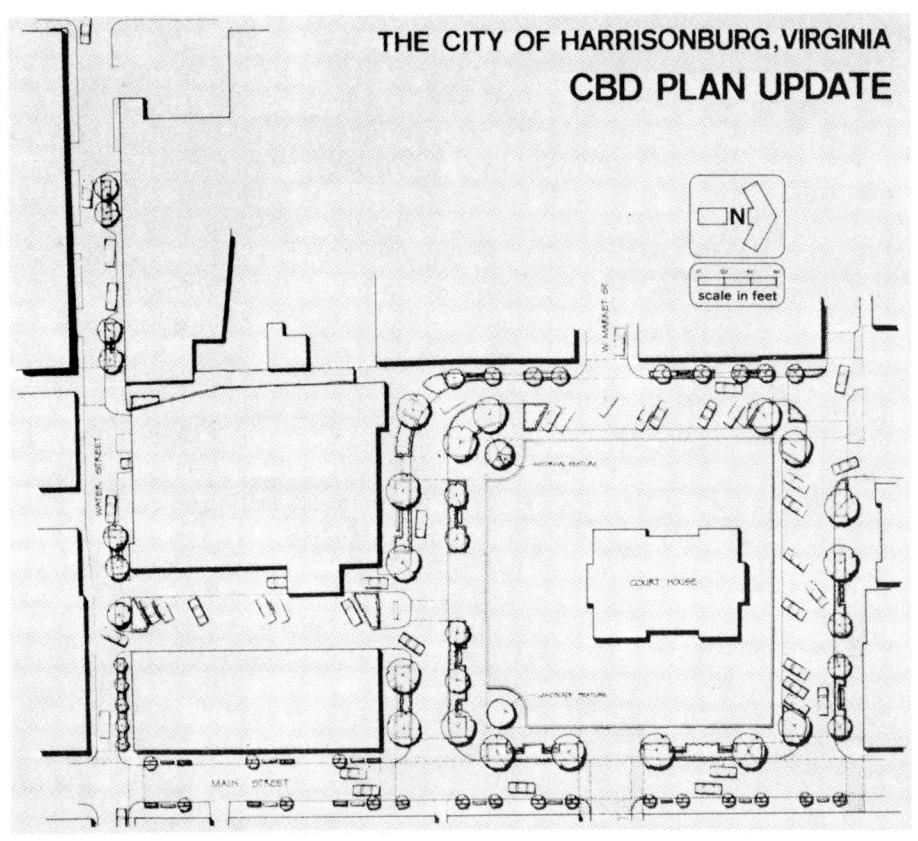

LANDSCAPE FEATURES / COURTHOUSE SQUARE
CITY OF HARRISONBURG, VIRGINIA

SECTION / COURTHOUSE SQUARE
CITY OF HARRISONBURG, VIRGINIA

CENTRAL BUSINESS DISTRICTS   167

EIGHT
PARKS AND RECREATIONAL AREAS

PARK AND RECREATIONAL AREA MASTER PLANS
Typical Examples

Identification and analysis of existing parklands, together with forecasts of population, economic changes, and recreational needs of the people, provide the basis for park planning. In the preparation of overall plans, careful attention is given to the function of each recreation area in the total system, to the types of parks needed in relation to residential neighborhoods and the community as a whole, and to the best distribution of needed recreation facilities among the various parts of the park system.

Complete master plans, in addition to locating special-use areas, also show the general arrangement of roads, parking areas, pedestrian walkways, buildings, and other recreational facilities. In addition, consideration is given to utility layouts, plantings, and preliminary grading schemes for the proposed park area. Development staging is also an important element of planning; a satisfactory, attractive, and completely usable facility should result as each stage is completed. Finally, maintenance costs and procedures are important elements entering into the designs of the master plans, and well-located and adequate maintenance areas are needed and should be a part of those plans.

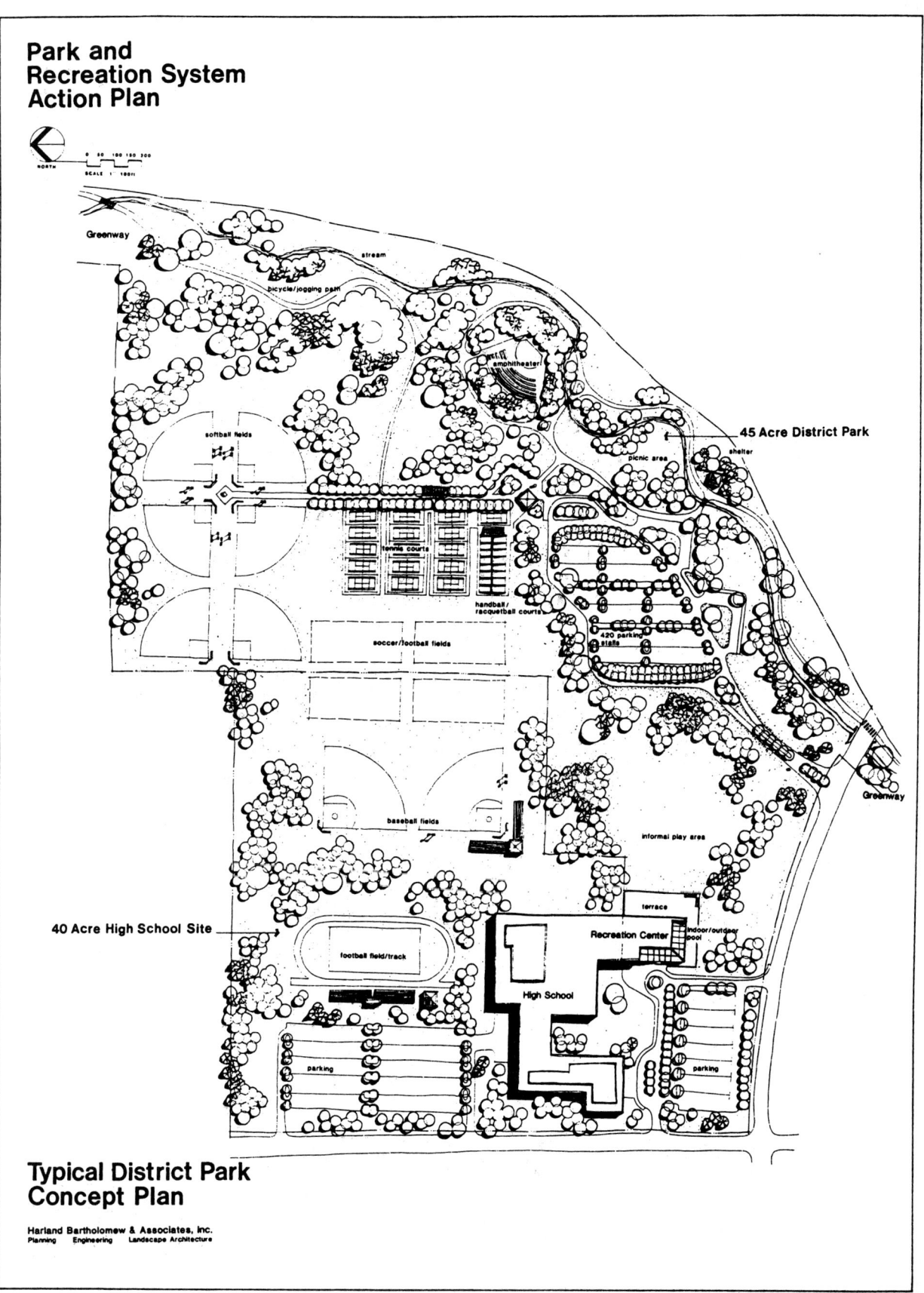

PARKS AND RECREATIONAL AREAS 171

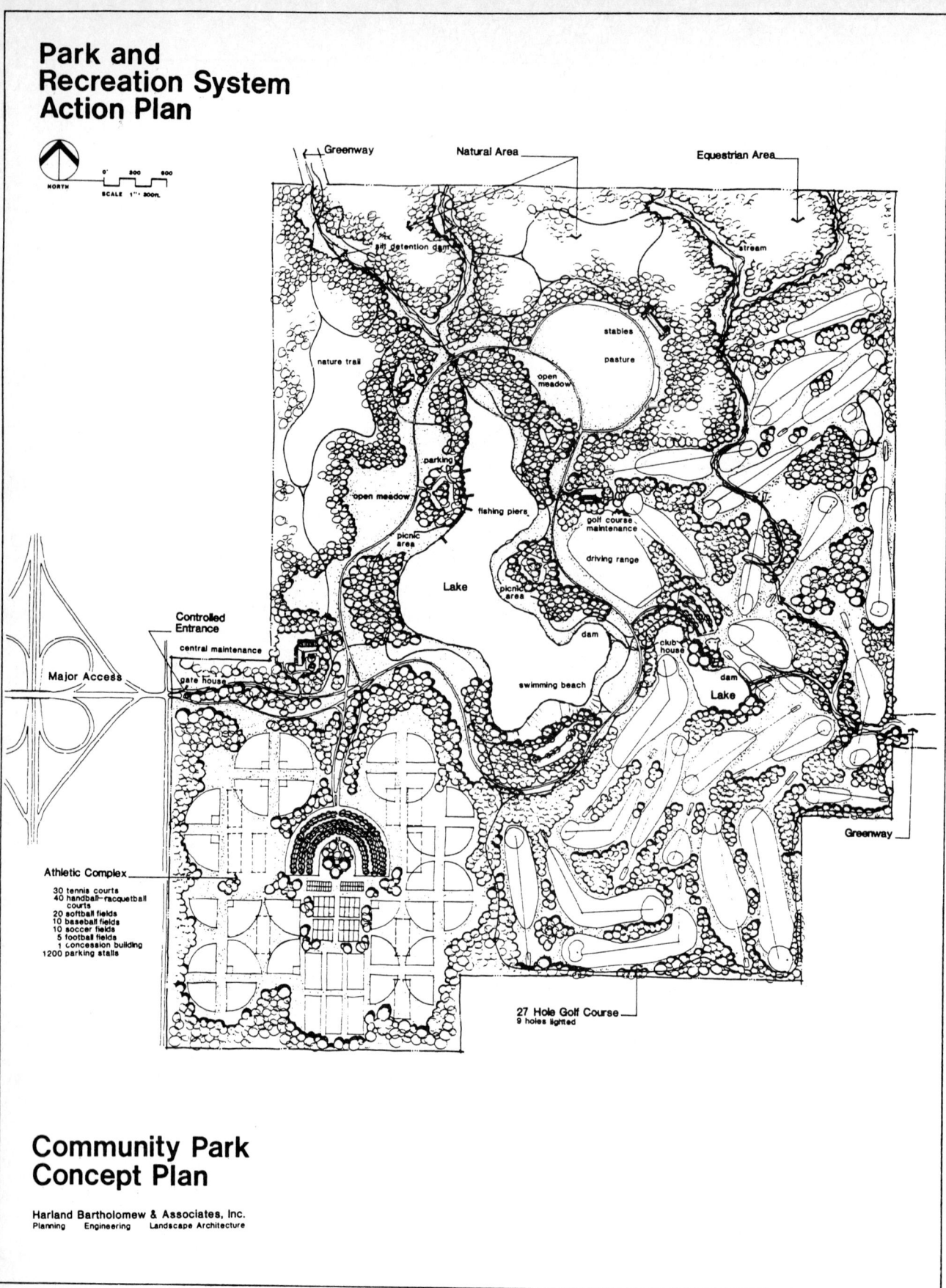

172 PARKS AND RECREATIONAL AREAS

Park and Recreation System Action Plan

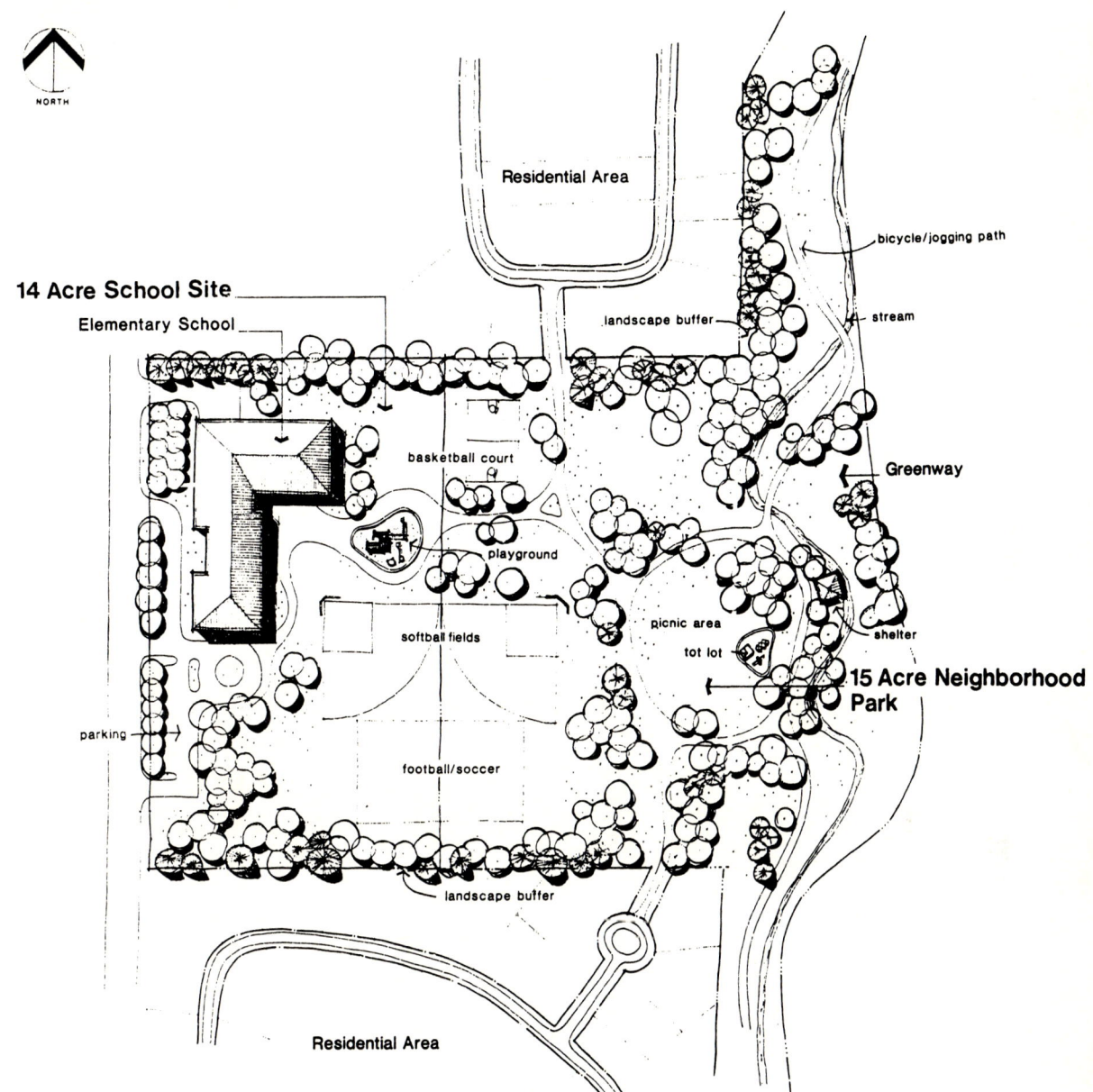

Typical Neighborhood Park Concept Plan

Harland Bartholomew & Associates, Inc.
Planning   Engineering   Landscape Architecture

CHALK BLUFF RECREATION AND CONSERVATION AREA MASTER PLAN
Clay County, Arkansas

The Chalk Bluff park site is located in Clay County in extreme northeastern Arkansas riparian to the St. Francis River, which forms the boundary between Arkansas and Missouri at this point. Piggott, Arkansas, with a population of 3300 (at time of study), is the largest town in Clay County, located about nine miles southwest of the site. St. Francis, Arkansas, population 350 (at time of study), is located approximately three miles south of the site. Access to the site is via a gravel road from St. Francis, which forms the western boundary of the park property. The County plans to pave this road soon. The site is about 55 acres.

The purpose of the Master Plan was to provide overall guidance for the future development of the Chalk Bluff site. It was meant to help create development that is as compatible as possible with the natural environment in a cost-effective manner. It was not a detailed technical plan, but rather dealt in concepts at this point: how to provide and control access, how to provide recreational and service facilities, and how all the facilities should relate to each other.

An interesting sewage disposal system called the "Clivus-Multrum" system was used on this project. The name means, literally, *inclining chamber*, and the principle of operation is that the waste undergoes controlled decomposition in a ventilating composting tank. This system is good where water supply is limited or unavailable or where, as in this case, the site should be disturbed as little as possible. This system requires less than half the space required for an aerated treatment tank system or a composting tank system—the two other systems that were considered.

The river overlook and pedestrian bridge also were interesting problems on this site. Because the area is environmentally sensitive, these facilities were designed in small components, built off site, then assembled on site, resulting in the least possible disturbance.

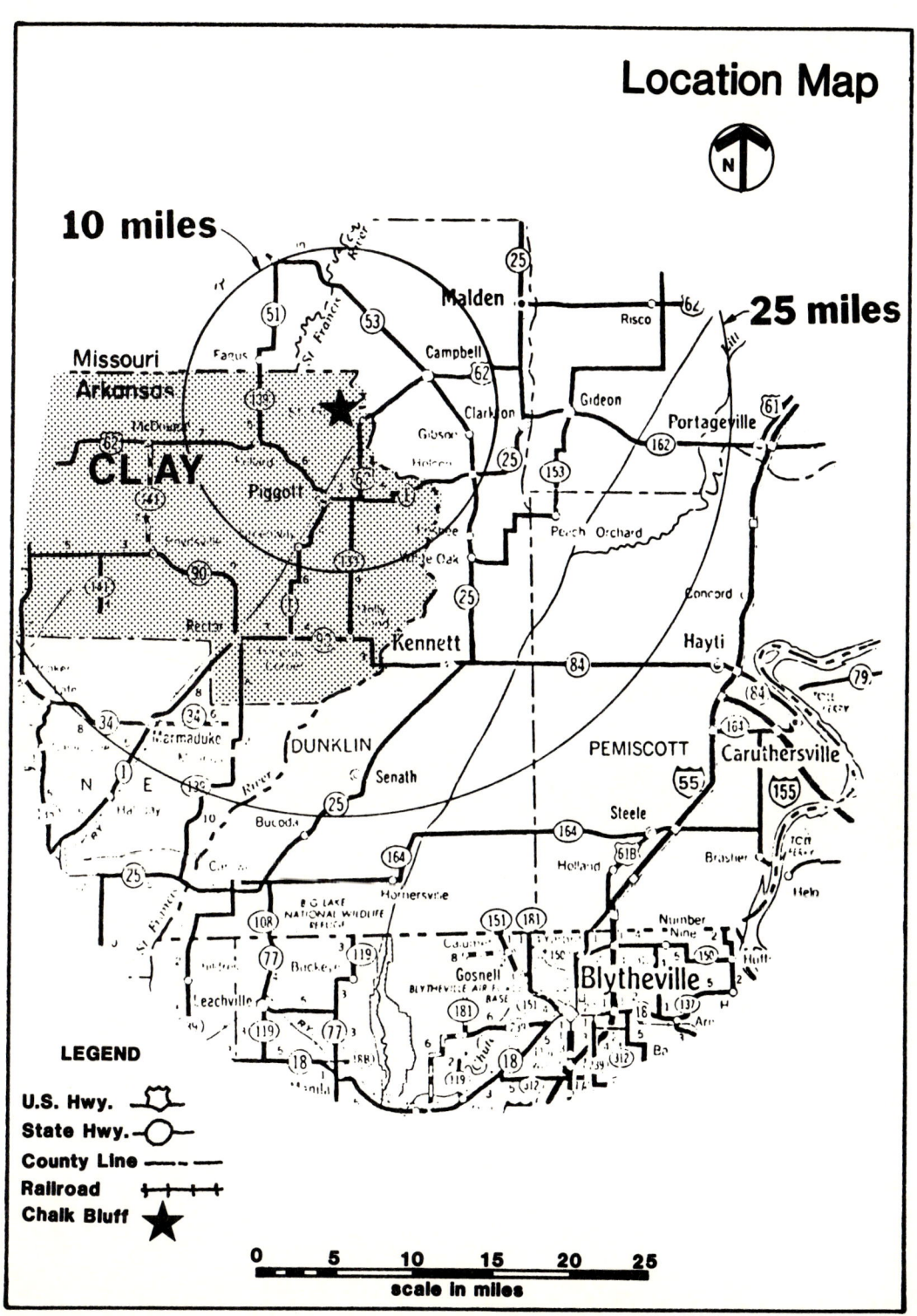

PARKS AND RECREATIONAL AREAS 175

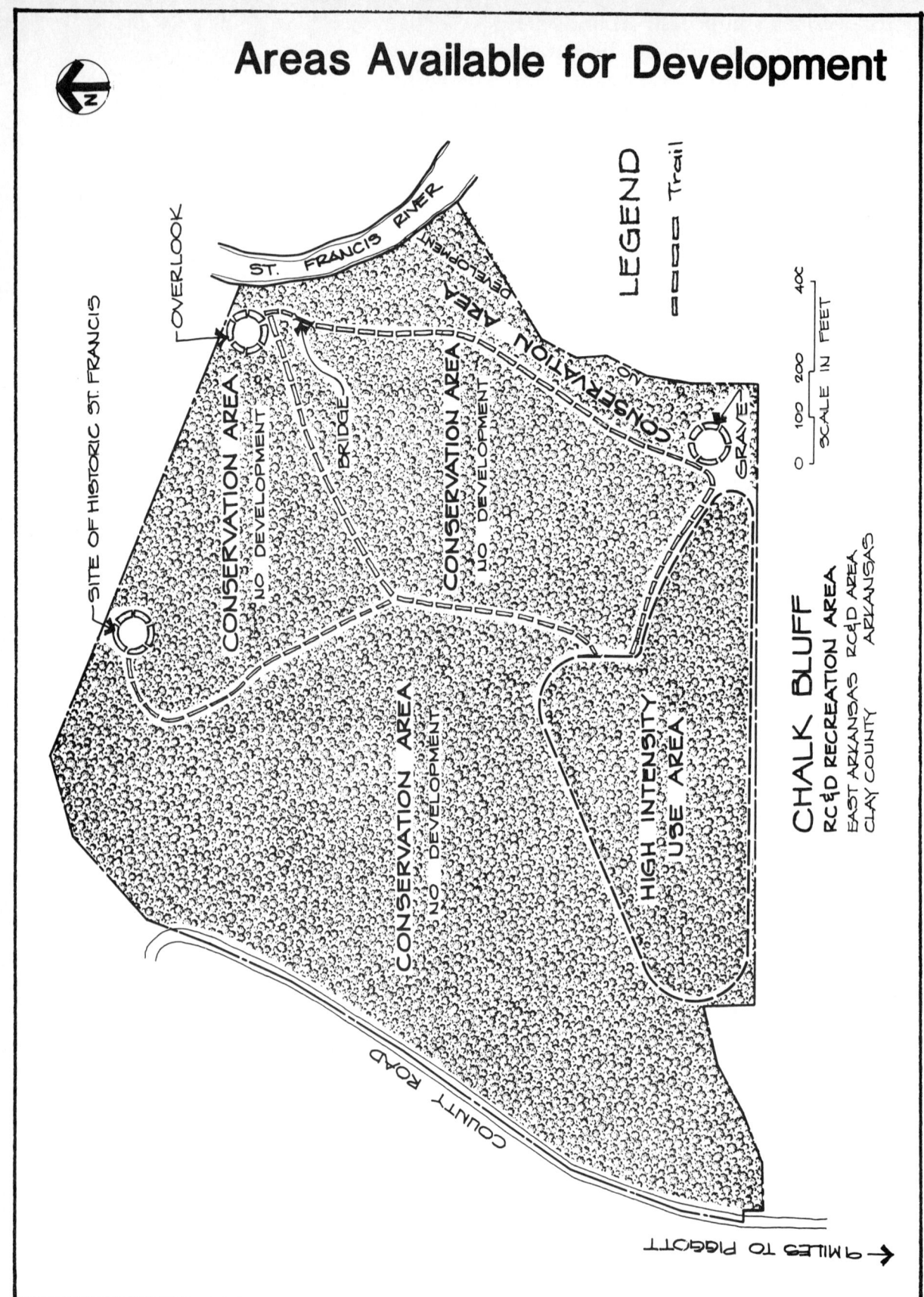

Physical Factors

PARKS AND RECREATIONAL AREAS

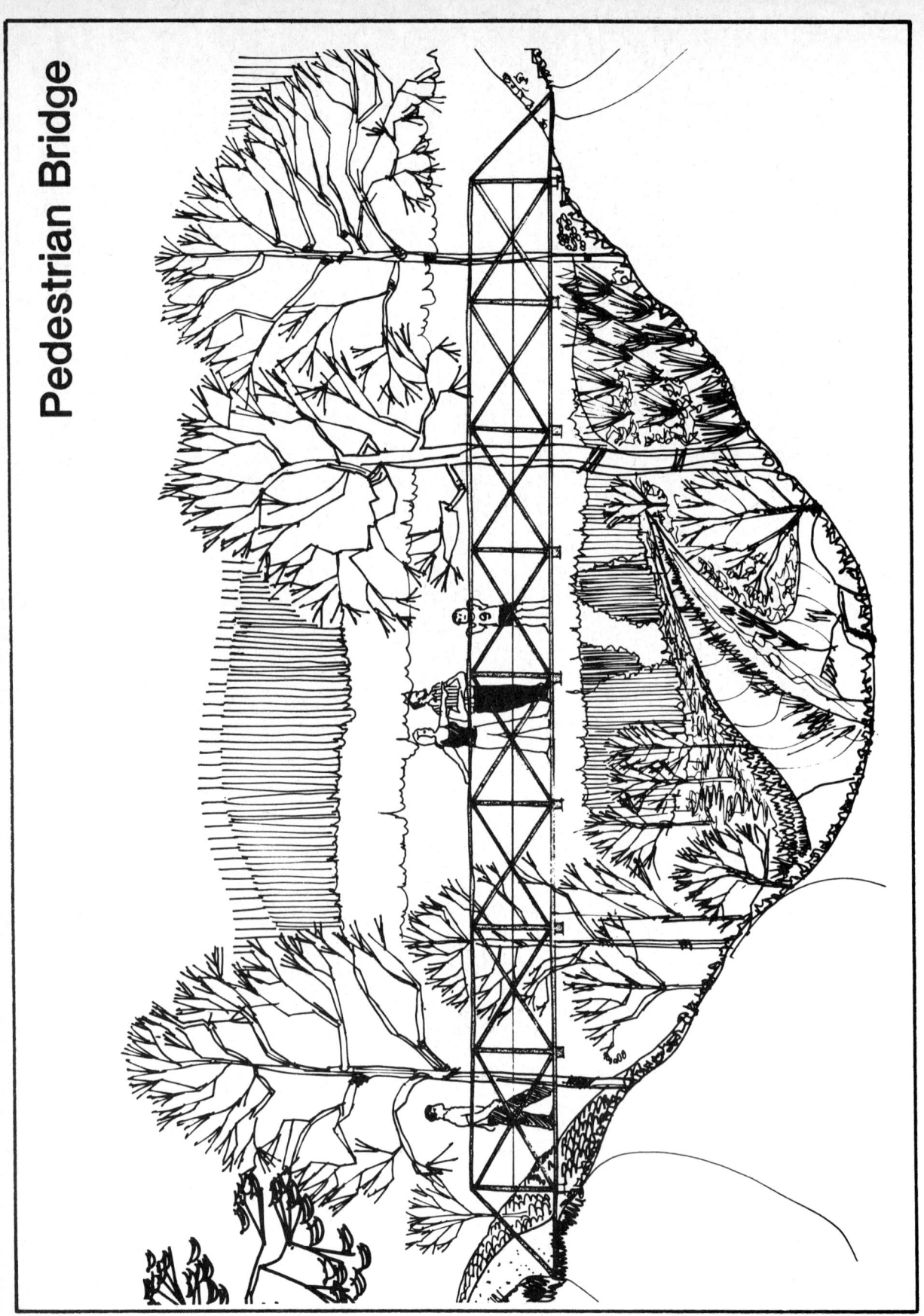

Pedestrian Bridge

178 PARKS AND RECREATIONAL AREAS

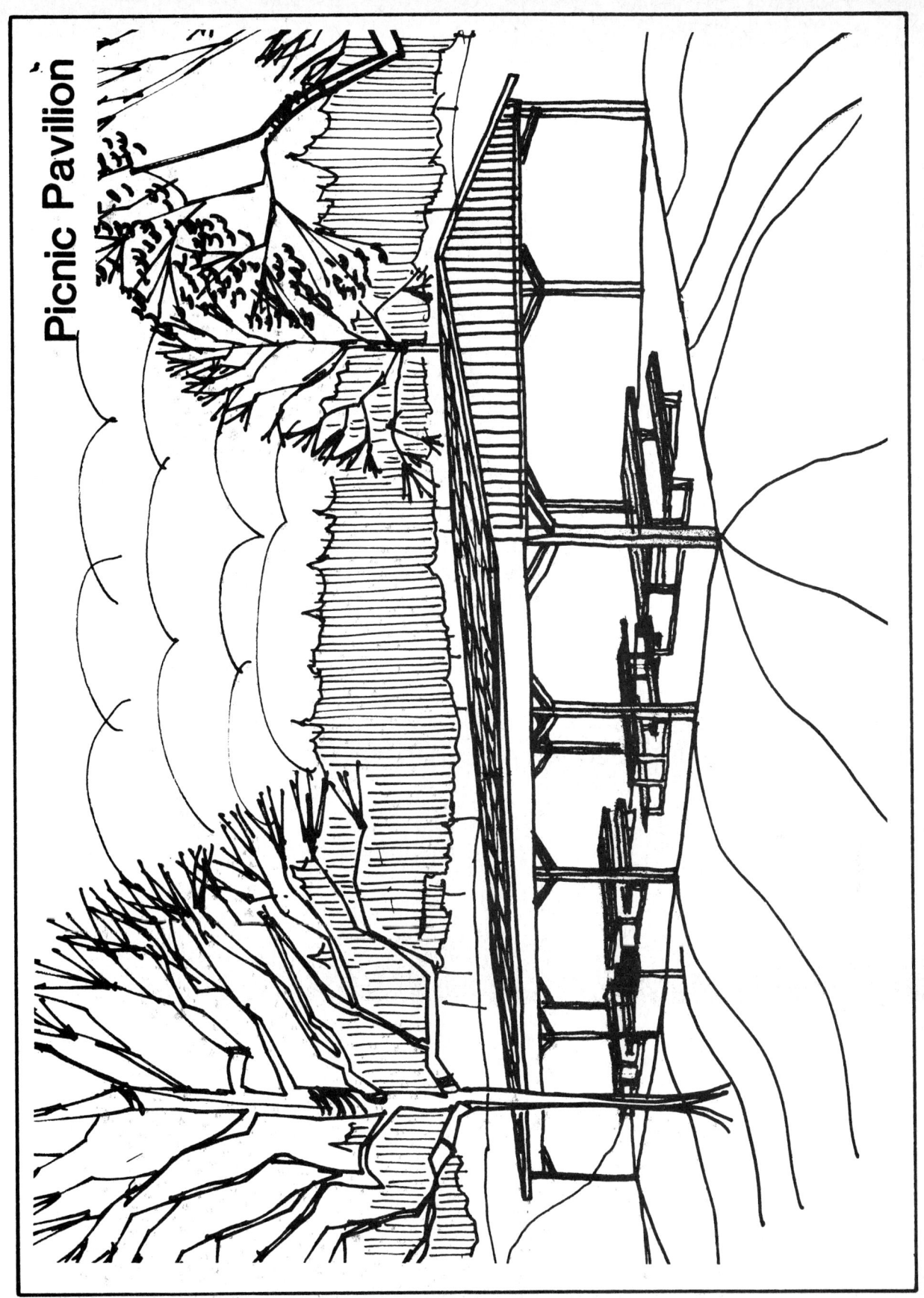

Picnic Pavilion

PARKS AND RECREATIONAL AREAS 179

Typical Road & Parking Lot Section

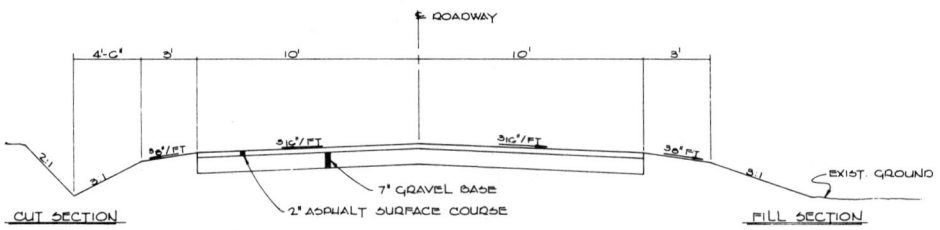

TYPICAL ACCESS ROAD SECTION

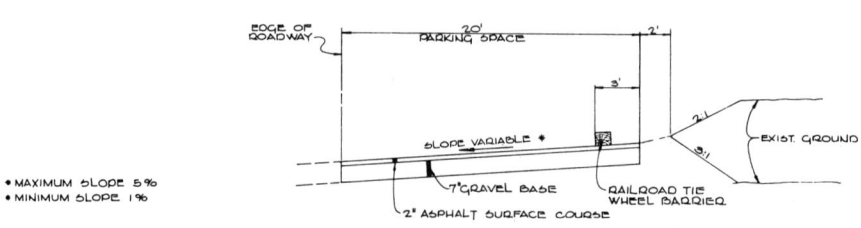

TYPICAL PARKING AREA SECTION

PARKS AND RECREATIONAL AREAS

Clivus Multrum System Diagram

PARKS AND RECREATIONAL AREAS 181

Restroom

182   PARKS AND RECREATIONAL AREAS

Observation Platform

PARKS AND RECREATIONAL AREAS 183

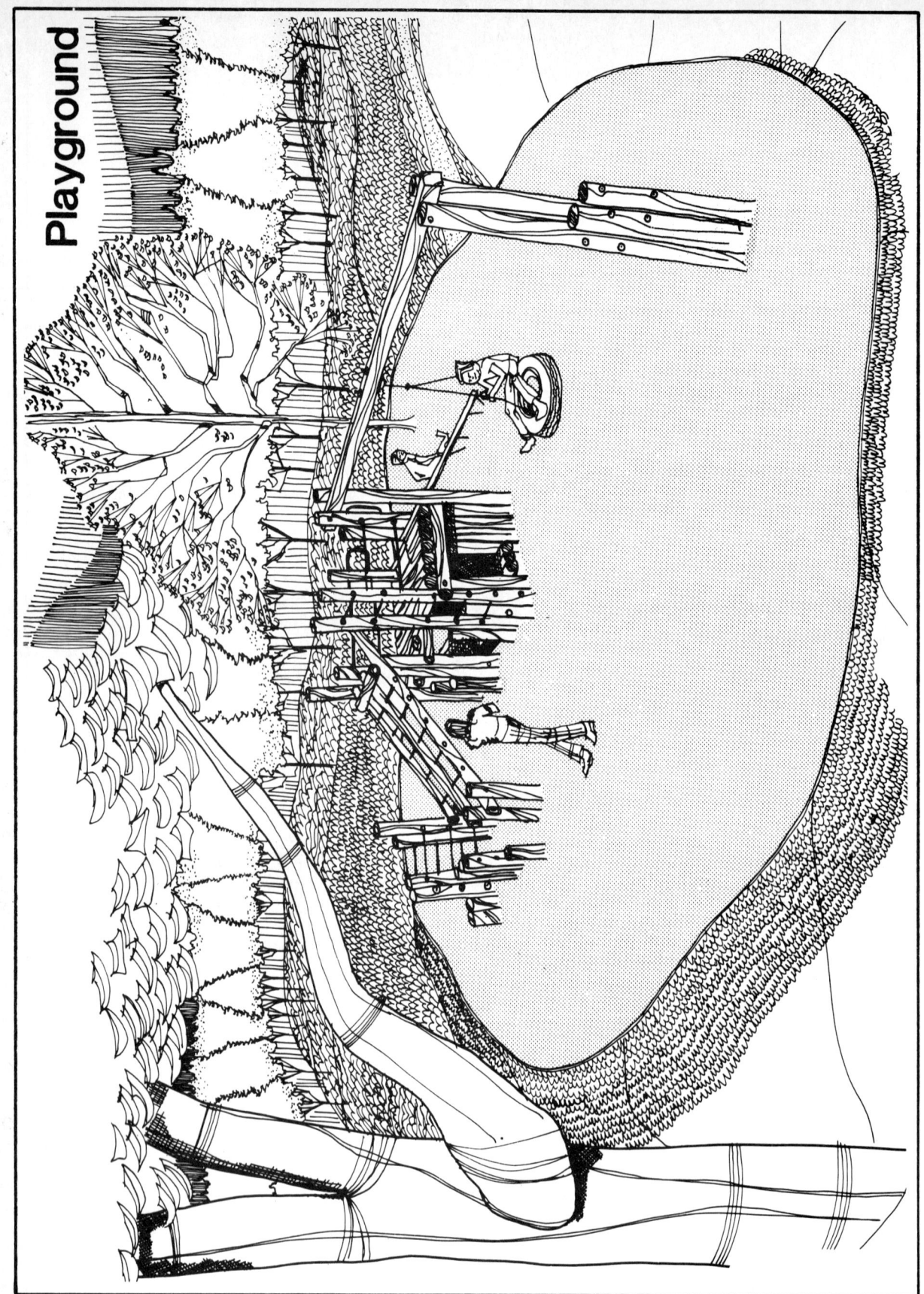

Entrance Sign

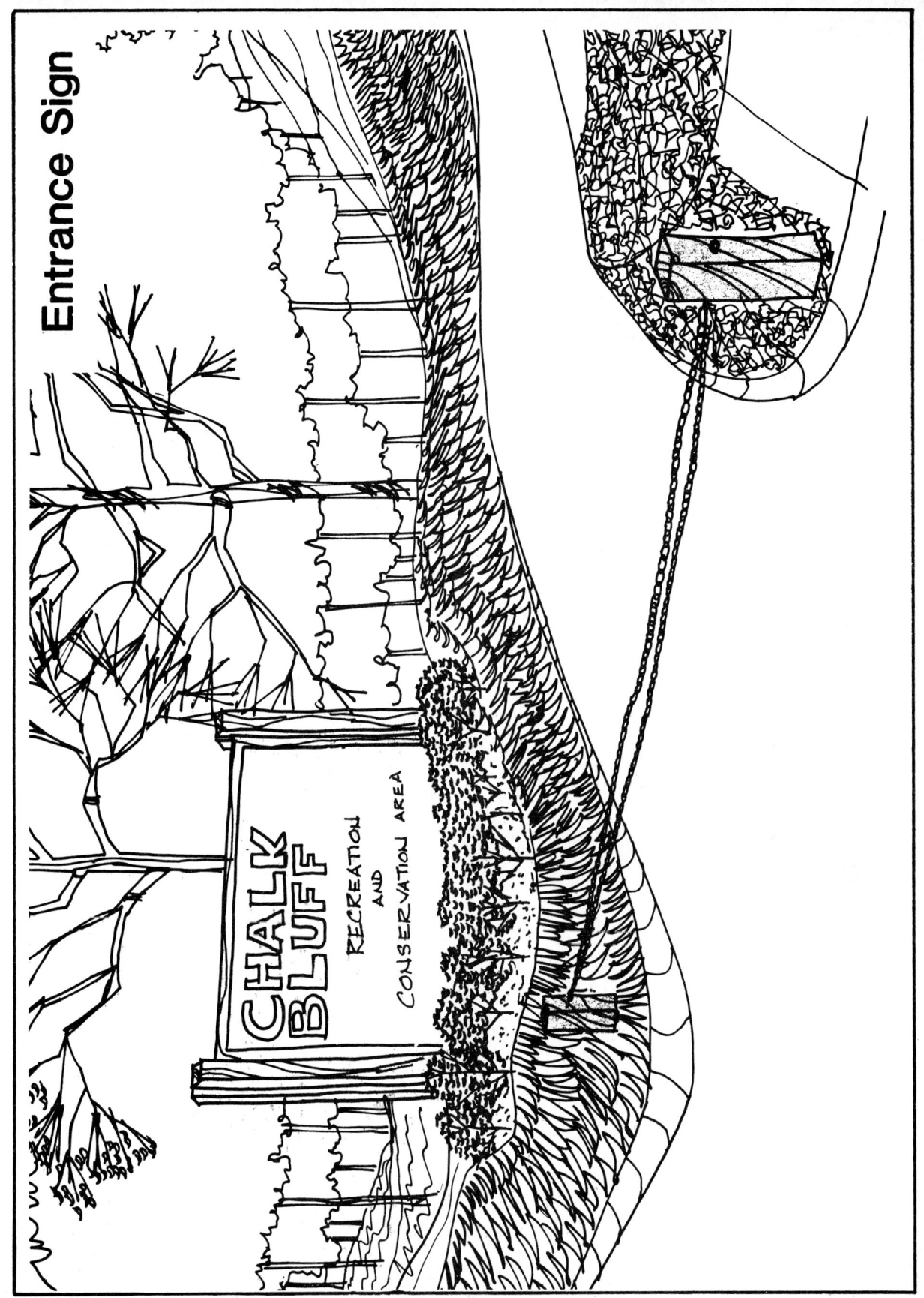

PARKS AND RECREATIONAL AREAS 185

Typical Signage

186 PARKS AND RECREATIONAL AREAS

Information Center

PARKS AND RECREATIONAL AREAS 187

Concept Plans

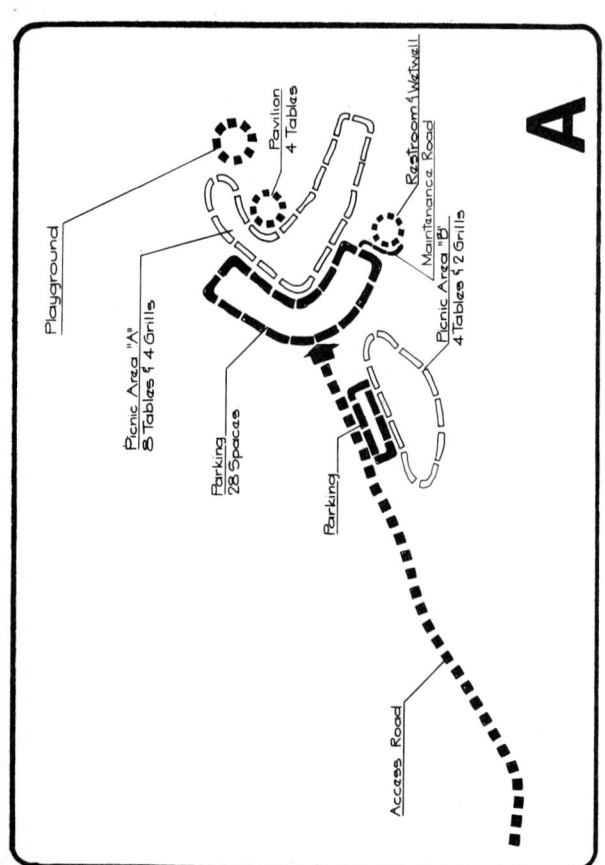

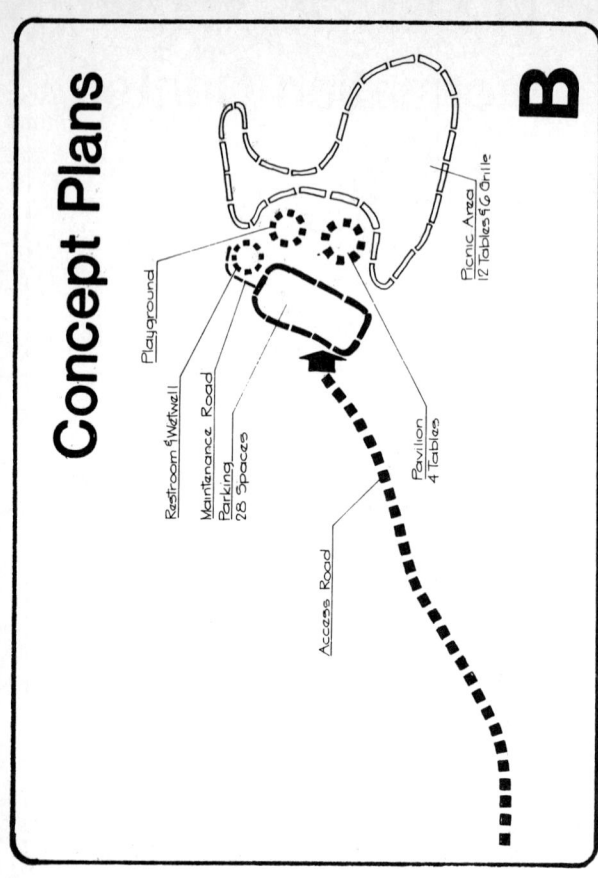

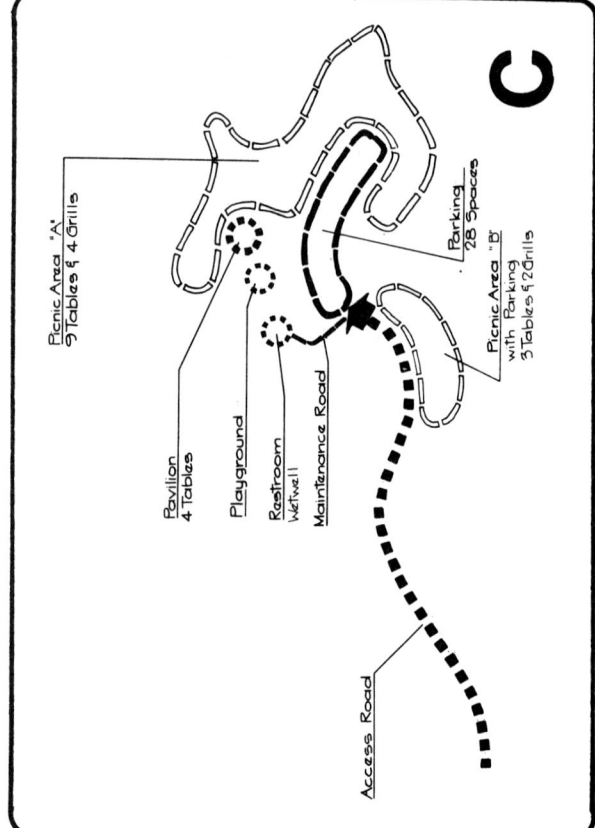

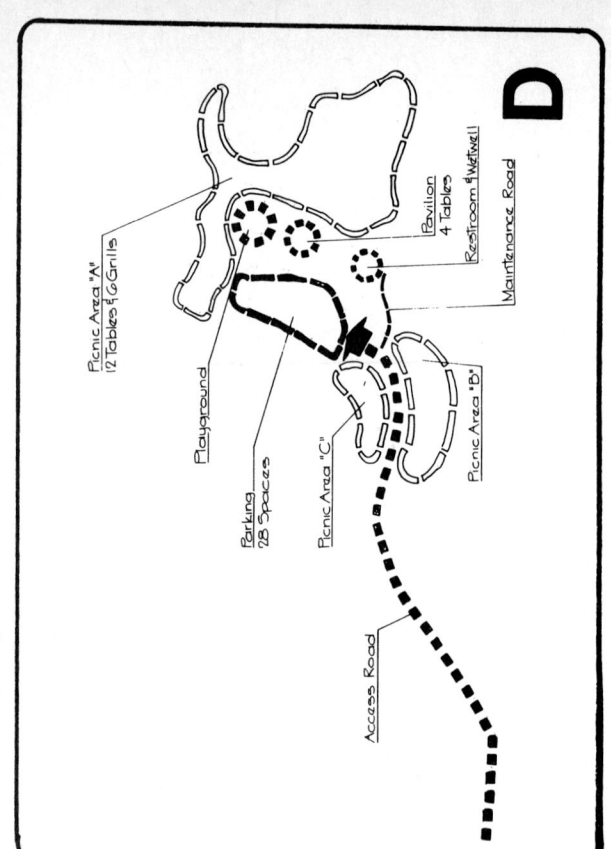

188 PARKS AND RECREATIONAL AREAS

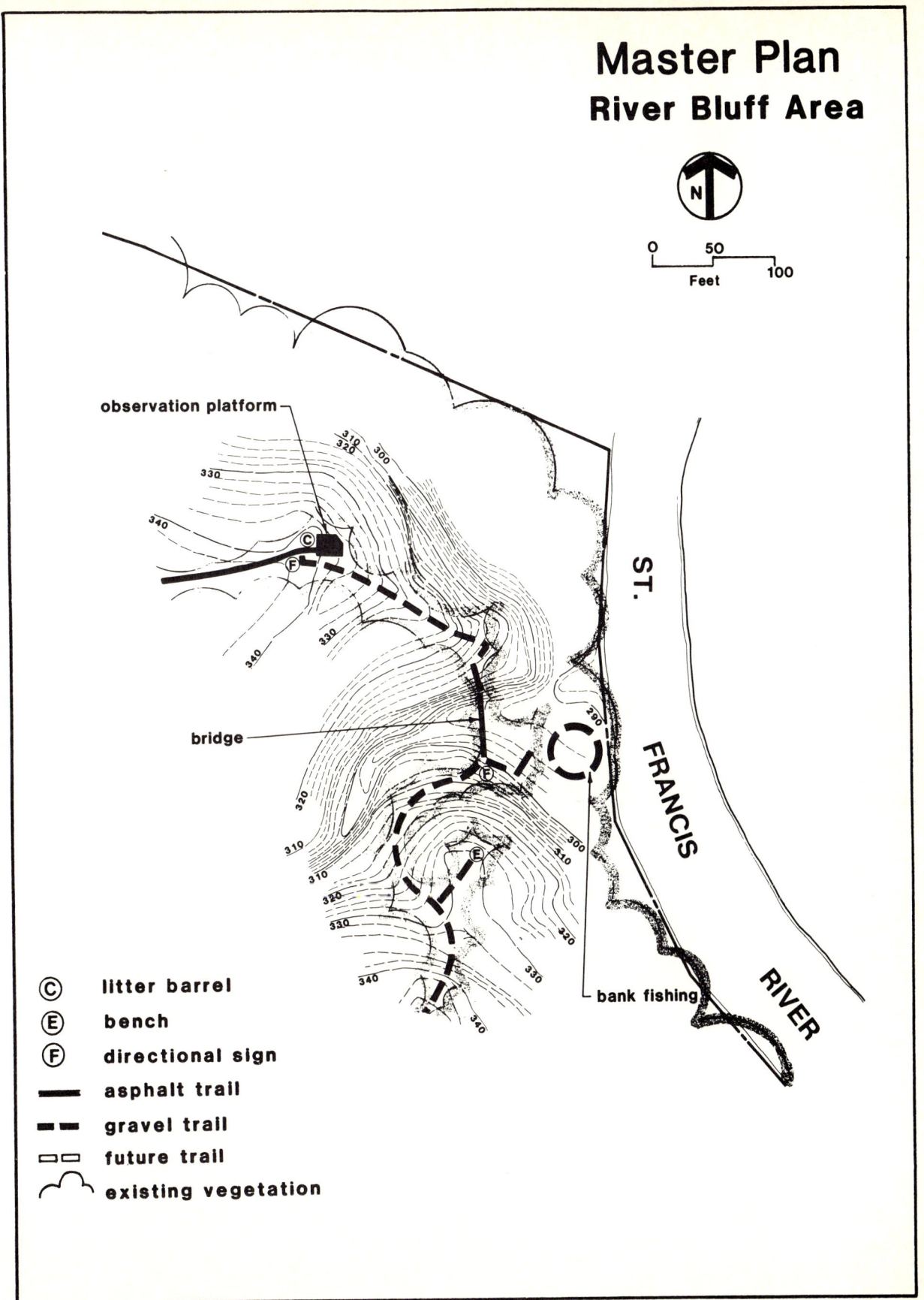

PARKS AND RECREATIONAL AREAS 191

LEDGES STATE PARK
Boone County, Iowa

The Iowa Conservation Commission contracted Harland Bartholomew & Associates to prepare an interpretive program and facilities plan for Ledges State Park, located near Boone, Iowa. The park, one of the largest in Iowa, contains over 1100 acres. In a state such as Iowa, where so much of the natural environment has been man-modified for farming, Ledges stands out with its diverse and contrasting natural features. This assignment included the development of architectural concepts for an earth-sheltered interpretive center, indoor and outdoor displays and exhibits, educational programs and interpretive concepts, and support amenities such as parking, trails, walkways, signage, and utilities.

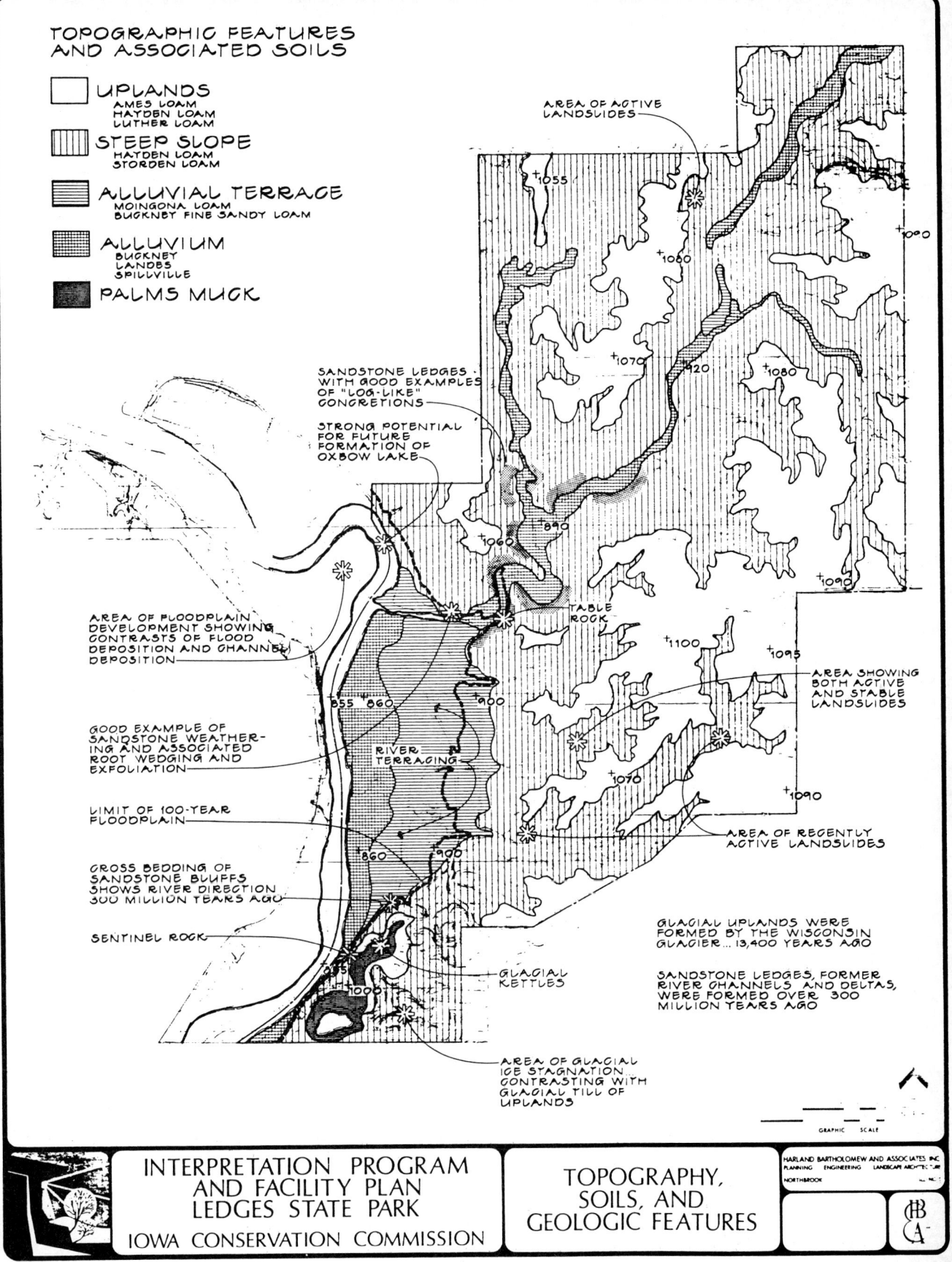

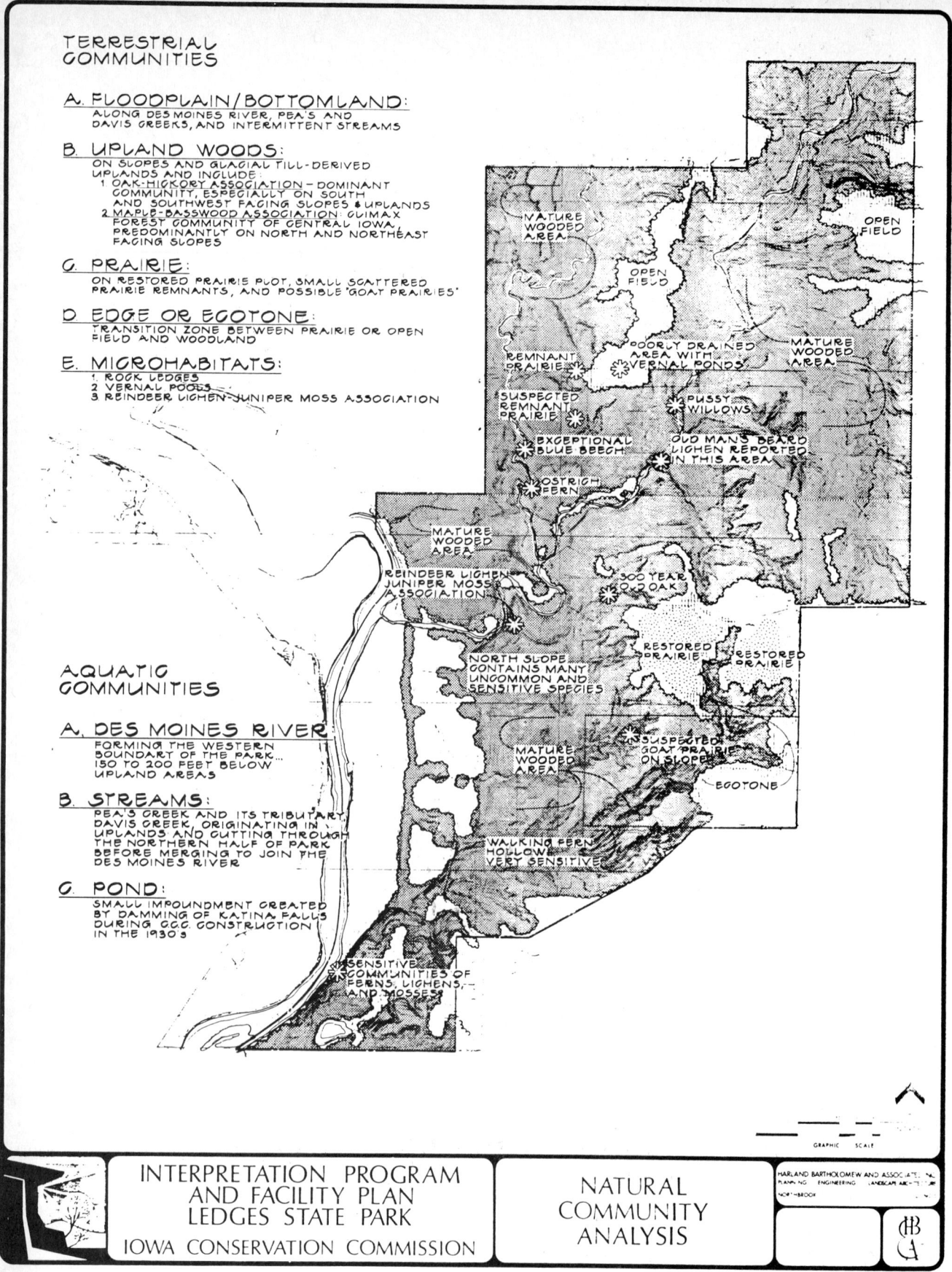

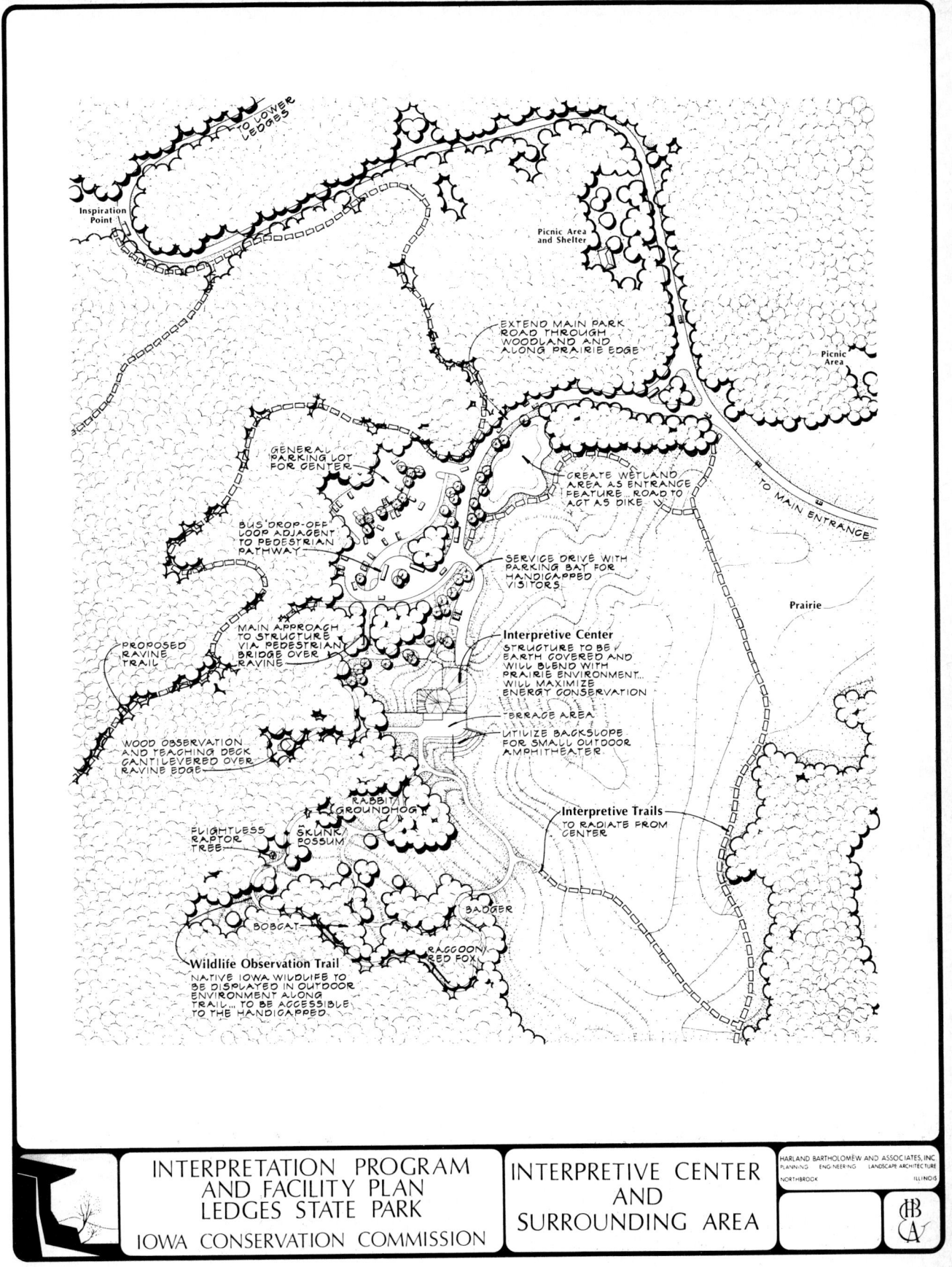

PARKS AND RECREATIONAL AREAS 195

South Exposure of Interpretive Center
INTERPRETIVE PROGRAM & FACILITY PLAN
LEDGES STATE PARK
prepared by
Harland Bartholomew & Associates, Inc.

Des Moines River Valley Overlook
**INTERPRETIVE PROGRAM & FACILITY PLAN
LEDGES STATE PARK**
prepared by
Herland Bartholomew & Associates, Inc.

PARKS AND RECREATIONAL AREAS 197

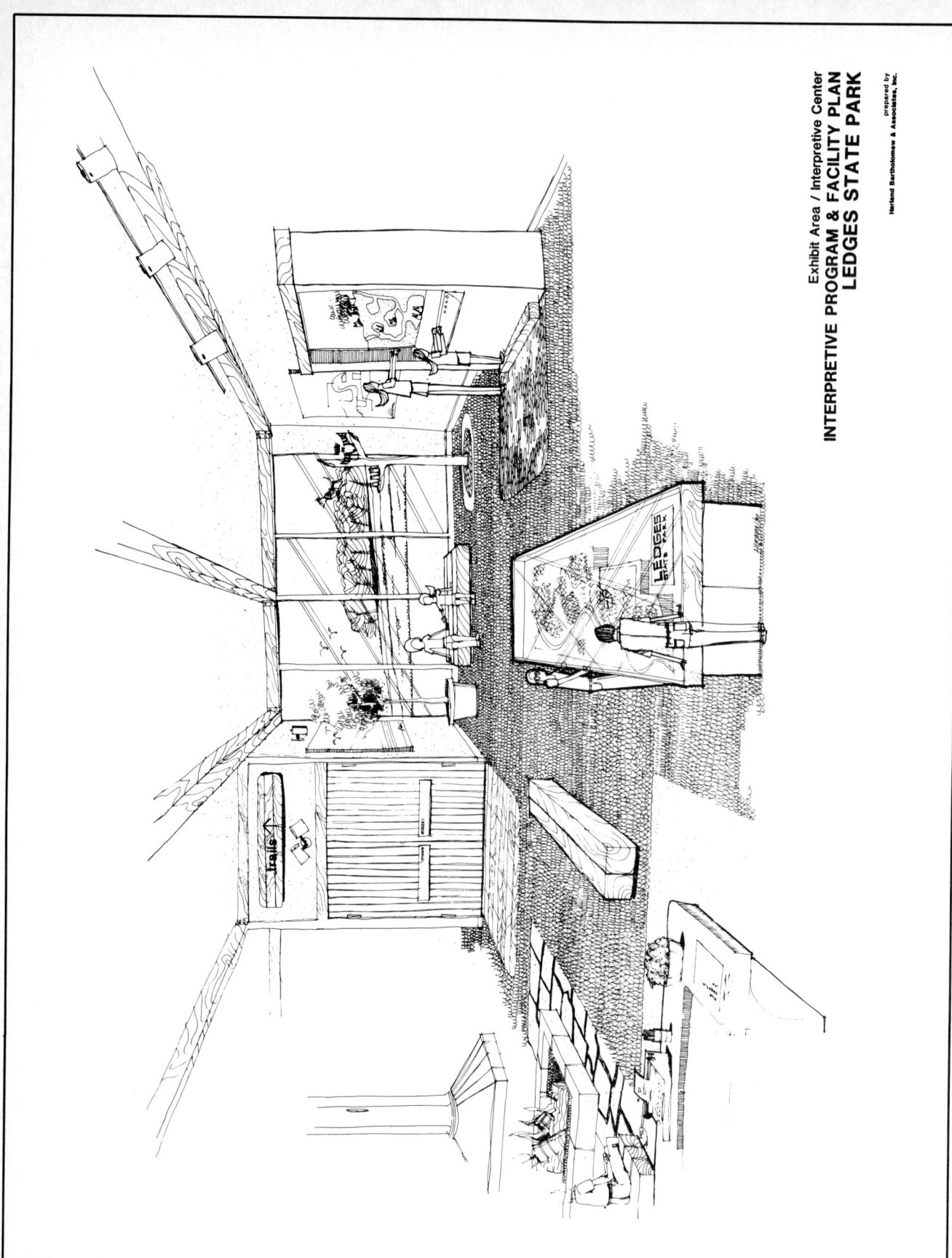

198 PARKS AND RECREATIONAL AREAS

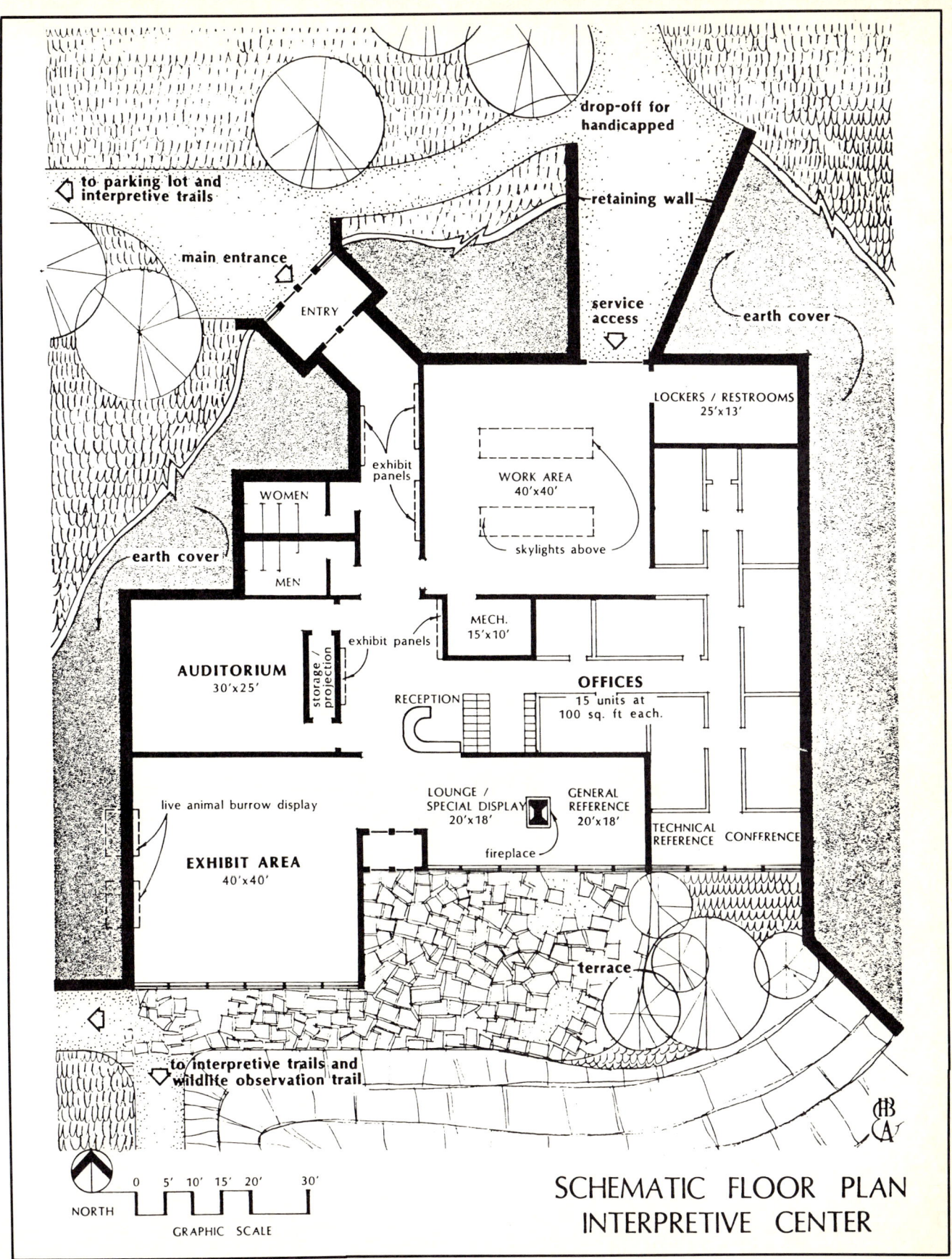

PARKS AND RECREATIONAL AREAS 199

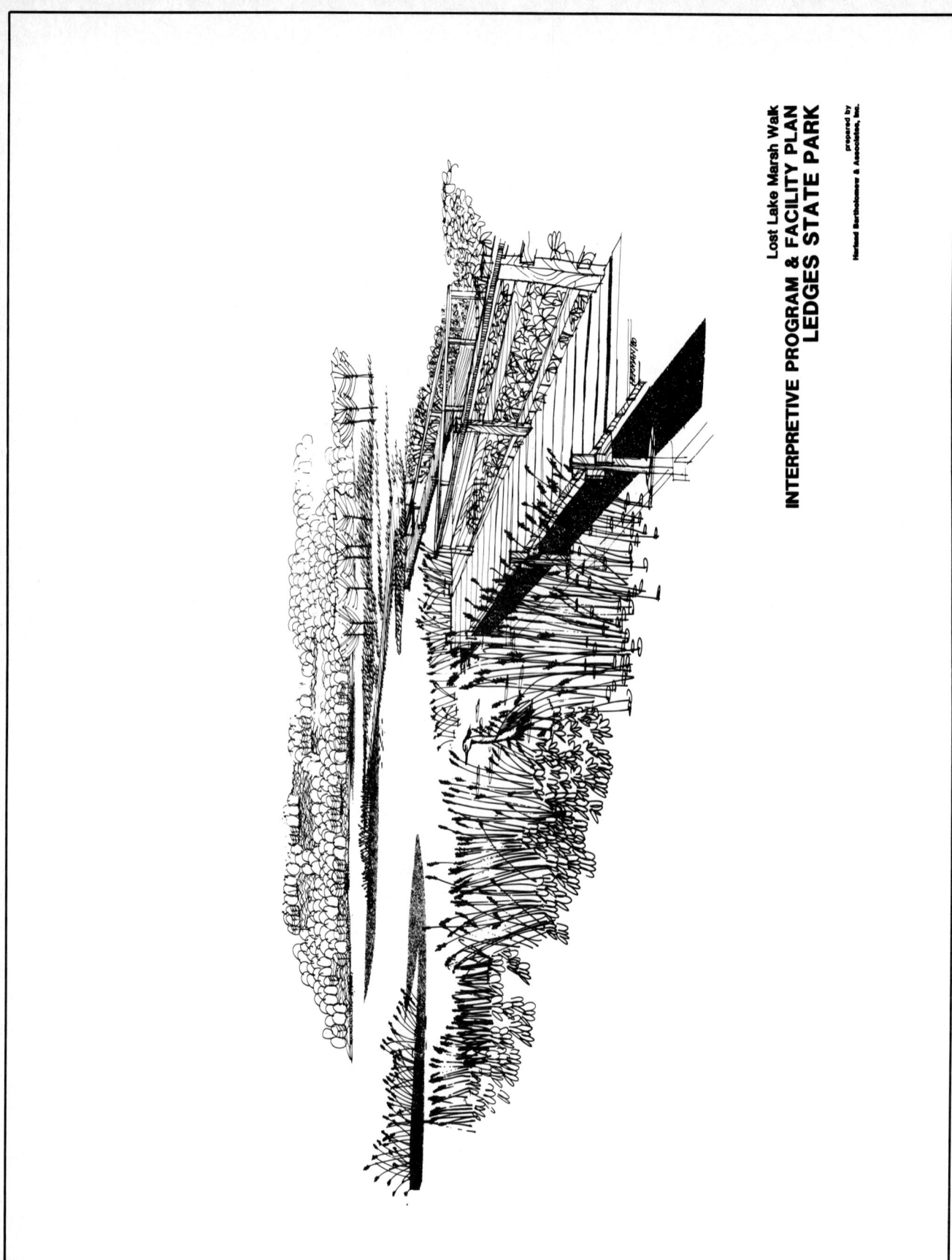

PARKS AND RECREATIONAL AREAS 201

RAVINIA PARK IMPROVEMENT PLAN
Highland Park, Illinois

Ravinia Park is a 38-acre outdoor music festival facility located north of Chicago, where during the summer months many internationally renowned musicians, theatrical and ballet companies, and other entertainers give live performances. The park includes a 3800-seat semi-open pavilion and general admission seating, facilitating attendances ranging between 10,000 to 20,000 persons.

These large attendances prompted the development of a traffic circulation and parking improvement plan for the Park. Harland Bartholomew & Associates was retained to analyze existing traffic and parking problems associated with Ravinia Festival events; prepare a traffic and parking improvement plan to submit to the City of Highland Park for a special-use permit; and prepare detailed parking lot landscape and engineering design plans to submit for bids and construction.

Specific design improvement proposals included the construction of pedestrian paths; separate turnaround areas for shuttle buses; and designation of specific areas for automobile, charter bus, and special visitor parking, including the handicapped.

Special consideration was given to the visual impact of the proposed improvements on the surrounding neighborhood. The shuttle-bus access drive to the Green Bay Bicycle Trail was constructed with Turfstone, a concrete paving stone that permits grass to grow between pre-cast holes in the blocks to provide some natural ground cover. Extensive planting provided a visual buffer between the shuttle buses and the surrounding neighborhood, and lighting for this area was designed to reduce the projection of glare to the surrounding property owners. All improvements were designed and installed to be compatible with the character of the adjacent residential neighborhoods.

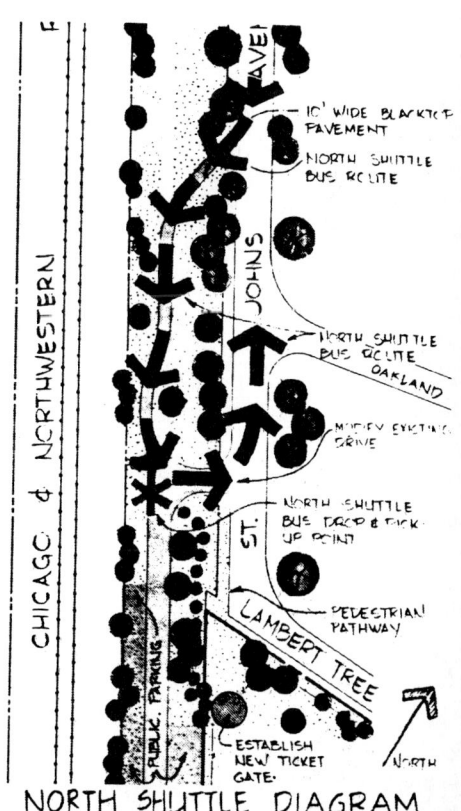

NORTH SHUTTLE DIAGRAM

FOR-MAR NATURE PRESERVE AND ARBORETUM
Genessee County, Michigan

For-Mar was originally established as a place for nature study, nature trails, arboretums, wildlife sanctuary, and conservation education. The long-range plan was structured to provide needed coordination among these varied uses, particularly nature study and the arboretum, while recommending specific improvements aimed at increasing the quality and quantity of outdoor education.

The proposed visitor center would provide orientation for both the nature preserve and arboretum. The nature preserve would include the development of interpretive trails, wildlife habitat areas, and a prairie restoration area. The arboretum provides tree and shrub displays of cultivated and Michigan plantings. Plant arrangements were carefully designed in response to environmental conditions such as drainage, soils, wind, and sun patterns.

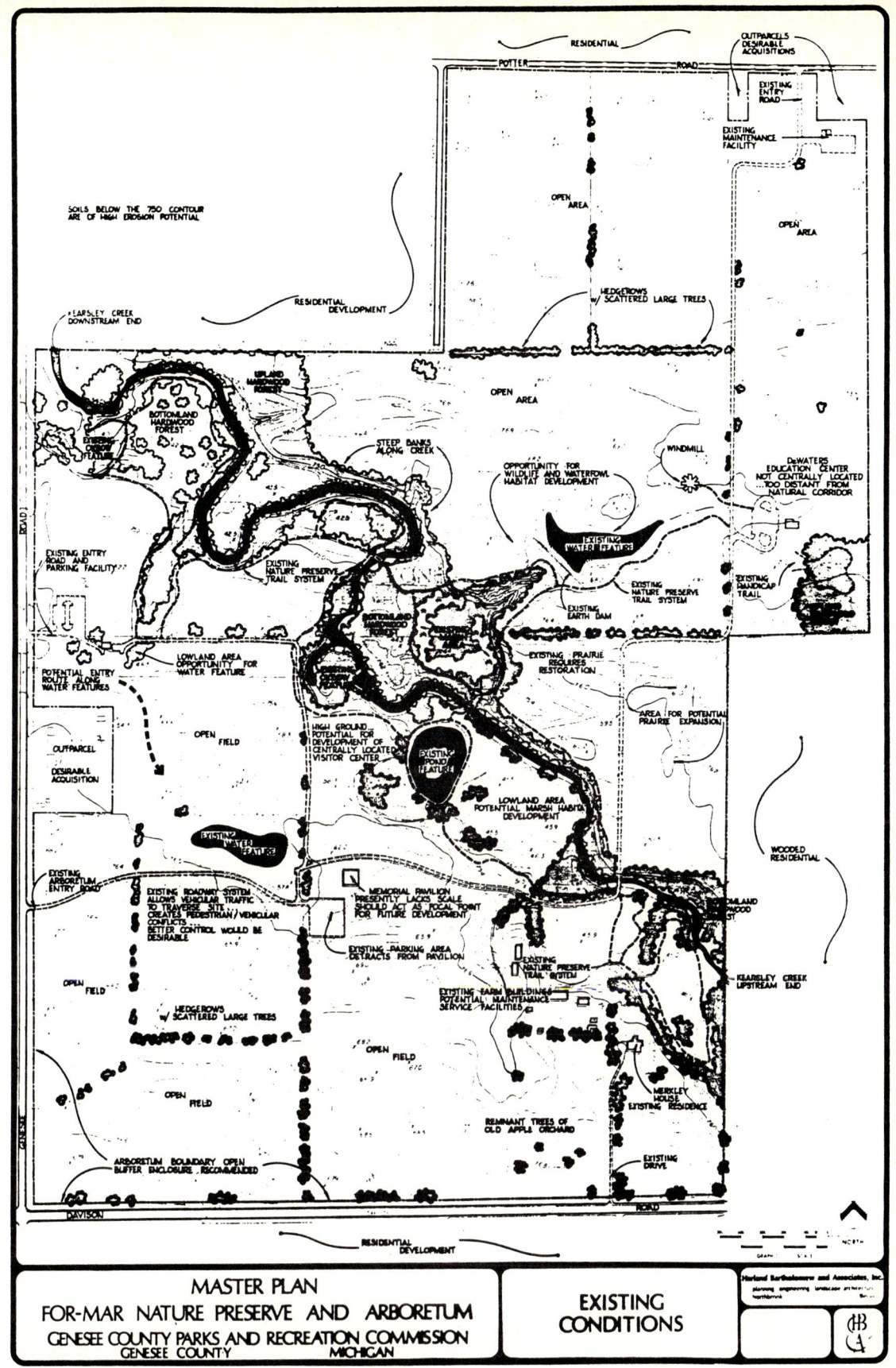

PARKS AND RECREATIONAL AREAS 205

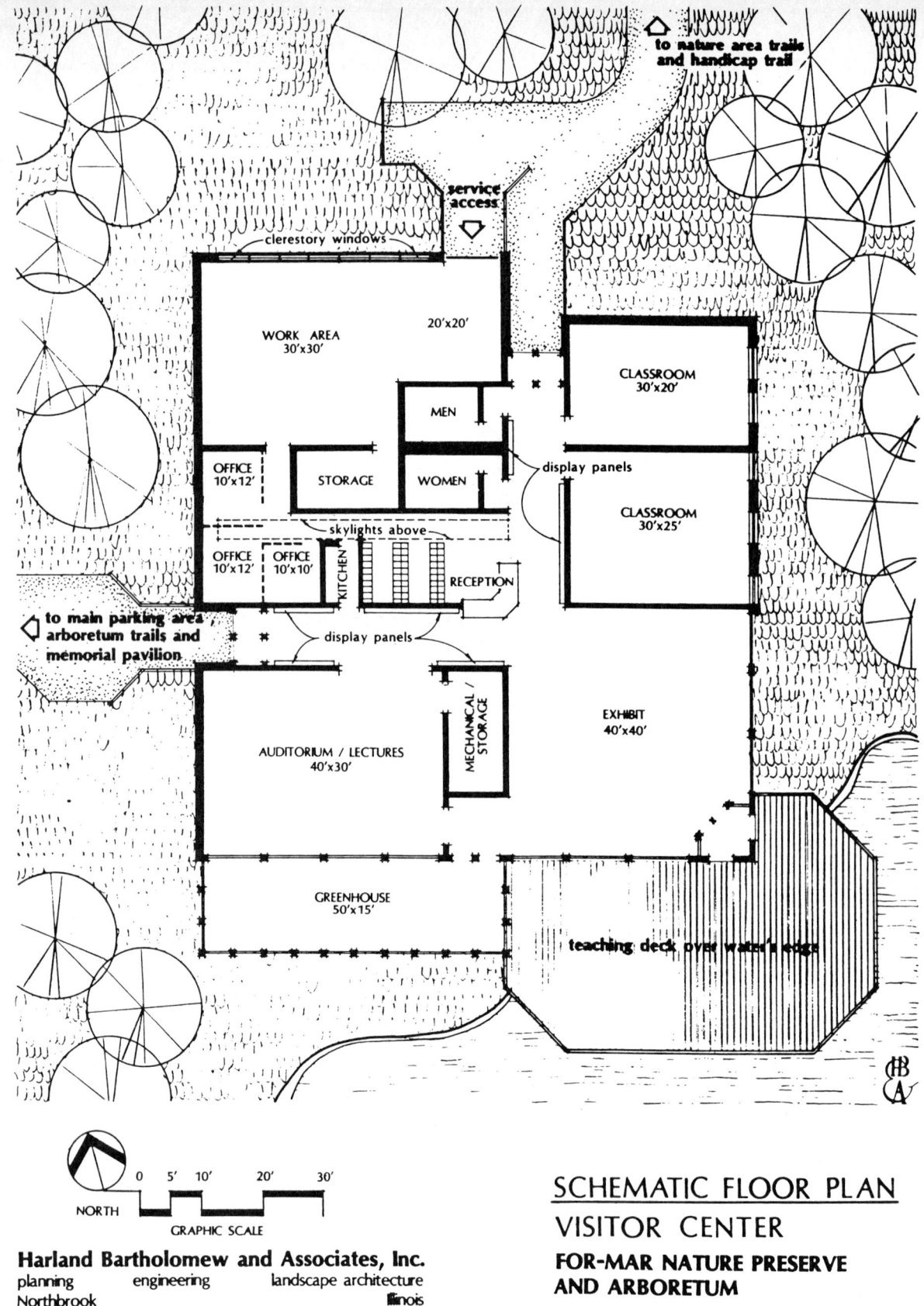

SCHEMATIC FLOOR PLAN
VISITOR CENTER
FOR-MAR NATURE PRESERVE AND ARBORETUM

Harland Bartholomew and Associates, Inc.
planning   engineering   landscape architecture
Northbrook   Illinois

FRANK HAMMOND PARK
Munster, Indiana

The Town of Munster, Indiana, is located south and east of Chicago, just east of the Illinois-Indiana state line. When the park was designed, the town had a population of about 18,000; the town has worked to preserve an overall low-density, good quality, residential character. Through land-use studies and controls, the town has been able to provide adequate business, industry, schools, parks, churches, and other institutions.

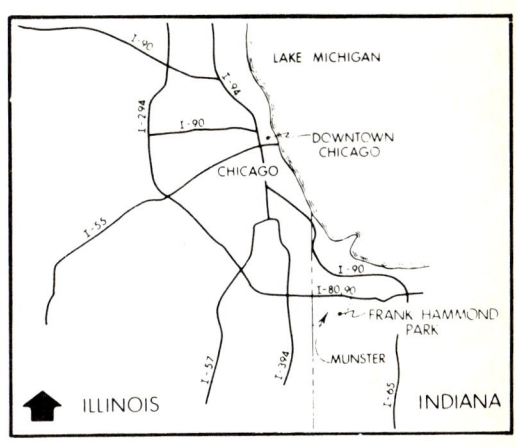

Harland Bartholomew & Associates provided a Master Site Plan for the park and detailed construction plans, including specifications and cost estimates for tennis courts, a paved running track, water supply system, storm sewer system, play areas, and landscaping. This 12-acre park was developed on a site adjoining an elementary school and was one of four city parks improved by the Town of Munster; HB & A provided detailed construction plans for all the parks.

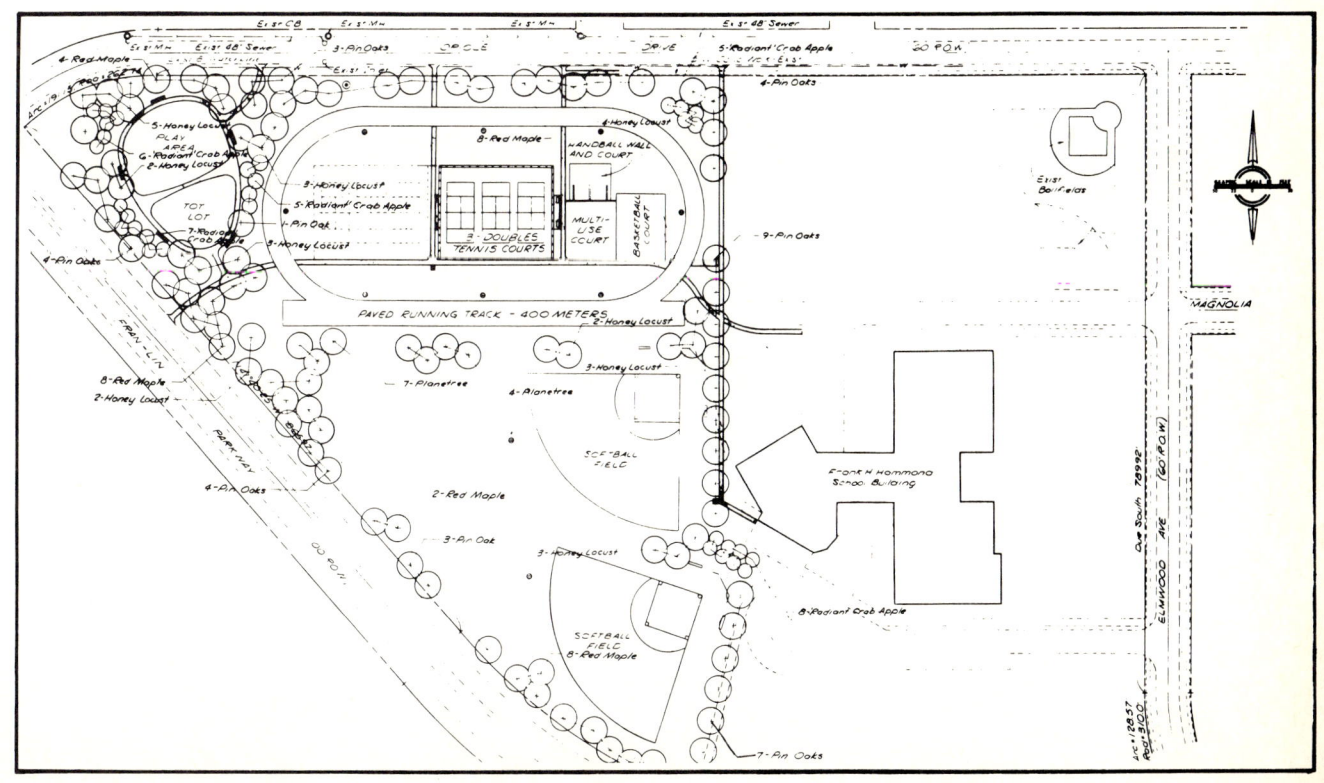

PERUQUE CREEK RECREATION STUDY
St. Charles County, Missouri

As part of the Peruque Creek Watershed Study, Harland Bartholomew & Associates was commissioned to prepare alternate concept plans for recreational development in conjunction with the proposed reservoir along Peruque Creek. The existing and future recreational supply and demand within the study area were analyzed as they related to the proposed development. Expected recreational activities were identified and sites evaluated accordingly. Recommendations were made for locating recreational development, and four alternate plans were prepared. A combination of sites was selected so that the sponsor would have flexibility in the development of the selected recreation concept.

Each of the plans contained provisions for swimming, fishing areas, boat launches, a maintenance center, and nature study. The plans varied in size and number of facilities. Two of the plans offered opportunities for camping.

In conjunction with the development of the recreation area, broader management practices were recommended. Methods to protect the lake perimeter and the watershed were suggested, and natural plantings to promote wildlife and to control soil erosion also were recommended.

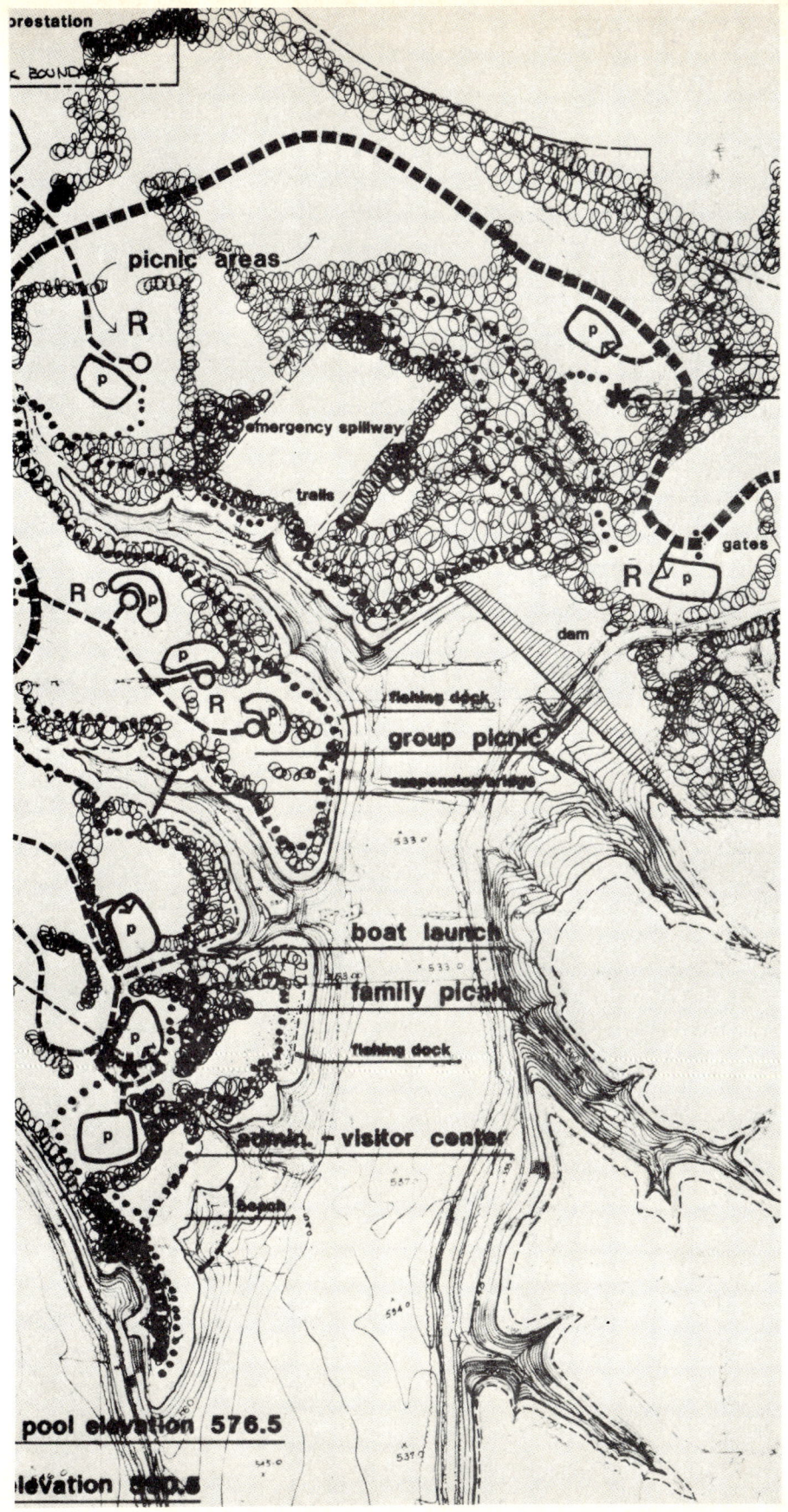

WOOD OAKS GREEN
Northbrook, Illinois

Wood Oaks Green is a 41-acre active recreation park, located on the western edge of Northbrook, adjacent to the Tri-State Tollway. The area suffered from a lack of recreational and open space, and the planned site was the last undeveloped tract in western Northbrook that could support such a facility.

After a series of meetings and public input, the Wood Oaks Master Plan was developed. Facilities in the final plan included baseball and softball fields, two soccer fields, 12 tennis courts, a "tot-lot," and a 50-foot-high sledding hill. Supporting elements included an elaborate path system, a hard-surface parking lot, landscaping, and the Park District's tree nursery.

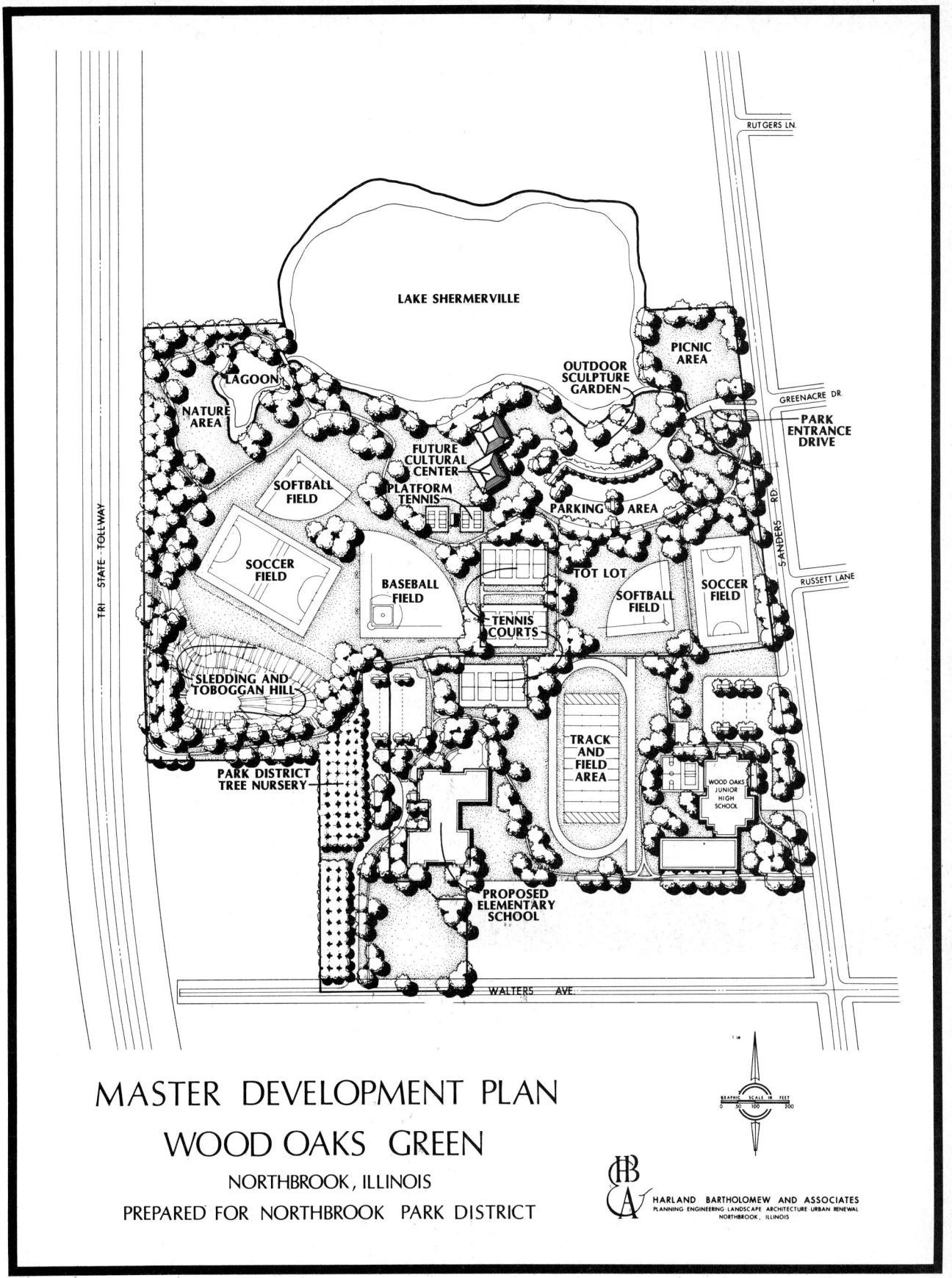

PARKS AND RECREATIONAL AREAS 211

OSMOND AND GAGE BROTHERS PARKS
Antioch, Illinois

The Village of Antioch is located in the Chain O'Lakes region of northwest Lake County, approximately 53 miles northwest of the Chicago Loop. Harland Bartholomew & Associates was asked to prepare master plans for the four park areas owned by the Village, two of which had been previously developed. The remaining two parks were undeveloped.

Osmond Park, situated northwest of the Central Business District, was to be developed as a unique passive-oriented recreational facility. Recreational activities planned include picnicking and fishing during the summer months and ice skating during the winter. The major focus of Osmond Park is an existing one-acre detention pond; the master plan calls for improving it through the reshaping of its shoreline and the construction of a new lagoon to provide an acceptable winter habitat for the pond's fish population. A picnic shelter would be constructed that could be converted to a warming station during the winter months. Other features would include a wood fishing deck (overhanging the pond's edge), a bridge, pedestrian walkways, a parking lot, and landscaped berms.

The concept for Gage Brothers Park called for the area to be used as an education-oriented facility that would be unique to the northern Illinois area. The focus of the park is a working, water-driven sawmill located along Sequoit Creek, which traverses the site. The park would function as an outdoor museum, relating the early history of the Antioch area. In addition to the sawmill, an arboretum containing trees that were utilized in the local timber industry would be planted. A self-guiding trail would interwind within the arboretum so that the park could be used without Park Staff present. Supporting elements would include an outdoor classroom, a parking area, and landscaping.

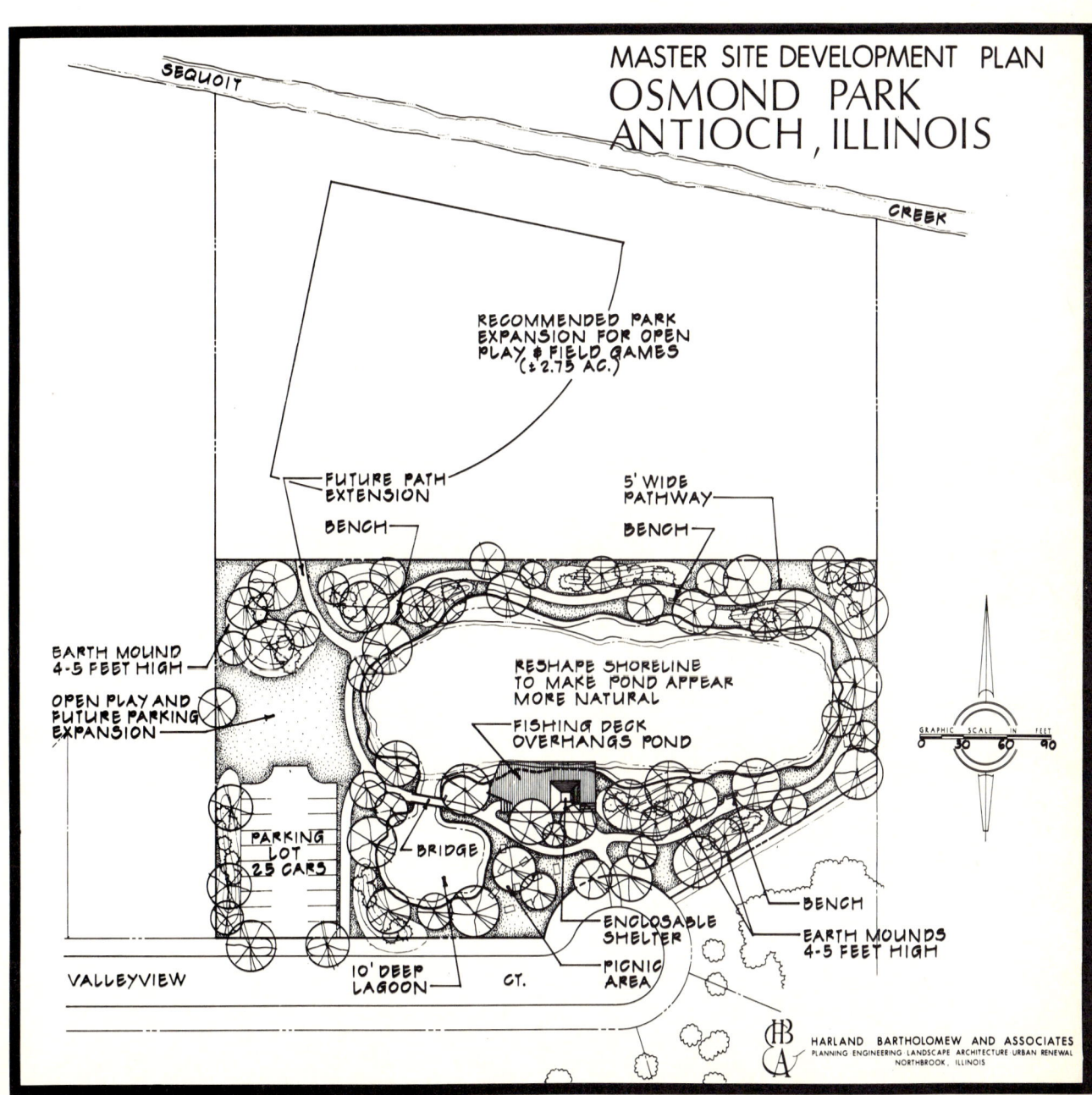

PARKS AND RECREATIONAL AREAS

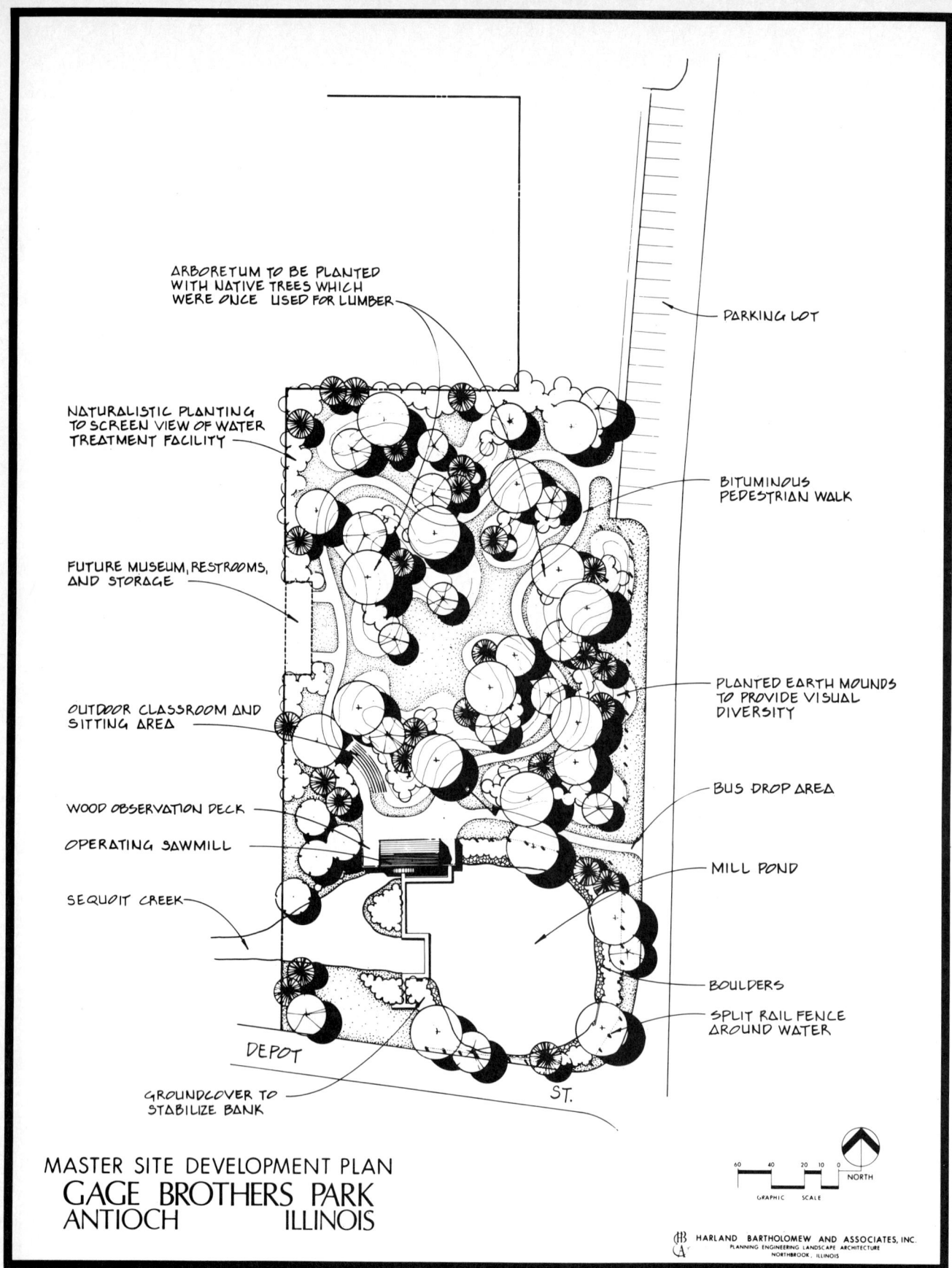

MASTER DEVELOPMENT PLAN
Roosevelt and Washington Parks
Waukegan Park District
Waukegan, Illinois

Washington and Roosevelt Parks are two of the oldest parks in Waukegan. Many of the site improvements made more than 50 years ago needed to be replaced and new facilities added. The land uses adjoining the park area had changed over the years, and new facilities were needed to serve the population in the adjacent areas. Maintenance and operation procedures had changed, and it was necessary to have park improvements planned to permit efficient management.

In the preparation of the Master Development Plan, a program was set forth that had the following goals and objectives:

1. Recognize and take maximal advantage of the natural features of the park areas and retain as many of the existing improvements as possible within the parks.

2. Re-establish the two parks as facilities providing the Waukegan community with a maximal contribution of usable open space near the downtown area.

3. Provide convenient physical access to the parks for both active and passive recreational purposes.

4. Re-establish the lagoon as a viable recreational asset and provide a program of continued management for the entire drainage system.

5. Develop a program of coordinated use between the neighboring schools and the parks.

6. Provide conveniently located park facilities for the senior citizens' housing complex.

7. Provide an attractive corridor along the entire length of both parks for use by pedestrians and bicyclists.

8. Establish an intensive planting and landscaping program to enhance the visual attractiveness of all areas in the parks.

ALLOCATION OF USE AREAS

The ravine areas of Washington Park would be used primarily for bicycling and hiking. The stream areas would be improved with several small lakes. The steep hillsides would be "non-use" areas except in those locations where stairways, paths, or other constructed facilities would permit vertical circulation from the bottom of the ravine to the upland areas.

In Washington Park, the intensive-use areas were along Washington Street where a patio, shelter, and bridge could serve the neighborhood population and the downtown workers and visitors. The high, relatively level area at Water and Juniper Streets was planned as an intensive-play area for the adjoining residential areas. With the construction of a ramp and deck system near the senior citizen housing, the area along Utica Street could become an intensive-use area.

When the lagoon in Roosevelt Park is rebuilt, one of the major recreational uses will be those passive activities that can be enjoyed along the shores, such as viewing, walking, casting, sailing model boats, and, in the winter, skating. The area in the western part of Roosevelt Park is planned for informal recreation, an open play lawn, and a picnic area. The promontory area with a bandstand and a "tot-lot" is planned to be renovated; the present uses of the area would continue.

MAJOR DETAILS OF THE PLAN

Lagoon and Stream Restoration. The lagoon in Roosevelt Park could be restored by several combined efforts. First, the lagoon needed to be dredged in such a way that approximately one-third of the lagoon basin just behind the dam would be eight to ten feet deep. The remaining two-thirds of the finished lagoon area would be dredged to allow a depth of approximately three to four feet. Second, the lagoon should be protected from excess sediment and nutrient inflow by two shallow retention structures. The stream channel should be regraded to improve the movement of water and runoff through the ravine. Certain areas along the stream would be widened, and aerators would be installed to provide water features and improved water quality. Erosion-prone areas would be lined with stones to minimize further erosion.

Ramps and Decks. These would be located adjacent to the senior citizens' housing projects along Utica Street. Constructed of wooden timbers, the ramps would have gentle slopes and be accessible by people in wheelchairs. At varying levels, platforms or viewing decks with benches could be constructed to provide views overlooking the ravine and lakefront. A structure for restrooms, maintenance storage, and operations should be located at the base of the system of ramps and decks. Proposed in the same area were the restoration of the natural artesian spring and the enlarged lake feature with spray fountains.

Terrace Shelter. To take advantage of the interesting views into the wooded ravine, it was planned that a terrace or deck be constructed. The terrace would project out over the steep hillside. Such a facility would be an attraction for the people of the neighborhood as well as the visitors and workers of downtown. A building that would provide a shelter area, restrooms, certain Park District offices, and facilities to be leased for food service would be an asset to this area.

Plaza. The plaza was planned as an urban passive park area. Landscaped walks, benches, night lighting, and points of major focus—such as fountains and/or sculptures—could be included. It was intended that the plaza serve as a gathering area for special neighborhood events and for certain citywide functions.

Suspension Bridges. Two suspension bridges were proposed. One would be located north of Water Street, in Washington Park, providing a connection between the Plaza, the Terrace Shelter, and the downtown area. The other bridge would span the ravine in the center of Roosevelt Park. In both areas, the bridges would permit easy access over the ravine and would allow an interesting and unusual view of the ravine. The bridges would be approximately 120 feet long and over 35 feet above the floor of the ravine, thus affording a walkway through the tree tops.

Recreational Areas. Other recreational areas were proposed within the two park sites. Additional and improved play equipment was advised for the area adjacent to Juniper Street in Washington Park and in Roosevelt Park along McAllister Street. A complex of courts for tennis, basketball, and paddle tennis were located in Washington Park along Juniper Street. Open areas for field games were planned throughout both Washington and Roosevelt parks. A sledding hill and basketball courts were located at the south end of Roosevelt Park.

IMPLEMENTATION

Phase I

1. Improve the lagoon, dredge existing siltation, repair dam, reshape and improve shoreline, add aerators.

2. Regrade existing stream bed to provide additional water features and construct siltation ponds.

3. Plant trees and, on open slopes, add ground cover to control erosion.

Phase II

1. Construct the ramp and viewing decks with restrooms and maintenance area located adjacent to the senior citizens' housing complex.

2. Construct the 12-foot-wide maintenance road.

3. Improve the crossing for those students west of the park who attend Andrew Cooke School.

Phase III

1. Construct the shelter and a concession area with terrace overlook, restrooms, picnic tables, and walkways.

2. Install the two suspension bridges.

3. Construct a downtown plaza with walkways and landscaping.

4. Develop additional picnic areas and open areas for lawn games throughout both parks.

5. Improve maintenance building.

Phase IV

1. Construct the eight-foot-wide pathway system with lighting and landscaping.

2. Develop the "tot-lot" in Roosevelt Park and improve parking and restroom facilities.

3. Construct the basketball courts and sledding hill at the south end of Roosevelt Park.

4. Restore the natural artesian well and add walkways and benches.

Phase V

1. Construct underpasses under Water Street and Belvedere Street, connecting the parks by means of this pathway system.

2. Develop the intensive-use area with tennis courts, basketball courts, multi-use courts, shelter, and play apparatus.

3. Construct the amphitheater and performance area across the lagoon.

4. Provide additional planting throughout both parks to supplement existing growth.

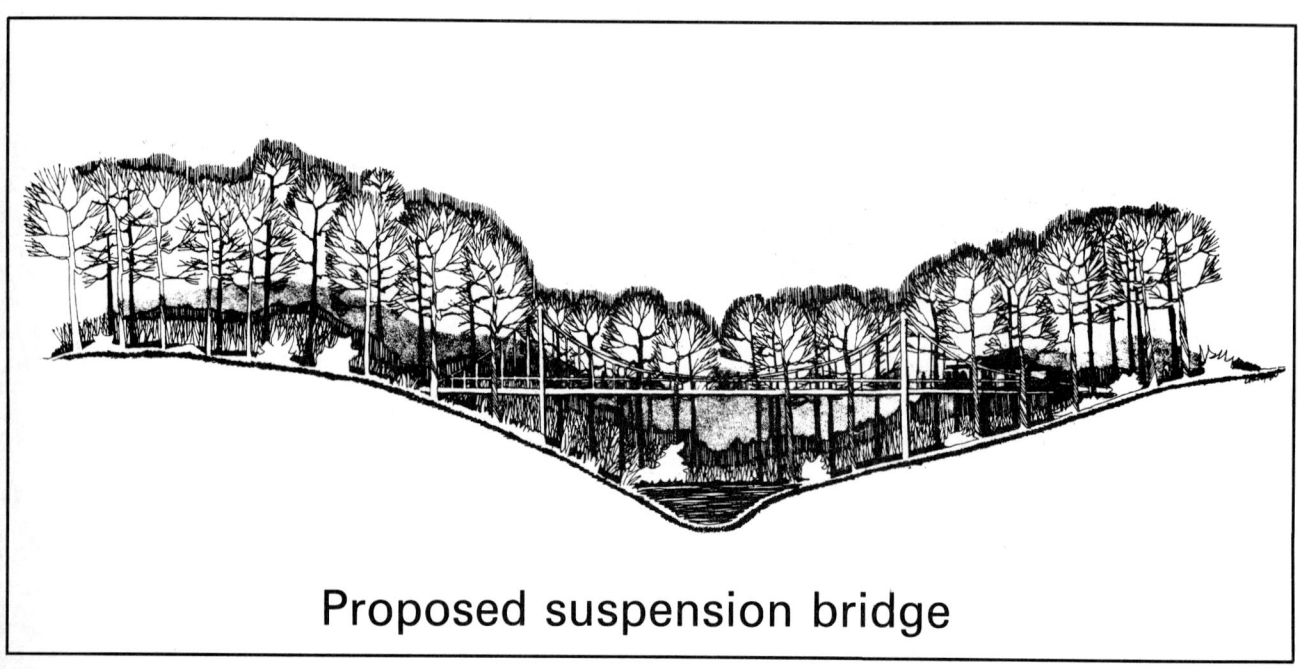

Proposed suspension bridge

220 PARKS AND RECREATIONAL AREAS

View of proposed ramps and viewing decks

PARKS AND RECREATIONAL AREAS

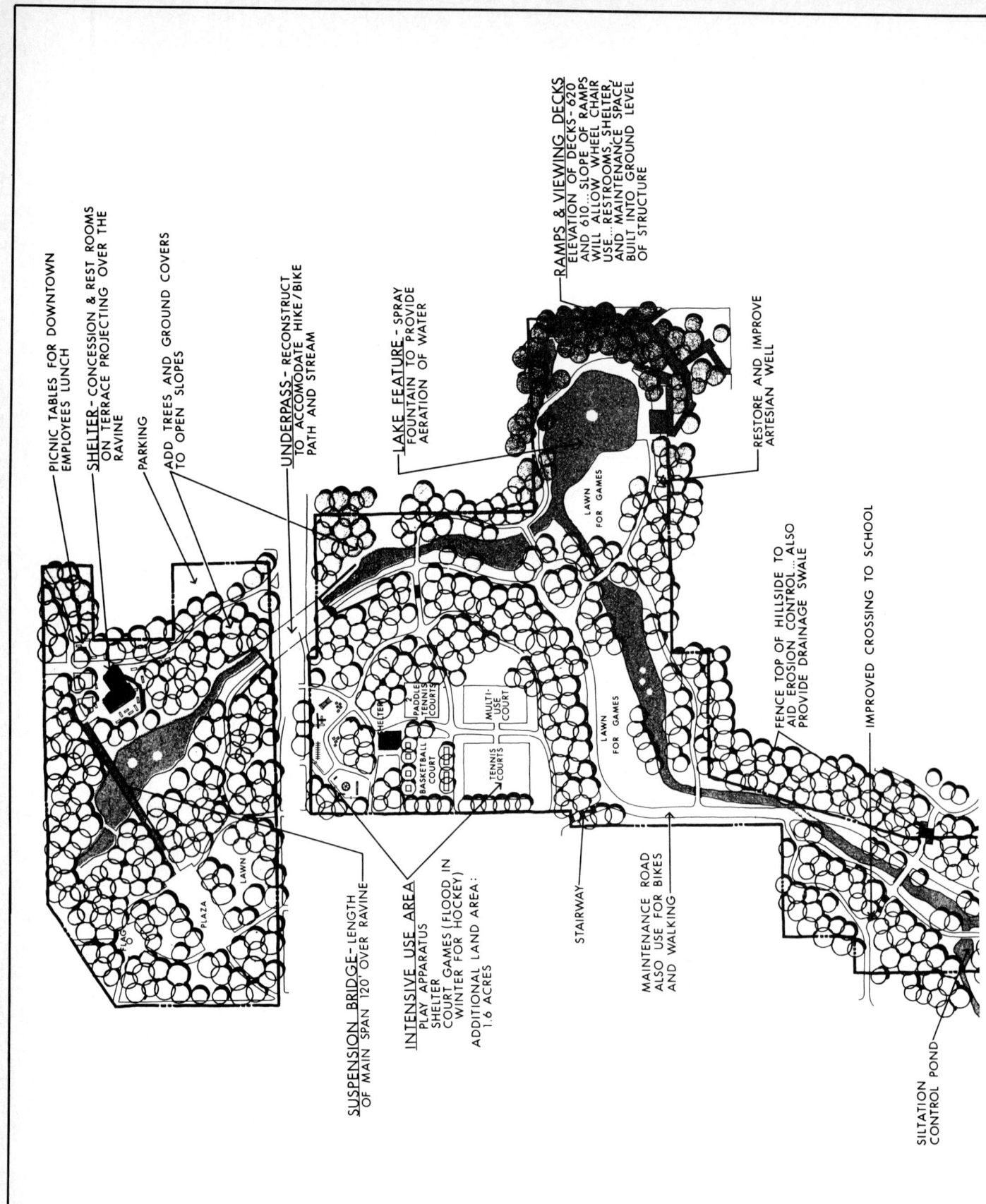

3. Construct a downtown plaza with walkways and landscaping.

4. Develop additional picnic areas and open areas for lawn games throughout both parks.

5. Improve maintenance building.

Phase IV

1. Construct the eight-foot-wide pathway system with lighting and landscaping.

2. Develop the "tot-lot" in Roosevelt Park and improve parking and restroom facilities.

3. Construct the basketball courts and sledding hill at the south end of Roosevelt Park.

4. Restore the natural artesian well and add walkways and benches.

Phase V

1. Construct underpasses under Water Street and Belvedere Street, connecting the parks by means of this pathway system.

2. Develop the intensive-use area with tennis courts, basketball courts, multi-use courts, shelter, and play apparatus.

3. Construct the amphitheater and performance area across the lagoon.

4. Provide additional planting throughout both parks to supplement existing growth.

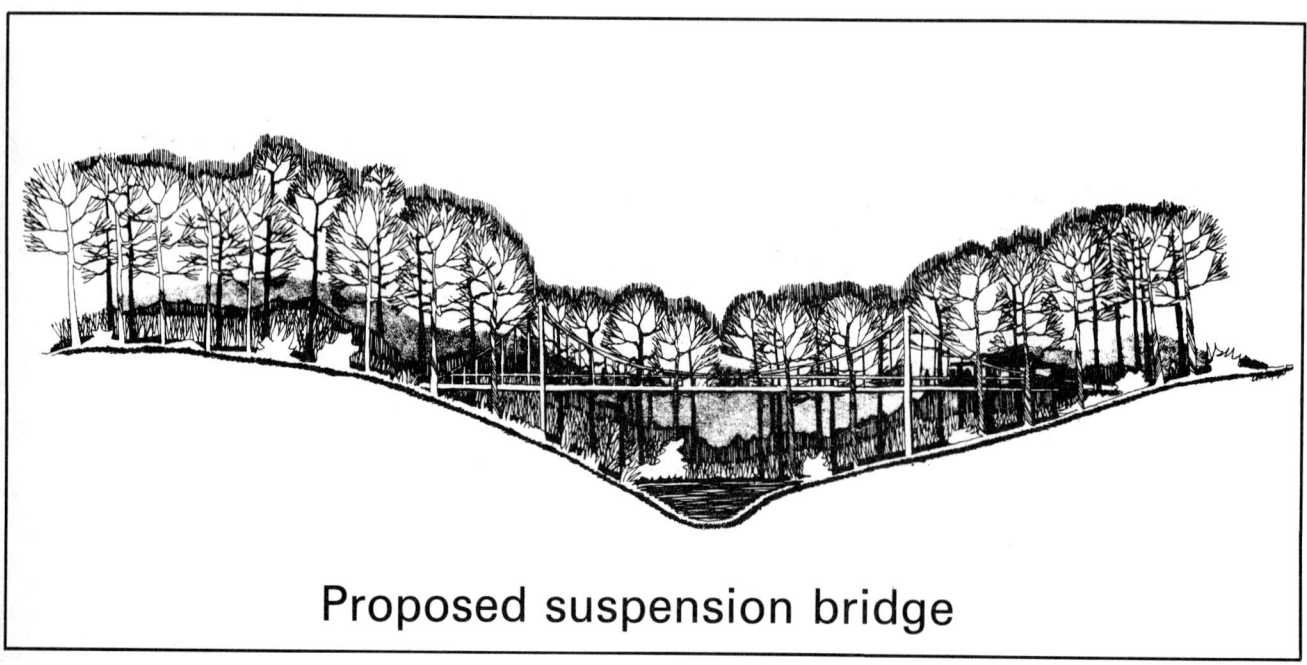

Proposed suspension bridge

View of proposed ramps and viewing decks

PARKS AND RECREATIONAL AREAS 221

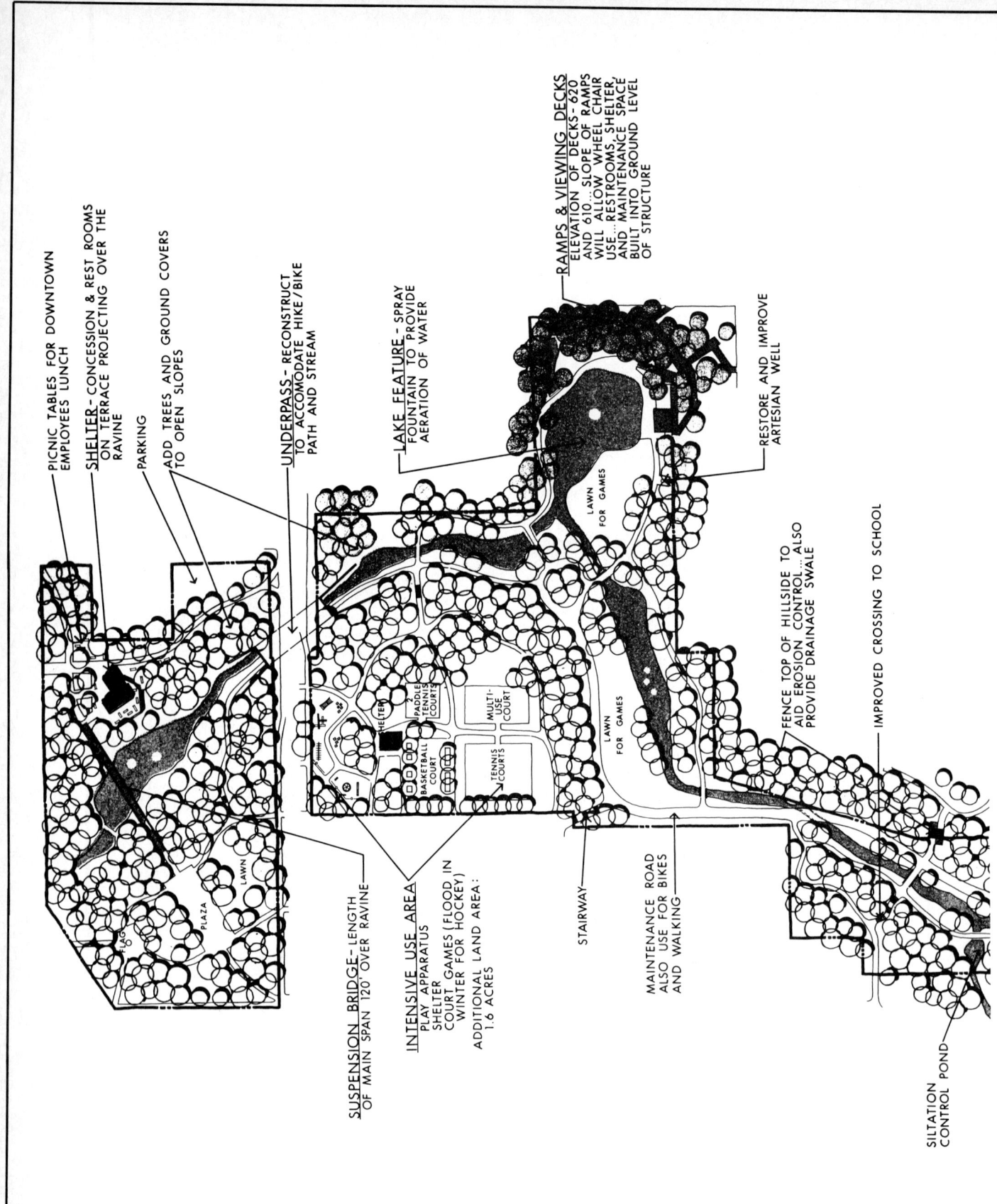

222 PARKS AND RECREATIONAL AREAS

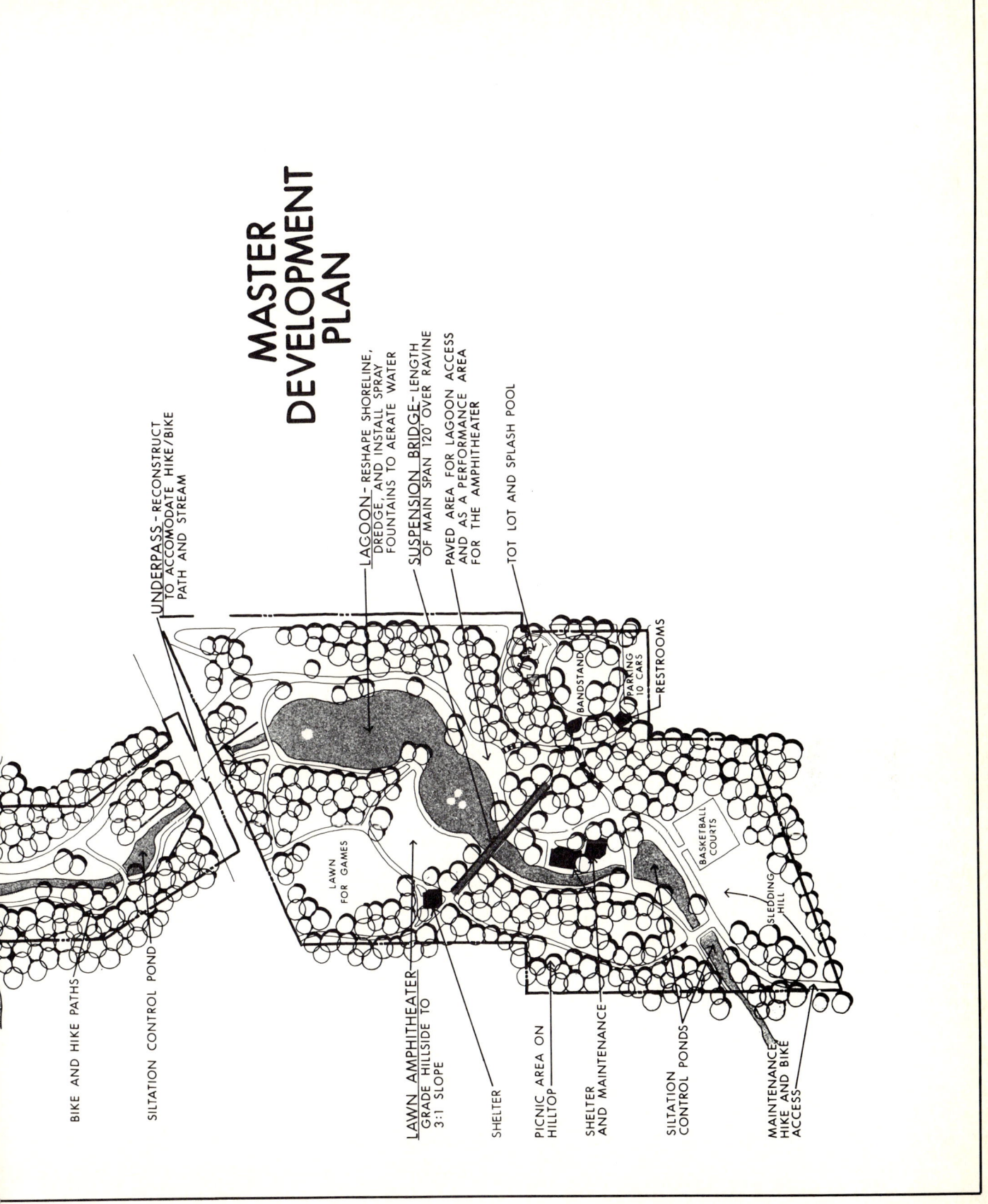

PARKS AND RECREATIONAL AREAS 223

MISCELLANEOUS LAYOUTS FOR PARKS

The park and recreational area plans on the following pages illustrate various forms for presentation. Some show new concepts for existing recreational areas; others indicate proposed improvements.

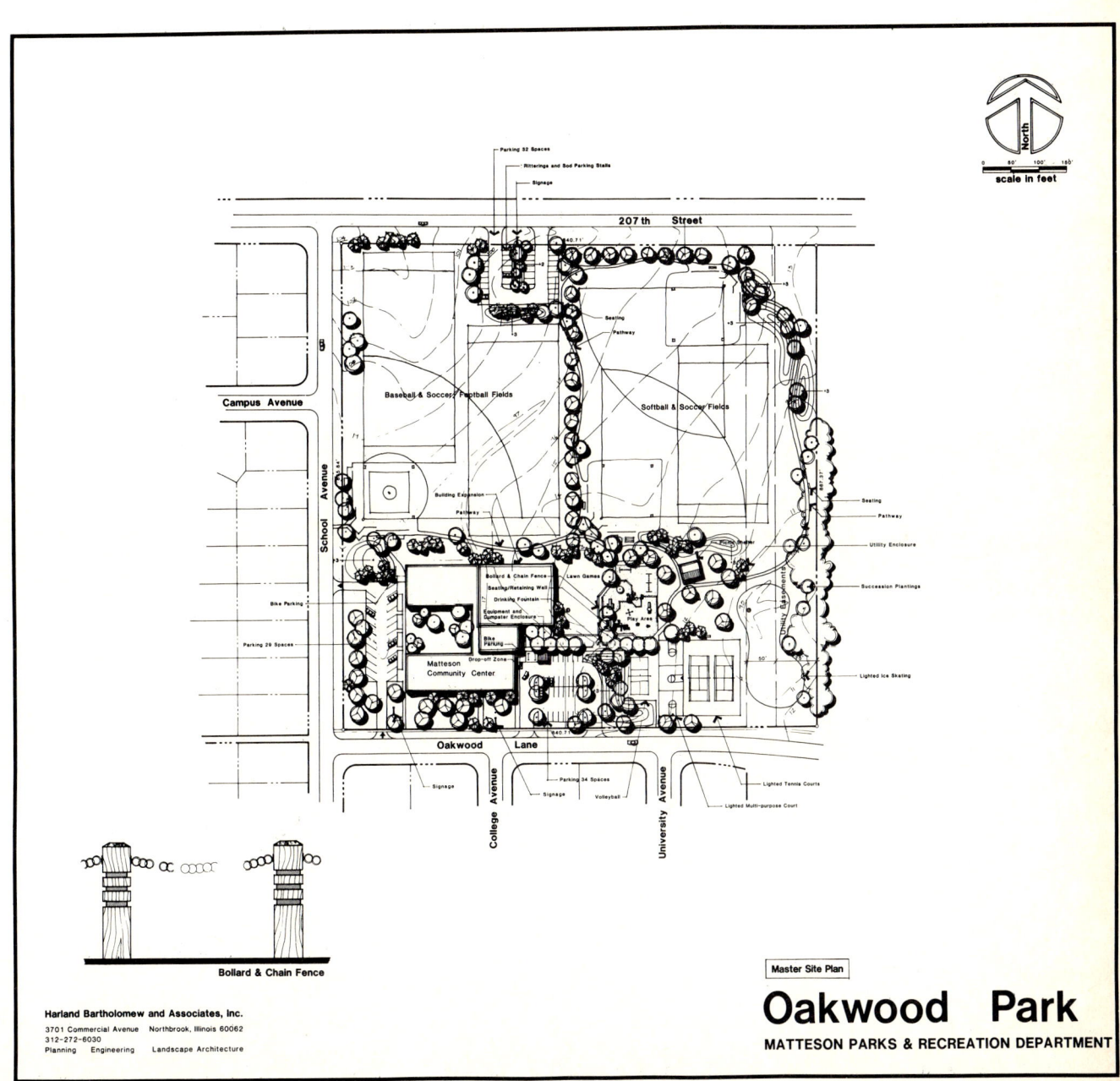

PARKS AND RECREATIONAL AREAS 225

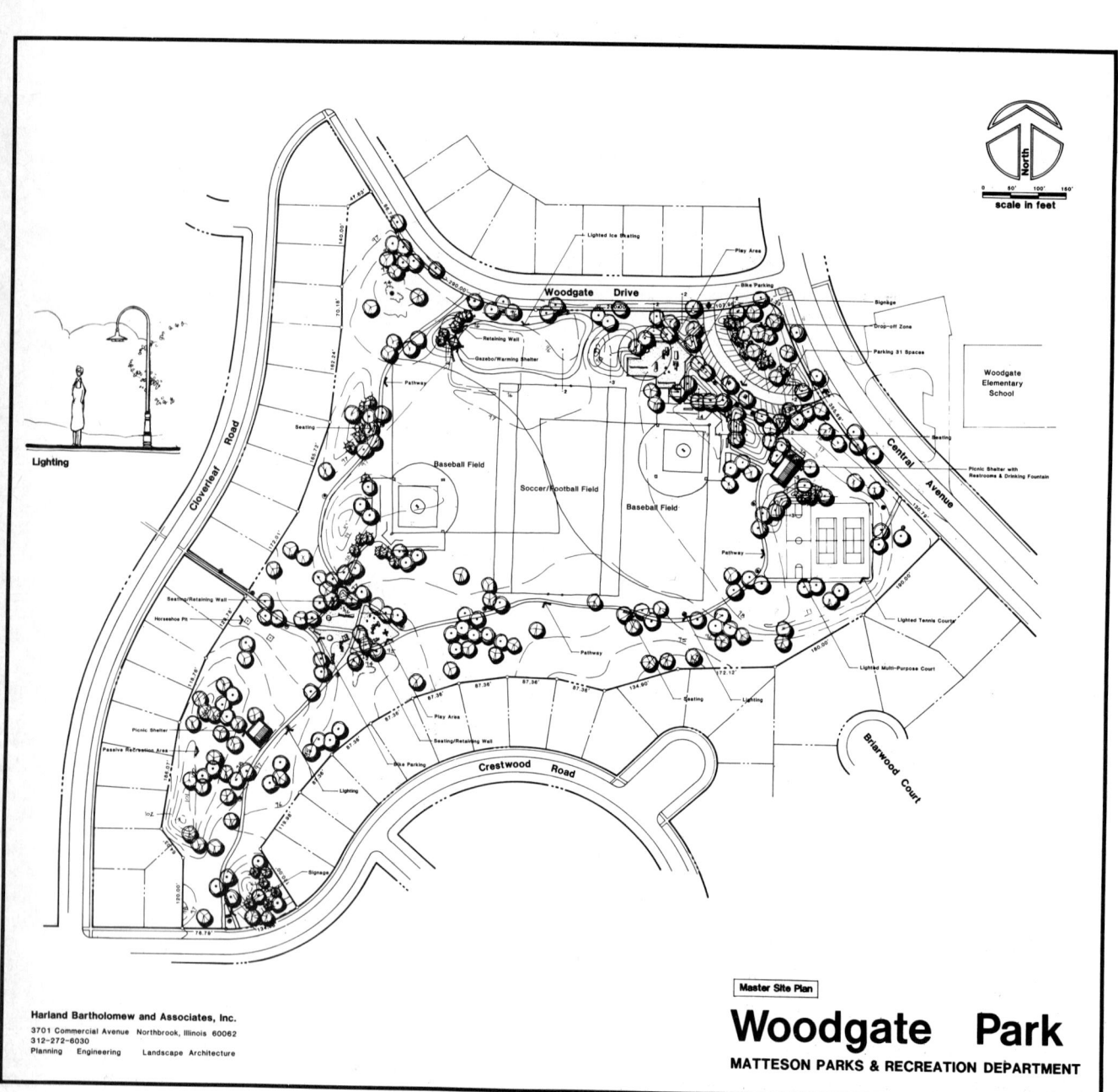

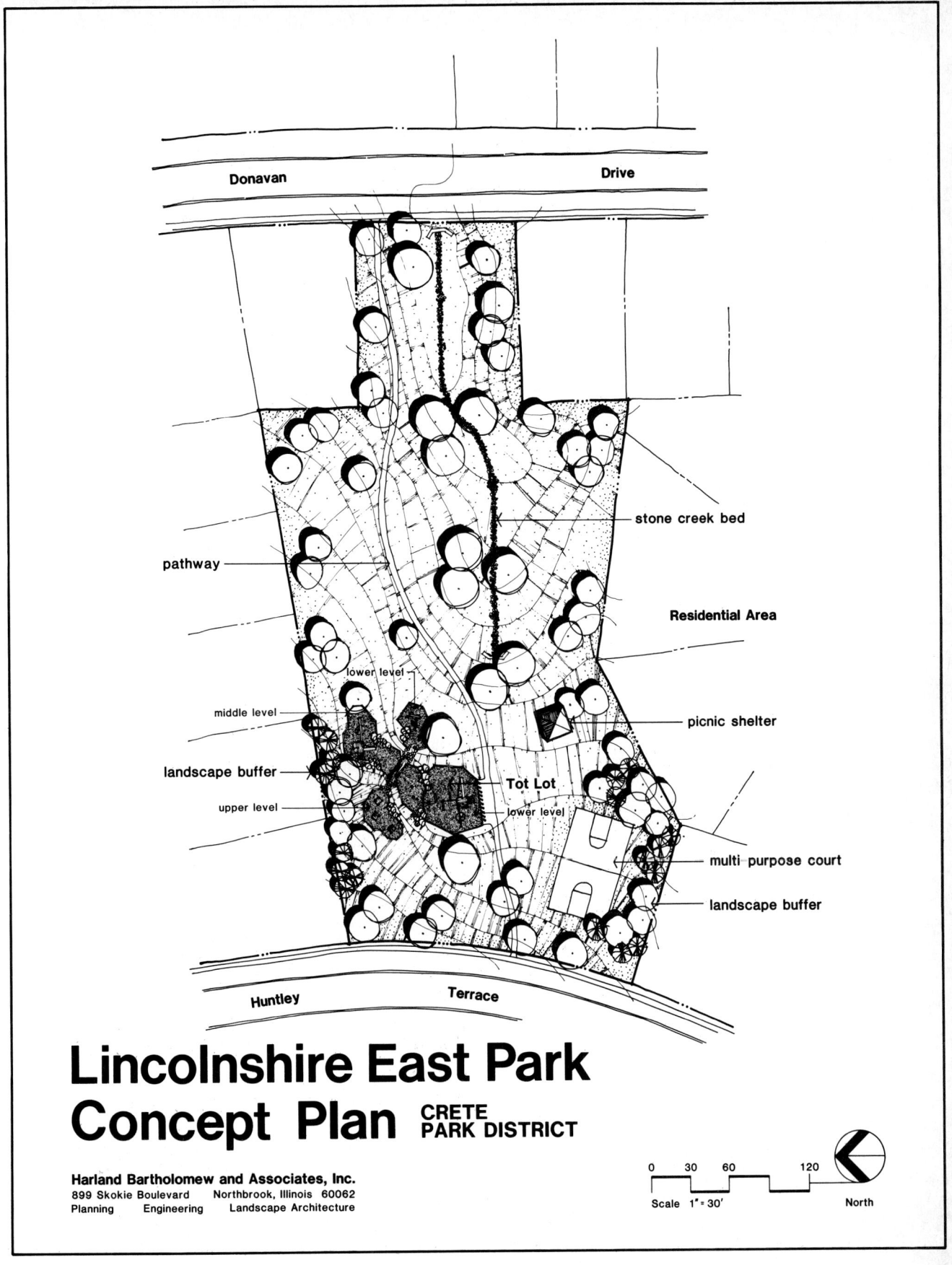

PARKS AND RECREATIONAL AREAS 227

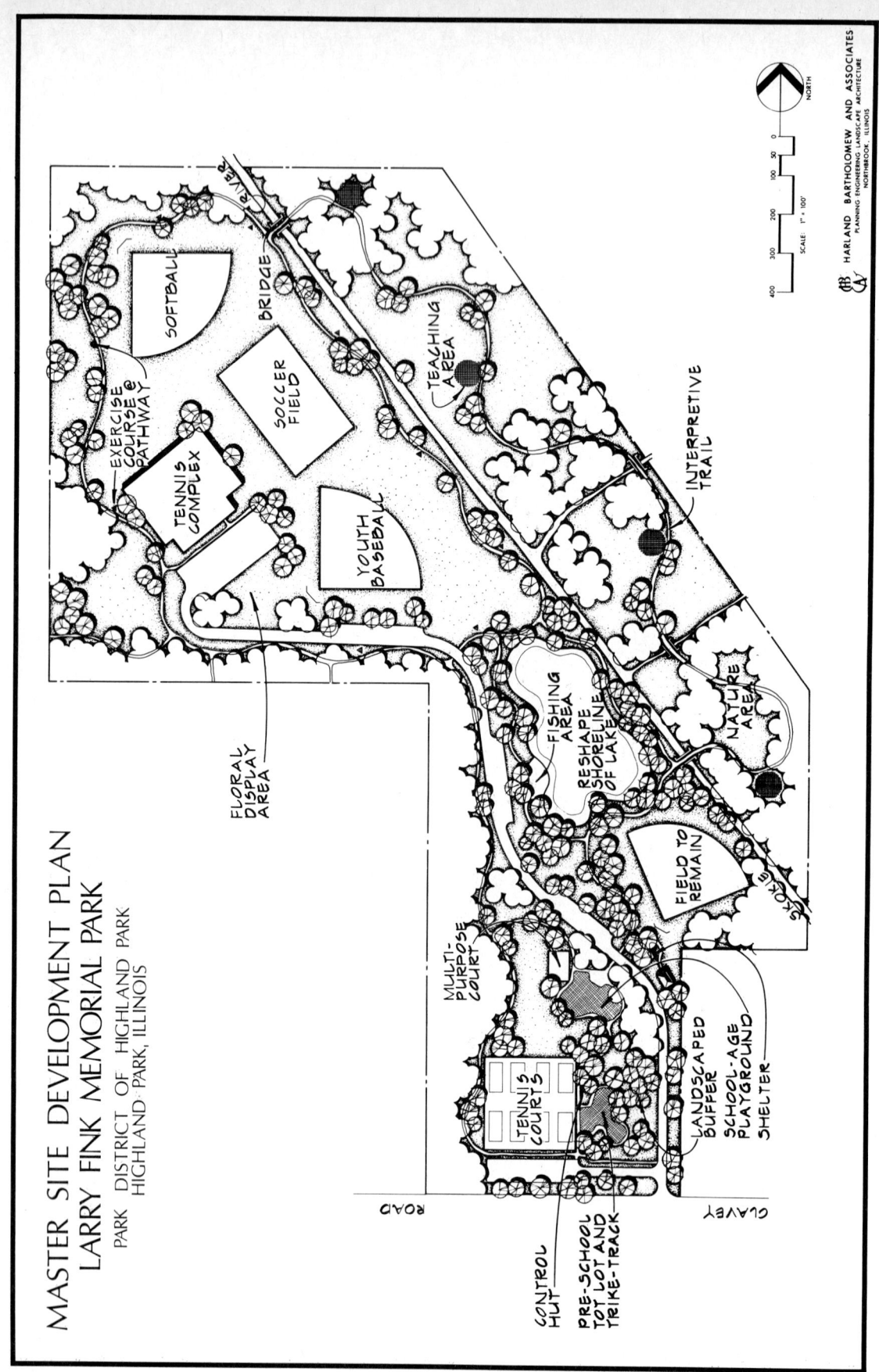

228 PARKS AND RECREATIONAL AREAS

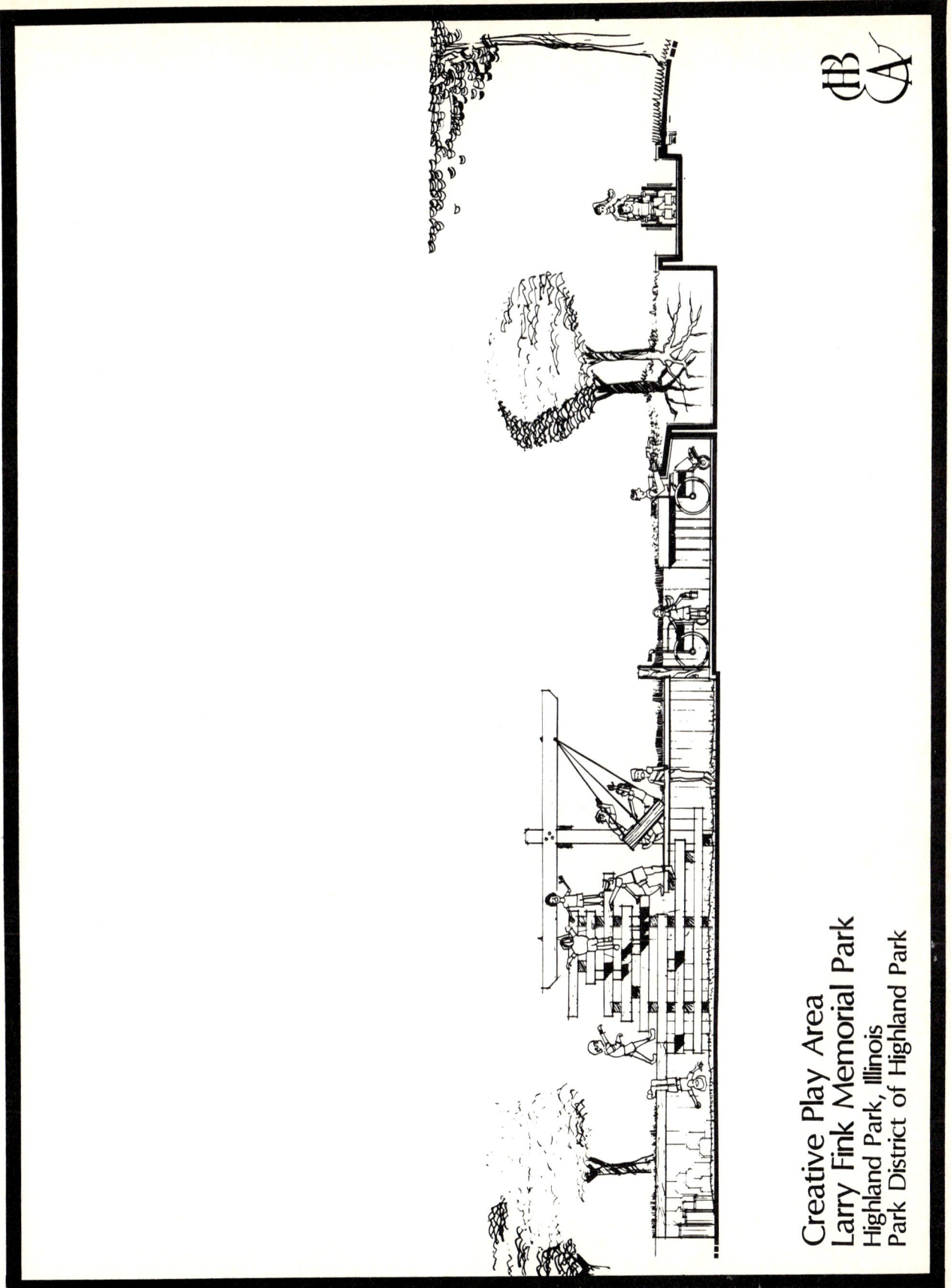

Creative Play Area
Larry Fink Memorial Park
Highland Park, Illinois
Park District of Highland Park

PARKS AND RECREATIONAL AREAS

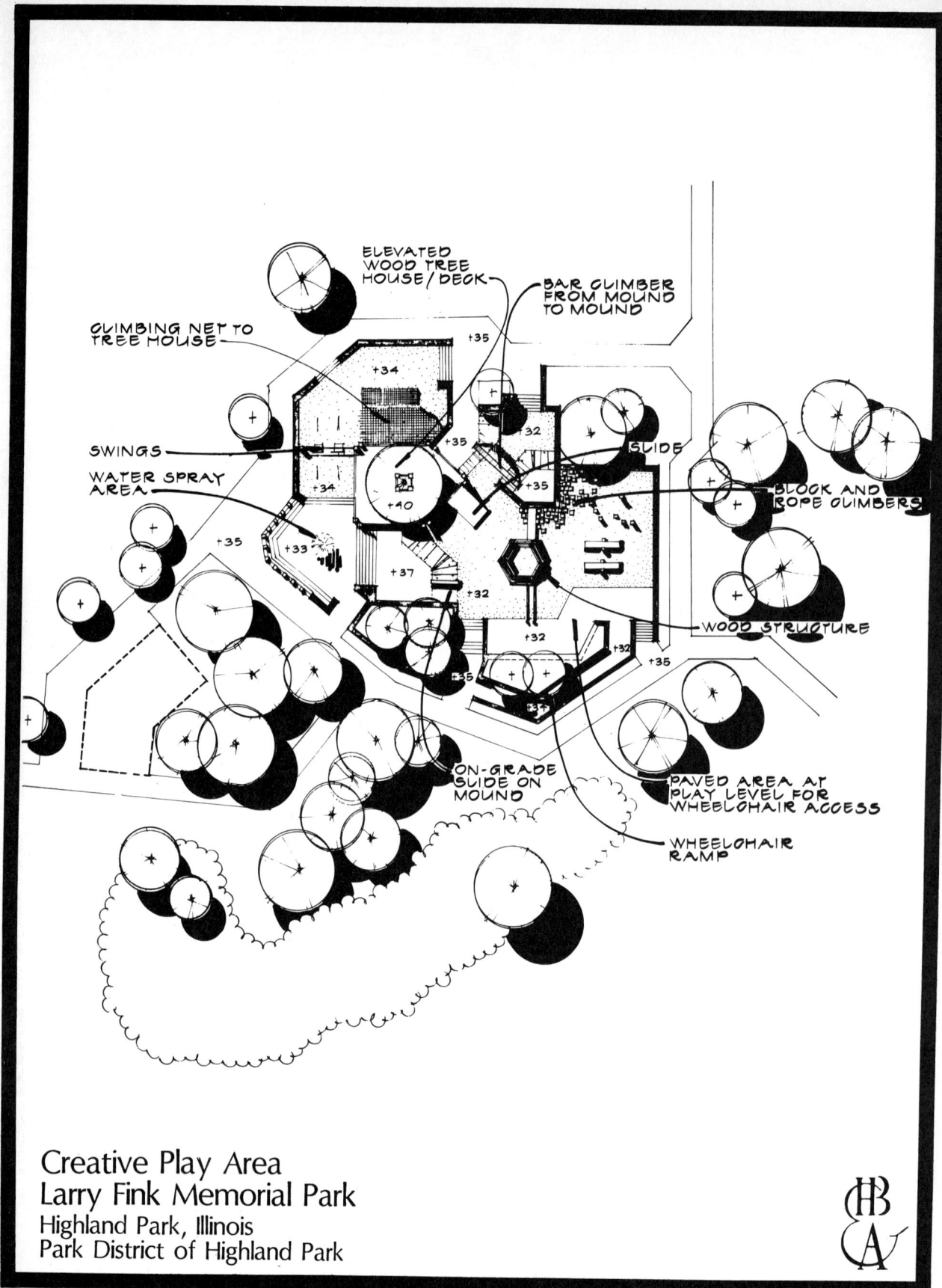

Creative Play Area
Larry Fink Memorial Park
Highland Park, Illinois
Park District of Highland Park

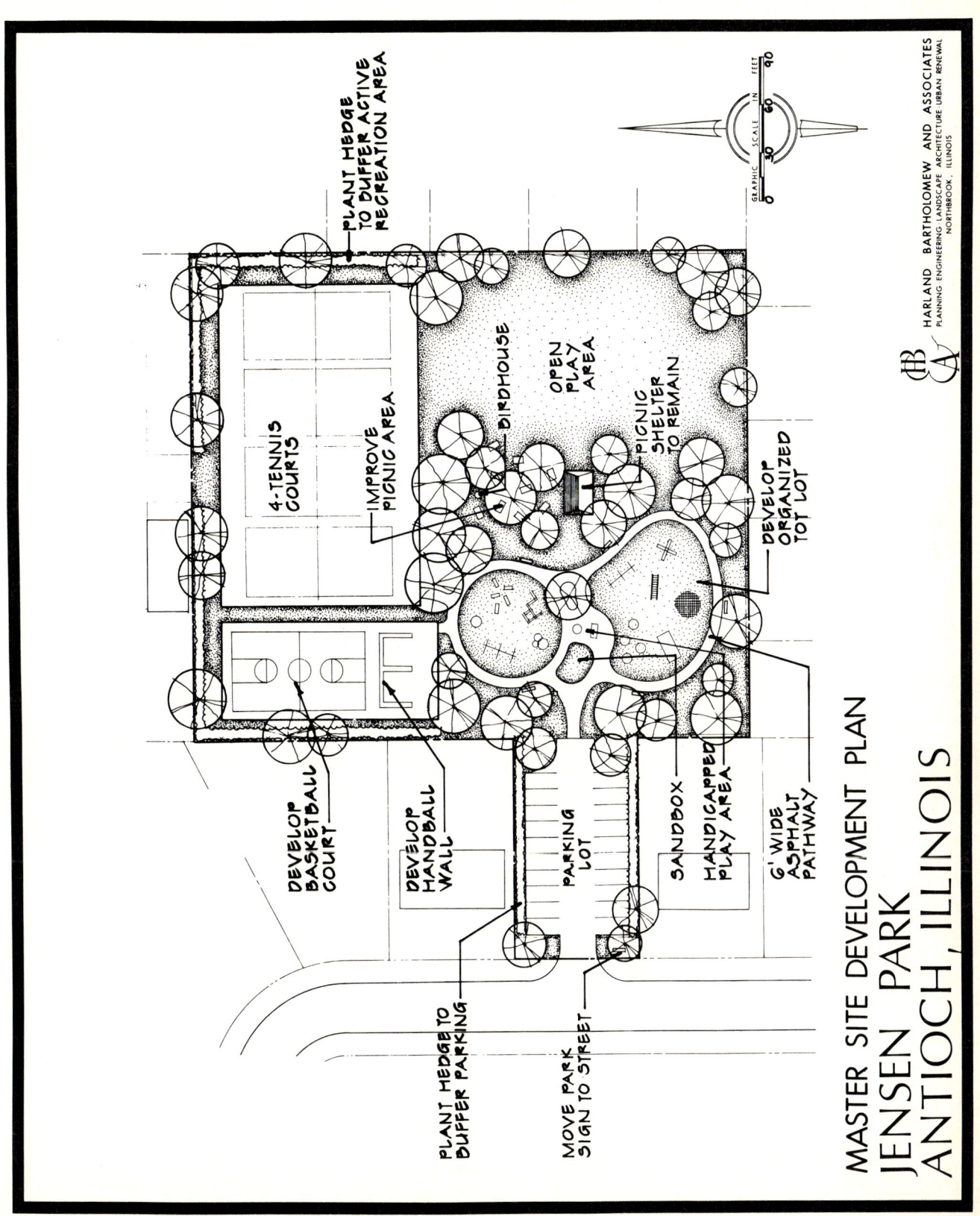

PARKS AND RECREATIONAL AREAS

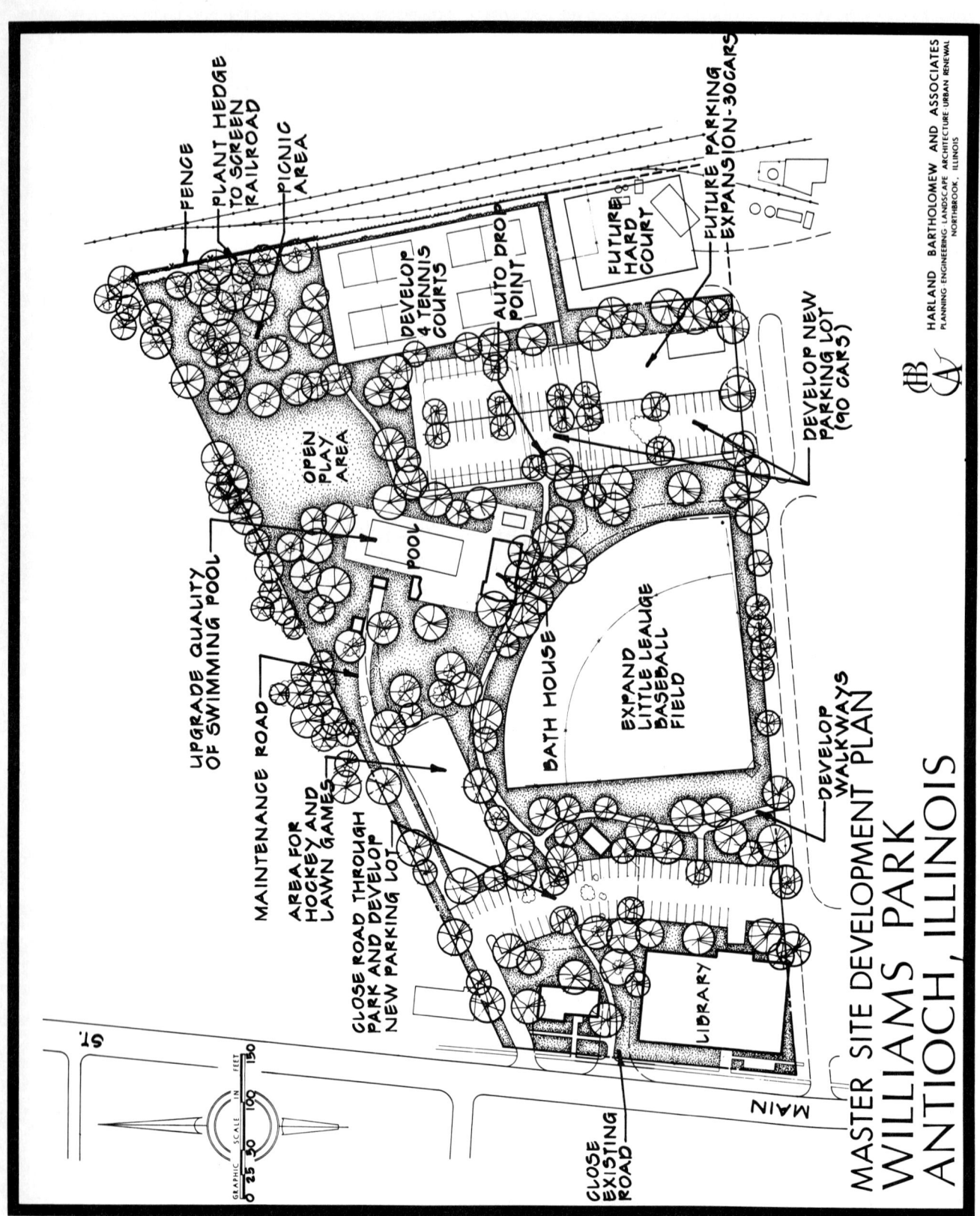

NINE
ENVIRONMENTAL ANALYSIS

ENVIRONMENTAL ANALYSIS FOR DEVELOPMENT ALTERNATIVES
Green Lake, Wisconsin

Green Lake is one of the deepest and most scenic lakes in Wisconsin. Seasonal recreational use has been great and will continue. Development standards are critically needed to protect the natural beauty and environmental quality people seek. Harland Bartholomew & Associates was asked to identify the ecological zones in the community and recommend uses and development standards for each zone.

The total land area is 320 acres in the city limits and five miles of lake shore. The population when the study began was about 1000 permanent residents with a strong seasonal influx. Seven ecological zones were identified based on natural land and water features and on past land uses: undeveloped forest; developed forest; and agricultural, urbanized, wetland, bay, and lake zones. The distribution of each zone was described, and recommended uses and development standards were developed for each zone. Principal uses are recreation, forestry, conservation/open space, residential, commercial, industrial, crop and livestock production, and extraction. Protection of water quality and aesthetic value of the lake was a prime consideration.

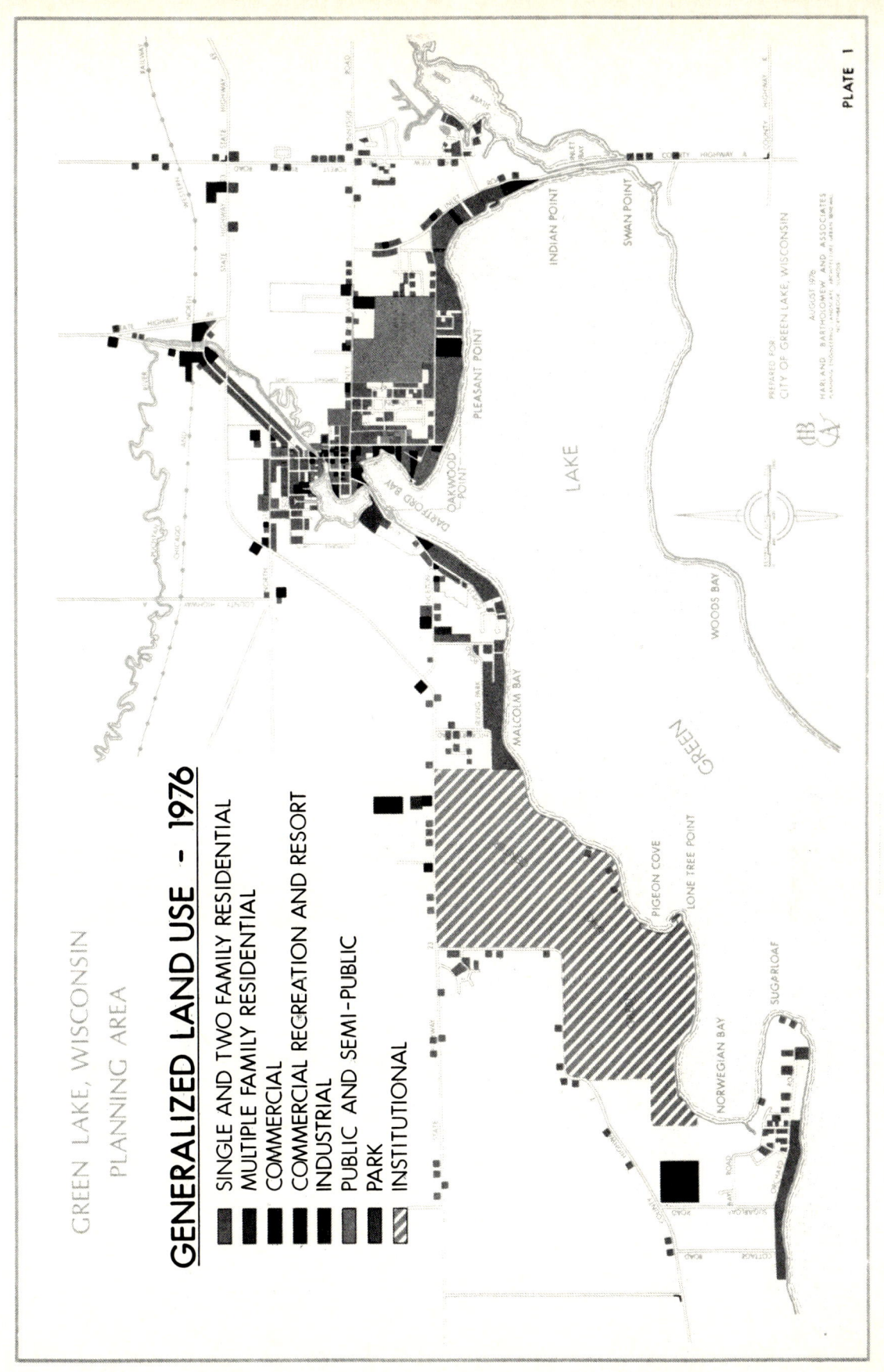

ENVIRONMENTAL ANALYSIS 235

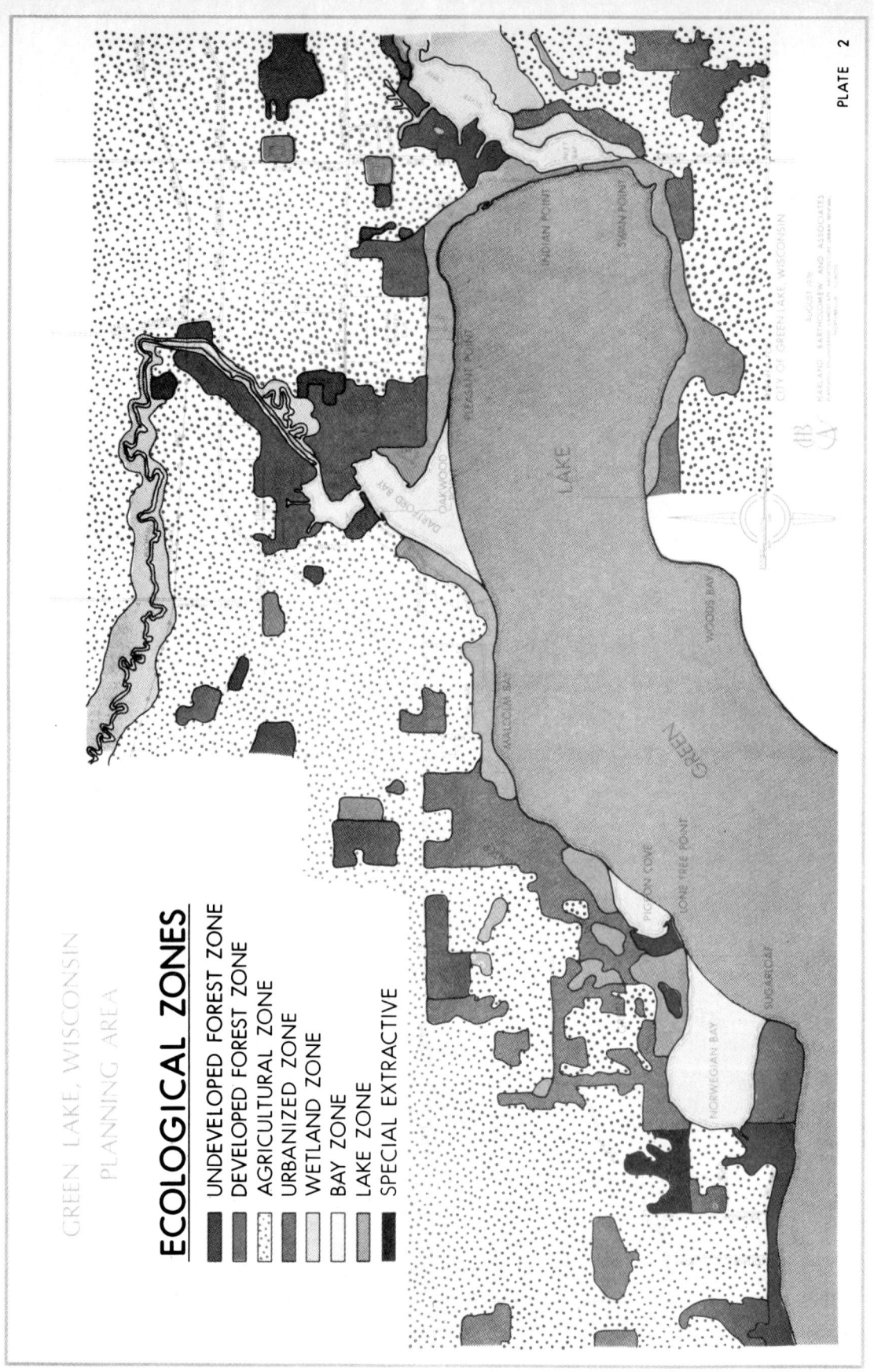

236 ENVIRONMENTAL ANALYSIS

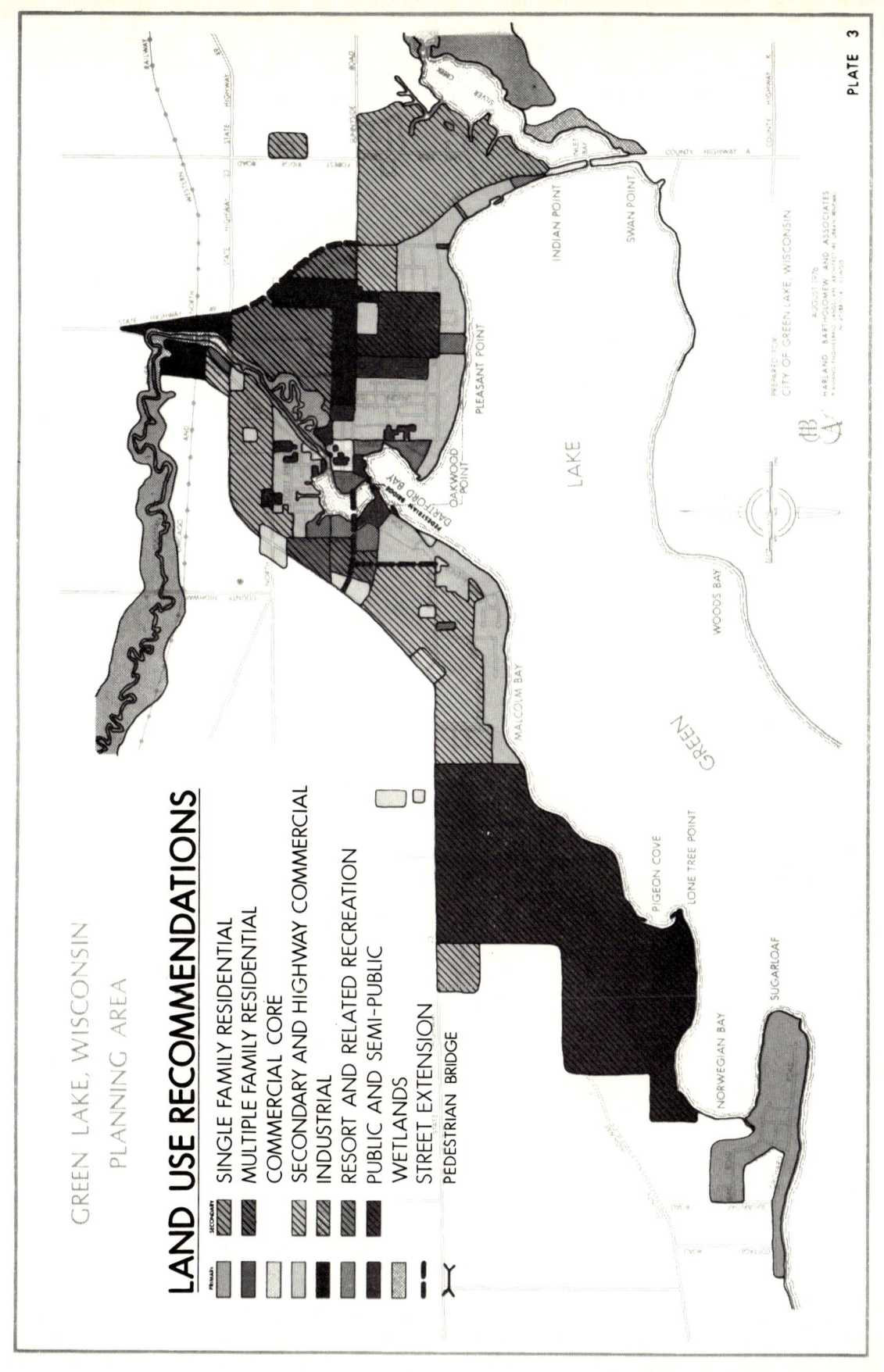

ENVIRONMENTAL ANALYSIS 237

TEN
TRANSPORTATION PLANNING

TRANSPORTATION PLAN UPDATE
South Bend Urban Area: South Bend, Mishawaka, and Elkhart, Indiana and Niles, Michigan

The South Bend Urban Area Transportation Plan is part of an overall interim study that includes preparation of a composite transportation plan for the region; refinement of the existing transportation plan for Elkhart; revision of the major route plan for Niles, Michigan; and revision of the major street and highway plan for the South Bend Urban Area.

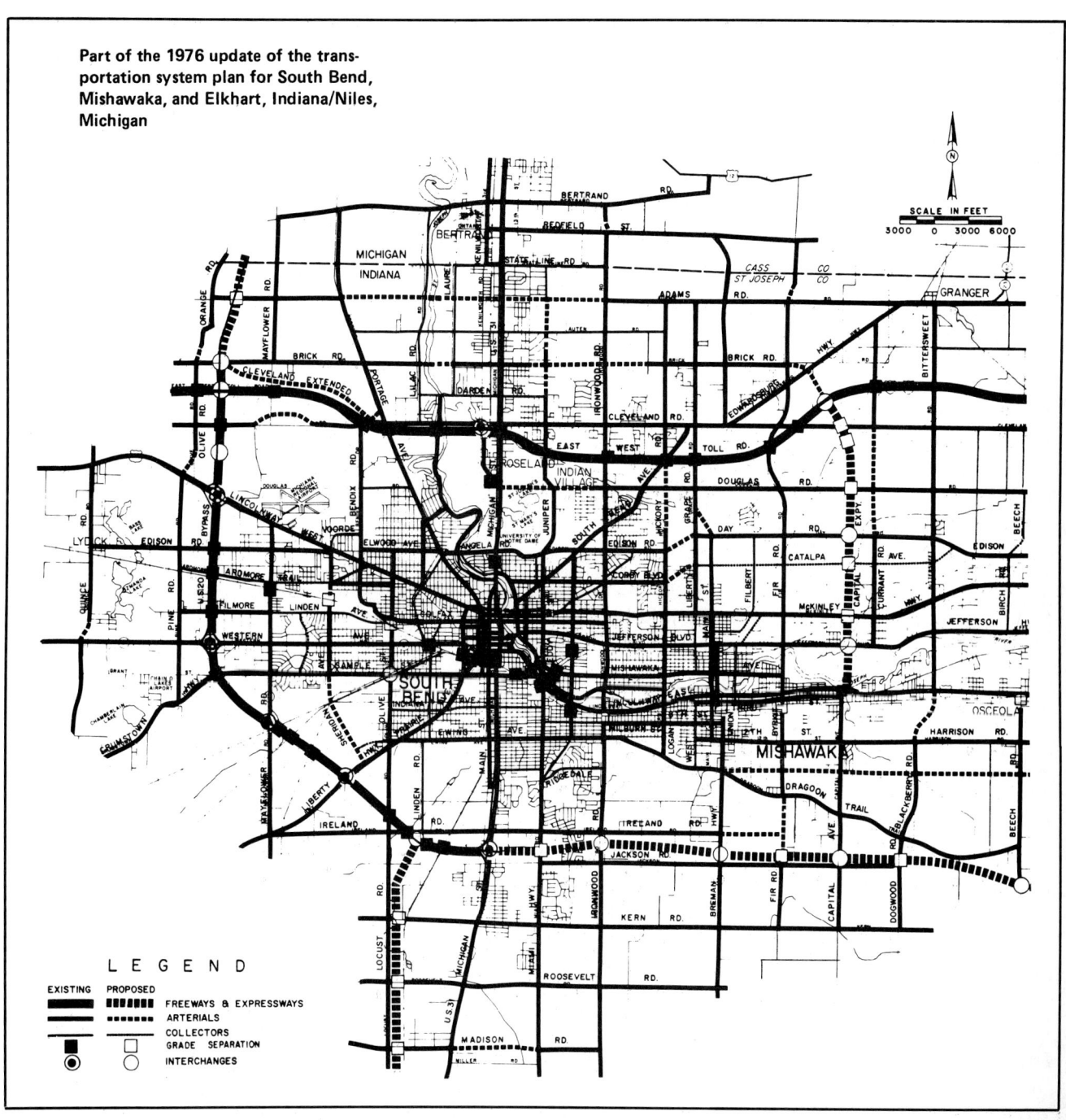

Part of the 1976 update of the transportation system plan for South Bend, Mishawaka, and Elkhart, Indiana/Niles, Michigan

U.S. 19 CORRIDOR STUDY
Pasco County, Florida

U.S. 19 is the only continuous major north-south route through west Pasco County, Florida, north of the Tampa-St. Petersburg metropolitan area. This highway consists of four through-traffic lanes, two in each direction, separated generally by a 40-foot grass median with turn lanes developed at intersections and at median openings. Because of the absence of other major highways, U.S. 19 must accommodate most of the north-south travel in west Pasco County, at times over 48,000 vehicles per day, on the four traffic lanes. With this heavy concentration of traffic, significant congestion and delay occur on U.S. 19.

A study was made; the objective was to determine short-range improvements to increase the vehicle-carrying capacity, safety, and operational characteristics of U.S. 19. The study comprised six elements: travel-time study, accident study, signal system study, intersection improvement study, parallel link analysis, and frontage road and widening evaluation. The parallel link analysis examined improvement to parallel roadways running several miles on either side of U.S. 19.

Following completion of the analysis, recommendations were made for widening intersecting streets to allow for additional green-light time to be allocated to U.S. 19. Double turn lanes were recommended at those locations that needed the additional capacity. Connecting segments of streets between subdivisions were recommended to allow access from one area to another. This traffic previously had to drive on U.S. 19. In addition to making these geometric improvements, it was recommended that widening U.S. 19 to six lanes would result in the greatest capacity and safety increase in the shortest period of time. Following completion of this study, approximately $6 million of federal funds from the 1978 Highway Act were allocated for improvements to U.S. 19.

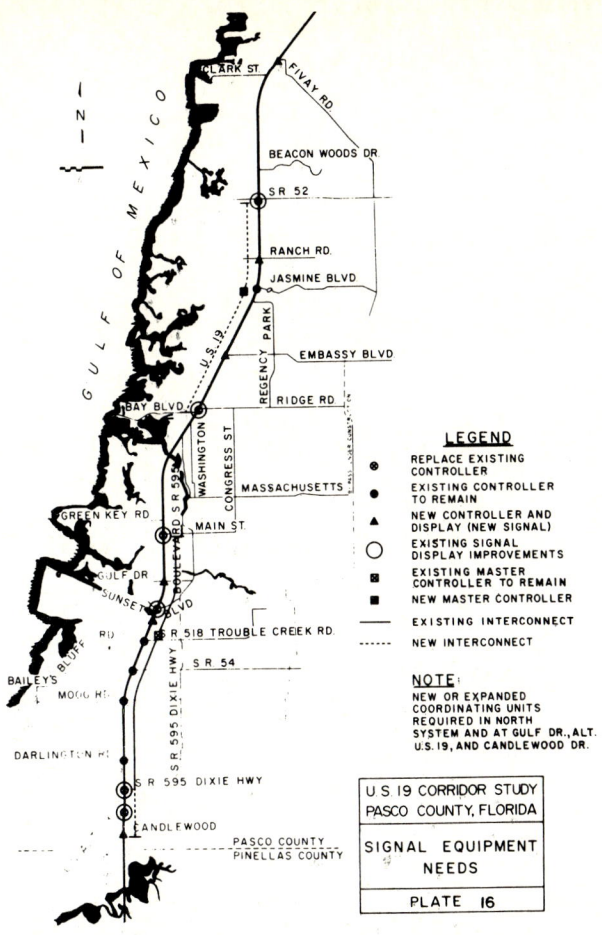

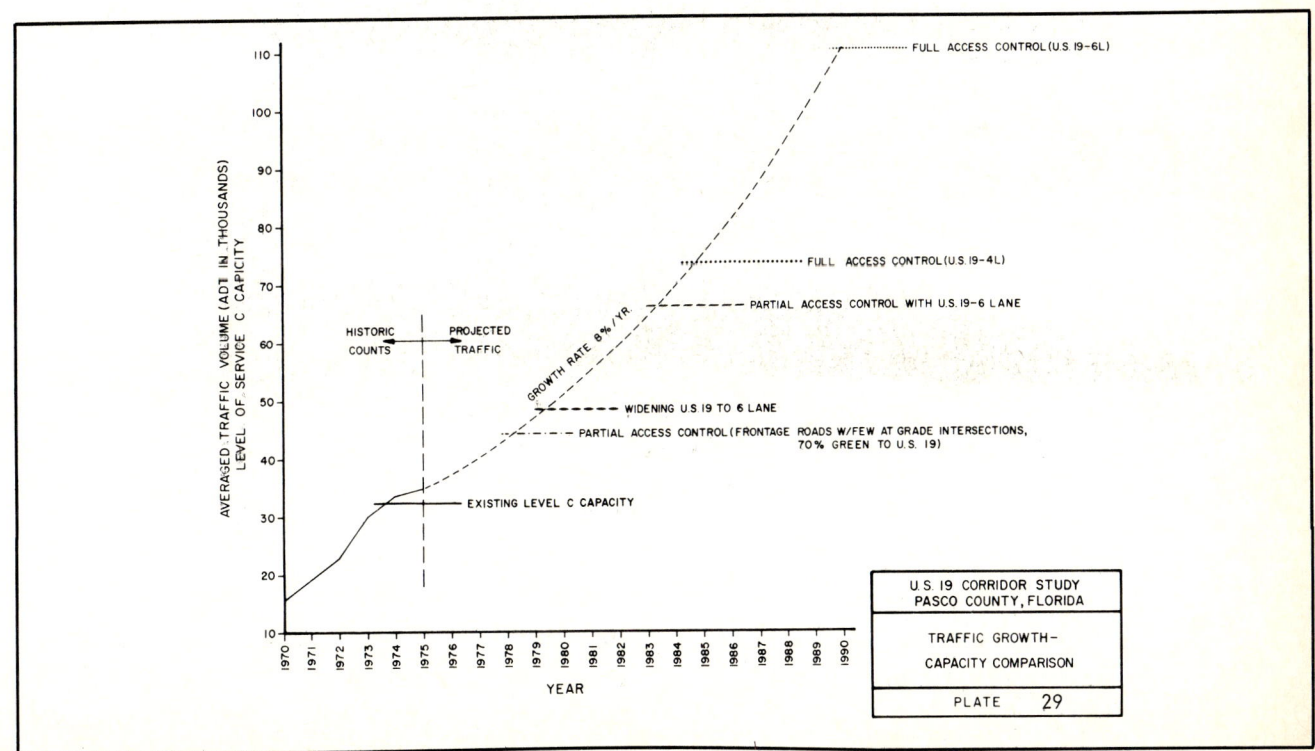

TRANSPORTATION PLANNING 243

CAMPUS TRANSIT PLAN
UNIVERSITY OF ALABAMA
Tuscaloosa, Alabama

Rapid expansion of University of Alabama facilities necessarily increased the distance between activity areas used by faculty and students. One result of this expansion was an increase in automobile and bicycle usage on campus, which contributed to congested and hazardous conditions on class days.

There was a need to discourage and possibly restrict vehicle use at certain campus locations. To replace over-use of vehicles on campus, a bus-shuttle system was recommended to provide service to all university activity areas in an effort to serve the internal campus needs while eliminating excessive movement, particularly between class hours. This system would serve two purposes: to transport on-campus residents between classroom buildings and housing facilities and to provide transportation service during the day for internal campus trips.

To facilitate movement between divergent areas of the campus, seven buses, each with a 33-passenger capacity, were recommended. These smaller buses require less space at stop locations and a smaller turning radius, which is important on narrow campus streets. The 33-passenger capacity would be adequate for meeting present and near-future campus needs.

CAMPUS TRANSIT PLAN
UNIVERSITY OF ALABAMA
TUSCALOOSA URBAN AREA TRANSIT STUDY

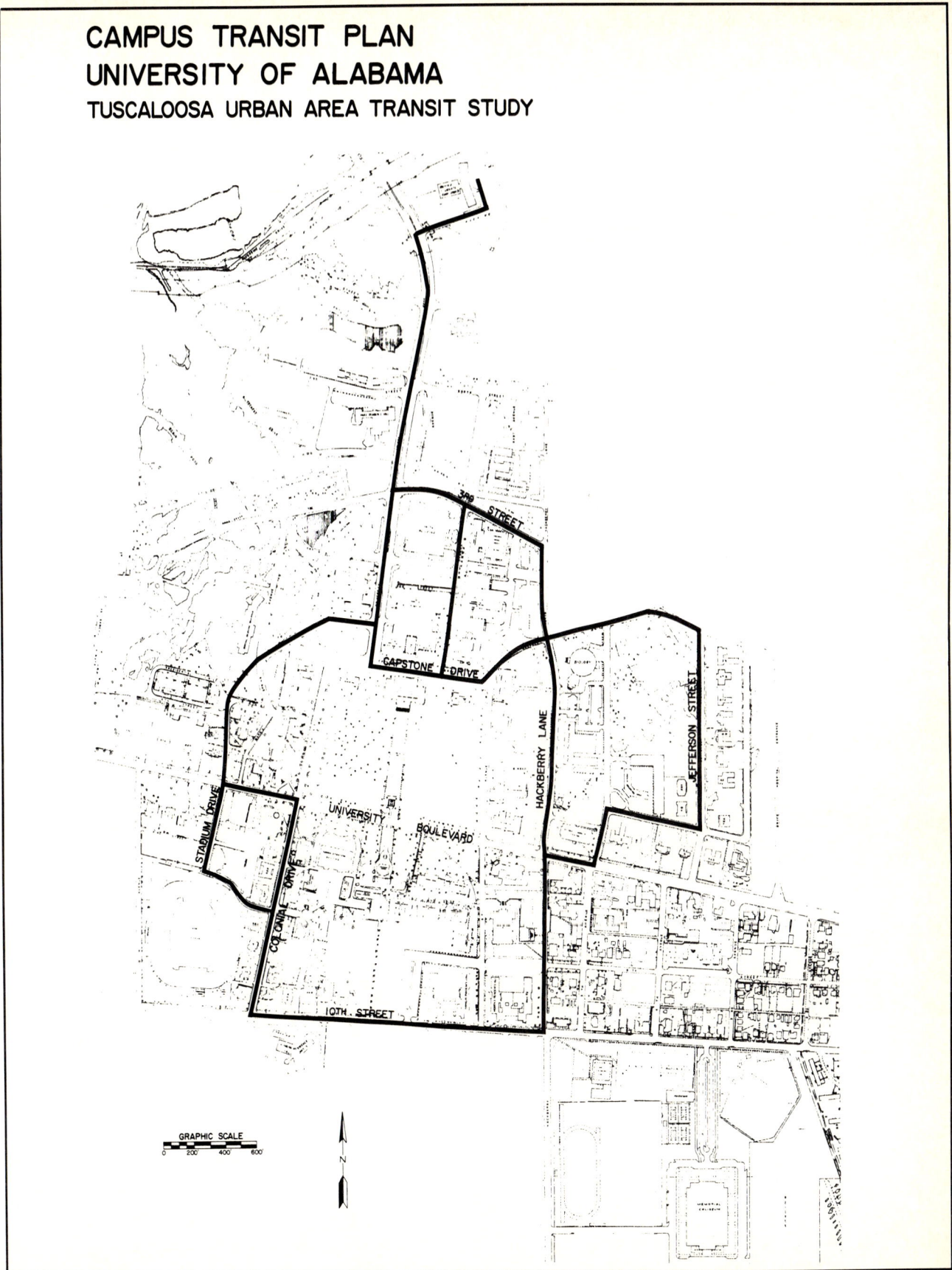

GOLDEN TRIANGLE REGIONAL AIRPORT MASTER PLAN
Columbus, Mississippi

This comprehensive plan included an analysis of existing airfield facilities and utilities and consideration of off-airport land use to determine maximum expansion capabilities. A noise study was done to determine compatible uses relative to the surrounding community. The final plan included a revised and updated Airport Layout Plan, recommendations for expansion of the aircraft parking apron, provisions for a separate cargo complex, and improvements to the airport terminal.

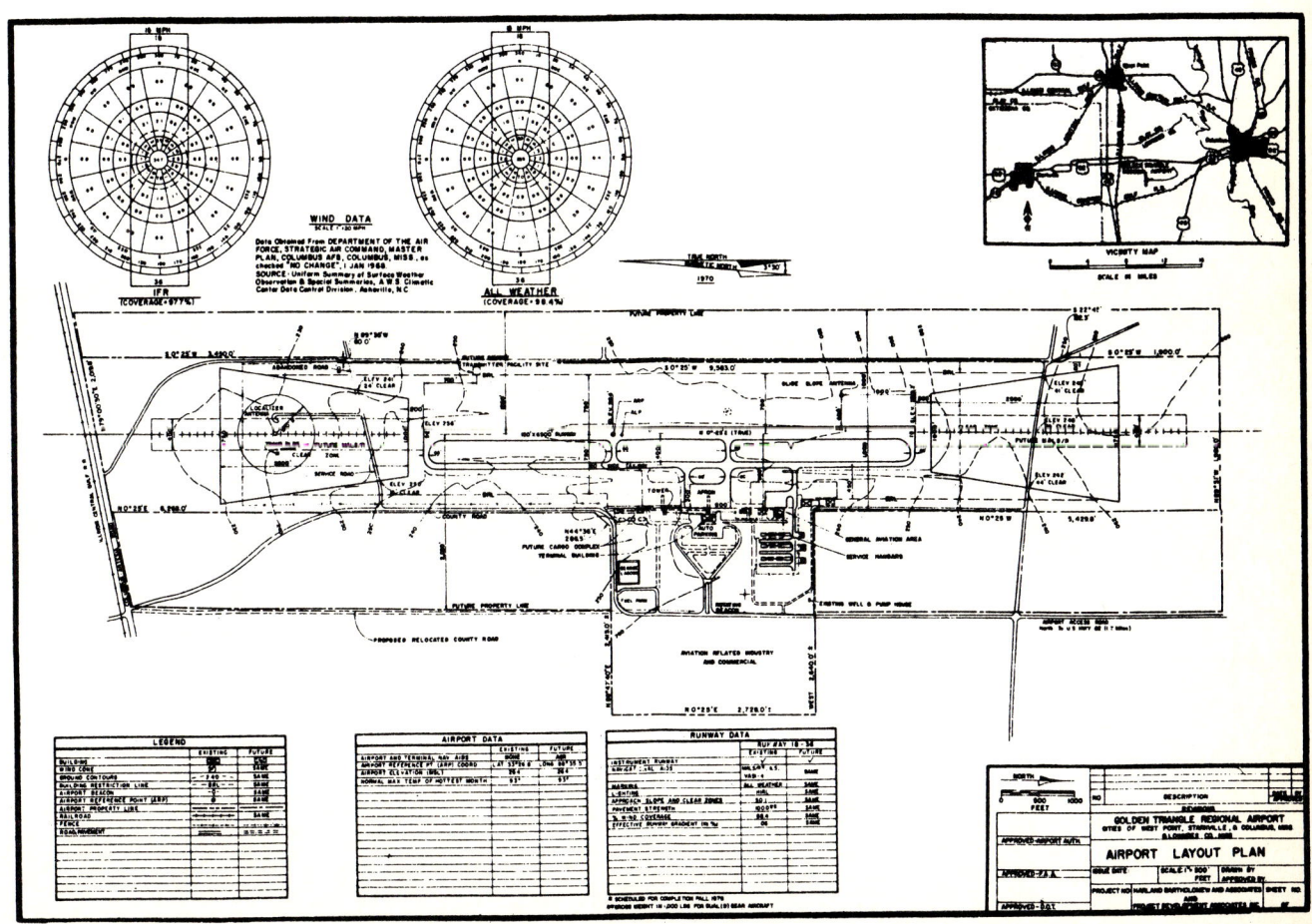

TRANSPORTATION PLANNING

SPRINGFIELD RAILROAD RELOCATION
Springfield, Illinois

The City of Springfield is located between St. Louis and Chicago. Five mainline railroad companies pass through but do not terminate in Springfield, nor do they provide major industrial service for the area. Therefore, recommendations involved consolidation and relocation as the most practicable solution for both the railroads and the city.

The community benefited by the solution in that the railroad was removed from the central city; the railroads benefited in terms of increased speeds and more efficient yard operations. The lines, which were generally at-grade through the city, were moved to a location south and east of the city to a grade-separated, fenced, common corridor.

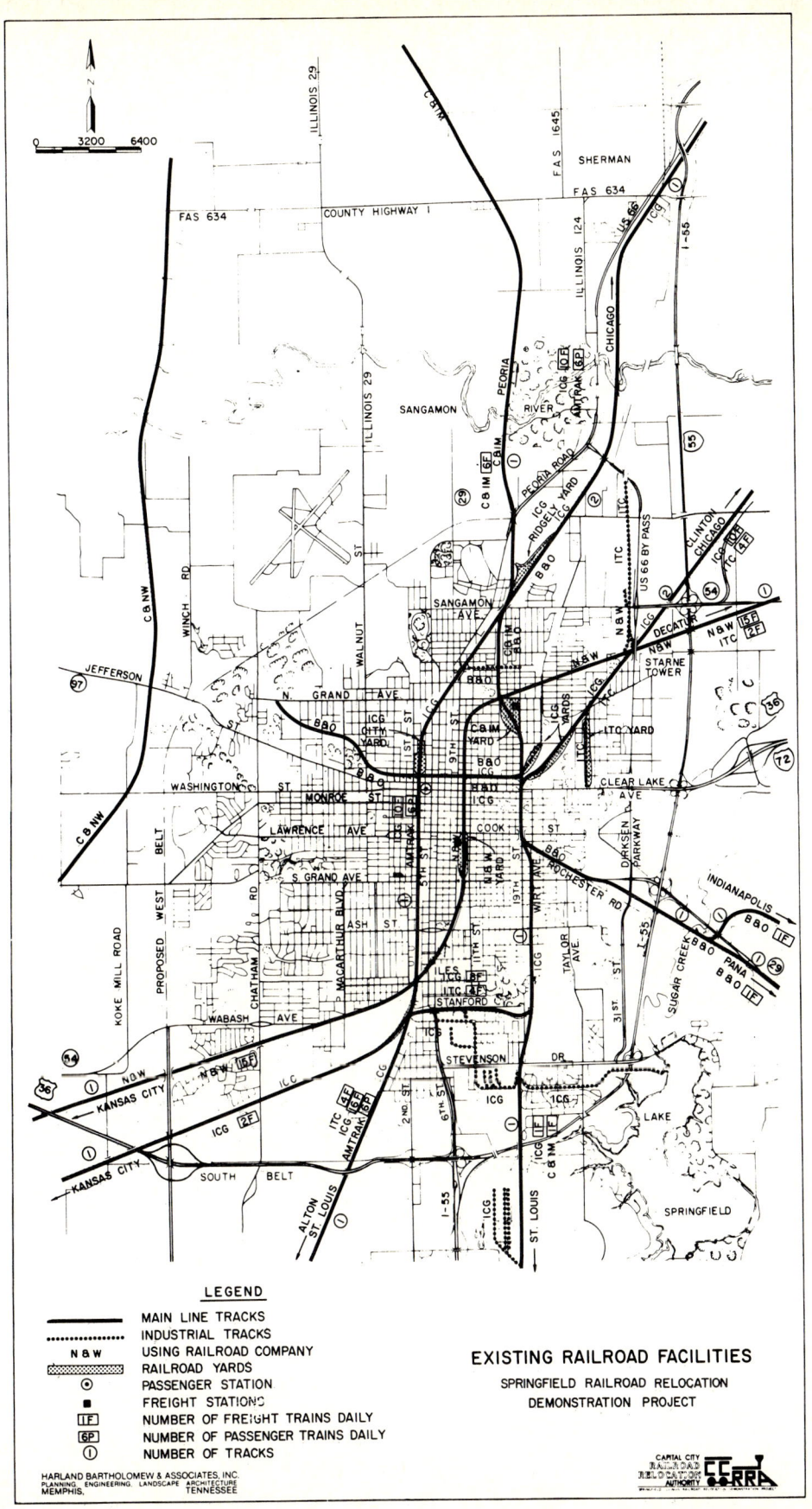

EXISTING RAILROAD FACILITIES

SPRINGFIELD RAILROAD RELOCATION
DEMONSTRATION PROJECT

TRANSPORTATION PLANNING 249

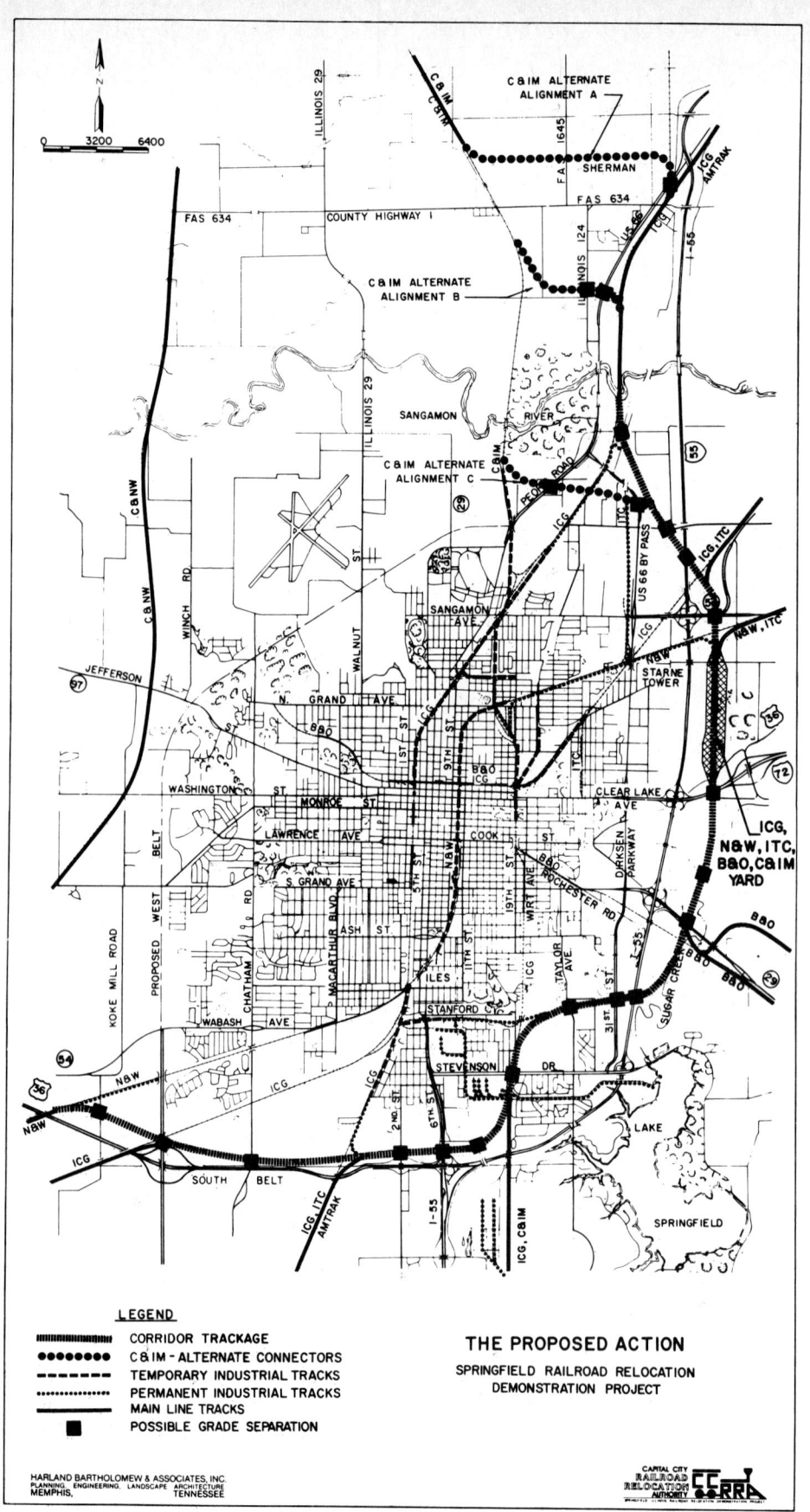

BROWNSVILLE-MATAMOROS RAILROAD RELOCATION DEMONSTRATION PROJECT
Brownsville, Texas and Matamoros, Mexico

The Brownsville-Matamoros project was handled as a binational transportation planning activity. Brownsville borders Mexico, and thus present and future Mexican planning alternatives were studied relative to the Brownsville planning. The overall study included a general social, economic, and environmental assessment of the area. Special technical studies included an air-quality analysis, a noise analysis, a vehicular-delay analysis, a railroad cost analysis, identification of port commodities and freight tariffs, an industrial survey, and a rail operations and needs analysis. Study results were documented bilingually in complementary planning reports.

Planning completed, a railroad relocation corridor to the east of Brownsville was selected. This route, which moved the railroad out of downtown Brownsville, allowed better development potential in the downtown area. A highlight of the project was the renovation of the Southern Pacific Rail Yard and Depot. The depot, built of adobe with a tile roof, was built near the turn of the century and resembles a California mission.

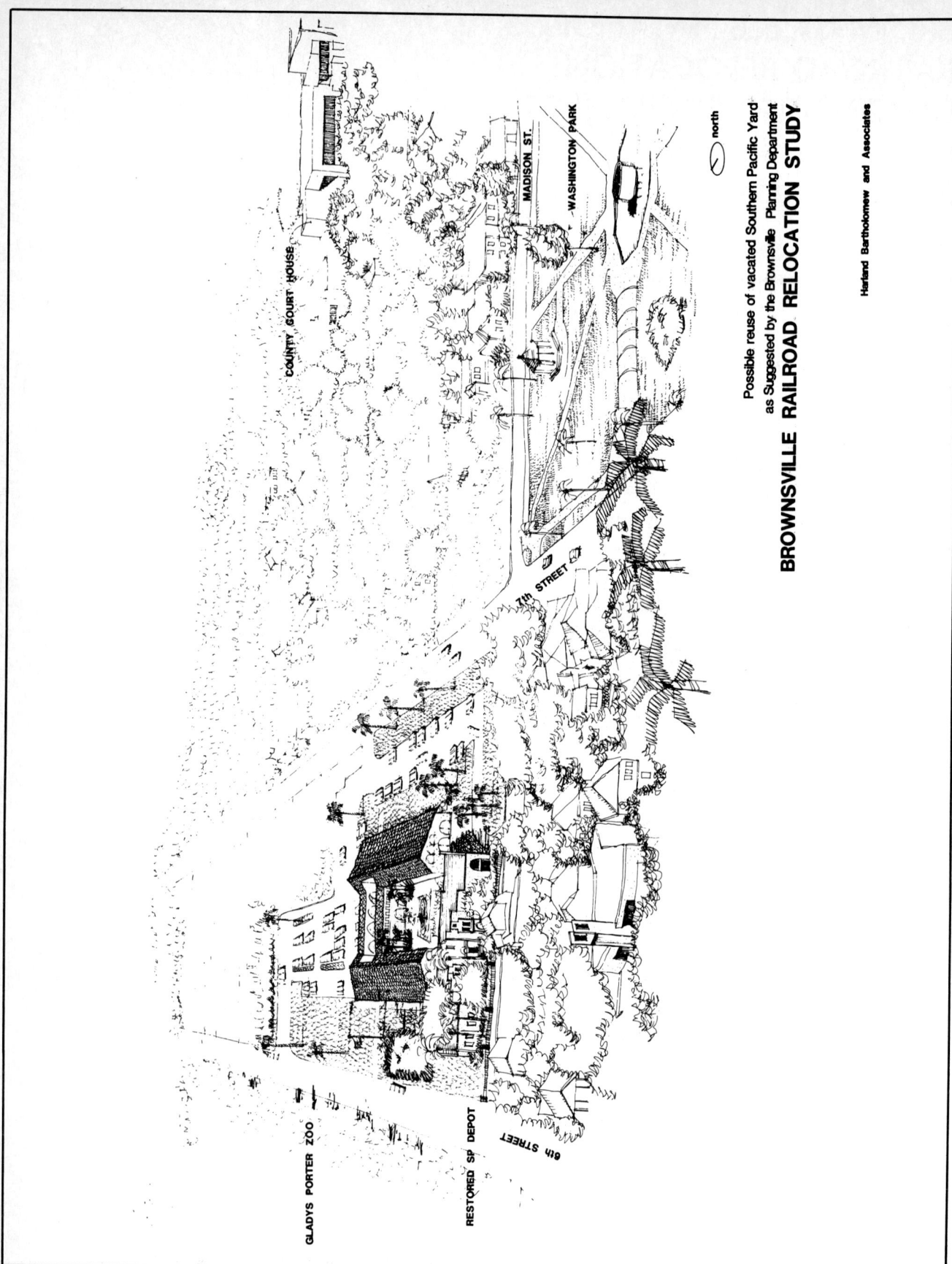

Possible Restoration of Southern Pacific Depot
BROWNSVILLE RAILROAD RELOCATION STUDY
Harland Bartholomew and Associates

GREENVILLE RAILROAD IMPROVEMENT
Greenville, Texas

In Greenville, Texas, land uses along the rail corridor were the major factor influencing the solution to railroad incompatibilities. The rail corridor under study passes through an area much less densely developed than the areas north and south of it. The development that has occurred is primarily commercial and industrial and is, therefore, not particularly incompatible with adjacent rail operations and facilities.

U.S. 69, which involves four at-grade crossings of two railroads, is the major north-south arterial across the corridor between the two parts of the city. The recommended solution in Greenville, therefore, became one of improving access for vehicles across the central rail corridor. To improve this access, a program of consolidation and grade separation within the central rail corridor was recommended. The program, which would be compatible with future planning, would align the Louisiana and Arkansas tracks to the present St. Louis-Southwestern alignment and would provide grade separation between these tracks and U.S. 69 to facilitate vehicular access across the corridor.

Artist's Conception of U.S. 69 Over the Railroads, on Embankment, Looking Southwest

TRANSPORTATION PLANNING 255

SAN ANTONIO DOWNTOWN "Y" PROJECT
San Antonio, Texas

Present day state-of-the-art structural systems and construction methods can provide economical solutions to the problems of erecting elevated roadways in an urban environment such as the Y-shaped Interstate highway junction in San Antonio with minimal disruption of traffic. This project is a three-lane, 40-foot-high structure supported by a single row of columns built on each side of—but not covering—the existing four-lane highways.

The construction sequence was arranged so that work began only on outbound lanes at the outer ends of all three segments of the Y. When construction reaches the interchange, work will shift to the inbound lanes. This sequence allows motorists to use the road as it is built, thus avoiding traffic stoppages.

The structure is a composite precast and cast-in-place system that can be erected from above using a launching truss.

T. Y. Lin International, San Francisco, developed the system. Harland Bartholomew & Associates developed the construction sequence method. Bill Shannon, Inc., San Antonio, was low bidder.

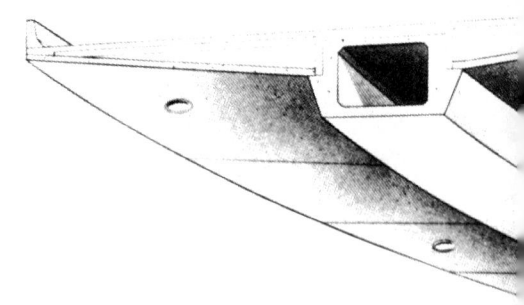

TRANSPORTATION PLANNING 257

ELEVEN
MILITARY PARKS

FORT CAMPBELL MASTER PLANNING
Fort Campbell, Kentucky

Fort Campbell is the home of the Army's famous 101st Airborne Division. The Fort is also a major training center for armored and infantry units as well as basic combat training. The Fort supports a major Army airfield. The installation occupies over 100,000 acres in Kentucky and Tennessee. The main built-up portion of the base is located about 10 miles north of Clarksville, Tennessee, and about 20 miles south of Hopkinsville, Kentucky. At the time of the planning, Clarksville had a population of about 52,000; Hopkinsville, 21,000.

The Master Plan for Fort Campbell described the future development of the installation under normal peacetime conditions. The plan analyzed land-use relationships, environmental setting of the installation, and utility systems required to service the installation. A Community Center complex was developed to provide convenient access to administrative, shopping, and recreation facilities. The complex included the expansion of the Post Exchange (PX), a new chapel, a child-care center, a hospital, and a cultural/recreation complex including music and drama buildings.

The Expansion Capability Study for Fort Campbell identified the maximal population that could be accommodated considering the limitations of housing, utilities, and other physical facilities, as well as the training capacity of the installation. Based on this maximal capability population, an expansion capability site plan was prepared showing the location of required housing, maintenance, training, community services, and other facilities on the post.

The Environmental Impact Statement (EIS) for the ongoing mission at Fort Campbell analyzed the probable impacts on the environment of the continued use of the post. Among the factors that were considered in the EIS were water and air quality, noise, socio-economic factors, land-use factors, ecology, history and archaeology, energy resources and conservation, and hazardous and toxic substances. A significant concern was noise impact from extensive helicopter operations in the area.

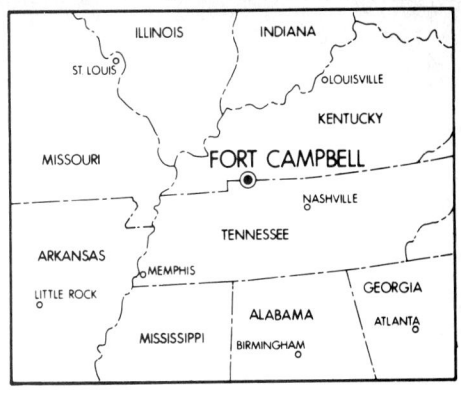

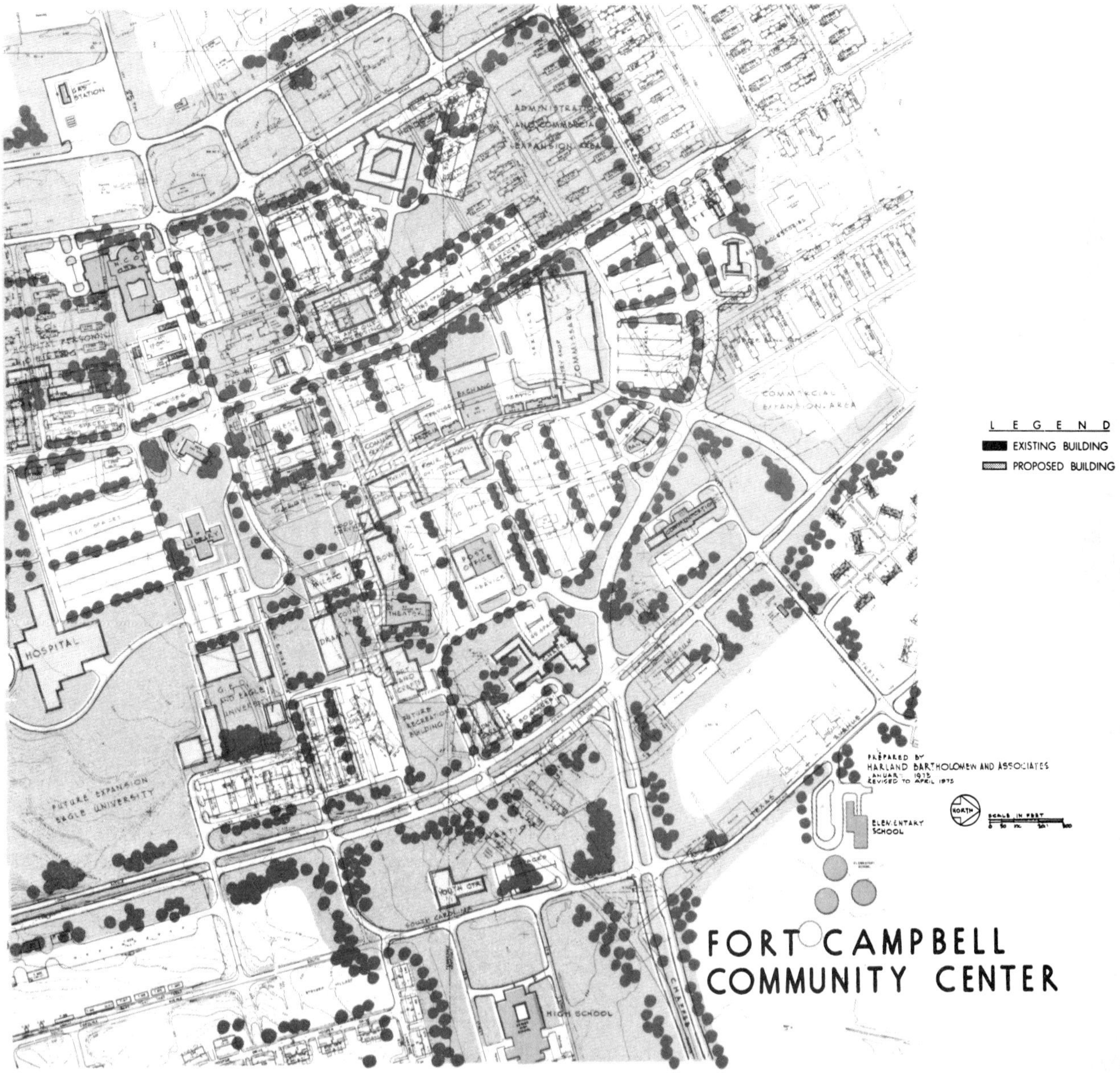

FORT CAMPBELL COMMUNITY CENTER

MILITARY PARKS

FORT SHERIDAN MASTER PLAN
Lake County, Illinois

Fort Sheridan, 25 miles north of downtown Chicago, is an administrative and logistic support center for a number of midwest Army activities. Construction of the original facilities began in 1889 and continued until 1915. A number of the original buildings are architecturally outstanding and have been included in the National Register of Historic Places.

The Master Plan takes into account not only the historical character of Fort Sheridan, but also the preservation of several heavily wooded ravines along the shore of Lake Michigan. Extreme care was taken in the development of the plan to keep these areas in their natural state. Another environmental consideration was prevention of severe erosion along the lake shore.

The plan provided for replacement of temporary World War II structures with new facilities, taking into account the limited land area and suburban setting of the post.

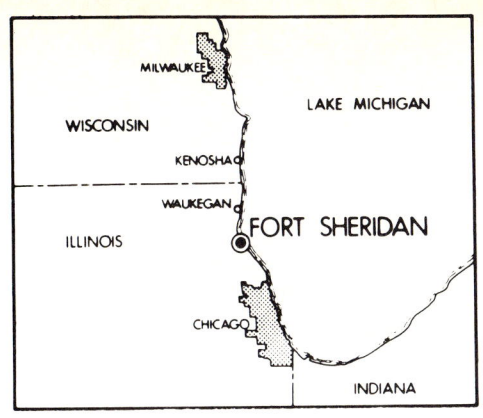

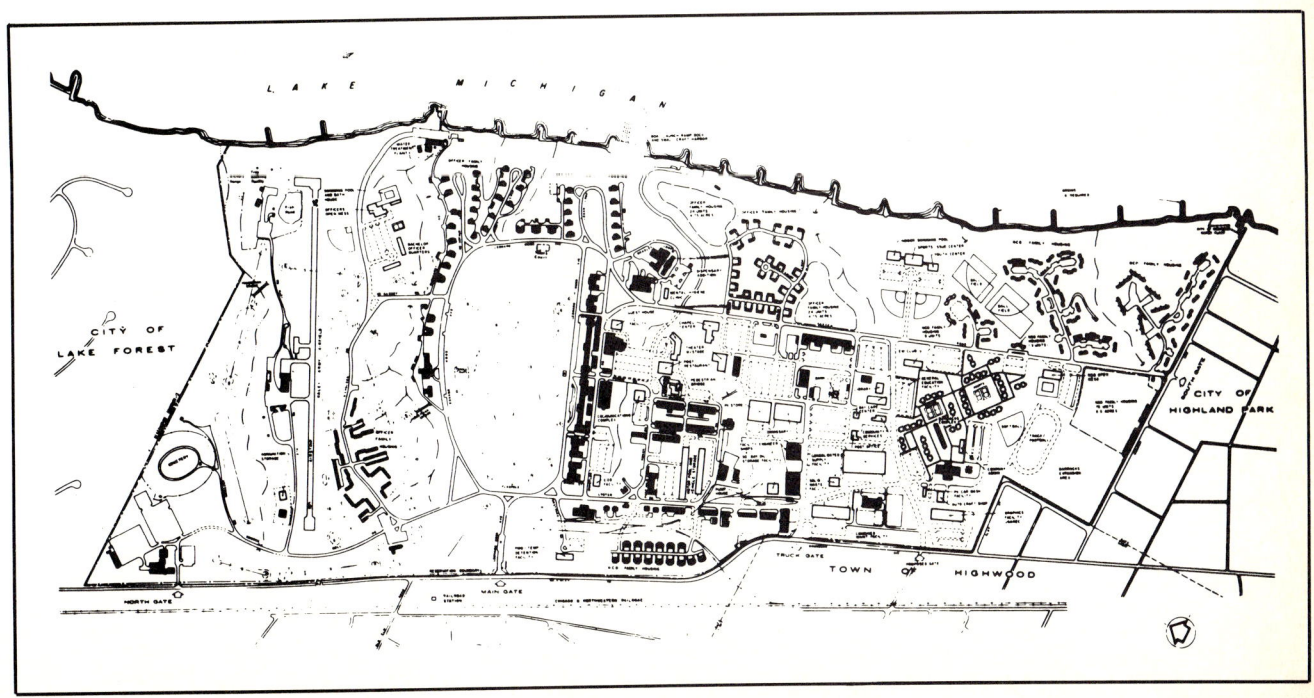

MILITARY PARKS 263

ROCK ISLAND ARSENAL MASTER PLAN
Rock Island, Illinois

The Rock Island Arsenal is located on a 950-acre island in the Mississippi River bordered by the cities of Davenport and Bettendorf in Iowa and Moline and Rock Island in Illinois. These four communities, referred to as the "Quad-Cities," have a combined population of over 200,000. The Arsenal employs approximately 7500 persons, about five percent of the Quad-Cities' total work force.

Established in 1862, the Arsenal has been an important center for the design, production, fabrication, testing, and storage of armaments since the Civil War. Manufacturing activities at the Arsenal have gradually declined and have been replaced by predominantly administrative functions. Today, the Rock Island Arsenal supports a limited industrial and research mission as well as various tenant commands.

The Arsenal has been designated a National Historic Place. The main historic area of the Arsenal features a series of ten limestone buildings constructed between 1872 and 1918 for manufacturing and assembly. While some industrial functions remain in these buildings, many of the historic shop buildings have been converted to administrative use.

The major objectives of the Master Plan were to retain the Arsenal's manufacturing capability, preserve and enhance the historical aspects, discourage unusually high concentrations of employment in certain areas, and to recognize and protect the original design.

The future development plan recognized the significant historical value of the Arsenal and attempted to achieve a realistic balance between today's requirements and the past heritage of the installation.

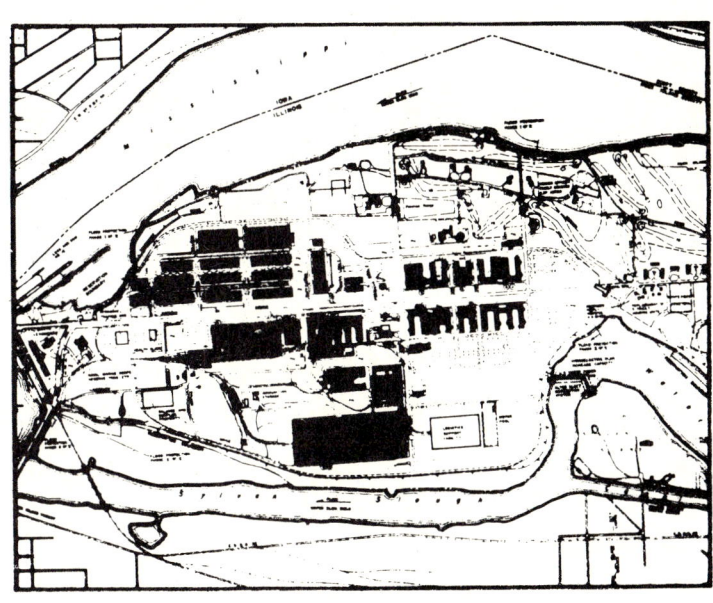

Sketch of Possible
Landscape Treatment of
Shop Building Courtyards

JEFFERSON BARRACKS NATIONAL CEMETERY
Saint Louis County, Missouri

Harland Bartholomew & Associates was contracted to prepare a long range Master Plan and subsequent construction drawings and specifications for the first stage of development of a 200-acre portion of Jefferson Barracks National Cemetery. The 200-acre portion of the cemetery was extraordinarily complex and required the effort of all disciplines of the firm. The presence of a dense white oak forest plus numerous sinkholes characteristic of a Karst topography posed obvious problems but created striking site planning opportunities. Because of steep slopes, shallow soil overburden, sinkholes, and other similar features, only about one-half of the undeveloped site was suitable for conventional gravesite areas. The remaining areas were left undisturbed except for occasional walkways or used for a limited number of carefully designed crypt burial facilities. A sizable creek running through the site plus highly erodible soil conditions posed significant design and construction problems. Because of the degree of technical analysis required for this project, the firm was presented a Merit Award by the American Society of Landscape Architects in their 1976 Professional Design Competition.

Jefferson Barracks National Cemetery is the nation's fourth largest national cemetery in land area and in the number of total interments. Of a total area of 307 acres, however, only 105 acres had been developed for use as gravesites prior to the study. Cemetery operations and projected interment rates were evaluated to provide sequential phases of improvements within the remaining undeveloped area that would serve the community beyond the turn of the century.

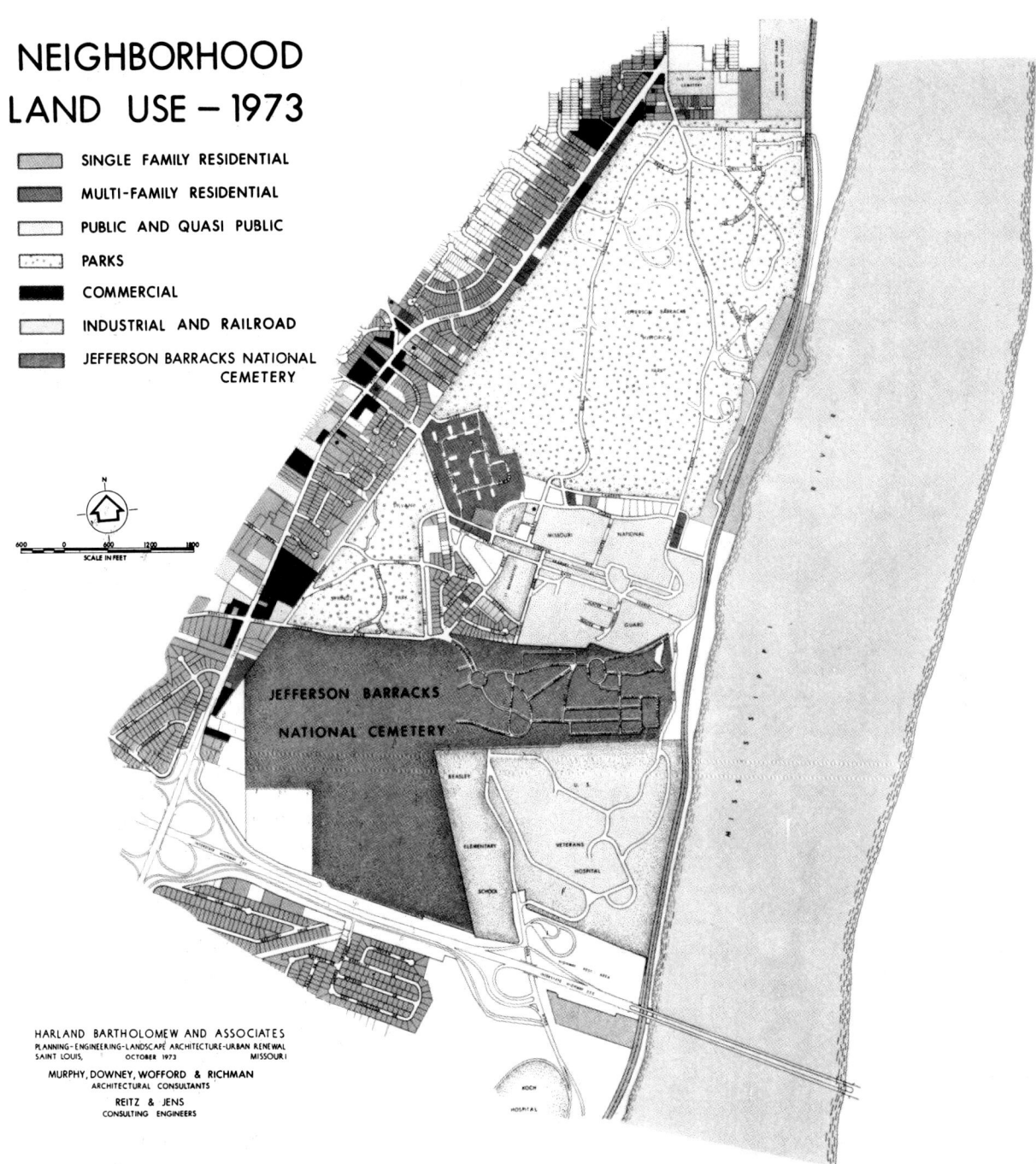

MILITARY PARKS 267

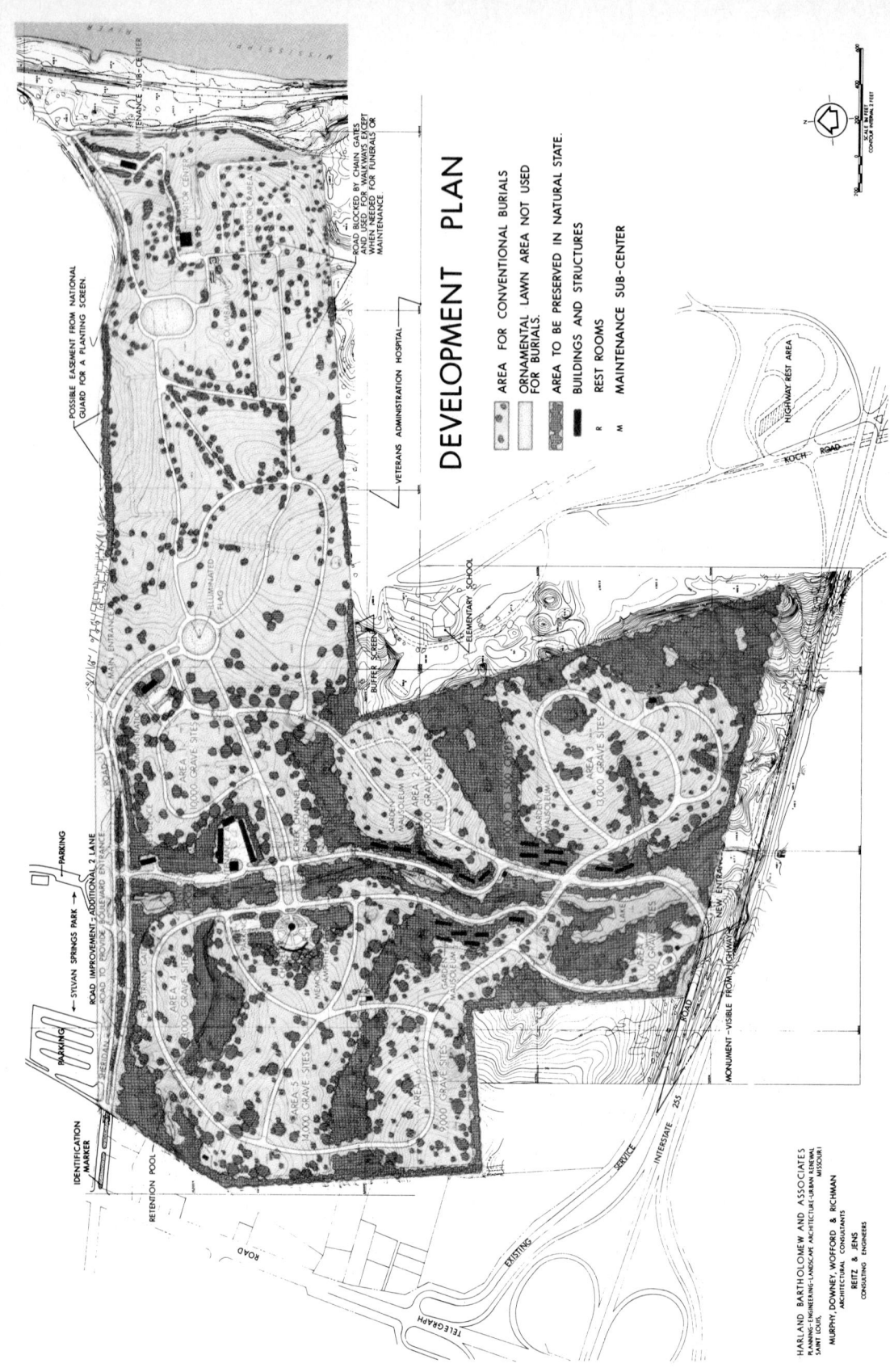

268 MILITARY PARKS

MILITARY PARKS 269

270 MILITARY PARKS

AIR INSTALLATION COMPATIBLE USE ZONES STUDY (AICUZ)
Glenview Naval Air Station
Glenview, Illinois

When the noise-impact zones and accident-potential zones are superimposed upon the air installation and the vicinity, the area within the boundary of these zones is defined as the AICUZ. The NAS Glenview AICUZ is composed of eight separate zones, portions of seven of which extend beyond the station boundary. The most extensive zones are to the north of the station reflecting the preferential runway policy.

Policies and programs in the AICUZ area would be considered in terms of three broad development objectives: (1) preventing incompatible development of vacant land, (2) where possible, remedying the problem of existing incompatible land uses, and (3) preventing any changes in compatible land uses that would make them incompatible. Each of these objectives is an integral part of the intent of the AICUZ program to direct future development in a way that benefits both the air installations and the surrounding communities of which they are a part.

AIR INSTALLATION COMPATIBLE USE ZONES STUDY
NAS GLENVIEW, ILLINOIS

LEGEND

■ NO NEW DEVELOPMENT

▨ RESTRICTED NEW DEVELOPMENT

▢ NO RESTRICTIONS

1. RESTRICTIONS ON USES SHOULD INCLUDE NO ABOVE GROUND GROWTH OR STRUCTURES THAT COULD INTERFERE WITH AIRCRAFT OPERATIONS AND NO USES THAT WOULD ATTRACT PUBLIC ASSEMBLY OTHER THAN THAT REQUIRED BY AGRICULTURE

2. RESTRICTION ON USES WHICH WOULD PRODUCE EMISSIONS INTO THE AIR THAT COULD INTERFERE WITH AIRCRAFT OPERATIONS

3. RESTRICTION ON COMMUNICATION ACTIVITIES WHICH WOULD PRODUCE TRANSMISSIONS (ELECTRICAL OR OTHERWISE), THAT WOULD INTERFERE WITH AIRCRAFT OPERATIONS

4. RESTRICTION ON USES THAT ARE PARTICULARLY LABOR INTENSIVE, UNLESS USES HAVE APPROPRIATE GROUND COVER RESTRICTION

5. RESTRICTION ON USES NOT PROVIDING ADEQUATE SOUND ATTENUATION

6. RESTRICTION ON USES THAT WOULD ATTRACT LARGE PUBLIC ASSEMBLY

NOTE: ZONE 1 - LESS THAN 65 L_{dn}
ZONE 2 - 65 L_{dn} TO 75 L_{dn}
ZONE 3 - GREATER THAN 75 L_{dn}

HARLAND BARTHOLOMEW AND ASSOCIATES
PLANNING-ENGINEERING-LANDSCAPE ARCHITECTURE-URBAN RENEWAL
NORTHBROOK, ILLINOIS

AICUZ / LAND USE OBJECTIVES

LAND USE CATEGORY	CLEAR ZONE ANY NOISE ZONE	APZ I NOISE ZONE 2	APZ I NOISE ZONE 1	APZ II NOISE ZONE 2	APZ II NOISE ZONE 1	NO APZ NOISE ZONE 2	NO APZ NOISE ZONE 1
RESIDENTIAL							
SINGLE FAMILY (LOW DENSITY)	■	■	■	■	■	5	5
SINGLE FAMILY (MODERATE DENSITY)	■	■	■	5	5	5	5
TWO AND MULTIPLE FAMILY DWELLING	■	■	■	■	5	5	5
MOBILE HOME PARKS OR COURTS	■	■	■	■	■	■	5
OTHER RESIDENTIAL	■	■	■	■	■	5	5
INDUSTRIAL / MANUFACTURING							
TEXTILE AND PLASTIC PRODUCTS	■	■	■	■	2	2	2
CHEMICAL AND PETROLEUM PRODUCTS	■	2,4,5	2,4	2,5	2	2,5	2
PROF. SCIENTIFIC AND CONTROLLING INSTR.	■	■	■	■	■	■	2
OTHER MANUFACTURING	■	■	■	2,5	2	2,5	2
TRANSPORTATION, COMMUNICATIONS AND UTILITIES							
RAILROAD, UTILITY AND STREET RIGHT-OF-WAY	■	3,5	3	3,5	3	3,5	3
COMMUNICATION	■	■	■	■	■	■	■
OTHER UTILITIES	■	■	■	■	■	■	■
OTHER TRANSPORTATION	■	■	■	■	■	■	■
COMMERCIAL / RETAIL TRADE							
WHOLESALE TRADE	■	4,5	4	5	6	5	
RETAIL TRADE	■	■	■	5	5	5	
EATING AND DRINKING PLACES	■	■	■	■	■	■	
PERSONAL AND BUSINESS SERVICES							
FINANCE, INSURANCE, REAL ESTATE AND PROF. SERVICES	■	■	■	■	4		
PERSONAL AND BUSINESS SERVICES	■	4,5	4	5	4	5	
REPAIR AND CONSTRUCTION SERVICES	■	■	■	5	4	5	
OTHER SERVICES	■	■	■	■	■	■	
PUBLIC AND INSTITUTIONAL SERVICES							
GOVERNMENT SERVICES	■	■	■	■	■	■	■
EDUCATIONAL SERVICES	■	■	■	■	■	■	■
CULTURAL AND RELIGIOUS ACTIVITIES	■	■	■	■	■	■	■
MEDICAL AND OTHER HEALTH SERVICES	■	■	■	■	■	■	■
CEMETERIES	■	■	■	■	■	■	■
OTHER PUBLIC AND INSTITUTIONAL ACTIVITIES	■	■	■	■	■	■	■
OUTDOOR RECREATION							
PLAYGROUNDS, NEIGHBORHOOD AND COMMUNITY PARKS	■	■	6	6	6		
NATURE EXHIBITS	■	■	■	■	■		
SPECTATOR SPORTS AND ENTERTAINMENT ASSEMBLIES	■	■	6	6	6	5	
GOLF COURSES AND RIDING STABLES	■	■	6	■	6		
OTHER OUTDOOR RECREATION	■	■	■	■	■		
RESOURCE PRODUCTION, EXTRACTION AND OPEN LAND							
AGRICULTURE (EXCEPT LIVESTOCK)	1						
LIVESTOCK FARMING AND FISHING	■	■	■	■	■	■	
FORESTRY AND MINING ACTIVITIES							
PERMANENT OPEN SPACE	1	6	6	6	6	6	6
WATER AREAS							

MILITARY PARKS

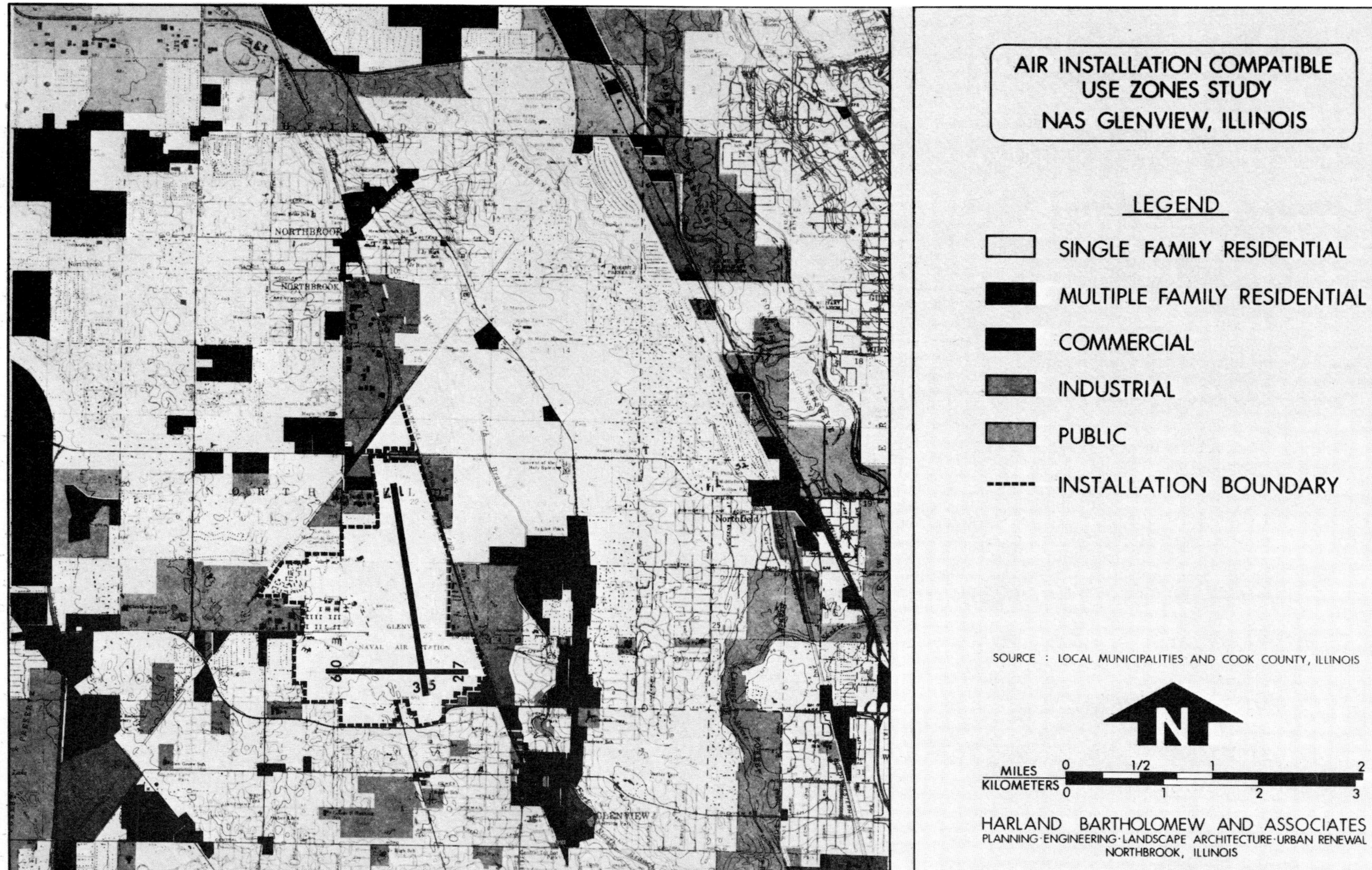

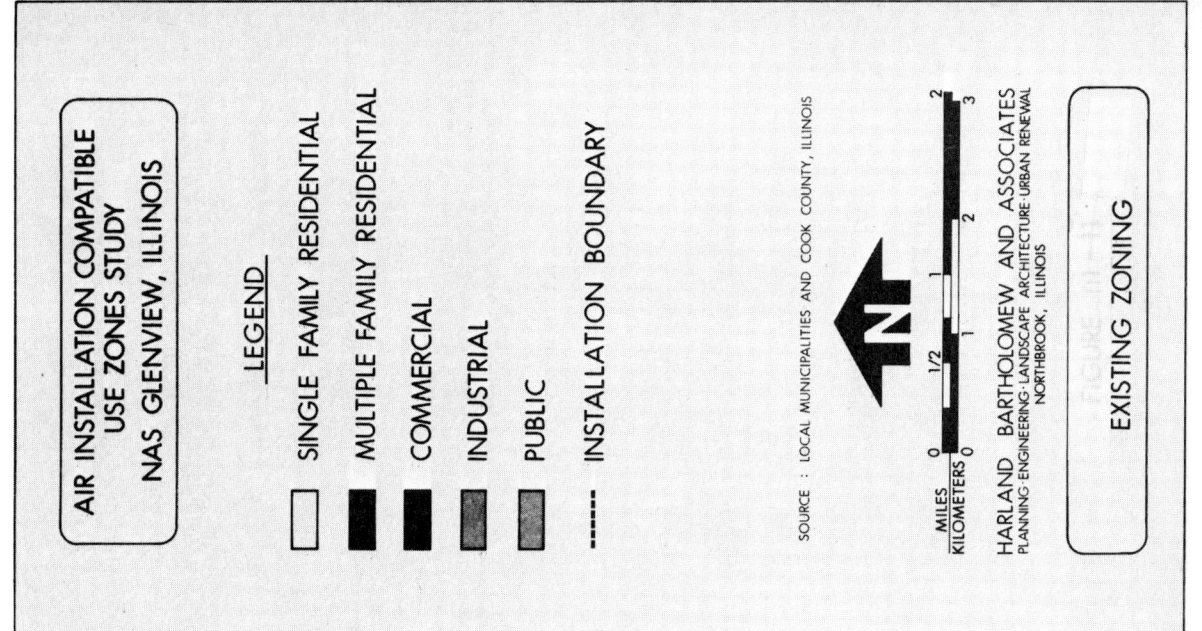

MILITARY PARKS 273

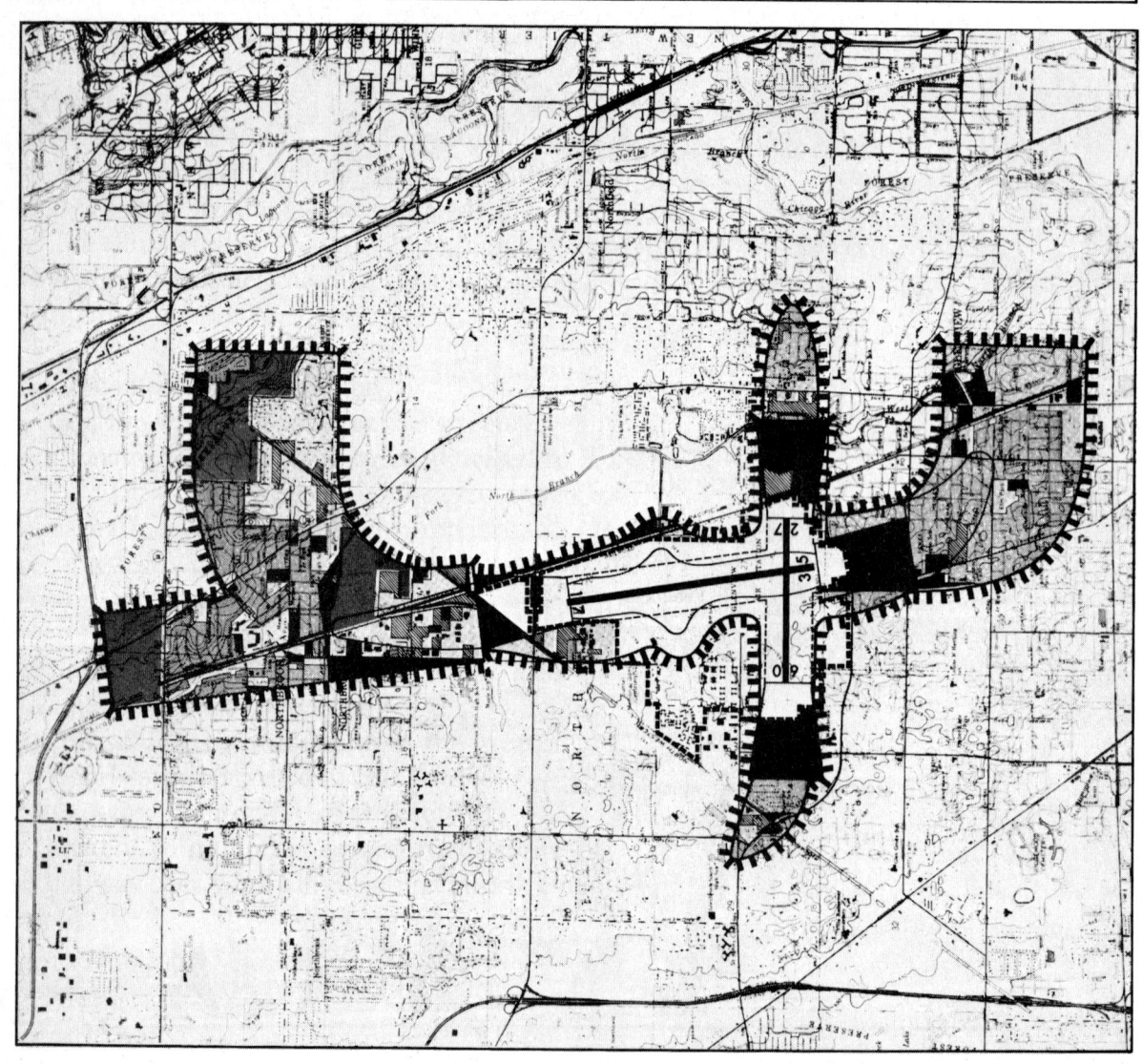

274 MILITARY PARKS

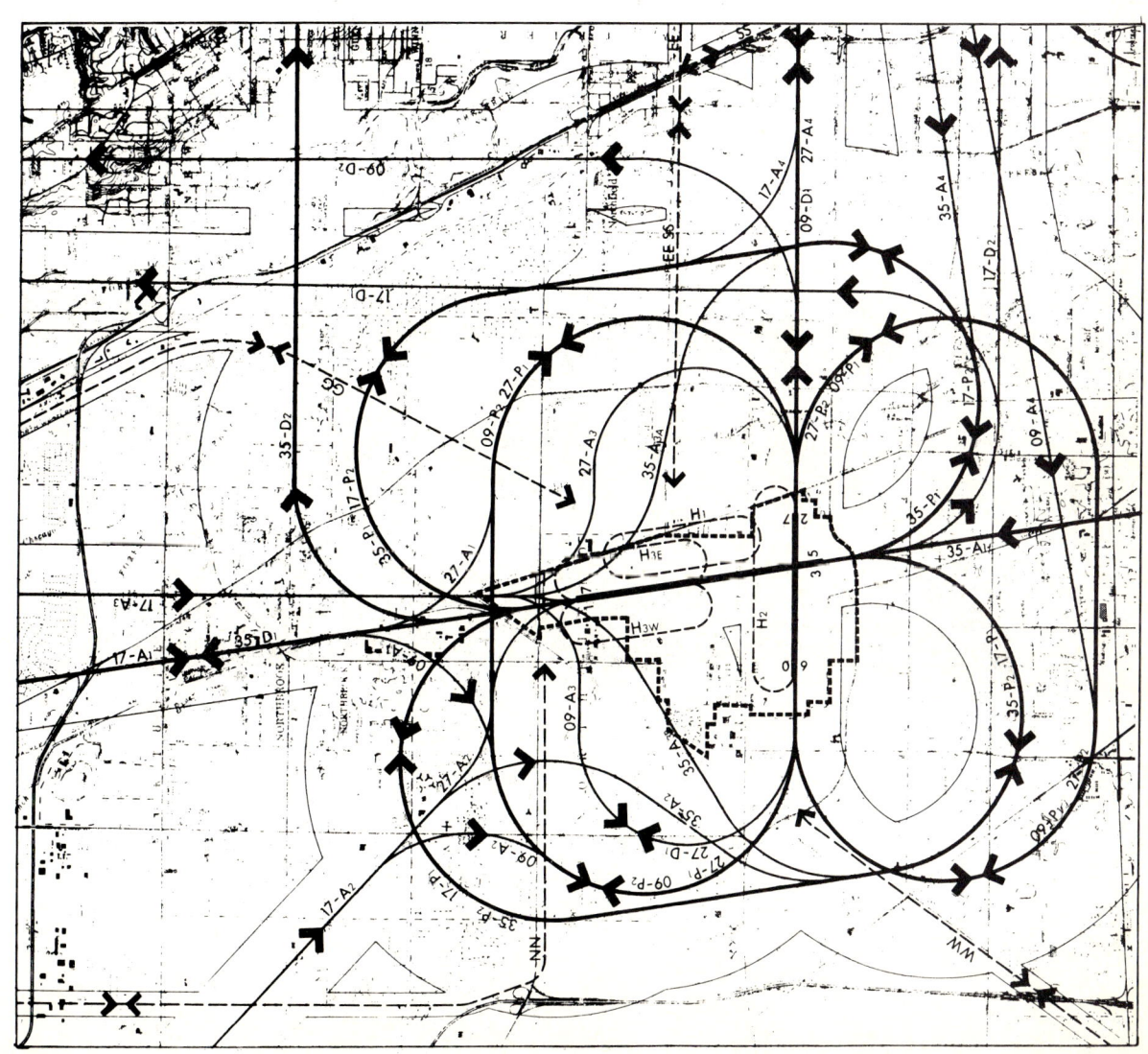

MILITARY PARKS 275

BASE EXTERIOR ARCHITECTURE PLAN
Naval Air Station
Meridian, Mississippi

Military installations have an economic, environmental, and visual impact on the communities in which they are located. And, the base itself affects the performance of those who work and live there. Many U.S. military installations were built decades ago, often under time pressure, and the buildings and grounds are in need of replanning and renovation.

The following is a schematic study of base problems with recommended solutions.

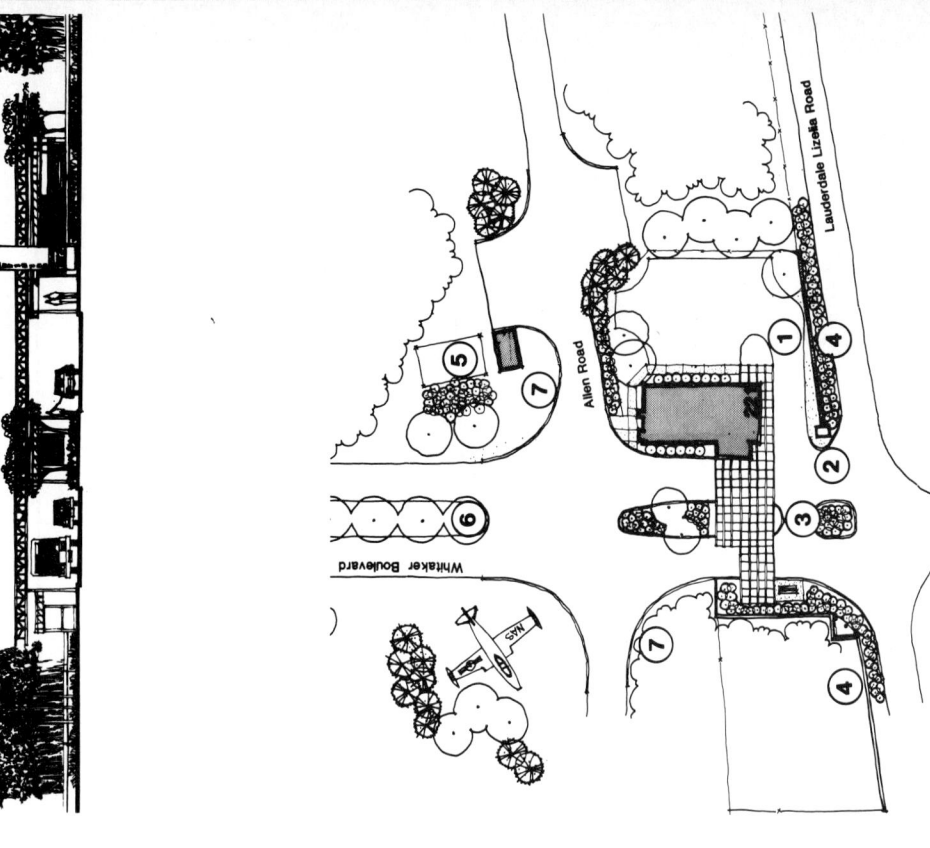

ENTRANCE

Problems

While the first impression of the main entrance is pleasant, the entrance area has several visual liabilities. Specific positive and negative elements include:

1. Large masses of pine trees surrounding the entrance give it a pleasant appearance.

2. The intersection of Lauderdale and Whitaker Roads, the driveway into the Gate House parking area, and the various small buildings all contribute to make the area cluttered and visually confusing.

3. Signing is overdone and out of date.

4. The kennel is obtrusive to the visual environment and could be more sensibly designed to meet security requirements.

5. Landscape detailing is overly fussy and not well designed.

Solutions

The primary objective is to simplify the many elements located in the entrance area while retaining the masses of existing pine trees. Specific recommendations include:

1. The Gate House parking lot driveway has been reoriented to access from Whitaker Boulevard thereby reducing the number of possible turning movements.

2. A new pylon entrance sign provides an up-beat image and impression of the station.

3. An overhead canopy has been introduced to visually tie together the Gate House, Sentry House and the bus stop. The canopy also provides for protection from the sun and rain. Lighting can be concealed within the canopy, reducing the number of overhead elements.

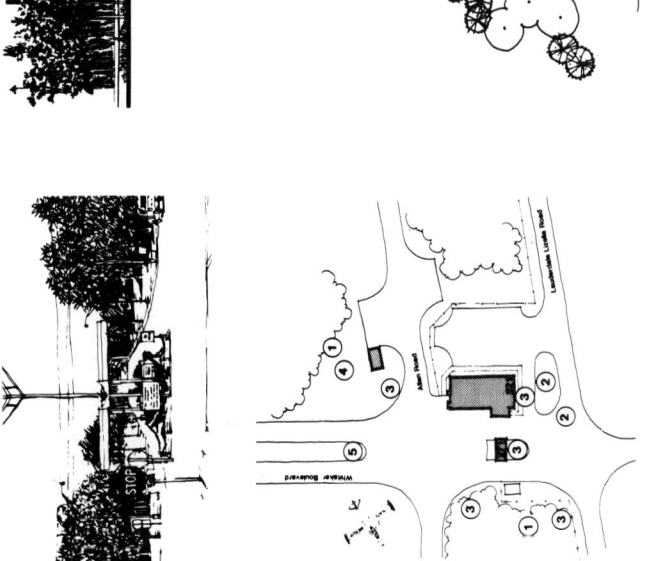

4. Low concrete walls used to screen parking areas and visually tie the various elements together.

5. Landscape planting (not total screening) and the use of black chain link fence to reduce the impact of the kennel.

6. Existing planter removed and replaced using compatible colors and materials to that now being used on the station's buildings. Planting would be reworked to reduce maintenance requirements.

7. Area signs would be removed and replaced with new directional and information panel signing.

MILITARY PARKS 277

utilitarian	Design or modify architectural elements to respond to climate--window overhangs, covered entries, reduce window size on south and west building exposures. Provide building ornamentation only to emphasize entries. Locate buildings with respect to solar orientation. Continue use of buff brick--paint all frame buildings a uniform buff color. Provide uniform reflective roof color.
visual quality	Design new or modify existing buildings to visually respond to early coastal style--large roof overhangs, covered porches, symmetrical design. Provide aesthetically pleasing site design--screened utilities and parking, group buildings to relate entries and create courtyards. Color code buildings to delineate functional/visual districts.
exposure	Determine design and material requirements relative to each exposure zone: Zone 1 Physically reflect early coastal style and respond to climate--smaller windows on south and east exposures, reflective materials, covered entries. Zone 2 Visually reflect early coastal style and respond to climate--smaller windows on south and west exposures, reflective materials, covered entries. Zone 3 Modify buildings to reduce energy and maintenance cost--window overhangs, covered entries, uniform color and materials.

Architecture/Site Planning

Base Exterior Architecture Plan for naval air station
MERIDIAN, MS

MILITARY PARKS

utilitarian

Complete secondary walk system; paint crosswalks.

Pave all existing natural pathways and gathering areas with durable materials.

Provide protection from sun and rain at gathering areas.

Provide functional site amenities that are vandal-resistant and located to prevent high maintenance.

visual quality

Complete overall walk system and provide Class I bike paths.

Provide covered walkways where pedestrian traffic is high.

Develop all pedestrian spaces (UEPH courtyards, HQ Building) with decorative paving and special amenities (i.e., decorative furniture, signing, lighting and screening devices).

Use decorative sidewalk paving material and special crosswalks.

exposure

Develop an overall pedestrian circulation system

Develop a hierarchy of sidewalk widths and materials:

Zone 1   Provide decorative paving and special amenities for walks and gathering areas--decorative furniture, signing and lighting.

Zone 2   Provide hard surface paving and functional amenities--protection from sun and rain, vandal-resistant furniture.

Zone 3   Provide adequate surface materials for walks (i.e., asphalt, shell, etc.).

Base Exterior Architecture Plan for
MERIDIAN, MS

Pedestrian Circulation

MILITARY PARKS

utilitarian

Design for functional use of plant materials—solar control, traffic control, erosion control.

Remove or relocate all plant materials that are improperly located (e.g. remove vines from perimeter fence).

Limit the variety of plant materials.

visual quality

Define visual areas through plant design.
Provide major visual elements along streets, walks, and building settings.
Screen major visual intrusions—parking, service areas, mechanical equipment.
Create special character plantings (parade field, HQ's building).
Define boundaries along First St. and Eleventh St.
Provide seasonal interest through the use of a variety of plant materials.

exposure

Delineate functional/visual districts.
Establish a range in design and type of material:
- Zone 1 Create aesthetic building settings, emphasize pedestrian and circulation routes, create special character, screen all obtrusions, provide seasonal interest.
- Zone 2 Define building entries, shade vehicular and pedestrian routes, provide specific solar control, traffic control and erosion control.
- Zone 3 Provide solar control, traffic control and erosion control.

Landscape Planting

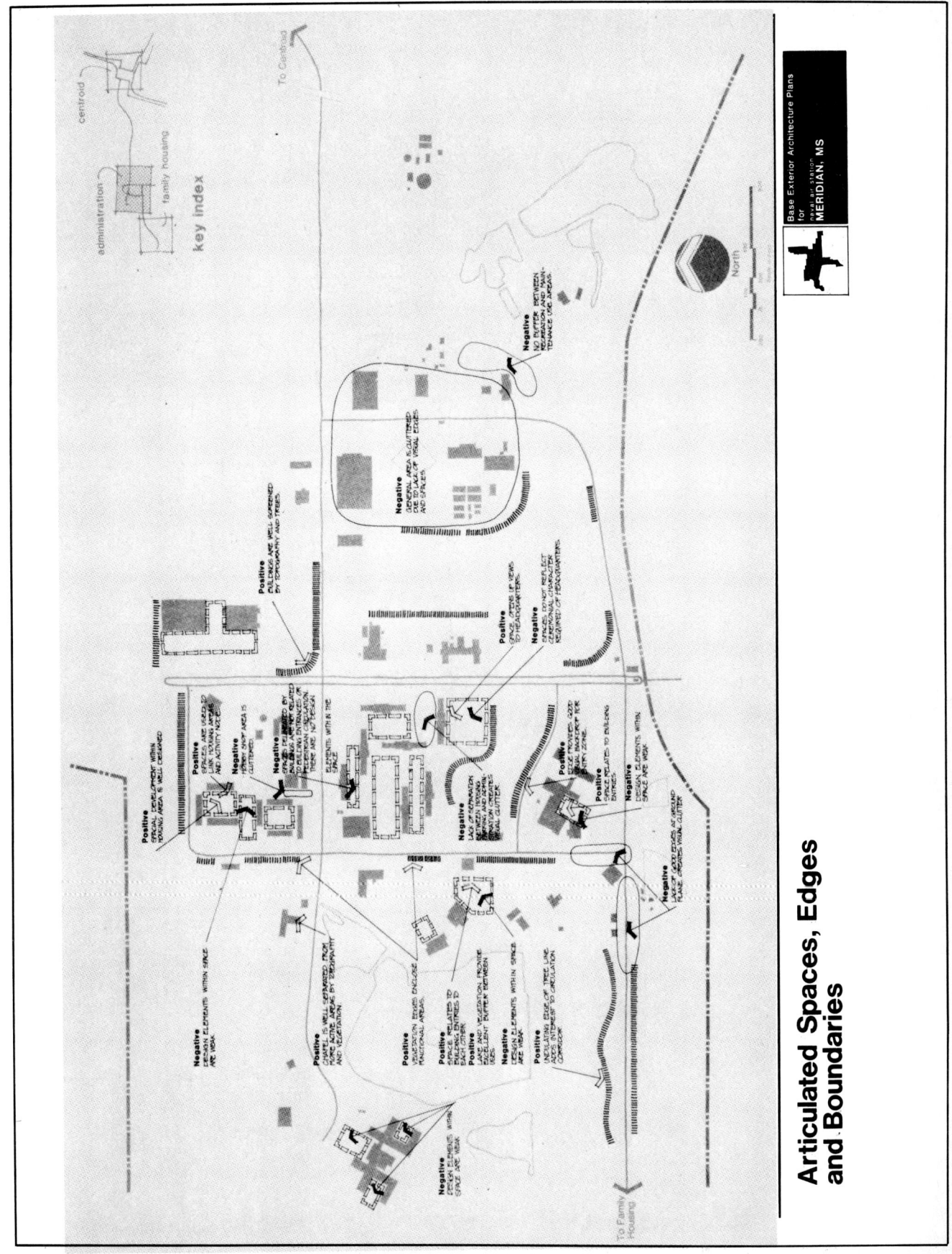

Articulated Spaces, Edges and Boundaries

MILITARY PARKS 281

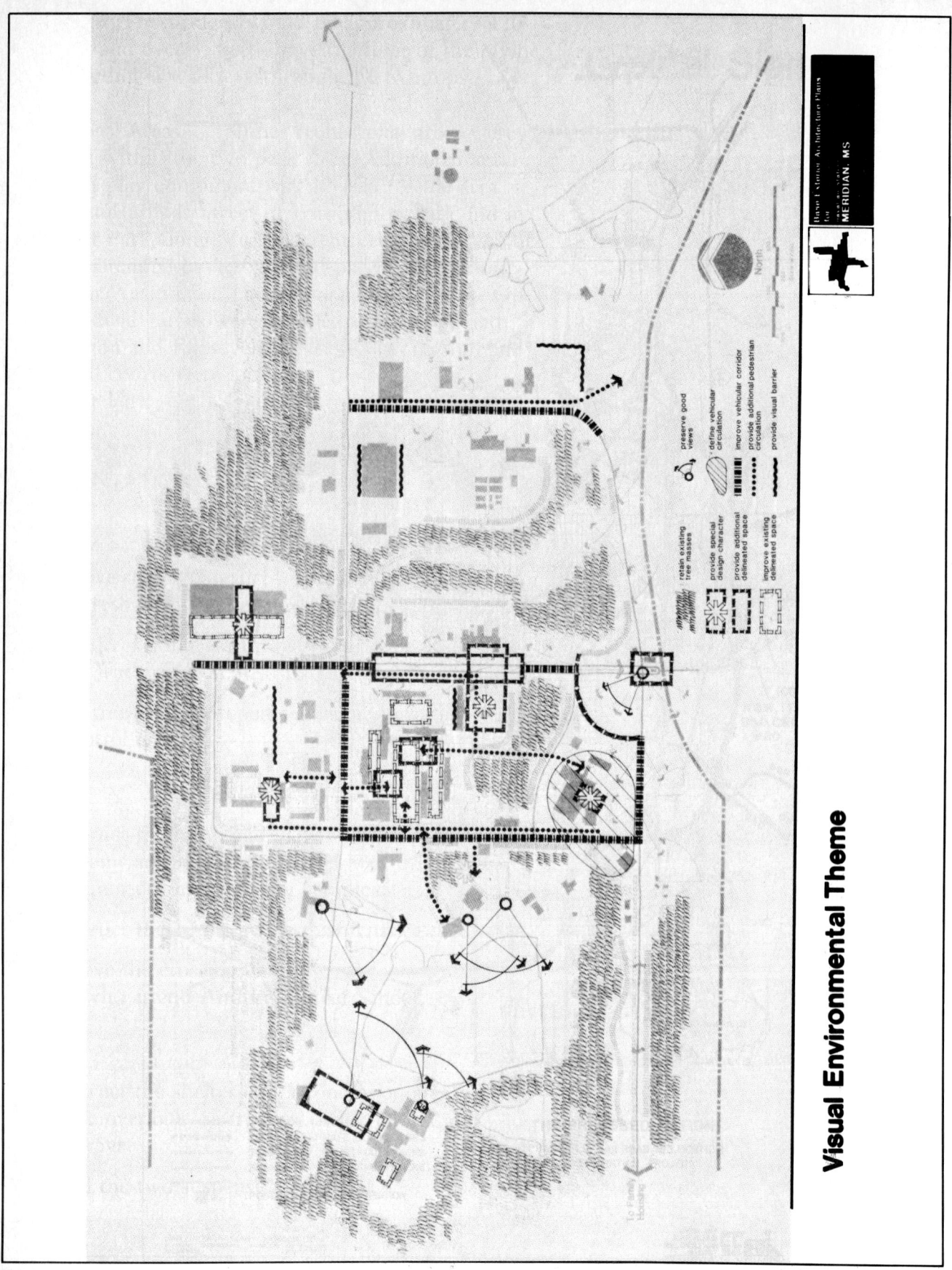

TWELVE
MISCELLANEOUS PROJECTS

COMMUNITY APPEARANCE AND PHYSICAL ENVIRONMENT
Cicero, Illinois

A very important objective of the comprehensive planning process is to provide an interesting and attractive environment in which people can live, work, and play. Unattractive environmental appearance can suppress incentive for the private improvement of property and for the location of new industry and business. Conversely, an attractive environmental appearance can stimulate growth and improvement.

Two important visual improvements of this plan were major street improvements and expressway corridor improvement.

MAJOR STREET IMPROVEMENT
CERMAK AND CICERO

MISCELLANEOUS PROJECTS

EXPRESSWAY PLANTING

DEPRESSED ROADWAY

AT GRADE ROADWAY WITH SCREEN PLANTING

DEPRESSED ROADWAY WITH TERRACED PLANTING

HARLAND BARTHOLOMEW AND ASSOCIATES
PLANNING·ENGINEERING·LANDSCAPE ARCHITECTURE·URBAN RENEWAL
NORTHBROOK, ILLINOIS
APRIL 1974

MISCELLANEOUS PROJECTS

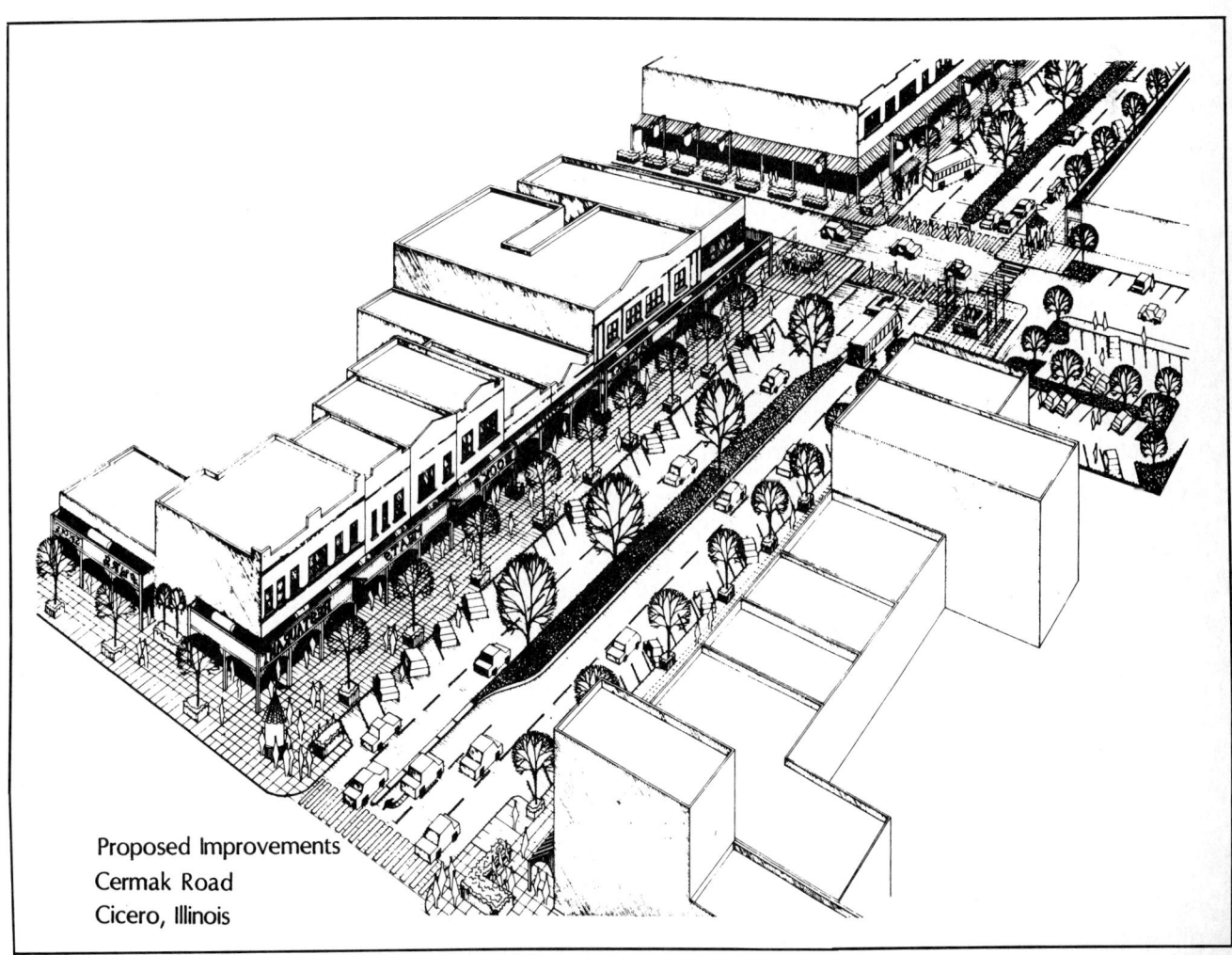

Proposed Improvements
Cermak Road
Cicero, Illinois

MISCELLANEOUS PROJECTS 287

RUSSELL HEIGHTS NEIGHBORHOOD IMPROVEMENT PROGRAM
Leeds, Alabama

The city of Leeds is located in the extreme eastern portion of Jefferson County, Alabama, approximately 15 miles east of downtown Birmingham. This city, with a population of approximately 9000, is one of several municipalities for which the Jefferson County Department of Planning and Community Development has the responsibility of planning and administering the Community Development Block Grant Program.

In an effort to concentrate improvements within the municipality, a low-to-moderate income neighborhood (eligible for CDBG funding) had to be identified and a three-year revitalization plan prepared. After an inventory and analysis of housing and environmental conditions was completed, the city was divided into seven neighborhoods. The local Citizens Advisory Committee selected the Russell Heights neighborhood for improvement. Over 44 percent of the residential structures in Russell were rated as dilapidated or in need of major repair. In addition, the neighborhood suffered from inadequate storm and sanitary sewers, poorly maintained streets, streets in need of design improvements, and a poorly maintained recreational area.

The revitalization plan focused on improving the least deteriorated portion of the neighborhood first. This area contained a junior high school and a city park which, with the planned improvements, could serve as an anchor and catalyst for future improvements in the neighborhoods.

Recommendations included street improvements, storm sewers, sidewalks, park improvements, and sanitary sewers. Additionally, the city officials were persuaded to begin demolition and clearance of vacant, dilapidated structures; and the County agreed to make available its existing residential rehabilitation program to eligible homeowners. The plan was accepted with implementation beginning in the fall of 1979.

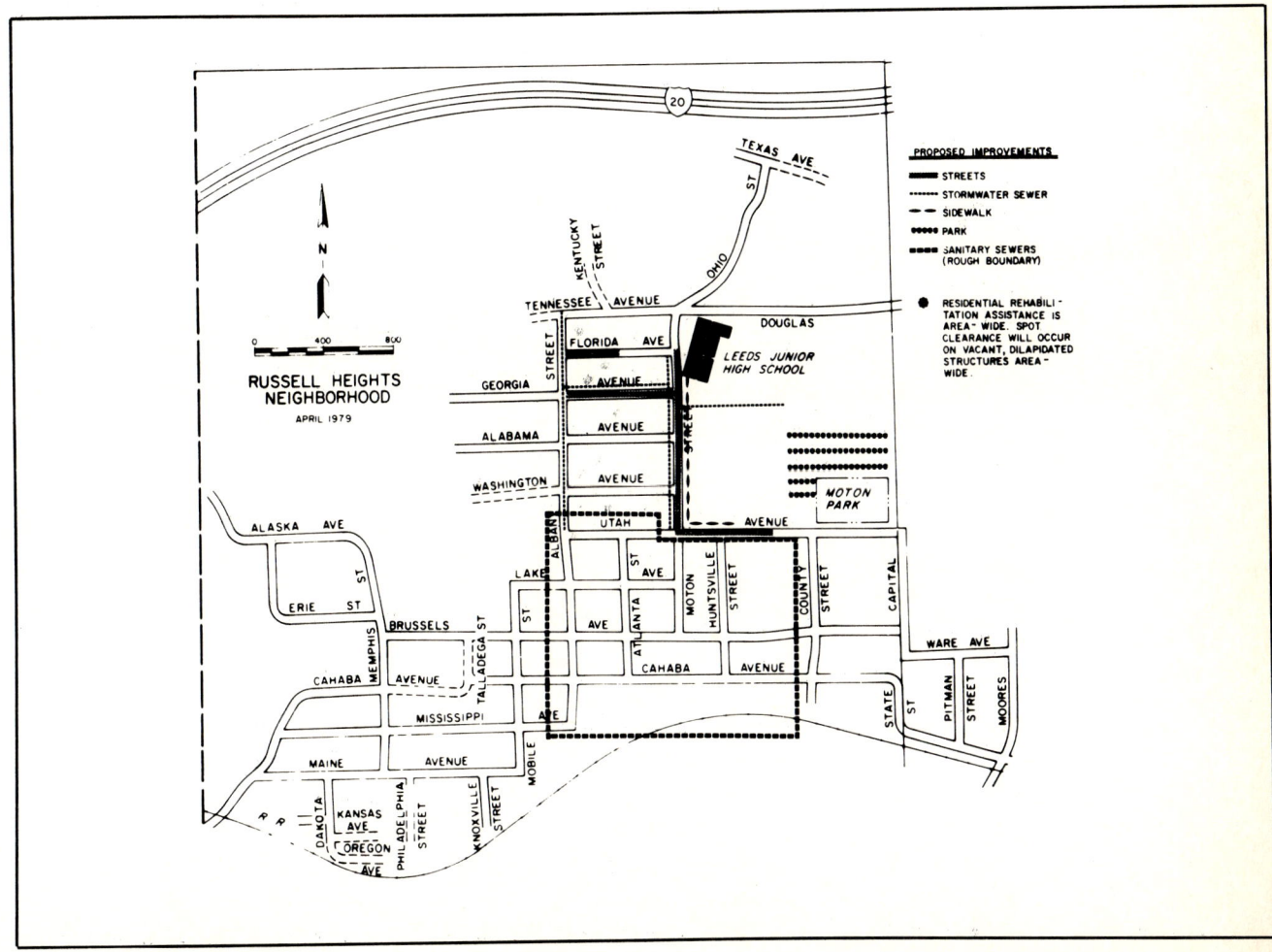

MISCELLANEOUS PROJECTS 289

SEWAGE TREATMENT PLANT
Perryville, Missouri

In 1938, Perryville's North Sewage Treatment Plant was constructed on a site southeast of Missouri 51 and U.S. 61. This plant, consisting of an Imhoff tank and trickling filter, served the city until 1955, at which time a second plant (south of Ganahl and Shelby streets) was constructed. These two plants served Perryville quite well until the late 1960s when city growth and one large water-using industry severely taxed the capability of these treatment plants to satisfactorily treat the sewage.

In 1971, planning was initiated for facilities that would meet the city's sewage collection and disposal requirements at the time of planning and into the immediate future. These efforts resulted in a bond issue being submitted to the citizens of Perryville in January 1973 to provide the local funding share of improvements to the collection and treatment facilities. The passage of this bond issue enabled the city to proceed with the preparation of detailed plans and specifications for the construction of the facilities. In August 1974, bids were received for this purpose and the construction started.

The construction of the South Pump Station (capacity 880 G.P.M.) with the 9100-foot-long South Interceptor (8″ to 15″ in diameter) permitted abandonment of the old (1955) South Sewage Treatment Plant by pumping sewage from that location east to the new Southeast Wastewater Treatment Plant. As an alternative to providing standby electrical power at this station, the old trickling filter tank at the South Treatment Plant was retained to be operated as a holding basin to receive flow from the pump station if power is interrupted.

The function of the 14,700-foot-long Northeast Outfall Sewer (12″ to 24″ in diameter) is to collect sewage from the entire city collection system and transport it southward to the new plant. Its construction permitted demolition of the old (1938) north sewage treatment plant and the elimination of three older lift stations in the city system. The Northeast Outfall Sewer can be extended northward to provide service for the proposed Industrial Park situated to the northeast of the city. The capacity of the Northeast Outfall Sewer at its upper reach is approximately 2.5 M.G.D.

The new Southeast Wastewater Treatment Plant provides secondary treatment at one location for all sewage generated in the city, removing 90 percent of the pollutants in the wastewater. The treated effluent is chlorinated prior to discharge to Cinque Hommes Creek. It is designed to serve a population equivalent to 9000 persons. The new treatment plant meets or exceeds the effluent requirements that have been set forth by the Missouri Clean Water Commission and the U.S. Environmental Protection Agency.

The wastewater treatment plant process units include pretreatment by screening, comminution (grinding), and grit removal. Primary treatment is provided by two primary clarifiers. Secondary treatment includes one trickling filter tower composed of plastic media, followed by a final clarifier. Post-chlorination facilities, which are automatically controlled, provide for disinfection of the plant effluent. Primary and secondary sludge is treated aerobically, and the treated sludge is disposed of on agricultural lands.

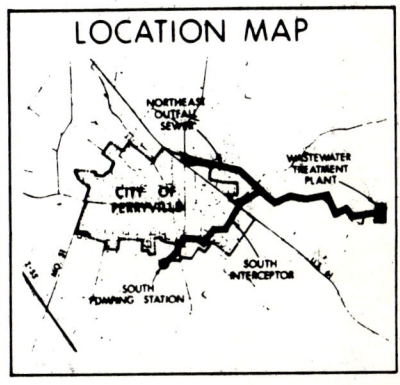

The plant has two electrical power sources to provide complete treatment should one of the incoming power sources fail. In addition to the facilities noted previously, a new administration building and laboratory are provided, together with a compressor building and garage facilities.

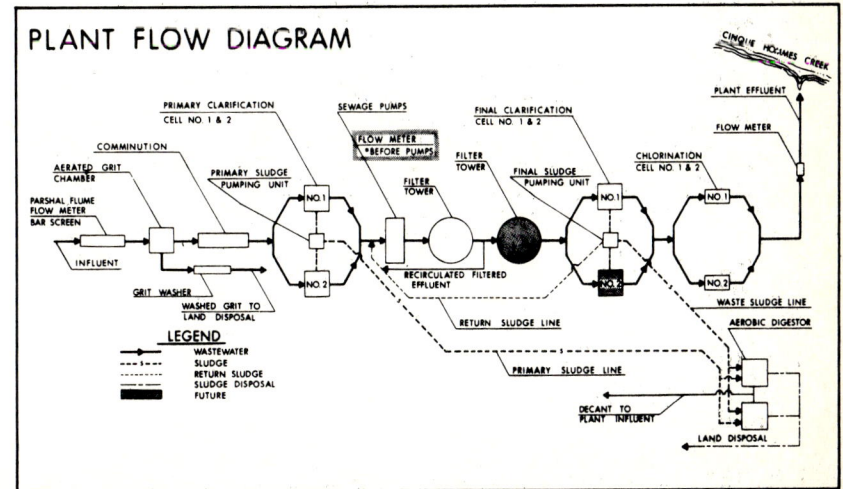

MISCELLANEOUS PROJECTS

SOUTHWEST PROVING GROUNDS
California and Arizona

Harland Bartholomew & Associates conducted comprehensive environmental studies of alternative sites for the Southwest Proving Ground facility for Chrysler Corporation near Phoenix, Arizona, and Thermal, California. Site investigations were carried out at each location for environmental factors that would constrain facility design. Published reports on geology, hydrology, soils, climatic data, plant and animal communities, and archeology were carefully reviewed for relevant factors. The HB & A environmental staff assisted engineering and design professionals at all stages of site evaluation and facility design. Environmental permits and documentation required at each site were also described.

In plans for the Thermal site, facilities were positioned to avoid an archeologically sensitive area and cause minimal disruption to a potentially significant archeological area. Erosion control in fine, sandy loam soils was particularly important in plans for the Phoenix sites. Dust control and protection and establishment of native vegetation were important on all sites.

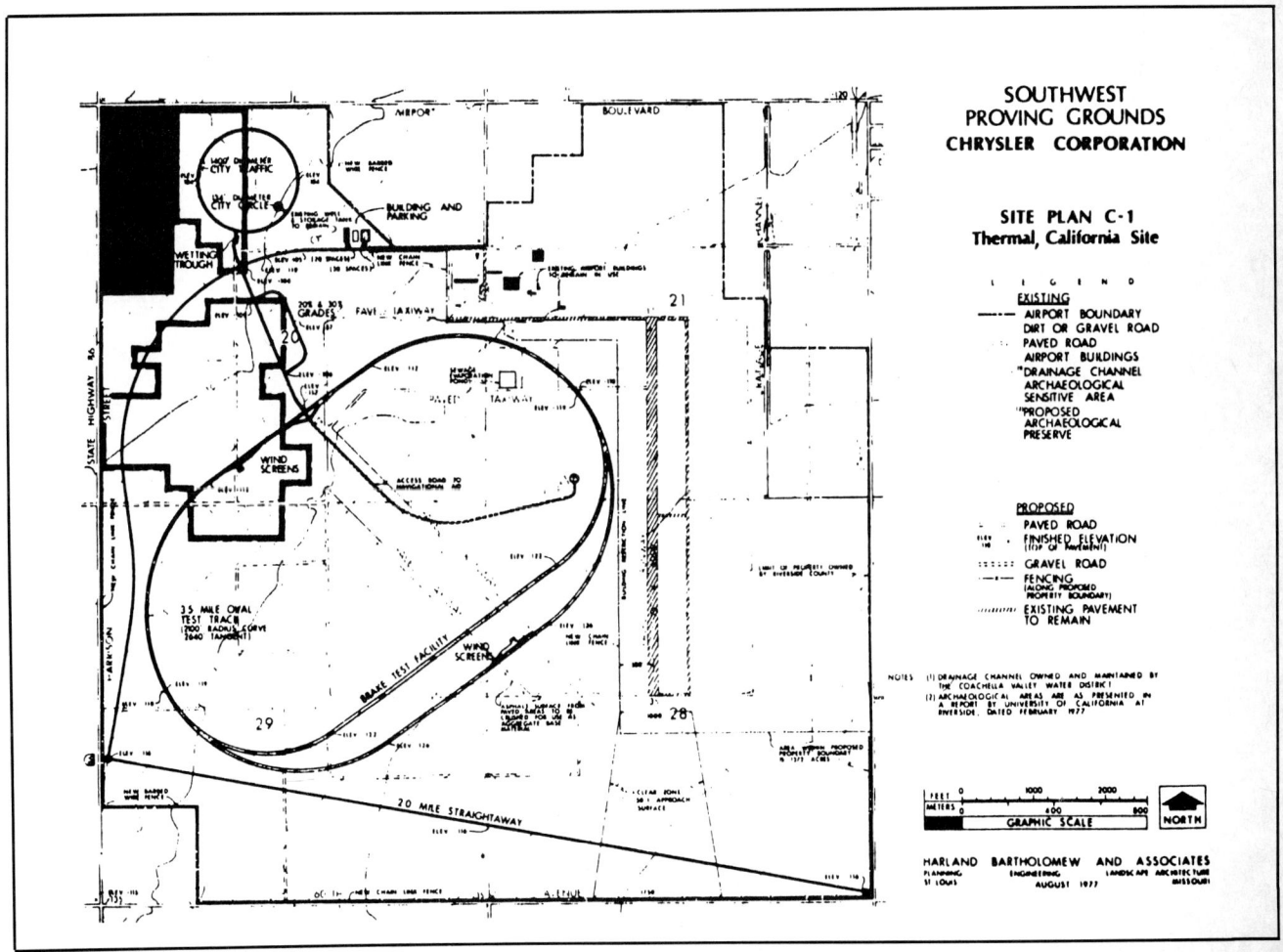

CLAYTON ROAD CURB PROJECT
Ladue, Missouri

The edge of the existing pavement and curb on Clayton Road had deteriorated to a dangerous level with much of the existing overlay displaced by freeze-thaw damage. As the loose overlay allowed water to penetrate the pavement, more surface course and base pavement damage occurred from freeze-thaw action. This created a self-perpetuating maintenance problem that threatened complete destruction of the roadway.

The project involved removal of the existing deteriorated lip curb and loose overlay, construction of over 15,000 lineal feet of new vertical curb, patching of the overlay, adjustment of 22 drainage inlets, and seal coating the pavement full width.

At the time of the project, Clayton Road traffic averaged about 20,000 vehicles per day. Thus, when the new curb was constructed, a new pathway also was constructed along the roadway. Ramps for the handicapped were provided at all drive and street entrances.

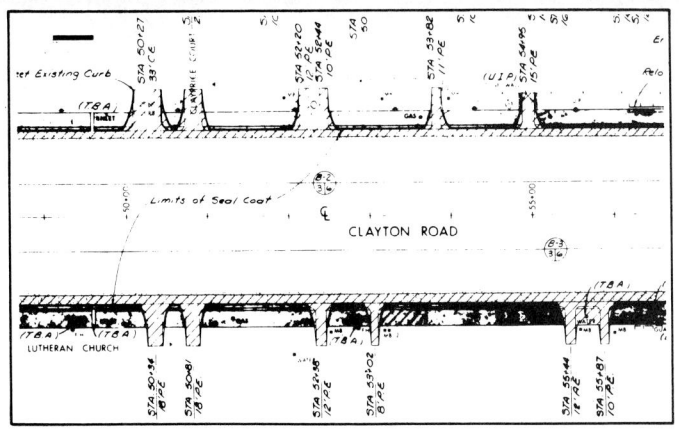
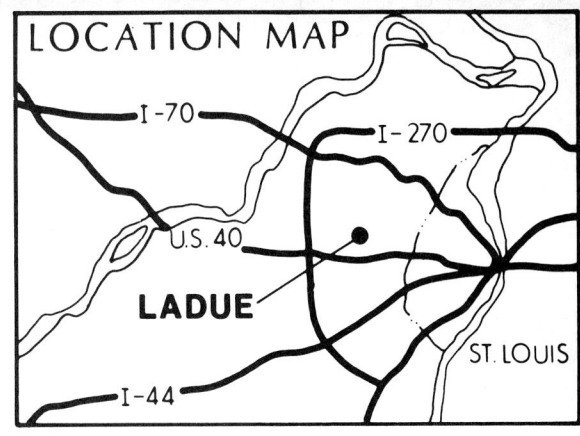

Before Improvement

After Improvement

MISCELLANEOUS PROJECTS 295

ALTO CRESPO
Urbanizadora Alto Crespo
Venezuela

Alto Crespo, a planned recreational community, is located on 425 acres outside of San Cristobal in the state of Tachira, Venezuela. The site is approximately 400 miles from the major city of Caracas, in a remote, mountainous area near the Colombian border.

Harland Bartholomew & Associates acted as project coordinator of a design team that included golf course architect Joseph L. Lee and the architectural firm James P. Chapman Associates. Hammer, Siler, George prepared the market study.

The team incorporated the dramatic natural beauty of the site into the design of a 582-unit residential community centered around a wide array of unique recreational facilities. Outdoor recreational facilities consist of an 18-hole championship golf course designed to enhance the entrances to the site with its spacious fairways and manicured tees and greens, tennis courts, olympic swimming and diving pools, a children's amusement park, a beach area, miniature golf, and simulated ski slopes and toboggan runs. Indoor facilities include tennis, squash, and handball courts; an intensive health club and medical evaluation facility; and a social club featuring a pro shop, locker room, and formal and informal dining facilities.

An information center located at the main entrance to the site incorporates an observation tower and auxiliary parking lots for those who use the internal transportation systems. A funicular railway is the focal point of the transportation system.

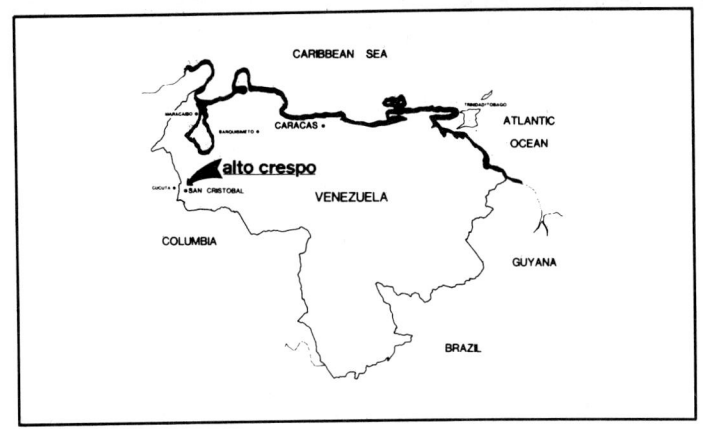

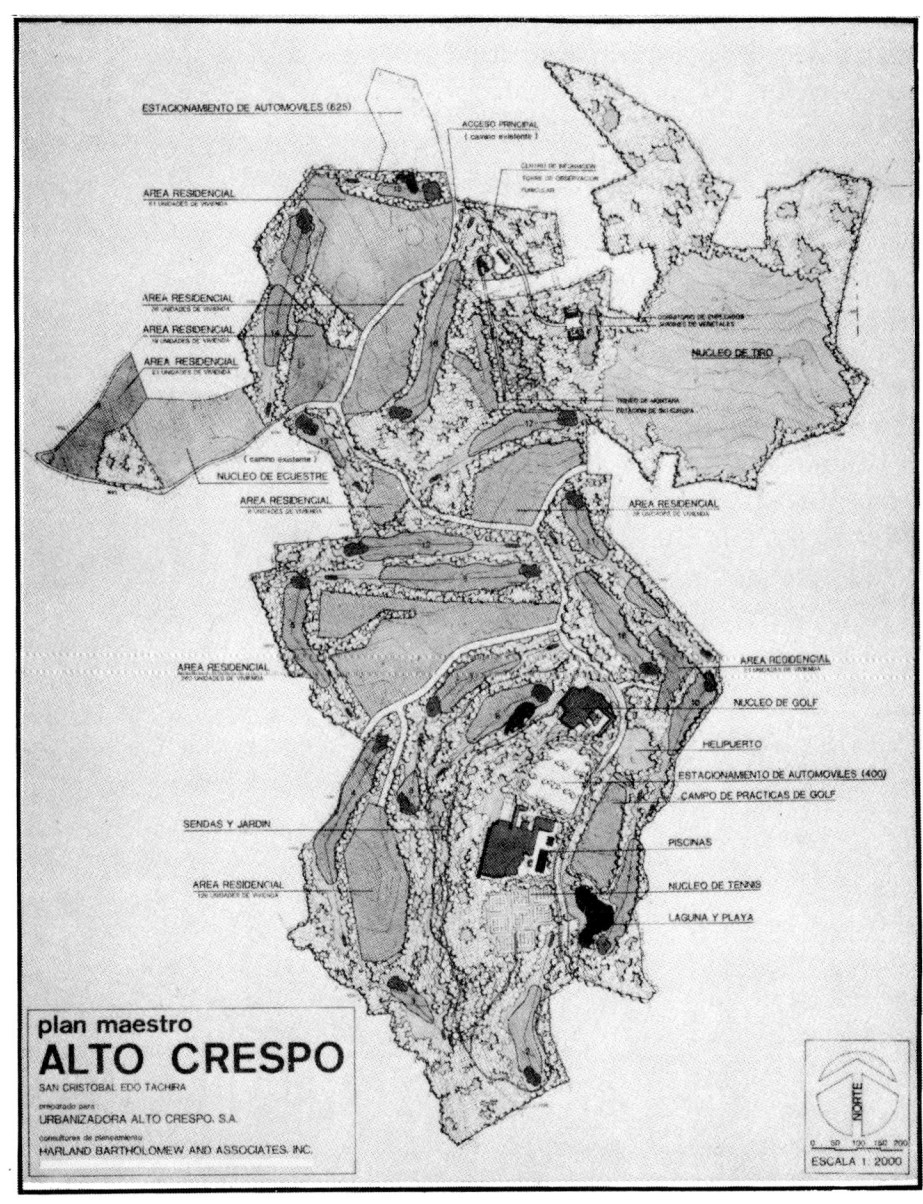

MISCELLANEOUS PROJECTS 297

DISTRICT 8 HEADQUARTERS SITE SURVEY ILLINOIS DEPARTMENT OF TRANSPORTATION
Madison and St. Clair Counties, Illinois

This project included an analysis of existing Department of Transportation space requirements, projection of future needs, and a two-part evaluation of alternative locations for new facilities. After preliminary screening of over 30 suggested sites, 11 were selected for detailed analysis. Utilities, soils, zoning, and land values were studied, and sample site plans, utilities plans, and development cost estimates prepared. The impact of a new facility on the surrounding community as well as the natural environment was assessed.

Special additional services provided to the client included: aerial photography, topographic mapping, soils analysis, architectural analysis of the existing facility, and organization and coordination of review committee actions.

The project was completed over a four-month period in order to minimize the effect of speculative pressures, and one of the preferred study sites was selected as the District's future headquarters.

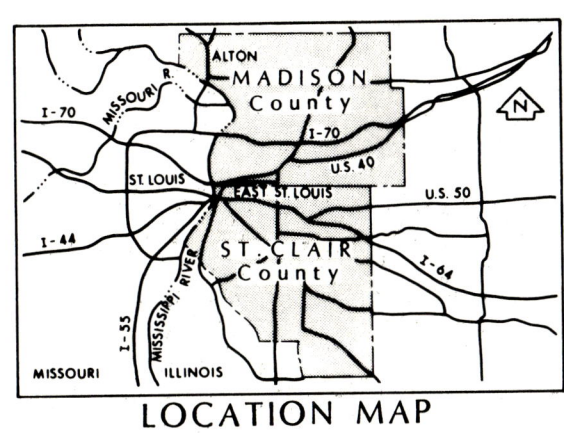

LOCATION MAP

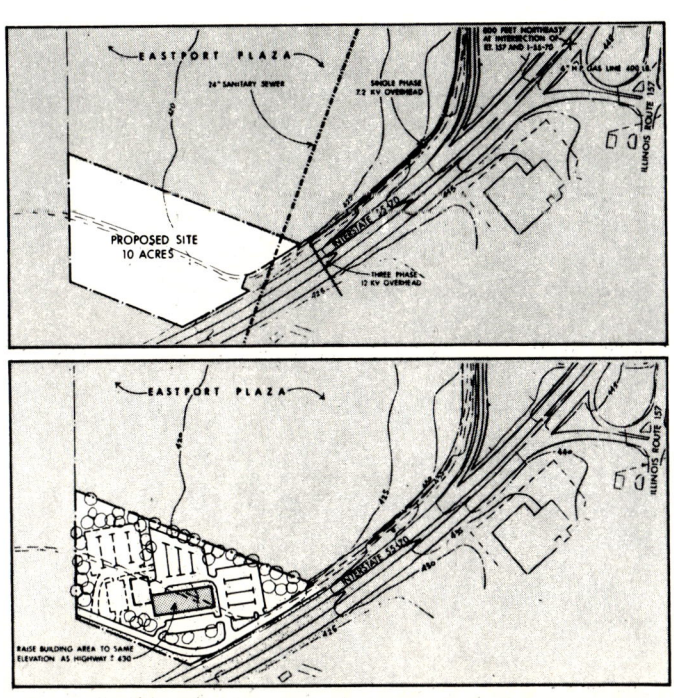

MISCELLANEOUS PROJECTS

TRANSPORTATION AND TRANSIT STUDY
Okinawa, Ryukyu Islands

The largest of the Ryukyu Island chain, Okinawa lies south of Japan between the North Pacific Ocean and the East China Sea. Mountains and forests cover the northern two-thirds of the island. The south is composed of rolling hills and contains most of the population.

Okinawa, Ryukyu Islands

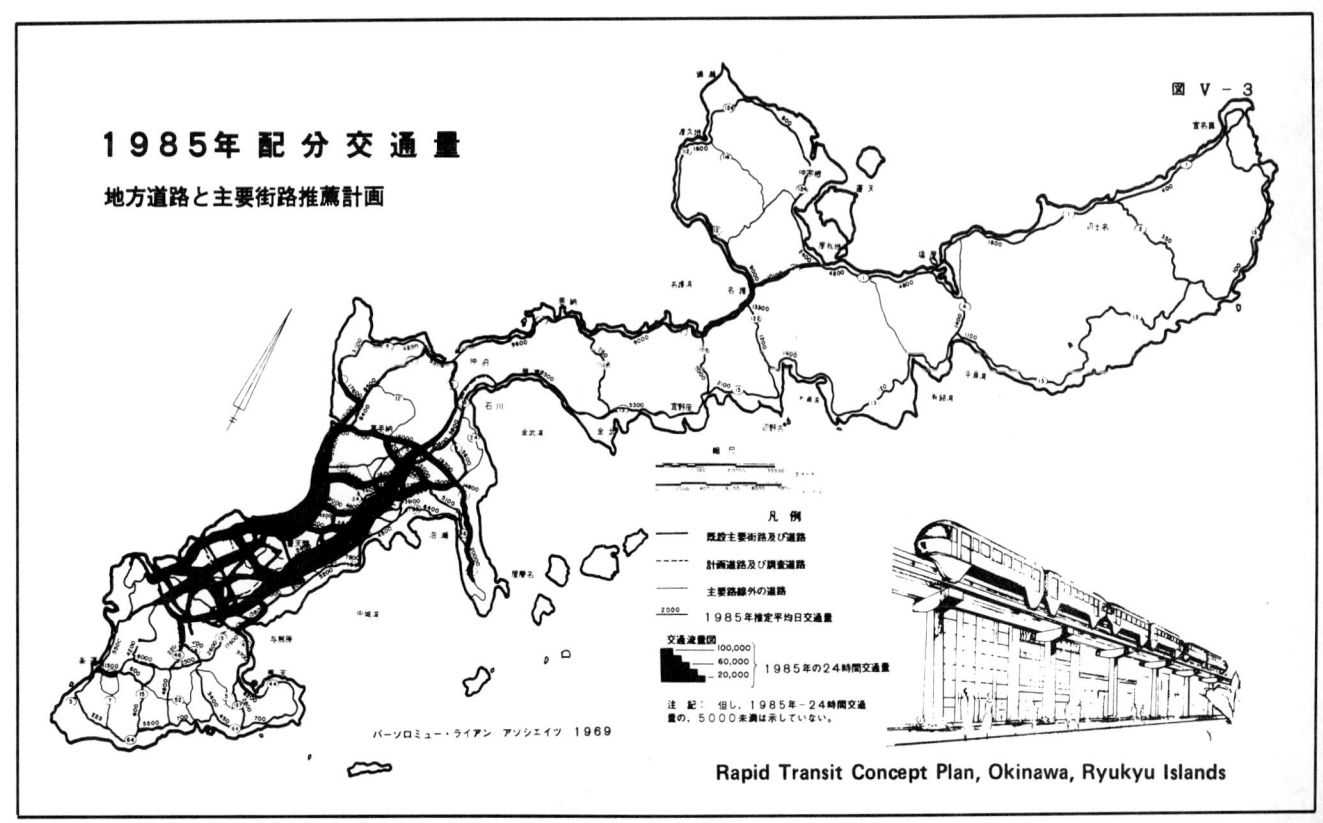

Rapid Transit Concept Plan, Okinawa, Ryukyu Islands

MISCELLANEOUS PROJECTS 301

THE CRITICAL PATH METHOD OF PROJECT SCHEDULING

The critical path method (CPM) of scheduling is a graphic tool that enables managers to see the elements of the project that are most critical to meeting the schedule. By using the CPM method, any or all the tasks within the project may be analyzed before, during, and after construction.

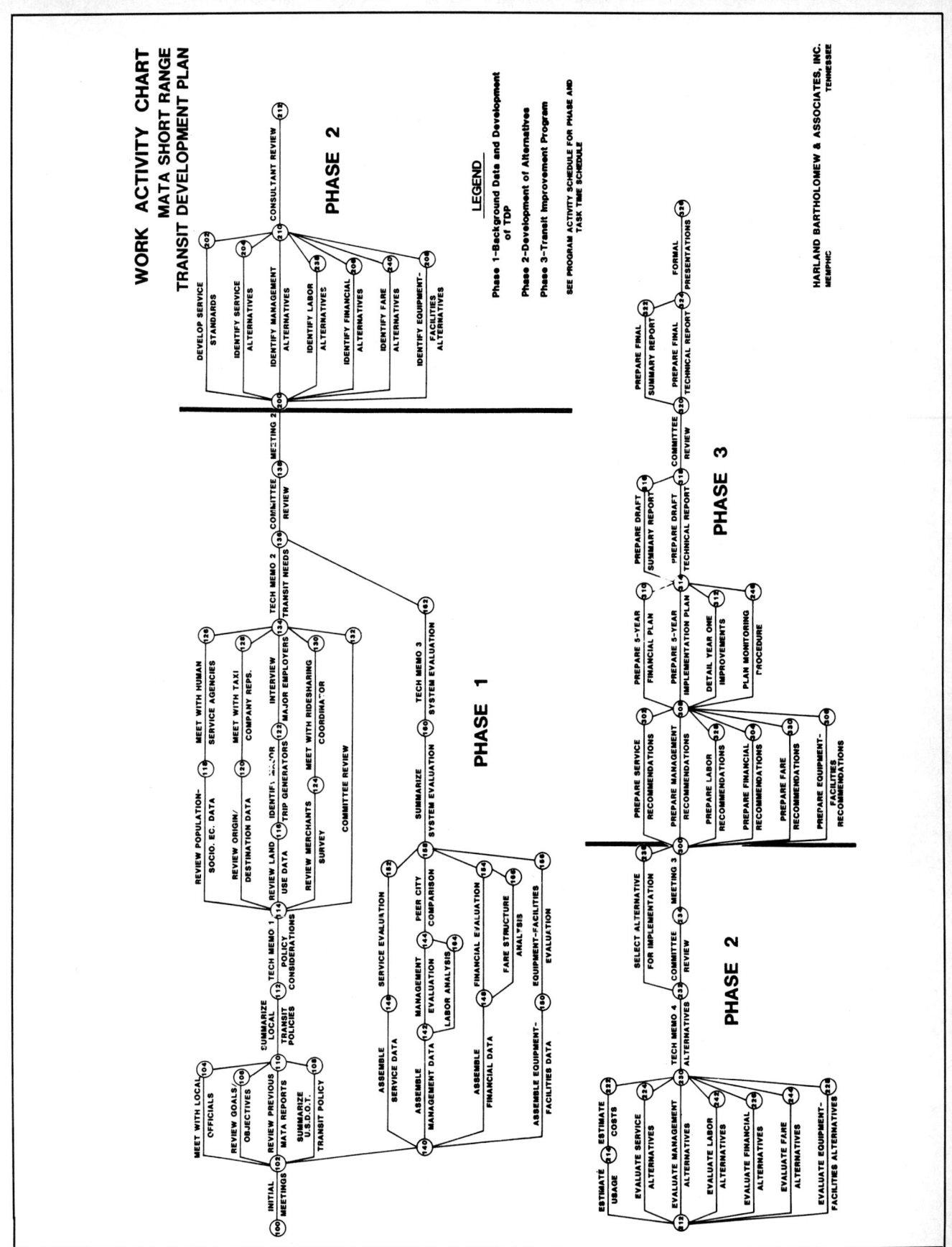

MISCELLANEOUS PROJECTS

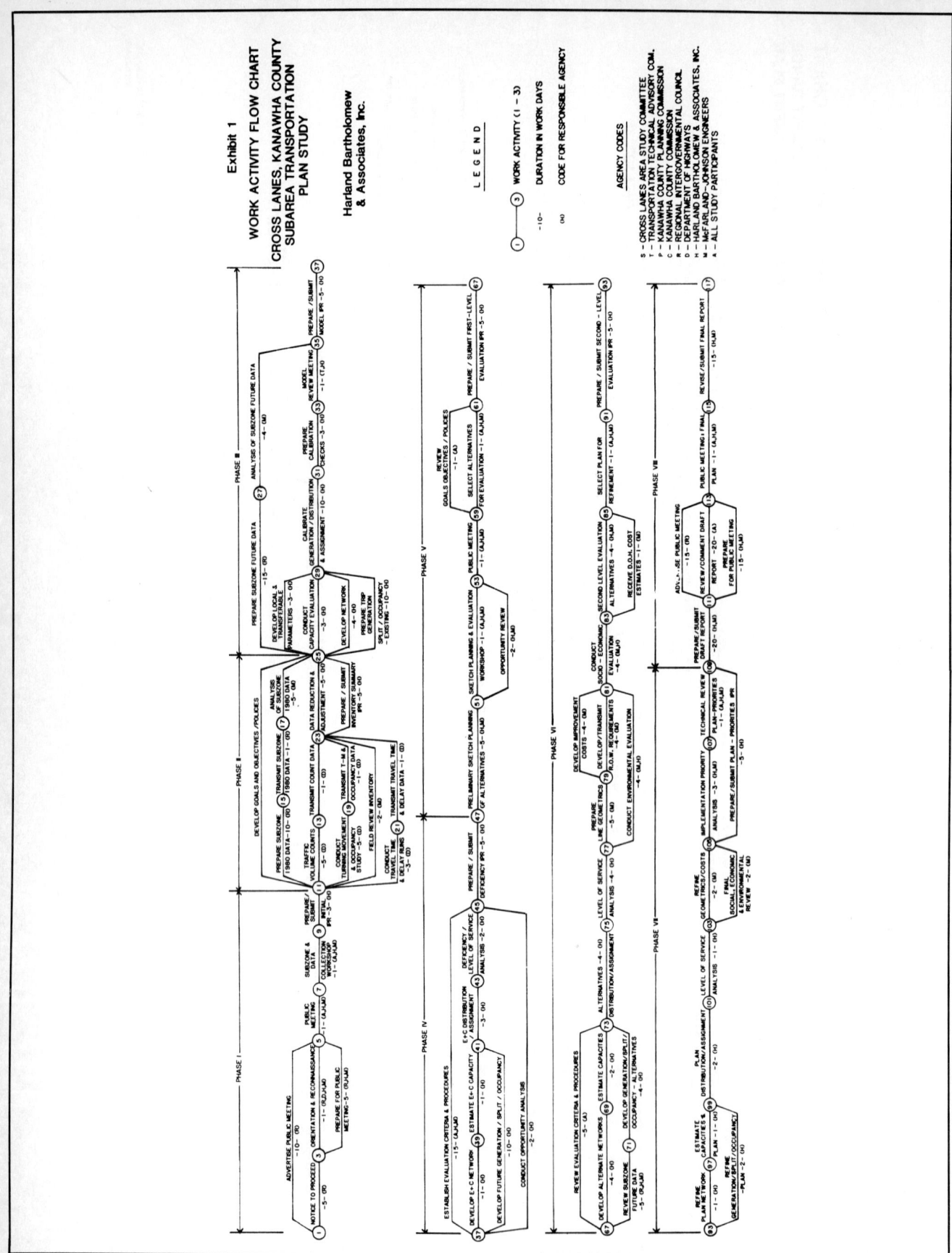

304 MISCELLANEOUS PROJECTS

Date Due

DEC 13 1980			

BRODART, INC.   Cat. No. 23 233   Printed in U.S.A.